Corinna Lenhardt
Savage Horrors

American Culture Studies | Volume 29

Corinna Lenhardt, born 1982, received her PhD in American studies from Universität Münster, Germany. Her research and teaching interests include African American and ethnic studies, race, gender, and popular culture.

Corinna Lenhardt
Savage Horrors
The Intrinsic Raciality of the American Gothic

[transcript]

D6

Bibliographic information published by the Deutsche Nationalbibliothek
The Deutsche Nationalbibliothek lists this publication in the Deutsche Nationalbibliografie; detailed bibliographic data are available in the Internet at http://dnb.d-nb.de

© 2020 transcript Verlag, Bielefeld

All rights reserved. No part of this book may be reprinted or reproduced or utilized in any form or by any electronic, mechanical, or other means, now known or hereafter invented, including photocopying and recording, or in any information storage or retrieval system, without permission in writing from the publisher.

Cover layout: Maria Arndt, Bielefeld
Cover illustration: Dagmar Fischer / photocase.de
Printed by Majuskel Medienproduktion GmbH, Wetzlar
Print-ISBN 978-3-8376-5154-6
PDF-ISBN 978-3-8394-5154-0
https://doi.org/10.14361/9783839451540

Contents

Acknowledgments 7

Abbreviations 9

Introduction 11

PART I:
The Gothic and the Savage Villain/Civil Hero Gotheme

What Is the Gothic? 27
1.1   The "Goth" in Gothic 29
1.2   A Working Definition 41
1.3   A Savage Villain/Civil Hero Gotheme? 52

British Origins of the Savage Villain/ Civil Hero Gotheme 57
2.1   The Villain 57
2.2   The Damsel in Distress 63
2.3   The Hero 67
2.4   Gothic Nationalism, or, the Gothic Gothic 69

PART II:
The Savage Villain/Civil Hero Gotheme:
WASP Origins and Iterations

Early WASP American Adaptations 77
3.1   Mock(ing) Villainy 77
3.2   Savage Villainy 82

Contemporary WASP American Iterations 101
4.1   Spotlights: The WASP American Gothic Novel Today 102

4.2	Shirley Temple, Sidney Poitier, and the Africanist Savage Villain Walk into the Woods….: Stephen King's *The Girl Who Loved Tom Gordon*	112
4.3	"Monster: Half Woman and Half Invention"—Karen Russell's *Swamplandia!*	128
4.4	Gothic Continuities and a Necessary Intervention (Interim Results)	137

PART III:
"You say I am wilderness. I am"— Black Origins and African American Reiterations

Innovation and Resistance: The SV/CH Gotheme in Black Writing, 1789 to 1861 143

5.1	*The Interesting Narrative of the Life of Olaudah Equiano, or Gustavus Vassa, the African, Written by Himself*	145
5.2	Gothic/Slavery: African American Slave Narratives	158
5.3	Early African American Novels: *Clotel* and *The Bondwoman's Narrative*	180

African American Gothic Today: Black Tradition and Reiterative Practices 203

6.1	Spotlights: The African American Gothic Novel Today	204
6.2	"Are You Afraid? You Should Be": Tony Morrison's *A Mercy*	221
6.3	"Pheenie Optimism"—with Zombies!: Colson Whitehead's *Zone One*	238

Epilogue: The American Gothic, Raciality, and the Possibility of Reiterative "Unthought" 253

Works Cited 259

Acknowledgments

As I approach the end of this project, I feel both happily and hopelessly indebted to the many wonderful people who helped me to make this happen. Maria I. Diedrich has guided me patiently and compassionately, since my first undergraduate seminar in American studies. More than merely passing on knowledge, she has not only reshaped my way of approaching the world but also modeled for me a life of searching, critical inquiry, and enthusiastic "eureka!" moments. *Savage Horrors* would not exist without her guidance, input, and support. In Katja Sarkowsky I have found another inspiring mentor and an absolutely remarkable interlocutor. Besides sharpening my understanding of ethnic studies, her invaluable feedback and input have very often helped me reconsider and reshape my arguments and ways of thinking. My colleague and best friend, Silja Fehn, has been the shining beacon in the gloom of daily PhDing. Without her constant encouragement and loving support, I would have given up this endeavor at innumerous instances.

Many chapters and work-in-progress versions of this book were read and commented on by the amazing American Studies colloquium at the University of Münster. Ina Batzke, Eric Erbacher, Lea Espinoza-Garrido, Linda Heß, Nic Lindenberg, Jesper Reddig, Alina Schumacher, and Anna Thiemann are among those whose sharp intelligence, challenging feedback, and heartfelt support shaped this book and its author. Chris Wahlig spent many hours expertly proofreading my manuscript, and I cannot thank her enough for making me look more professional than I would have ever managed on my own.

I am also indebted to my larger academic network, especially the many fiercely intelligent and creative members and friends of the Association for Research in the Fantastic (Gesellschaft für Fantastikforschung), including Tobias Haupts, Christine Lötscher, Lars Schmeink, and Simon Spiegel. The American Studies Association and the German Association for American Studies have helped professionalize me in the field of American studies, offering me a forum for exchange and networking. My students at the College of William and Mary and the University of Münster have been the best teachers any scholar could ever ask for. Their questions and ideas (re)shaped my arguments and concepts time and again, and I cannot thank them enough for probing into my research.

My family has been extraordinarily supportive through the years: My parents, Ralf and Angelika Lenhardt, with their support and unflinching belief in me, are the backbone of this project. Danke, dass Ihr mich auf die teure Schule geschickt habt! Ich liebe Euch über alles. My brilliant and incredibly funny, patient, and loving husband Sandro and my beautiful, sharp-witted daughter Liv fill my life with more laughter and love than I could ever ask for. Ich danke Euch unendlich.

Abbreviations

AM Toni Morrison's *A Mercy*

EH Charles Brockden Brown's *Edgar Huntly*

LM James Fenimore Cooper's *The Last of the Mohicans*

P Edgar Allan Poe's *The Narrative of Arthur Gordon Pym, of Nantucket*

S Karen Russell's *Swamplandia!*

SV/CH Gotheme Savage Villain/Civil Hero Gotheme

TBN Hannah Crafts's *The Bondwoman's Narrative*

TC Victor LaValle's *The Changeling*

TG Stephen King's *The Girl Who Loved Tom Gordon*

TIN Olaudah Equiano's *The Interesting Narrative of Olaudah Equiano, or Gustavus Vassa, the African, Written by Himself*

TKM N. K. Jemisin's *The Killing Moon*

UTC Harriet Beecher Stowe's *Uncle Tom's Cabin*

WASP White Anglo-Saxon Protestant

Z Colson Whitehead's *Zone One*

Introduction

> "You say I am wilderness. I am. Is that a tremble on your mouth, in your eye? Are you afraid? You should be." (Toni Morrison, A Mercy 155)

In his 1992 text-based painting *Study for Frankenstein #1*,[1] African American artist Glenn Ligon combined into one artwork, measuring 30 1/8 x 20 in., the complex, interwoven history of race and racialization[2] in the Gothic writing tradition, past and present, European and North American, Black and white. The present study requires roughly 300 pages to do the same. *Study for Frankenstein #1* consists of one sentence from Mary Shelly's world-famous 1818 Gothic novel *Frankenstein*, which is repeated four times. The stenciled black letters on white canvas become increasingly blurry until they cease to be legible, creating a thick black smear: "Sometimes I wished to express my sensations in my own mode, but the uncouth and inarticulate sounds which broke from me frightened me into silence again." Ligon is well-known for frequently drawing from the writings of African American authors, leaders, and activists,[3] and he has quoted a few texts by white authors

---

[1] The title of the painting is intentionally misleading. It implies that this version is not only a study and an incomplete version of Ligon's "Frankenstein" but also that this is the first in a series of studies. However, expanding on the notion of a Frankensteinian monster as a loose assembly of parts, Ligon has composed numerous versions of this painting, differing mainly in size and line breaks, under the exact same title (*Study for Frankenstein #1*). I am referring to the 30 1/8 x 22 in. version of the painting, which is currently owned by the Saint Louis Art Museum, St. Louis, Missouri.

[2] When speaking of "race," I want to evoke "the now wide understanding that race is an arbitrary social construct, a shifting and contradictory category that is constantly being constructed and reconstructed, and that is far from an 'innate' or 'natural' biological fact" (Henry and Tator 118). My understanding of "racialization" is based on Robert Miles' conceptualization of the term as "a process of categorization, a representational process of defining an Other (usually, but not exclusively) somatically" (75). In line with Didier Fassin, I believe that racialization conceptualizes "how to do races with bodies" (421).

[3] His text-based paintings include quotes from Zora Neal Hurston ("I feel the most colored when I am thrown against a sharp white background"), Ralph Ellison ("I am an invisible man"), James Baldwin, Malcolm X, and Richard Pryor.

that are explicitly concerned with race and racism (e.g., Jean Genet's 1959 play *The Blacks* and Richard Dyer's 1988 watershed essay "White"). At first glance, *Study for Frankenstein #1* "seems to be his only use of a text by a white author that does not manifestly address racial themes" (Young 221). Yet, by choosing *Frankenstein*, Ligon "draws Shelly into the orbit of these authors, white and black, who write explicitly about race" (ibid.), and, in doing so, he uncovers the thematic undercurrents of race and racialization generally and of Blackness more specifically at the heart of the iconic Gothic novel.

Figure 1 Study for Frankenstein #1

Glenn Ligon, *Study for Frankenstein #1*. 1992. Oil stick and gesso on canvas, 30 1/8 x 22 in. Saint Louis Art Museum, St. Louis, Missouri, U.S.A.

Frankenstein's monster has been described and discussed by numerous scholars as a heavily racialized character, most comprehensively in Elizabeth Young's book-length study *Black Frankenstein: The Making of an American Metaphor*. Although yellow-skinned, black-haired, and black-lipped in Shelly's novel, the monster "was painted blue in nineteenth-century stage incarnations, and tinted green in twentieth-century cinematic ones, [but] the monster's color nonetheless signifies symbolically, on the domestic American scene, as black" (Young 5). The long cultural afterlife of Frankenstein's monster in the United States can thus be understood as one instantiation of what Toni Morrison referred to as "American Africanism," the discursively fabricated "brew of darkness" and of "rawness and savagery, that provided the staging ground and arena for the elaboration of the quintessential American identity" (*Playing* 44). *Study for Frankenstein #1* forcefully evokes this "brew of darkness" and dyes Frankenstein B/black. That is, Frankenstein's monstrosity is rendered a matter of racial Blackness by the extensive use of a black-colored oil stick. The letters discursively blend racial Blackness and black color-coding (B/blackness)[4], becoming increasingly smudged and difficult to contain in the stencils' faintly visible outlines, until, reflecting the ending of *Frankenstein*, both the text and the monster are "lost in darkness" (Shelly 324) and in impenetrable B/blackness. Thus, Ligon renders visible both the racialized discourse out of which *Frankenstein* (the novel and the icon) was created and the racialization that *Frankenstein* has initiated (and continues to initiate) itself.

By making race and racialization visible in the discursive materiality of Shelly's novel, Ligon's (re-)creation of Frankenstein's monster, as an instantiation of anti-Black racial discourse, integrates the Gothic novel into the longstanding history of discursive construction, visually (including literarily) depicting Black men as monstrous threats that must be policed, battled, overcome, and punished (beaten, incarcerated, tortured, lynched) by white men. Adopting a broad perspective, he engages with the history of anti-Black racism, by showing how the white discursive gaze creates "*the Nigger* [as] possessing only the nature of a savage *thing*, driven almost solely by his animal intuitions and lust for violence," until the Black man is completely stripped of the "sociological, historical, or economic causes for his behavior" (Curry 197, original emphasis). That Ligon created his version of a visibly B/blackened Frankenstein in 1992, the year of the Rodney King riots in Los

---

4   In my study, I refer to people of African descent as "Black" and "African American." However, "African American" implies residence in the U.S., while "Black" functions as an umbrella term for all individuals who are part of the Black Atlantic and African diaspora. Especially in the context of early Black writing and slave narratives, the term "Black" helps capture the fluidity and movement of Black identities and texts throughout the Black Atlantic. The capitalization of "Black" is not a political decision but a pragmatic one; in a study dealing with Gothic fiction, a clear differentiation between references to the color black and Black peoples ensures comprehension.

Angeles,[5] implies both the actuality and continuity of the racist discourse of the Frankensteinian Black male as a "savage *thing*" (Curry 197).

Yet, Ligon's Frankenstein does more than visualize white discursive violence. Located narratively on the brink of the monster's rebellion against his creator, the painting's blackness must also be read as conquering the white canvas, representing the survival and triumph of B/blackness over whiteness and the normative order of clear-cut and white-framed discursive stencils. Thus, Ligon's painting achieves to voice what Shelly's monster cannot: its "own sensations in [its] own mode." This mode consists chiefly of Shelly's (racialized) Frankenstein as a basis on which political dimension and actuality can be balanced with a unique aesthetic in a powerful painting. Joining the large group of writers, filmmakers, artists, and musicians who have adapted and/or worked with Frankensteinian material, Ligon created a new, discourse-strategic version of the monster that self-reflexively and critically highlights and functionalizes its history of racialization and anti-Black racism as part of the visual legacy of the Gothic icon. Once we have encountered Ligon's *Study for Frankenstein #1* and connected it to the iconic Gothic novel, we can no longer dismiss the monster's discursively inscribed Blackness. In other words, we cannot think of *Frankenstein* outside its racialized box. In this respect, Ligon has created a contemporary African American portrait of Frankenstein, by "studying" its racialized (and racializing) textual origins in nineteenth-century British Gothic fiction.

My interpretation of Ligon's painting sheds light on one important aspect of his artwork: his quotation and deconstructive reworking of a Gothic icon to depict the hateful racialized discourse underlying the construction of the monstrous Black male body. Other possible contexts, such as Ligon's engagement with homosexuality and homophobia (Young 225) and the discussion on the possibilities and limitations of what he calls a "post-black" aesthetic (Golden 14), have been excluded from my argument. I do, however, argue that highlighting Ligon's creative engagement with the Gothic vis-à-vis race and raciality is essential to better understand not only *Study for Frankenstein #1* but also the Gothic. Indeed, the underlying strategy—Ligon's complex creative unpacking and deconstructive reworking of the Gothic icon's racialization—is archetypal of a branch of literature and art we call "African American Gothic" and what we tend to consider under the umbrella notion of "the American Gothic."

---

5 Triggered by the legal acquittal of four officers of the Los Angeles Police Department for usage of excessive force in the arrest and beating of Rodney King, widespread violent unrest began on April 29, 1992 in South Central Los Angeles, a region with a majority population of African American and Hispanic peoples. The Rodney King case received national media coverage, primarily because the excessive violence of the police force was videotaped by a witness.

In this study, I inquire into and extensively survey the relation of the American Gothic—both White Anglo-Saxon Protestant (WASP) and African American in origin—to race and raciality, from its origins in eighteenth-century Britain to the American Gothic novel in the twenty-first century. As many African American artists and writers, such as Toni Morrison, Colson Whitehead, and Glenn Ligon, have repeatedly and successfully drawn attention to the problematic relation of the (American) Gothic to race and raciality, my study is far from the first to adopt a critical perspective on this relation.[6] However, it differs significantly from preceding studies in terms of scope and consequences. By focusing on race and raciality in a range of Gothic texts and socio-cultural contexts, I delineate the intrinsic raciality that is discursively sedimented and conventionally encoded in the Gothic's uniquely binary structure. This finding remarkably contrasts the traditional approach to race in Gothic fiction, which is summarized by Bienstock Anolik and Howard as

> [an] examin[ation of] texts in which Gothic fear is relocated onto the figure of the racial and social Other, the Other who replaces the supernatural ghost or grotesque monster as the code for mystery and danger, becoming, ultimately, as horrifying, threatening and unknowable as the typical Gothic manifestation. (2)

I argue that there is no typical Gothic manifestation that is not already racialized or racializing. Whether a ghost, monster, or undefined lurking presence, the entities that are employed to create Gothic atmospheres and hauntings in fiction are intrinsically connected to discursive racialization. Additionally, based on my discussion of the earliest Gothic texts, I create two divisions of racialization: the Gothic other and the Gothicized Black abject. Arguing that we must account for a crucial discursive shift from one type of Gothicized savagery to the other—that is, from the Native American Savage Villain to the Africanist Savage Villain as the thingified Black abject—I employ Sabine Broeck's notion of white abjectorship to discuss the Gothic. The abject Gothicized Black presence in WASP American Gothic literature must be understood as having a destructive and lasting impact on

---

6 Works that focus on the Gothic's discursive strategies of racial othering include Judith Halberstam's *Skin Shows: Gothic Horror and the Technology of Monsters*, which attributes the preference of Gothic authors for monstrous otherness to race, class, gender, and sexuality; Howard L. Malchow's *Gothic Images of Race in Nineteenth-Century Britain*, which explores racialized Gothic tropes in the context of European nationalism and imperialism; Kathleen Brogan's *Cultural Haunting: Ghosts and Ethnicity in Recent American Literature*; Edward H. Jacobs' *Accidental Migrations: An Archaeology of Gothic Discourse*; Dani Cavallaro's *The Gothic Vision: Three Centuries of Horror, Terror and Fear*; Andrew Smith, William Hughes, and Jonathan Taylor's *Empire and the Gothic: The Politics of the Genre*; and Ruth Bienstock Anolik's *The Gothic Other: Racial and Social Constructions in the Literary Imagination* and *Demons of the Body and Mind: Essays on Disability in Gothic Literature*.

the cultural discourse in the United States. Yet, as Ligon's *Study for Frankenstein #1* makes abundantly clear, this is only one aspect of the Gothic.

The Gothic, I argue, must be understood as an ultra-adaptable, discursively active writing strategy whose racialized (and racializing) quality can also be employed creatively and critically by historically and culturally marginalized groups and individuals. More precisely, I claim that consistent and thorough inclusion and visualization of race and raciality are required in discussions of (American) Gothic texts—and the "brew of darkness" that Ligon draws upon and carves into the white (intertextual) background—to fully understand the potentials and limitations of one of the most consistently popular types of fiction (and art). A focus on race and raciality, which arguably predetermine and predefine other categories of (external and self-)identification, such as gender and class, requires rethinking of the (American) Gothic as the appropriate genre for the excluded, marginalized, and silenced. However, such a focus all too often entails including, centering upon, and voicing only the needs and stories of WASP protagonists that are presumed to be underprivileged.[7] In other words, a substantive working definition of the (American) Gothic must include the subversive, and even deconstructive, strategies of an artist such as Glenn Ligon, who strategically uses the Gothic as a reference and point of departure to claim his voice in the art scene, political discourse, and hybrid historiography of the United States.

It is for this purpose that I introduce the notion of the "Gotheme." "Gotheme" is a neologism loosely based on Roland Barthes's semiological notion of "myth" and is directly derived from Claude Lévi-Strauss's notion of "mythemes" (Lévi-Strauss 206ff.). It describes an irreducible, unchanging unit of signification that always consists of a dichotomy, of which the destructive element is foregrounded against the foil of its only potentially corrective counterpart. In my study, the concept of

---

7   The American Gothic in scholarship is commonly understood as the internalized and psychologically sophisticated evolution of its generic British parent, which is defined solely by its settings and props. The American Gothic is thought to have translated the British Gothic's weariness "of Enlightenment values" (Sage 8) and critical inversion of rationality (see Morrow and McGrath xiii) to meet the needs of the North American readership. On American soil, and thus in a culture of self-proclaimed reason and rational realism, adapted conventions of the Gothic flourished, as Leslie Fiedler, Teresa A. Goddu, Alan Lloyd-Smith, and others have argued extensively, because the American myth does not reward everyone who pursues happiness and success with riches. To depict the terror-inspiring underside of the American Dream—the racism, sexism, and capitalism that keeps anyone who does not fulfill the ideal (WASP) man, who achieves success with hard work and self-reliance, American writers have turned to the Gothic. This apparent need for adaptation and re-mythologization also means that the American Gothic is both perceived as distinct from the British Gothic—and thus no longer understood as a literature-specific concept or literary genre—and as being open to other forms of cultural production, including the visual arts. In Part I of my study, I will critically engage this perspective on the (American) Gothic.

the Gotheme replaces the so-called "laundry list definitions" of the Gothic, which synchronically and diachronically describe the stereotypical props, settings, and characters (e.g., items as diverse as a haunted castle, the pitch-black interior of a spaceship, trap doors, an evil monk, Frankenstein, Edward Cullen, an innocent maiden, and Marilyn Manson) as they appear in texts that are deemed "Gothic." Similarly, Gothemes describe recurring plots, scenes, props, character types, and locales at the core of ultra-adaptable Gothic imagery, as dichotomies of contrasting elements; the horror of being incarcerated needs the foil of freedom, chaos needs harmony, and the dark villain needs a fair hero. It is in this binary construction of the Gothic that its explosive potential lies: Gothemes are sedimented discursive patterns as well as interpellated messages that need to be "appropriated" (Barthes 119), thus allowing the discourse to be changed. I will not employ (or defend) a structuralist approach to literature. Rather, my understanding of the specifically structural conventionality of Gothic novels implies careful dissection of repetitive and constantly replicating structural elements.

This study will closely analyze the (re-)iteration[8] of a central Gotheme and its implications, which are unique to American culture: the Savage Villain/Civil Hero (SV/CH) Gotheme. It originates in the early British Gothic, in which the essential gulf between hero and villain is composed of colonialist imagery with visual racial underpinnings;[9] against the hero's highlighted whiteness and chivalrous nature, the villain stands out as "the terrible and fearsome 'other' who symbolizes the dark self of the colonizer and assures him of his own moral integrity and identity" (Althans 69). The reader of late eighteenth- and early nineteenth-century British Gothic fiction expected (and continues to expect) a violent clash between two larger-than-life characters and between civil values and savage anarchy. Gothic texts

---

8   The terms "iteration" and "reiteration" are derived from Jacques Derrida's notion of "iterability." In his essay "Signature Event Context," iterability is introduced in the context of a linguistic sign that has to be repeatable in order for us to recognize it as such, but every repetition is different. Judith Butler synthesizes Derrida's concept with Foucault's concept of discourse and her notion of performance, arguing that we act through the utterances we make, not due to the intention or will of an individual speaker but the effect of sedimentary historic conventions and meanings (discourses), which are (unintentionally) quoted and repeated in every act of speech. This ongoing practice of quotation and reiteration is open to resistance, resignification, and change. By consciously altering the quoted discourse, that is, by consciously influencing the process of reiteration, the subject can leave its passively quoting position and become a discourse-altering agent. For clarity's sake, I distinguish between "iteration," intentional or unintentional quotation of a discourse (e.g., in Gothemes) in a new context, without an effort to critically alter it, and "reiteration," or intentional quotation of a discourse (e.g., in Gothemes) in a new context that alters the discourse (see also Chapter 2).

9   This writing strategy has been discussed in relation to the notion of "Imperial Gothic." Patrick Brantlinger suggests confining the Imperial Gothic to the period between 1880 and 1914, which roughly represents the heyday of the British Empire.

written during this time use an interesting device: The climactic moment in which the villain loses both his morality and the fear of God is marked by a change in the vocabulary used to describe the villain. As the angry, loathsome man betrays his humanity, his brow darkens, his eyes blacken, and his skin turns deep red, until he resembles a "savage, inhuman monster" (Walpole, *Castle* 108; see also Walpole, *Castle* 22, 94).

Early North American writers, most famously Charles Brockden Brown in the first fully-fledged American Gothic novel *Edgar Huntly; or Memoirs of a Sleep-Walker* (1799), imported the Gothic mainly from England, keeping the motif of savagery to depict the loss of civilized and pious human qualities within the Gothic villain. However, instead of just acting and looking *like* a savage, due to his uncivil immorality and blasphemy, the villain was blended with eighteenth- and early nineteenth-century America's personification of absolute wilderness: the ignoble "Indian" savage. The motif rose in popularity, due in part to the ongoing success of the now unique American Gothic, and the evil or ignoble savage was increasingly adapted and Gothicized, until it encompassed African and African American peoples as well, producing a perfectly horrid image of darkness: the Africanist Savage Villain.[10] This shift from one type of Gothicized savagery to another must be understood as a monumental shift from Gothic otherness to the Gothicized Black abject. Sabine Broeck explained the discursive process of white abjectorship in this ontological repositioning of the Black body as a savage thing:

> To come into being, the European subject needed its underside, as it were: the crucially integral but invisible part of the human has been his/her *abject*, created in the European mind by way of racialized thingification: the African enslaved, an unhumaned species tied by property rights to the emerging subject so tightly that they could—structurally speaking—never occupy the position of the dialectical Heglian object as other, has thus remained therefore outside the dynamics of the human. ("Legacies" 118, emphasis in the original)

The alteration of the Gotheme in early American Gothic writing doubtlessly led to the creation of many thrilling texts for a fast-growing and almost exclusively WASP readership. While the white Civil Hero offers room for identification and condensed enactment of the contemporaneous ideology of WASP Americanness, the semantic extension of the Savage Villain has been narrowed so far as to exclude the entire WASP readership; to WASP Americans, villainous savagery is entertaining because it is not only "easily avoidable" (Balchin 254) but also racially and ontologically impossible. As I will show in great detail, a stereotypical motif as successful

---

10 The first part of the concept, "Africanist," goes back to Toni Morrison's watershed exposure of the "Africanist presence" in the fiction of seminal white American writers, as well as in American culture (Morrison, *Playing* 6). For more on this, see Chapter 4.

and problematic as the SV/CH Gotheme is open to criticism, creative rewriting, revision, and deconstruction by those it denigrates as being evil and thingified savages.

To undertake such a vast, interdisciplinary project, I mainly offer a starting point for better comprehension of the Gothic's (often highly problematic) relation to race and racialization, by carefully dissecting the WASP American Gothic tradition before delineating the Black/African American Gothic. My focus on the African American Gothic must not be mistaken as only a pragmatic choice; rather, as I describe in detail, the African American Gothic tradition not only offers the opportunity to trace the unique Gothic tradition born in 1789 in the Black Atlantic, outside of the WASP American context, but it also consists of a stream of literature that actively, strategically, and continuously reacts to the WASP American Gothic tradition from the 1830s onward. Understanding that the rethinking of the (American) Gothic has direct impacts on the core concerns of Gothic Studies and American Studies (especially on current debates following the intervention of Afro-Pessimism[11]), I carefully consider the complexity (i.e., the historical and cultural diversity) of the concept(s) it involves.

To make sense of the contemporary cultural plurality and generic hybridity of the (American) Gothic and to critically dissect the notions of the Gothic and American Gothic, this study closely reads WASP and African American Gothic novels, written by male and female American authors, from the interconnected perspectives of New Historicism, Critical Race Theory, and Gender Studies. Special attention is paid to the historical, cultural, and sociopolitical contexts that formed the texts under scrutiny, while the state and prospects of the U.S. literary market and its strategies for acquiring an audience/customers are questioned. Given my special interest in the (American) Gothic's relation to race and raciality, I evaluate the texts' constructions of race and raciality in particular, and, given the Gothic's highly gendered binaries (e.g., the male hero/villain and the damsel in distress), I trace its intersection with gender.

The notion of "text" underlying this study is that which is applied in poststructuralist American Studies, thus making it inclusive and open to the utmost extent. Derived from the semiological approach of Roland Barthes, "text" is a cultural praxis and is therefore not limited to literary works or even to written text. Since American culture can be understood as "those stories that Americans tell one another in order to make sense of their lives" (Mechling 4), text becomes the medium,

---

11   I use the uppercase and hyphenated term "Afro-Pessimism" to differentiate between the critical intervention of Afro-Pessimists, writing from the perspective of Black Studies, such as Saidiya Hartman, Hortense Spillers, Frank B. Wilderson III, and Jared Sexton, and the afropessimist approach to the postcolonial state and potential of the African continent, which was especially prevalent in the 1980s and 1990s.

ritual, and spatial vehicle for storytelling. Application of this open, holistic notion of text places strong emphasis on the interconnectedness and intertextuality of the texts and the stories they tell. Drawing on Mikhail Bakhtin's key differentiation between monologic and dialogic works of literature, poststructuralist Julia Kristeva (*Desire*) emphasizes texts' intertextuality, which replaces traditional notions of intersubjectivity, thus relocating meaning from the author-produced text to the reader who is actively involved, not only with the text in question but also with the complex network of texts invoked in reading and writing processes. Although the implications of intertextuality are acknowledged, this study is limited to the discussion and comparison of intertexts and literary traditions explicitly suggested by the examined texts.

Despite its roughly sketched, radically open notion of "text," the main focus of this study is on a very narrow selection of literary texts: published print novels. This limitation might be surprising, but it is applied due to the unique character of the subject under study. The (American) Gothic has its origins in literature, specifically the English novel, and only over the course of the Gothic novel's success story have its leitmotifs evolved into the transmedial and transcultural conventional structures, motifs, and tropes with which we associate it today. I trace and analyze the Gothic's historical development and construct a working definition of the (American) Gothic to be examined, through the close reading and analysis of contemporary WASP American and African American Gothic novels. It is my hope that future research will take the next step and transfer this new notion of the literary American Gothic to contemporary American film, digital media, and so on, as well as to the many other ethnic variations of the contemporary American Gothic.[12]

I have divided this study into three parts, each of which has been further subdivided into various chapters. "Part I: The Gothic and the Savage Villain/Civil Hero Gotheme" establishes a working definition of the Gothic and, by tracing the fixation on race and racial otherness in early British Gothic traditions, situates race and raciality as a key convention of the Gothic. More specifically, Chapter 2, "What Is the Gothic?", analyzes the notion of the Gothic both diachronically (i.e., etymologically and with regard to its conceptual history) and synchronically (i.e., with regard to the multitude of explanations and definitions prevalent in the field of Gothic Studies today). Engaging with the heated debate surrounding the definition of the Gothic means entering and making sense of a rapidly growing field of study that all too often dwells on a difficult-to-decipher, overly ornate style and/or which dismisses not only the need for but also the possibility of defining its subject. As one

---

12   In my own research, I have applied this theoretical framework to contemporary American Indian Gothic fiction and film as well as to the Gothic long poems of Asian–Canadian author Larissa Lai (see Lenhardt's articles "Wendigos," "Washington's Troops," and "As Bones").

is unable to comprehend the Gothic in terms of a "large, irregularly shaped figure" (Williams 23) and a "Frankensteinian process" that results in a "textual monster" (Kilgour 4), I develop a new discourse-strategic working definition of the Gothic that aligns with and extends recent scholars' work to renegotiate the (American) Gothic from a postcolonial perspective.[13] I then narrow down the vast continuum of dichotomic structures and motifs used in Gothic writing strategies to the key SV/CH Gotheme, thereby integrating it into my working definition.

Chapter 3, "British Origins of the Savage Villain/Civil Hero Gotheme," delineates the origins of the racialized and racializing Gotheme in early British Gothic literature. By examining classic early British Gothic literature (including but not limited to *The Castle of Otranto*, *The Monk*, and *Melmoth the Wanderer*), I link the early Gothic's fascination by juxtaposing racially overdrawn characters, in terms of either savagery or civilization, to two contradictory versions of the myth of the "savage" Goths. The early Gothic seems to originate in hierarchically and exclusionarily structured discourses of race, belonging, and nationality. The staging of dichotomous characters in racialized terms, of either their villainous savagery or their heroic, civil virtues, creates a visibly marked and genuinely politically active national narrative produced by a young British nation, deeming itself to be under multilateral attack. I conclude Part I by tracing how the success of nationalistically inspired racial stereotypes, especially the juxtaposition of the racialized savage villain and the civil hero on British soil, triggered the migration of the SV/CH Gotheme across the Atlantic. Here, the SV/CH Gotheme will be utilized within another national narrative that opposes the British Gothic endeavor.

In "Part II: The Savage Villain/Civil Hero Gotheme: WASP American Origins and Iterations," the process of migration, adaptation, and translation of the early British Gothic's intrinsic raciality (within the SV/CH Gotheme) in WASP American literature is examined. The driving force of this part of the study is a hypothesis derived from my analysis of early British Gothic texts: If the SV/CH Gotheme, and thus raciality, is a conventional constant in past and present American Gothic novels, then the American Gothic must be understood as intrinsically racialized and racializing. This is a potentially devastating result with far-reaching implications, particularly for current debates in American Studies triggered by the intervention of Afro-Pessimism.

Chapter 4, "Early WASP American Adaptations," provides a basis for a rather pessimistic outlook on nineteenth-century white Gothic literature. This chapter illustrates how the British Gothic's racial other was adapted and how there was a momentous cultural shift from the initial type of Native American Savage Villainy to the Africanist Savage Villain, as the Gothicized Black abject, which swallowed and

---

13   See Cavallaro (2002), Theo D'Haen (1995), Edwards (2002), Hogle (2002), Jacobs (2000), Khair (2009), Lee (2009), and Smith et al. (2003).

replaced the Native American other, due to greater political, social, and cultural urgency and actuality. Eventually, WASP American Gothic literature focused solely on the Africanist SV, and the noble savage became the stock stand-in character used to depict the Native American other in WASP American literature.

In Chapter 5, "Contemporary WASP American Iterations," the transition to the contemporary WASP American Gothic is traced and used to analyze the continuous presence of the racialized and racializing SV/CH Gotheme in a number of recent WASP American Gothic novels. To increase the depth of this necessarily selective survey, I provide a close reading of two contemporary mainstream bestsellers that are heavily pervaded with Gothic motifs and, more importantly, climactically constructed around the SV/CH Gotheme: Stephen King's *The Girl Who Loved Tom Gordon* (1999) and Karen Russell's *Swamplandia!* (2011). Both novels have Gothic undertones and focus on the coming-of-age of a female protagonist who is involuntarily left to her own devices in the North American wilderness. The fully iterated SV/CH Gotheme in these novels, as well as in the broader North American literary landscape, indicates the continuous consistency of conventional early WASP American Gothic writing strategies in WASP American fiction. Discussion of the way in which the continuity of race and racialization in WASP American Gothic texts—specifically, the dehumanized and Gothicized Black abject (i.e., the Africanist Savage Villain)—directly fuels the arguments of Afro-Pessimism and thus concludes this section of the study, thereby motivating my critical engagement with African American literature in the third section. There, I explore whether the racialized WASP American Gothic patterns—and, most importantly, the SV/CH Gotheme—are conventional, and therefore potentially changeable, or if they are essential and intrinsic to the Gothic and, much like the rules of chess, definitive and invariable.

"Part III: 'You say I am wilderness. I am'—Black Origins and African American Reiterations" continues the discussion of the Afro-Pessimistic implications of the previous section and examines the SV/CH Gotheme in Black Atlantic and African American texts from the nineteenth century to the early twenty-first century. The underlying premise of the third section is that if African American Gothic texts are intrinsically racialized and racializing and if the central SV/CH Gotheme cannot be reiterated outside the boundaries of race—that is, if intra-discursive emergence of "unthought" is impossible or undesirable—then the core of the Gothic might indeed be race/raciality. Reflecting the structure of the previous chapter, I trace the SV/CH Gotheme in early Black/African American texts, before examining the Gothic in contemporary African American novels.

Chapter 6, "Innovation and Resistance: The SV/CH Gotheme in Black Writing, 1789 to 1861," argues against scholarship that theorizes the African American Gothic as a merely reactive "anti-gothic" (Smethurst 29) type of writing. Instead, I trace a uniquely Black Gothic tradition stemming from Olaudah Equiano's *The Interesting Narrative*. In doing so, I establish an alternative point of origin for the American

Gothic, beyond the cultural and geographic boundaries of WASP-dominated North America and within the Black Atlantic. In subsequent analyses of nineteenth-century and contemporary African American Gothic texts, I delineate the continuous presence of the SV/CH Gotheme in complex reiteration contexts and in terms of discourse-strategic efforts. I also identify the way in which it is strategically utilized, reiterated, and critically (re-)integrated into two writing traditions, self-reflexively and significantly complicating both the Gotheme and the Gothic writing strategies. In particular, Toni Morrison's gloomy recourse to seventeenth-century plantation life in *A Mercy* (2008) and Colson Whitehead's post-apocalyptic zombie wasteland in *Zone One* (2011) are analyzed in depth. These bestselling works coincide in their fictional discussion of Afro-Pessimistic assumptions and Black ontologies from within and vis-à-vis the Gothic writing strategy. In my analysis of Morrison's and Whitehead's creative and reiterative exploitation of the intrinsic raciality of the SV/CH Gotheme, I discuss the possibility of a discursive "unthought," that is, of the Gothic performed outside the conventional discursive boundaries of race and racialization.

Taken together, the three parts of *Savage Horrors: The Intrinsic Raciality of the American Gothic* establish and subsequently answer four consecutive questions:

What is the Gothic, and what is the core of the diverse texts categorized as American Gothic?

Is this core the racialized and racializing SV/CH Gotheme?

If so, how is the SV/CH Gotheme employed in Gothic novels by African American authors, who, according to WASP American Gothic conventions, belong in the racial category of the abject (i.e., the Africanist Savage Villain)?

Is creative and discursive "unthought" possible? In other words, is it possible that future Gothic texts will establish a binary of villainy and heroism, without instantaneously equating villainy with monstrous Blackness (that is, the Gothicized Black abject/the Africanist Savage Villain) and heroism with white civility (which is often directly conflated with white supremacy)?

All four questions reflect the central dilemma of contemporary Gothic scholarship: What do we talk about when we discuss *the Gothic*? Is the old umbrella term still helpful for summarizing the variety of reiterative efforts by non-WASP American writers and artists? Only by seeking to define the Gothic can we describe and analyze the core of all (American) Gothic works and either retain the umbrella term or permanently reject it due to irreconcilable differences. But what if this core also acts as a divisor? What if, at the core of the Gothic, a racialized and racializing structural convention has tainted Gothic texts with racialization, denigration, and white abjectorship since the eighteenth century? What would the "American" in American Gothic signify then?

PART I:
The Gothic and the Savage Villain/ Civil Hero Gotheme

What Is the Gothic?

> "I perceive you have no idea what Gothic is; you have lived too long amidst true taste, to understand venerable barbarism."
> (Walpole, "Letter" 469)

In 2018, the most comprehensive and authoritative online bibliography of Gothic scholarship, *The Sickly Taper*,[1] lists close to 12,000 articles, monographs, and anthologies explicitly concerned with the Gothic. Surfing from page to page, skimming through the lists of scholars and their publications, *The Sickly Taper* offers us a first glimpse at the truly monstrous proportions of the field of Gothic studies.

We find ourselves confronted with a history of Gothic research that easily covers one hundred and forty years and every topic imaginable, from Munson A. Havens' *Horace Walpole and the Strawberry Hill Press* (1901) and Edith Birkhead's now classic *The Tale of Terror* (1921), through Berenstein's *Gender, Sexuality, and Spectatorship in Classic Horror Cinema*, to Marilyn Manson, the cyberpunks, and beyond. We meet scholars working in such diverse areas as the English Gothic, Scottish, German, Russian, Asian, and the many subcategories of the American Gothic, such as New England Gothic, Southern Aristocrat Gothic, Frontier Gothic, and Local Color Gothic, African American, Chicano American, and most recently, Native American Gothic. Gothic is not only a global, transcultural phenomenon, but it also seems to be internally pluralistic to the utmost degree. Female Gothic, Feminist Gothic (not to be confused with Gothic Feminism[2]), Post-Feminist Gothic, and Male Gothic must all be taken into account, let alone New Gothic, Neo Gothic, Postmodern, and Postcolonial Gothic, Anti-Gothic and Aftergothic, a handful of Gothic Revivals, and we could easily go on and on. Adding to our bewilderment, the Gothic is far from being limited to prose fiction. Instead, we learn about Gothic drama and poetry, Gothic art, film, even websites, and the Gothic's uncanny power to invade a wide variety cultural forms to produce "generic hybrids" (Gamer 12, 23).

---

1   *The Sickly Taper* was founded by the late Gothic scholar Frederick S. Frank and is today run by the Department of English Language, Literature, and Creative Writing at the University of Windsor (Ontario, Canada), under the direction of Carol M. Davidson.
2   Cf. Birkerts.

Facing this dilemma of ever-multiplying Gothics, it is not surprising that the question "What is the Gothic?" has become more and more important in recent years. In fact, it has become outright fashionable to start one's discussion off with just that question,[3] so that it gradually replaces its predecessor, "Why, yet another publication on Gothic fiction?" Surprising indeed, however, is the ubiquitous atmosphere of satiation in most recent publications. Instead of attempting to answer the by now truly haunting question, by analyzing the multiplicity of possible answers and by stripping away the typically over-ornate style in which they are presented, recent scholarship shrinks from defining the Gothic. No longer interested in providing their own (however culturally and temporally limited) definition, in the face of innumerable critical claims and counterclaims, Punter and Byron argue representatively that it should be up to the individual "student and reader to evaluate these claims and to find out for themselves which of the many definitions and descriptions seem most apposite" (xviii).[4] Understanding the Gothic to be both omnipresent and imprecise, Anne Williams' influential study, *Art of Darkness: A Poetics of Gothic*, warns against the "Dangers of Defining 'Gothic'" and reminds "the reader of Justice Potter Stewart's memorable standard for the obscene, which in effect stated: 'I can't define it, but I know it when I see it'" (14).[5]

This disregard for the value of both ontological and working definitions, that is, for the scholarly need to stipulate and limit one's very specific field of inquiry, by disclosing the underlying theoretical assumptions and categories used to organize the inquiry, has led scholars such as Rintoul to conclude that "[c]learly, studying the Gothic has no *best* approach" (709, original emphasis). Capitulating as this may seem, we are not left without guidance from our Gothic studies' predecessors. We can fall back on the by now common ground of etymology, before trying to subdue the "large, irregularly shaped figure" (Williams 23) with a working definition. How far this etymological consensus will help us in our quest for a working definition of "the Gothic" will have to be evaluated critically.

---

3   See Marilyn Michaud's pointed discussion of recent scholarship's focus on the question; she shows how leading scholars such as Fred Botting, Jerrold E. Hogle, Robert Miles, Marie Mulvey-Roberts, and David Punter use this question as a starting point for an attempt at defining the Gothic (Michaud 1, also her second footnote).
4   Among other recent studies that foreground approaches to the Gothic, rather than ways of defining it, are: Catherine Spooner and Emma McEvoy, Marilyn Michaud, and Richard S. Albright.
5   See also Williams' subchapter, "On the Dangers of Defining 'Gothic'," 12–24.

1.1 The "Goth" in Gothic

The majority of contemporary scholars of the Gothic, among them David Punter and Glennis Byron, Fred Botting, Robert Miles, and Robin Sowerby, agree that a solid basis can be laid for describing the complex nature of the Gothic, by describing the term's historical and mythological origins, before turning to Gothic's origins as a genre.

Historically, the adjective "Gothic" relates to members and practices of the Goths, a Germanic tribe of Scandinavian origin whose two branches, the Ostrogoths and the Visigoths, harassed the Roman Empire for centuries.[6] In the absence of early written accounts and with only a limited number of cultural artifacts, we cannot reconstruct a complete and reliable history of the Gothic people; more important to our interests, however, is the fact that we can reconstruct the cultural myths that developed around a people known from the start only via legends and myths.[7]

Mythologically, the undocumented history of the Gothic people and their culture has proven to be ultra-adaptable to changing political and aesthetic ideologies. Most strikingly, the term "Gothic" has been used to mark one end of a bipolar opposition from the European Renaissance onwards. When the early Renaissance drew the line between privileged forms of cultural production, which abided by the classical rules derived directly from ancient Greek and Roman high cultures and the disregardable cultural lapse that was the Dark Ages, everything medieval, barbarous, superstitious, ignorant, and irrationally wild became conflated with the

---

6   According to their own legend, documented in retrospect in AD 551 in the Late Latin *Getica* (also known as *De origine actibusque Getarum* [*The Origin and Deeds of the Goths*]) by the Roman-Gothic historian Jordanes and backed by recent archaeological findings, the Goths left their native Scandinavian shore around the turn of the eras and sailed in three ships, under their king Berig, to the Baltic Sea's southern shore. Here, they defeated the Vandals and other Germanic tribes of the area and settled. Conquering and settling successively until the seventh century, the Goths moved thousands of miles across the map of Europe, breached the Roman Empire's border during the third century, took Rome in AD 410, and established kingdoms in France and Italy, before arriving at the Black Sea, as Jordanes claims, under the fifth king after Berig, and after various adventures. (In fact, recent research into the history of the Goths has successfully established the hypotheses that Jordanes' account is only an interpretative summary of an older written account of the origin of a barbaric people, the *Origo Gothica*, written by the Roman intellectual Cassidor around AD 519. See Wolfram. For a more detailed summary of "Pre-Gothic Gothic," see also Sowerby.

7   Discussing the mythological underpinnings of Jordanes' *Getica*, David Punter and Glennis Byron point to Samuel Kliger's *The Goths in England: A Study in Seventeenth and Eighteenth Century Thought*. Kliger shows how Jordanes' account is shaped by his aim of glorifying his own ancestry, the Thracian tribe, which he identified as the more impressive tribe of the Goths. What is more, he aimed to create a unified notion of a commonly shared northern identity and used the term "Gothic" in an extended sense to homogeneously embrace all tribes now called "Tutonic" or "Germanic." See more recently Peter Heather.

barbaric Roman-slaying Goths.[8] John Dryden's 1695 definition that "[a]ll that has nothing of the Ancient gust is call'd a barbarous or Gothique manner" (119, 40) had long become common knowledge by the eighteenth century. As Punter and Byron summarize for eighteenth-century England, this polarized "equation of the Gothic with a barbaric medieval past served not only to establish through difference the superiority of the more classical traditions of Greece and Rome, but also to confirm the virtues of the equally civilized, ordered and rational present" (4).

In England, the rise of Greek- and Roman-inspired neoclassicism also gave rise to an alternative and, in many ways, even contradictory version of the Gothic myth. Following the revival of the reception of Tacitus, who was regarded first and foremost as Rome's greatest historian, and his account of the Germanic tribes in his AD 98 *Germania* (*terminus post quem*), the barbaric slayer became coupled with his noble twin. Although Tacitus argued that the Goths were the most visible of the Germanic tribes, it is the very common conflation of "Gothic" with all Germanic or Teutonic tribes that made this text so important to the Gothic mythological tradition. Talking about the Germanic people in general, Tacitus is understood to describe only the Goths when he draws the picture of a pre-modern society's brave and virtuous people. Their blue eyes sparkling with spite, their hair red, their bodies tall, strong, and very apt for physical combat, the Germanics/Goths are pictured as a just and noble race that has always existed in close touch with nature, honors its women, and elects its chiefs "parliamentarily" at a communal gathering (Tacitus I,4; II). "During the eighteenth century, however, the Gothic also began to be invested with a set of different and contradictory values in both aesthetic [...] and political terms" (Punter and Byron 4). In the process of (re-)claiming a native England origin, i.e. of mythologizing the country's origin for a political and literary nationalist agenda, politicians (both Whig and Tory), writers (e.g. James Thomson in his poem "Liberty"),[9] and historians (e.g. Charles-Louis de Secondat Montesquieu in *Spirit of the Laws*, translated to English in 1750) had narrowed the dominant myth of the Gothic people down to their pre-parliamentary qualities; qualities that were understood

---

8   The few then-known manifestations of the 700-year-long Gothic past, mainly architectural influences and a few fully-fledged Gothic buildings, such as the Mausoleum of Theodoric just outside Ravenna, Italy, became, though not seldom wrongfully attributed, chief examples of the Goths' atrocious ending of the golden age of classical antiquity and the even more atrocious imposition of their disordered, barbaric style. The great artifacts that we today associate with the Goths, precious gem-encrusted eagle brooches, the gold crowns of Visigothic Spain, and, most importantly, the Silver Bible, *Codex Argenteus*, the sixth-century AD copy of four gospels in the Gothic language, were unknown at least to the vast majority of scholars and laymen.

9   In his poem, Thomson, for example, writes of the Goths settling Britain that they "brought a happy government along; / Formed by that freedom which, with secret voice, / Impartial nature teaches all her sons" (Thomson 4.682-4).

to be the dominant character traits of the English who understood themselves as the Goths' contemporary descendants.

It becomes apparent that the two Gothic sides of one barbaric coin, that is, the native parliamentarian and his evil twin, the barbaric slayer of classic antiquity, are not born within an ideological vacuum; rather, it is the British nation-building efforts of the seventeenth and eighteenth centuries, and especially that of England, that evoke a mythological Gothic past in direct relation to contemporary developments, which, in turn, foster the spread of the myth and its popularity. I am referring particularly to the necessity of a legitimizing, national narrative of a British Empire that had to face immense political and social changes within the Georgian era.[10] Consider, for example, in this respect, events and ongoing developments, such as the Agricultural Revolution, the accelerating Industrial Revolution, the Act of Union (1801), the wars with the thirteen American Colonies (1765-1783) and with Napoleonic France (1793-1802), and social reform movements under politicians such as Robert Peel and campaigners like William Wilberforce and other members of the so-called Clapham Sect, Thomas Clarkson, as well as Quakers like Elizabeth Fry, that began to bring about radical change in areas including the abolition of slavery, prison reform, and social justice. While in the process of imagining the British nation, as in Benedict Anderson's terminology, colonial racism "was a major element in that conception of 'Empire' which attempted to weld dynastic legitimacy and national community" (Anderson 150), it was not the only element. Though peppered with colonial racialized imagery, the rise of early Gothic fiction exemplifies at least two other ways in which we can perceive late eighteenth- and early nineteenth-centuries British nationalism: Firstly, Gothic fiction effectively conflated villainy and violence with Catholicism (c.f. villains such as Shedoni, Ambrosio, and the Inquisition), thus promoting British Protestantism and the legitimacy of the protestant king. Secondly, early Gothic outsourced the catholic villainy to foreign places and races such as Spain, Italy, and Orientalized Arabia. Especially in the wake of the French Revolution, xenophobic veins, fueled by anxieties about possible revolutionary upheavals on British soil, turned the Gothic into a racialized political propaganda tool seemingly[11] outside of the immediate context of colonialism.

Politically, late seventeenth- and eighteenth-century England was divided between the Tories (court party) and the Whigs (country party). Strikingly, both par-

---

10   The Georgian era takes its name from and is defined as spanning the reigns of George I (enthroned in 1714), George II, George III and George IV, and it is often extended to include the short reign of William IV, which ended with his death in 1837.

11   A political reading of early British Gothic fiction within the direct framework of Colonialism and Empire politics in general, and of Walpole's Whig-style strategies in *The Castle of Otranto* in particular, is discussed in Chapter 3.

ties connected contemporaneous politics with the Goths and their presumed primitivism. On one side,

> the Gothic is associated with the barbaric and uncivilized in order to define that which is other to the values of the civilized present [Tories]. Alternatively, the Gothic is still associated with the primitive but the primitive has now become identified with the true, but lost, foundations of a culture [Whigs]. The Gothic past is consequently seen as retaining not only more power and vigour than the present, but also, in a strange way, more civilized values. (Punter and Byron 5, the attributions in squared brackets are mine)

While the Tories used the barbaric Gothic myth to construct a self-legitimizing pre-Reformation medievalism and to overcome threats to the unbroken bloodline of the divinely blessed monarchy, the Whigs constructed the English houses of parliament and the constitutional monarchy in terms of a pre-parliamentary Gothic ancestry. By the time the Whigs blended Gothic history with the reception of Tacitus' *Germania* and their political present, it was common, albeit contested, ground that the English derived their "idea of political government," as Montesquieu argues in his vastly influential *Spirit of the Laws* (1748, English 1750), from the Germans and their "beautiful system [...] invented first in the woods" (162/61). This common eighteenth-century practice dates back to the late seventeenth century and the ultimate ideological clash of Tories and Whigs during the 1688 deposition of the Catholic James II, in favor of the Protestant William and Mary and dubbed the "Glorious Revolution" by the victorious Whigs. Here, the need for a new, Gothic national identity reached a first political peak. After installing the new Protestant regime, the Whigs continuously faced threats to the legitimacy and authority of a monarchy that was no longer sacredly tied by an unbroken bloodline. The positive, pre-parliamentary mythology of the Goths (and their British descendants) ultimately legitimized and fixed the political need for a patriotic national identity, and for Whig-style politics.

In the wake of the French Revolution, the Gothic heritage myth of the English nation was transformed into a powerful propaganda tool for legitimizing the presumed moral supremacy of the English (British) over the French, barbaric other. In his virulent tract, *Reflections on the Revolution in France* (1790), Edmund Burke uses the English Gothic heritage to invent a foundational narrative for England's nobility and civilized order that (Gothically) leans toward the monarchy, nobility, the Church, and the morals and manners of the gentleman:

> This idea of a liberal descent inspires us with a sense of habitual native dignity, which prevents that upstart insolence almost inevitably adhering to and disgracing those who are the first acquirers of any distinction. By this means our liberty becomes a noble freedom. It carries an imposing and majestic aspect. (Burke 276)

The Revolution of 1688, brought about by what Burke repeatedly calls "a just war," and its unwritten constitution are constructed as being both an agreement among civilized parties and the basis for preserving this supreme civilization. In stark contrast, the French Revolution is evoked as the epitome of an atrociously irrational and immoral nation of barbarians:

> The fresh ruins of France, which shock our feelings wherever we can turn our eyes, are not the devastation of civil war: they are the sad, but instructive monuments of rash and ignorant counsel in a time of profound peace. They are the display of inconsiderate and presumptuous, because unresisted and irresistible authority. The persons who have thus squandered away the precious treasure of their crimes, the persons who have made this prodigal and wild waste of public evils (the last stake reserved for the ultimate ransom of the state), have met in their progress with little, or rather with no opposition at all. (Burke 283)

These patriotically inspired revivals of the Gothic myth quickly triggered a Gothic revival in art and architecture;[12] no longer associated with barbarous anti-classicism, Gothic became the latest craze and a natural, lasting signpost for Great Britain's Gothic ancestry and national identity. However successful the Gothic national myth initially was in England's late seventeenth to early eighteenth centuries, it soon came under unexpected attack from its closest ally, nationalism.

> To be British was to be Protestant, with both identities drawing strength from the deep wells of residual anti-Catholicism. The Catholic became the convenient other "British" identity. Britain's identity was of a modern, progressive nation transforming itself, and the world, through commerce and science, a progress guided by the advanced condition of its constitution and government, in sharp contrast to Europe, figured as despotic, backward, feudal, Catholic, and Gothic. (Miles, "Eighteenth-Century" 15)

The strong Catholic overtones of the Gothic style rivaled its role in Britain's national myth. As a result, the old dichotomy of the Gothic moved center stage once more. While the Gothic is always conflated with primitivism, it is also always "identified with the primitive for specific ideological purposes" (Punter and Byron 5). It is used either to define the negative other, the dark foil against which a present culture's civilized achievements stand out most brightly, or as the naturally fertile but now

---

12   While the many extreme Gothic makeovers of rich Whig aristocracy's private homes, most famously Lord Cobham's Gothic Temple, also known as the Temple of Ancient Liberty, and Horace Walpole's papier-mâché and trompe l'œil project, Strawberry Hill, make nice anecdotes, undoubtedly, the rebuilding of the Houses of Parliament, after the fire of 1834, in architect Charles Barry's design of a building in the Perpendicular Gothic style marks the highly visible, however late peak, of Gothically legitimized English nationalism.

spoiled and lost ground from which the present culture's greatness once grew. In Great Britain, and especially in England, these two interpretations of Gothic primitivism have existed side by side in a tense balance from the Renaissance onward. It is within the center of this tense balance that the Gothic as a literary genre first took shape, which brings me to the second and final point of mutual agreement among scholars of the Gothic.

Defining a point of generic origin for the literary Gothic has become a very repetitive business. The Gothic, in its most narrowly defined sense, is an English literary genre, which was coined as a literary "in" expression, if not invented from scratch as a genre, by Horace Walpole's 1764 "Gothick story," *The Castle of Otranto*, and which drew to a close when Mary Wollstonecraft Shelley's *Frankenstein: or, The Modern Prometheus* (1818) and Charles Robert Maturin's *Melmoth the Wanderer* (1820) were published. Recognized forerunners of the Gothic literary genre are first and foremost the early eighteenth-century Graveyard Poets—the earliest poem attributed to the Graveyard School in turn is Thomas Parnell's "A Night-Piece on Death" (1721)—and their contesting of Augustan moderation. Other often quoted influences include Friedrich Schiller's first drama, *Die Räuber* (1781, premièred 1782), and:

> the German materials that flooded into 1790s London, such as the plays influenced by Schiller's electric *The Robbers*, or the novels Isabella Thorpe recommends to Catherine Morland as being perfectly "horrid" in Jane Austen's *Northanger Abby* (1818). But as Coleridge argues in *Biographia Literaria* (1817), such materials are themselves imitations of English originals. (Miles, "Eighteenth-Century" 11)[13]

Chief examples of the back-and-forth exchange between the English Gothic romance and Germany's *Schauerliteratur* are the light fiction works by Christian Heinrich Spieß, Carl Gottlob Cramer, and Christian August Vulpius, an example of which is Vulpius' 1798 version of the uncanny robber, *Ronaldo Rinaldini*.

The rise of Gothic fiction in England coincided not only with the revival of the Gothic myth as a fashionable statement of patriotism but, most strikingly, also with the steady acceleration and massification of the book market, due to the industrialized improvement of its means of production. The eighteenth-century English book market was based on the marked industrialized improvement of its means of production and could thus rely on a well-functioning production and distribution network, which for the first time enabled a larger, though still limited, percentage of gentry and upper-class people to physically and financially access a growing

---

13 "I will read you their names directly; here they are, in my pocketbook. Castle of Wolfenbach, Clermont, Mysterious Warnings, Necromancer of the Black Forest, Midnight Bell, Orphan of the Rhine, and Horrid Mysteries" (Austen 37). For commentaries on the "horrid novels," see Michael Sadleir or Bette B. Roberts.

variety of reading materials, including novels, pamphlets, newspapers, and magazines. Favorably set in a country that stressed the need for religious and political participation through the independent study of texts,[14] the surge of commercialization and industrialization established the need for both an informed and educated working public and a homely sphere of (presumed) leisure and privacy. Staying in "the cradle of privacy" (Chartier 363f) and the leisure of their homes, and thus having the time and money to enjoy being entertained by a novel or a magazine without having to educate themselves about political issues, were the gentry and upper-class women. Understanding that women needed education and guidance in the sphere of their private homes as well, that is, stressing the emotional capabilities and responsibilities of England's women, the many erupting romance and pulp fiction publishing houses quickly turned them into their sole target audience. The literary Gothic entered the market during the first bonanza period of journalism and pulp fiction and helped turn popular fiction first into a profitable trade and finally into a lasting success story.

The epicenter of this accelerated circulation and massification of the young literary market was undoubtedly the infamous Minerva Press, founded by William Lane in the late eighteenth century. Recognizing the possibilities of cheap and widely circulating popular fiction, Lane's publishing house not only concentrated nearly exclusively on hastily produced and poorly imitated sentimental and Gothic fiction (Ann Radcliffe's vastly successful romances quickly became the often-copied prototype) but also established a network of privately-owned libraries as its prime market. Minerva Press also utilized the novelty of professional authorship, by employing mostly female authors at very low wages. Among Lane's stable of writers were Regina Maria Roche (*The Maid of the Hamlet*, 1793; *Clermont*, 1798), Eliza Parsons (*The Castle of Wolfenbach*, 1793; *The Mysterious Warning*, 1796), and Eleanor Sleath (*The Orphan of the Rhine*, 1798); six of the Northanger's "horrid" seven were published by Minerva. A large number of titles were published anonymously, including such novels as *Count Roderic's Castle* (1794), *The Haunted Castle* (1794), *The Animated Skeleton* (1798) and the response to Matthew G. Lewis' uproar-causing and sales-boosting *The Monk* (1796), and *The New Monk* (1798). Note, however, that "the public taste for Gothic was not restricted to the novel, but it was here that it was at its most significant" (Punter 8). Minerva Press helped turn the Gothic novel into a widely distributed and financially rewarding success; it also assisted in the genre's unparalleled defamation.

While the Gothic myth was still considered patriotic and fashionable in English high culture, Gothic romance's cultural descent began as both contemporaneous authors and literary critics increasingly dismissed it as being dangerously irrational, feminized pulp fiction.

---

14   For a condensed summary see Ana Vogrinčič (107).

> In effect, the positive, idealized meanings of Gothic were channeled into chivalry and architecture, while the glamorously negative ones were poured into the Gothic novel, so that it soon gained a reputation, much like Lord Byron's, of being mad, bad and dangerous to read. (Miles, "Eighteenth-Century" 17)

Eighteenth-century critics, who oftentimes were authors active in the Romantic movement themselves and who had therefore a close-meshed self-interest in dismissing pulp fictional Gothic efforts,[15] stressed the value of and the need for 'useful' literature that could foster the moral and political education of its readership, by illustrating good moral behavior and basic political principles. Gothic writing, on the other hand, could achieve neither and, instead, would only encourage irrational impulses. While Aristotle's *Poetics* must be mentioned as the often-quoted origin of some of the rules of drama, rules that Horace Walpole also claims to have adopted as the underlying plot structure of *The Castle of Otranto*,[16] the predominant resort of high-culture proponents and Gothic romance opponents was Horace's *Ars Poetica*. In his highly influential 1750 essay, Samuel Johnson elaborates on Horace's "incredulus odi" principle,[17] by stressing the didactic impulses that literature concerned with real life, and real life only, can and must have on the minds of "the young, the ignorant, and the idle." Authors "mingle good and bad qualities in their principle personages […] as we accompany them through their adventures with delight" (Johnson 54); the depiction of heroically stylized villains, however, will damage the morality of readers and must be criticized sharply. Samuel Taylor Coleridge in his review of Lewis' *The Monk* also stresses Horace's "incredulus odi" phrase. Faced with the bestselling success of the "horrible and the preternatural," Coleridge can no longer rely on the rational dismissal of everything "unbelievable" and consequently introduces "satiety" as the remaining means of terminating the ills of what now has to be considered "the popular taste":

> We trust, however, that satiety will banish what good sense should have prevented; and that, wearied with fiends, incomprehensible characters, with shrieks,

---

15   Aside from the brief discussion of Samuel Johnson's and Samuel Taylor Coleridge's anti-Gothic arguments below, Clara Reeve's *The Progress of Romance, Through Times, Countries, and Manners* (1785) and Thomas Mathias' *The Pursuits of Literature* (1798) can be consulted as widely received contemporaneous discussions of the (Gothic) romance. For a compilation of relevant essays and newspaper articles and/or reviews, see Clery and Miles (173ff.).

16   In his preface to the second edition of *The Castle of Otranto* (1765), Walpole insists that *Otranto* obeys Aristotle's three unities of time, place, and action (Walpole 9–14).

17   Horace, line 188. The line reads "Quodcunque ostendis mihi sic incredulus odi," which can be translated as "Scenes put before me in this way move only my incredulity and disgust." Johnson paraphrases freely: "What I cannot for a moment believe, I cannot for a moment behold with interest or anxiety," implying that the probability of a literary text determines its didactic usefulness.

murders, and subterraneous dungeons, the public will learn, by the multitude of the manufacturers, with how little expense of thought or imagination this species of composition is manufactured. (Coleridge 194)

Although the English literary market remained dominated by pragmatic and didactic genres, such as political treatises, self-educational manuals, sermons, and religious tracts, long into the nineteenth century, Minerva-style popular fiction, with its base depictions of violence, crime, and the world outside of the conduct books, continued to win more and more readers. What is more, it won over more and more women readers. A nation that was to the utmost degree culturally anxious about the female propensity for sentimental, emotional, and mentally destabilizing romance felt itself increasingly dominated by a female reader- and authorship. Satiety, apparently, could not be expected from female readers.

While contemporaneous critics like Johnson and Coleridge helped draw a first, albeit tentative, canonical line between the high Romantics' great poetry, which was naturally a male sphere dominated by writers such as themselves and the pulp fictional "species of composition," it was twentieth-century literary criticism that established the narrow yet influential canon of *The Great Tradition*,[18] a high-cultural genealogy traceable from Austen through Eliot, James, and Conrad, dismissing Gothic romance as Romantic poetry's "illegitimate cousin" (Hume 282). Moreover, echoing the earliest Renaissance reception of medieval Gothicism, Gothic romance was dismissed as being wildly irrational, a "dim, shapeless fiction [which] lacks the unifying clarity of the Romantic Imagination as articulated by several great poets in their greatest poetry" (Williams 6). Northrop Frye's *Anatomy of Criticism* (1957) and *The Secular Scripture* (1976) provided yet another nail in the coffin of the Gothic's cultural respectability. In his discussion of the romance, substantially identical to Gothic romance, Frye points out its misty, diffuse, and intuitive style; the Realistic novel, on the other hand, is marked by its jejune focus on manners, morals, and society. The romance, therefore, must be defined by its "feminine" qualities, whereas the Realistic novel, in contrast, by male spheres and rational sobriety (Frye 23). Unsurprisingly, Frye moves the (Gothic) romance, overladen with emotional excess (a key "feminine" quality written for a predominantly female readership), to the lowest rung of the critical ladder. At the core of Fyre's argument, Fred Botting argues

---

18　See Frank R. Leavis' *The Great Tradition: George Eliot, Henry James, Joseph Conrad* (1960). While Leavis is one of the most influential critics arguing for a Romantic tradition without the Gothic, other Anglo-American critics have tried to establish what they considered to be a more inclusive Romantic canon. Yet, guided by the central premise that "great fiction is Realistic fiction," the Gothic tradition is not (and cannot be) accounted for. Ian Watt's 1957 *The Rise of the Novel* and Wayne Booth's *The Rhetoric of Fiction* (1961) are two often-quoted cases in point. See the more detailed discussion of the "twentieth-century keepers of the House of Fiction" versus the Gothic novel in Williams (1ff).

by quoting Herry J. Pye's 1786 *Commentary*, lies a key concern of eighteenth-century criticism:

> The disturbance of boundaries between proper reality and unreal romantic identification [...] disrupts the order discriminating between virtue and vice: mimesis finds itself distorted by the fanciful effects of romance so that readers, instead of imitating paragons of virtuous conduct, are possessed of "a desire of resembling the fictitious heroine of a novel," thus losing any sense of reality. (Botting, "In Gothic" 9)

It goes without saying that for Pye it was the young and the female readers who were threatened by (Gothic) romance's enticing fantasies. A thorough revision of this hostile conflation of the Gothic with presumed "feminine" qualities of excessive emotionality, i.e., pulp fiction's "little expense of thought," began in the 1960s with the rise of Gothic studies as a genuine field of scholarly interest that coincided with the literary and cinematic mass-market revival of the Gothic in the U.S. However, while everyone working in the field of Gothic studies (then and now) would stress the wrongful and exclusive dismissal of the Gothic romance of the late eighteenth and early nineteenth centuries as high Romanticism's "neurasthenic cousin, or, a Madeline Usher, always in the process of disappearing but never permanently buried" (Williams 3), it cannot be concluded that the field of Gothic studies has reached a sustainable consensus concerning the defining qualities of its subject matter.

Before we can evaluate the analytical potential of this minimal consensus, an important methodological note should be added. It is critical to mention the scholarly convention of foregrounding the English tradition of the Gothic, of even claiming that we are dealing with "a most indigenous phenomenon" (Williams 13). Just as a mythological focus on the Goths has led us seemingly inevitably to the British Isles, the generic origin of the literary Gothic is identified with British, even English, literary productions of the eighteenth and nineteenth centuries. While the focus on the English construction of the Gothic myth theoretically anticipates England's central role in the subsequent production of the Gothic genre and might therefore seem circular, this indeed retrospectively formulated argument should not be dismissed due to its seemingly narrow perspective. European romanticism in general used mythological allusions to construct a positively primitive national identity; however, the conflation of national identity and a presumed Gothic ancestry is uniquely British. Furthermore, the essentially tense split of the Gothic myth in Great Britain and its conflicting political adaptations cannot be found anywhere else in Europe. The English literary Gothic genre, which grew out of this complex mythological climate, in turn proves to initially be a uniquely British phenomenon. That said, a generic history of the Gothic must nevertheless accommodate the manifold influences and modifications undergone by the English genre, in the wake of becoming a bestselling export hit. Even if I define the Gothic most narrowly as a historic genre which lasted from 1764 to 1820, that is, from *The Castle of Otranto* to *Melmoth the Wanderer*, I need to not only accept a very strong and inflexible notion of "genre," but I also need to account for the vast spectrum of texts which were produced in this very limited period of time, by authors as diverse as Horace Walpole, Ann Radcliffe, Ludwig Tieck, E.T.A Hoffmann, François-Thomas-Marie de Baculard d'Arnaud, José de Urcullu, Alessandro Manzoni, and, not least, by the innumerable avatars of Minerva-style pulp fiction.

What, then, can be gained from a scholarly consensus, which highlights the English literary tradition and its conversion of Gothic mythology? In fact, if one wanted to derive a definition of the Gothic only from this two-fold consensus, one would most likely argue that the Gothic is an English literary genre (1764–1820), which is ideologically highly adaptable, as it essentially shimmers between the two mythological poles of the evil Goth and the good Goth. Given this two-fold consensus, which is repeated and only slightly modified in numerous publications on the Gothic, it is surprising that only the premise of a very strong and narrowly enclosed English literary genre has generated related hypotheses and interpretations, which either stress the tight boundaries of the Gothic genre or which dismiss them as exclusive and improperly centered on an English canonical perspective. The mythological Goths, however, remain covered merely superficially (though in great detail), that is, without extensive theoretical consequences. It is not exaggerated to claim that the Goths' mythological presence has mainly become a means to either establish or reject an etymology of the traditionally, i.e., since Walpole, capitalized term "Gothic." In her chapter, "The Goths in History and Pre-Gothic History," Sowerby goes so far as to claim that it:

> is well known that the use of the term "Gothic" to describe the literary phenomenon that began in the later eighteenth century has little, if anything, to do with the people from whom it is derived. Nevertheless a companion to the Gothic should contain some mention of the historical Goths and some discussion of the strange history of the term and its uses before Horace Walpole [...]. (15)

While she dismisses the importance of the "Goth" in "Gothic," Sowerby nevertheless capitalizes the term, thus re-creating the previously dismissed lineage. In contrast, critics such as Stevens, Ellis, and Davenport-Hines stress the presumed independence of the literary tradition from its mythological eponym by lowercasing the "gothic."

The derived double nature of Gothic's mythological (and etymological) origin, i.e., its intrinsic shimmering between its associations with both "the barbaric and uncivilized in order to define that which is other to the values of the civilized present," and with a primitivism that "has now become identified with the true, but lost, foundations of a culture" (Punter and Byron 5), is stated frequently but with little influence on the analysis to follow. "Primitivism," "barbarity," and "wilderness" are mere buzzwords used to describe the English cultural and oftentimes propagandistic struggle with Catholic Europe, with France in particular, and the Enlightenment. Punter and Byron's discussion of "Civilization and the Goths" is simultaneously a case in point and notable exception to this rule. Conflating the Gothic myth first with primitivism and then with "the other," Punter and Byron argue that "throughout the developing political use of the term [...] the Gothic always remains the symbolic site of a culture's discursive struggle to define and claim possession of the civilized, and to abject, or throw off, what is seen as other to that civilized self" (5).

Primitivism is, for Punter and Byron, among other instances, utilized in counter-discourses to the Enlightenment, to Modernism, and to Imperialism. It is traceable, for example, in the recurring "ghosts of the past" (53) in postmodern literature, in the "return of the imperial repressed" (49) in imperial and in postcolonial contexts, and in the contemporary Gothic subculture's testing of boundaries between the normal and the other (63). If we conflate the Gothic myth with primitivism, which we in turn conflate with otherness *per se*, it becomes dubious of what the value of the primitive and, ultimately, of the "Goth" in "Gothic" (capitalized) might be. Indeed, have not many recent publications focusing on the Gothic "other"—*The Gothic Other. Racial and Social Constructions in the Literary Imagination*, eds. Ruth Bienstock Anolik and Douglas L. Howard (2004), *Postfeminist Gothic: Critical Interventions in Contemporary Culture*, eds. Benjamin A. Brabon and Stéphanie Genz (2007), Tabish Khair's *The Gothic, Postcolonialism and Otherness. Ghosts from Elsewhere* (2009), and Katrin Althans' *Darkness Subverted: Aboriginal Gothic in Black Australian Literature and Film* (2010) to name just four—established notions of "Gothic otherness," without (at least explicitly) detouring via the primitive Goths?

I claim that the etymological consensus is essential for defining the Gothic (thus capitalized); in itself, however, it is not a sufficient definition. It is essential to understand that the Gothic, from day one, has been a fundamentally racialized strategy, which established its view of primitivism in terms of racially explicit savagery. This holds true as much for the politically motivated Gothic, which Botting, Ellis, Miles, and others stress, as for the literary Gothic, which Walpole's *Castle of Otranto* helped to initiate. Differentiating between primitivism in the above sense and the Gothic's essential emphasis on the savage qualities of its thus racialized villains not only stresses the importance of deciphering the racial discourse underlying the Gothic tradition, a central undertaking personified most markedly by the scholars focusing on "Imperial Gothic,"[19] but it also changes the way we think of the (Ame-

---

19   Patrick Brantlinger suggests confining the Imperial Gothic to the period between 1880 and 1914, which roughly represents the heyday of the British Empire; colonial and postcolonial approaches to the Gothic employ a similar focus for the analysis of younger texts.

rican) Gothic. When it comes to defining the Gothic, to providing an answer to the question, "What is the Gothic?," scholars working in the tradition of this consensus have to make a decision: Can we still define the Gothic as a genre, or has it become something else? From the 1970s onwards, and increasingly in the course of reader-response criticism and the ongoing re-evaluation of genre theory, most scholars have opted for the latter, going to great pains to establish individual notions of and approaches to what this "something else" could or should entail. The methodological reason for this choice is apparent. Only if we drop the closely meshed barriers of the genre can we account for the manifold hybrid manifestations of the Gothic through time and (data) space, culture and ethnicity, class and gender.

However, for the majority of scholars, this does not necessarily entail negating the generic origin of the Gothic "something else" in eighteenth-century England. In the process of sub-categorizing the Gothic, the minimal consensus remains surprisingly untouched. After 1820, it seems the genre ceased to exist, while the Gothic has continued to exist ever since—not as a genre but as "a mode" (Punter and Byron 26), "an aesthetic" (Gamer 4; Miles, *Gothic* 1ff.), "an irregularity" (Williams 23), or as something completely else. Defining this Gothic as "something else," on the one hand, and the relationship between the myth-based English generic ancestor and its worldwide descendants, on the other, are arguably the major points of scholarly disagreement. Unfortunately, these are also the points central to a sustainable definition of the Gothic.

1.2 A Working Definition

> "If it looks like a duck, swims like a duck and quacks like a duck, then it probably is a duck." (The duck test, possibly coined by James Whitcomb Riley, 1849–1916)

I propose that the "something else" in question essentially has to account for the enormous creative, cultural, and political agency inherent in Gothic literary texts written by and for historically and culturally marginalized individuals and groups. It also has to display the creative, cultural, and political agency inherent in innumerous Gothic texts written *about* these people. I will, therefore, refer to the Gothic as a writing strategy and define it as follows: The Gothic, etymologically and thematically derived from the mythologized "Goths," is a writing strategy that employs a stable canon of Gothemes, that is, of conventionalized motif/trope binaries, and (re)iterates a dominant discourse of otherness or abjection. When reiterated from the perspective of those peoples conventionally either denigrated or abjected, this writing strategy can, however, also produce highly culturally and politically active texts, which not only envision a counter-narrative to the dominant discourse but also aim to change this discourse altogether. The Gothic trades and quotes stereotypes, yet it also has the potential to quote with a twist. This twist can either describe a new context, genre, etc., in which the conventions are employed, or it can describe the discourse-altering reiteration the author undertakes. In other words, while some Gothic texts, consciously or not, repeat old and painfully racialized stereotypes in new contexts, therefore strengthening the underlying discriminating discourse, other Gothic texts function as consciously critical narratives that make visible and aim to change the hateful discourse.

As a strategy, the Gothic is ideologically and generically ultra-adaptable. As a matter of fact, Gothic novels today hardly look like their generic English ancestors. The contemporary Gothic is strategically called upon in a great variety of text types and genres so that "generic hybrids" (Gamer 12, 23) have long become the norm, replacing fully fledged and often one-dimensional *Schauerromane*; and, yet, all these diverse texts critically and consciously employ Gothic writing strategies, thereby entering into a dialogue with Gothic's multilayered history, with each other, and, last but not least, with readerly expectations and literary market needs around the world.

Note that my working definition of the Gothic as a writing strategy mainly rests on three theoretical concepts—Gotheme, (re)iteration, and the discursively constructed other/abject—all of which need clarification.

The term "Gotheme" is a neologism that I base loosely on Roland Barthes' semiological notion of "myth" and more immediately on Claude Lévi-Strauss' notion of "mythemes" (*Structural* 206ff.). A Gotheme, therefore, describes an irreducible, unchanging unit of signification that always consists of a dichotomic opposition pair, of which the destructive element is foregrounded against the contrast of its only potentially corrective counterpart. The use of Gothemes in a fictional text is a writing strategy; it also inevitably determines whether this text is primarily, substantially, or marginally perceived as "Gothic." Gothemes themselves, however, are not strategic in any way. If we leave close-meshed structural anthropology behind and tie Gothemes to a Foucauldian notion of "discourse," we can conceive them as discursive patterns that perform an intrinsically sedimented discourse through binary opposition pairs. In Gothic fiction, the essential oppositions, for example, the opposition between the Savage Villain and the Civil Hero, remain unaffected throughout the story. The fundamental clash is not reconciled, since binary oppositions are not evened out by an identity-sustaining synthesis. If both a synthesis of opposing forces is refused and the destructive element of the Gotheme is continuously foregrounded, the text will inevitably end with a projecture of violence, destruction, and anxiety—the often-quoted "chill factor" (Banta 1) that readers of the Gothic crave.

In my study, the concept of the Gotheme restructures what Diane Long Hoeveler has dismissed as "that old critical trap—the generic laundry list" (104) of the Gothic. Laundry lists of the Gothic aim at defining the Gothic, by indiscriminately listing recurring plots, scenes, settings, props, and characters synchronically and diachronically as they appear in media deemed "Gothic." To a certain extent, they "duck test" the Gothic: If it looks like Gothic (props, setting), plots like Gothic and its characters act like Gothic, then it probably is Gothic. This approach is commonly understood as being only a little younger than the first Gothic novel. In as early as 1797, an anonymous letter to the editor of the *Spirit of the Public Journals for 1797* satirically lists, particularly for the "desirous" female author, the ingredients for the perfectly terrific Gothic novel:

> In the mean time, should any of your female readers be desirous of catching the season of terrors, she may compose two or three very pretty volumes from the following recipe:
>
> Take— An old castle, half of it ruinous.
> A long gallery, with a great many doors, some secret ones.
> Three murdered bodies, quite fresh.
> As many skeletons, in chests and presses.
> An old woman hanging by the neck; with her throat cut.
> Assassins and desperadoes "quant suff."
> Noise, whispers, and groans, threescore at least.
>
> Mix them together, in the form of three volumes to be taken at any of the watering places, before going to bed. (qtd. in Clery and Miles 184)

Despite its satirical and dismissive origins that represented the Gothic as "a kind of mass-produced fiction-by-numbers" (Gamer 9), the laundry list approach flourished in twentieth- and early twenty-first-century Gothic research and remains one of the most prevalent methods applied to Gothic literature today. And while it is a fair guess to assume that laundry list scholars as diverse as Dale Baily, Jerrold E. Hogle, Fred Botting, Allen L. Smith, Slobodan Sucur, Jeffrey N. Cox, Victor Sage, James Watt, and Eric Savoy (among many others) run into severe problems when faced with the contemporary Gothic's generic, cultural, and (trans)national plurality, they argue that quite the opposite is true. Within the context of American Gothic, Savoy claims respectively that the "formal adaptability and innovative energy of American Gothic" is "nowhere [...] more evident than in the strange tropes, figures, and rhetorical techniques" ("The Rise" 168). Each cultural context is understood to produce its own set of features which quickly become defining for this specific Gothic literature.

The concept Gotheme incorporates two key aspects of the laundry-list approach into the Gothic, by conceptualizing recurring plots, scenes, props, character types, and locales as culturally specific and ultra-adaptable motifs that depend on both a diametrical opposition and a widely-received publishing history, i.e. a mainstream standing. The truly sturdy Savage Villain/Civil Hero Gotheme, which my present study mainly focuses on and which I claim is a key Gotheme in Gothic literature *per se*, can be traced in contemporary and early U.S. American literature just as much as it can in Walpole's *The Castle of Otranto*, dating back to England's earliest notions of the Goths (see above and Chapter 3). If we think of another canonical Gothic feature, the claustrophobically "antiquated or seemingly antiquated space" (Hogle 2) that Gothic plots are set in,[20] it becomes clear that this setting works only in binary opposition to a contrasting space of the open outside. The horror of being incarcerated in a Gothic castle requires the possibility of freedom of movement outside, to make it the terrible exception to the rule of normality which it presents itself as to the reader. This contrasting element of normality is established through both the frame narrative and a customary Gothic feature, which was first introduced by Irving Malin for the context of the American Gothic: the "voyage into the forest."[21] This often climactic voyage "represents movement, exploration, not cruel confinement" (Malin 106); however, we should not confuse it with a happy ending. The voyage into the forest takes place within the Gothic plot's logic and is "usually erratic, circular, violent, or distorted" (ibid. 105). The binary opposition of claustrophobic and open spaces, which I conceptualize accordingly as the Gotheme Claustrophobic Space/Open Space, is performed continuously and self-reflectively in the Gothic text up to a point, where the polarity of these two elements, as well as of confinement and voyage, "shrink to one point of horror" (ibid. 107). If we now compare the Gotheme Claustrophobic Space/Open Space, for

---

20   Hogle's list of "antiquated or seemingly antiquated space[s]" includes "a castle, a foreign palace, an abbey, a vast prison, a subterranean crypt, a graveyard, a primeval frontier or island, a large old house or theatre, an aging city or urban underworld, a decaying storehouse, factory, laboratory, public building, or some new recreation of an older venue, such as an office with old filing cabinets, an overworked spaceship, or a computer memory" (2).

21   Despite the fact that Malin does not mention him or one of his texts, I would argue that Malin's analysis of the "voyage into the forest" directly refers back to D.H. Lawrence's depiction of the American forest and its potential for an American Adam's heroic quest. Mogan, Sanders, and Karpinski argue that marveling "at the subversive duplicity of classic American literature, Lawrence located the source of its energies in the American forest" (15). Indeed, it is the clash between the questing hero and America's wilderness that lies at the heart of Lawrence's understanding of the frontier myth and of American identity *per se*: "When you are actually in America, America hurts, because it has a powerful disintegrative effect on the white psyche. It is full of grinning, unappeased aboriginal demons, too, ghosts, and it persecutes the white men, like some Eumenides" (Lawrence, "Studies" 51).

example, to Hogle's above-mentioned laundry list of "antiquated or seemingly antiquated space[s]," the methodological advantages of our new notion stand out most vividly. I understand the term Gotheme as a chance to summarize under a common denominator a highly diverse bundle of necessarily context-specific instantiations of, for example, antiquated spaces such as the Castle of Otranto, Northanger Abbey, Stephen King's nameless but famous pet cemetery, and Colson Whitehead's post-apocalyptic rendering of downtown Manhattan, Zone One.

In addition to considerably reducing the number of items of our laundry lists, the introduction of the notion Gotheme offers another big advantage: It helps me to avoid the "Levy fallacy" and, therefore, to account for the survival of the Gothic outside of England and after the 1820s. In his influential study of 1968, *Le Roman "Gothique" Anglais, 1764–1824*, Maurice Levy restricts the Gothic most narrowly to a handful of English literary texts that were produced between 1764 and 1824. Even three decades after *Le Roman "Gothique" Anglais*, Levy still only reluctantly sympathizes with the majority of scholars who define the Gothic in a way that includes Emily Brontë's "Wuthering Heights, Charlotte Brontë's fiction, or certain novels by Dickens" ("Gothic" 3); and Levy still questions whether he must be "equally tolerant when this unique epithet is used in relation to the works of Stevenson, Wilde, Conrad, Saki, Graham Green, Somerset Maugham and a few others" (ibid. 3). His fallacy is that he bases his defining criteria for identifying Gothic literature on two, strictly content-related features, which he derives from a very limited number of supposedly archetypically "Gothic" texts only: architecture and the sublime. By focusing especially on the use of the castle-motif as a key criterion for Gothic fiction, Levy is forced to strip the "unique epithet" off many texts—including Mary Shelley's *Frankenstein*—which we today would invariably recognize as being canonically Gothic. Due to the same line of reasoning, Levy also cannot acknowledge any Gothic writing tradition outside the English context (and outside his narrow timeframe). Levy explicitly argues against an American Gothic literature, mainly due to the fact that the texts in question lack the specific English Gothic architecture (castles); since they also fail to depict Britain's national and political ethos, the American texts cannot even be labeled "sublime." If highly context-specific literary motifs are extracted from a text, universalized as being the prototypical feature(s) of a genre, and ultimately used to "face check" presumably Gothic texts stemming from other cultures, times, and authors, the use of a however narrow laundry list definition of the Gothic is tautological and of no avail.

My notion of Gotheme takes the Levy fallacy into account by refraining from stating prescriptive feature bundles. Gothemes, such as Savage Villain/Civil Hero or Claustrophobic Space/Open Space, are umbrella terms for dichotomically related motifs/tropes and their specific histories of instantiation. I share Teresa A. Goddu's observation that "once imported to America, Gothic's key elements were translated into American terms, and its formulas [...] unfixed" (266) and believe that the notion of Gotheme can help us conceptualize the evolution of Gothic motifs and tropes within texts that are still, and unquestioningly so, perceived as being Gothic fiction. Motifs and tropes have been adapted to suit U.S. needs, the conventional dichotomies and techniques of bundling these evolved motifs and tropes, however, have remained unaffected. While the notion Gotheme methodologically anticipates conventionalized dichotomies in a Gothic text, it does not determine the analysis to follow. Whether or not a Gotheme is actualized in a specific text, and what form the involved motifs take, is never predetermined but always open for analysis.

My notion of Gotheme, though derived mainly from Lévi-Strauss' structural anthropology, is fully intertwined with the clearly post-structural concepts of iterating and reiterating discourses, especially discourses of otherness and of the Black abject. While I am very conscious of the theoretical gap I am bridging, I am convinced that at least Lévi-Strauss will not turn in his grave upon publication of my study. In *The Raw and the Cooked: Introduction to a Science of Mythology* (*Le Cru et le Cuit*, 1964), Lévi-Strauss makes a statement that continues to puzzle many critics, as it can be understood as foreshadowing a Foucauldian notion of "discourse": "I therefore claim to show, not how men think in myths, but how myths operate [literally: "think themselves"] in men's minds without their being aware of the fact" (*The Raw* 12).

A discourse, according to Paul-Michel Foucault's key definition in *Archaeology of Knowledge* (1969), is a materially evident praxis of social speech (thinking, writing, speaking, and acting in general), a praxis that not only reflects (social) objects by thinking, speaking, writing, etc. but that systematically creates these (social) objects. Foucault's examples of social objects include insanity, sexuality, and normality, and their related individual and collective subjectivities. Discourses form and order our perceptions of the world; however, they require continuous repetition, a "doing," to remain intact. Foucault intends to uncover this active prerequisite by reconstructing a discourse's constitutive rules, its formation, and transformation into different discourses. He focuses on four dimensions: the dimension of the objects, of utterance modalities, of terms/notions, and of applied strategies. In his later work, most prominently in "Orders of Discourse" (*L'Ordre du Discours* 1971), Foucault stresses the fact that a definition of discourse should also include the social mechanisms of exclusion, i.e., the instruments and processes of control, working through exclusion, limitation, and regulation of access.

The terms iteration and reiteration are derived from Jacques Derrida's notion of iterability. In his essay, "Signature Event Context," iterability is introduced in the context of the linguistic sign that has to be repeatable, in order for us to recognize it as a linguistic sign, but where every repetition is essentially a repetition with a difference (context, speaker, mindset, tone of voice, etc.). Following her earlier argument from *Bodies That Matter*, Judith Butler synthesizes in *Excitable Speech. A Politics of the Performance* Derrida's concept of iterability with her own notion of performance and Foucault's concept of discourse: The fact that we act through the utterances we make (i.e., that our speech has the performative power to change the world) is not due to the intentionality or the will of the individual speaker. Rather, it is the effect of sedimentary historic conventions and meanings (discourses), which are (unintentionally) quoted and repeated in every single act of speech. This ongoing practice of quotation and reiteration is open to resistance, resignification, and change. By consciously altering the quoted discourse, i.e., by consciously influencing the process of reiteration, the subject can leave its passively discourse-quoting position and become the discourse-altering agent. For clarity's sake, I distinguish between "iteration," the intentional or unintentional quotation of a discourse (sedimented, for example, in Gothemes) in a new context, without an effort to critically alter it, and "reiteration," the intentional quotation of a discourse (sedimented, for example, in Gothemes) in a new context with a discourse-altering intention.

Whether or not these discourse-altering reiterations of Gothemes in contemporary U.S. American Gothic texts can also be understood in terms of the postcolonial paradigms of either "writing back" or "rewriting," or should rather be labeled as "created-anew," is a constantly resurfacing concern of the analyses to follow. The implications for the umbrella-term "American Gothic" would in all three cases be profound.[22] If the African American texts in our corpus purely write back to the dominant master narrative in the way Ashcroft, Griffith, and Tiffin envision it, for example, by reversing a Gotheme such as the Savage Villain/Civil Hero Gotheme, in order to place the villainy with whom it rightfully belongs—the white oppressor—, then they rephrase conventionalized Gothemes only, and we can safely dismiss well-established American Gothic sub-versions, such as "African American Gothic," in favor of the all-encompassing umbrella term. If, however, reiteration should be closer to the rewriting paradigm and entail a creative intertwinement of transcultural Gothemes with culture-specific motifs/tropes (which include plots, scenes, settings, props, and characters), the notion of one "American Gothic" could come under severe pressure. Lastly, if a text in my corpus does not fall back on the conventionalized dichotomies that I have titled "Gothemes" but instead creates a totally new *horror from scratch, we will have to drop the notion of "Gothic" and replace it (*horror) with a more fitting, culture-specific term and acknowledge that creative and discursive "unthought" of the racialized conventions of the Gothic is actually possible (see also Chapters 5.4 and 8).

---

22 Note that I do not want to suggest conflating African American studies and postcolonial studies in any way: "The experiences and cultural productions of people of African descent in the United States differ markedly and profoundly from those of persons from colonized or formerly colonized lands. [...] My purpose, then, is not to blur the distinctions between postcolonial and African American literary studies but rather to identify points of correspondence and build bridges between them" (Gruesser, *Confluences* 2).

My working definition of the Gothic, combined with my primary focus, the Savage Villain/Civil Hero Gotheme, also ties in with recent Gothic scholarship on race and discursive otherness. Indebted to the important pioneer work by gender-focused scholars of the Gothic,[23] it is Toni Morrison's famous treatise, *Playing in the Dark. Whiteness and the Literary Imagination* (1992), which today is commonly understood as the trigger for the first wave of Gothic scholarship explicitly concerned with Blackness, race, and the U.S. American experience. Confronted with an American Gothic tradition that had conflated villainy and monstrosity with Blackness early on, and equipped with her own, unique (African) American Gothic novel *Beloved* (1987), Morrison wonders "why [...] a young country repelled by Europe's moral and social disorder [...] devote[s] its talents to reproducing in its own literature the typology of diabolism it wanted to leave behind" (36). Overflowing with images of damnation, hell, and monstrosity, these early American texts evoke a nightmare scenario in what we today might call "Gothic" terms. Faced with the dense wilderness of nature, with fears of damnation and feelings of helplessness, the Puritans defined their newly gained American identity against the seemingly demonic, mainly Native American otherness that they encountered. They also color-coded their struggles, by depicting their newly gained American identity and their religious faith in images of whiteness and bright light surrounded by blackness, which the Puritans ascribed to nature and to the Native American.

The founding myth and its obsession with the dichotomy of light and dark, white and black became "institutionalized in the United States in the form of

---

23 Eve Kosofsky Sedgwick's *The Coherence of Gothic Conventions* (1976), though theoretically based on Freud and the methodology of New Criticism, tackles topics and tropes that would soon become key foci of gender studies (e.g., she analyzes the "male paranoid plot" in contrast to "the maternal or monstrous plot") (ix). Two years later, Sandra Gilbert and Susan Gubar's influential study, *The Madwoman in the Attic: The Woman Writer and the Nineteenth-Century Literary Imagination*, was published, revolutionizing Gothic scholarship. Gilbert and Gubar's mixing of deconstruction techniques and feminist criticism spawned an entire generation of feminist and gender-sensitive Gothic criticism. Michelle Massé's *In the Name of Love: Women, Masochism, and the Gothic* (1992), Susan Wolstenholme's *Gothic (Re)Visions: Writing Women as Readers* (1993), Diane Long Hoeveler's *Gothic Feminism* (1998), and Diane Wallace and Andrew Smith's recent anthology, *The Female Gothic: New Directions* (2009), are among the many influential studies that understand themselves in direct relation to Gilbert and Gubar. Triggered by feminist analyses, the construction of masculinity started to appear in Gothic scholarship in the late 1990s: Cyndy Hendershot's *The Animal Within: Masculinity and the Gothic* (1998) relates male fears of incarceration directly to dominant power structures, Andrew Smith's *Victorian Demons: Medicine, Masculinity, and the Gothic at the Fin-de-Siècle* (2004) analyzes male fears in terms of sociology and medicine, and George Haggerty's important study, *Queer Gothic* (2006), establishes both a transgressive notion of homosexual encounters in British Gothic literature and a work of reference for the scholarship on Queer Gothic which followed and still continues to follow his lead.

slavery" (Cassuto 3). The black skin color of the enslaved Africans, and later of the growing African American population, was equated with an animalistic wildness and put forward as an argument for the mutually beneficial 'peculiar institution.' In Toni Morrison's words, "[i]t was this Africanism, deployed as rawness and savagery, that provided the staging ground and arena for the elaboration of the quintessential American identity" (*Playing* 44).

Morrison's *Playing in the Dark*, while undoubtedly very influential, coincides chronologically, and regarding focus and method, with a number of other publications. Kari J. Winter's study, *Subjects of Slavery, Agents of Change: Women and Power in Gothic Novels and Slave Narratives* (1992), for example, connects and discusses both the depiction of slavery in Gothic literature and the Gothic in slave narratives; and David Mogan, Scott P. Sanders, and Joanne B Karpinski's anthology, *Frontier Gothic. Terror and Wonder at the Frontier in American Literature* (1993), establishes the American wilderness as the central trope of American Gothic fiction, as it is at the very heart of the frontier myth, the "most popular origin myth" (Limerick 323) of American self-mythologization:

> The gothic wilderness is a profoundly American symbol of an ambiguous relationship to the land, of an alienation that was first articulated when, in the words of Peter N. Carroll, the Puritans perceived "beneath the florid plenty of the New World [...] the Devil lurking in the wilderness." (Mogen, Sanders, and Karpinski 20)

Later publications to follow the lead of Morrisson, Winter, and others include Teresa Goddu's *Gothic America: Narrative, History, and Nation* (1997), Robert K. Martin and Eric Savoy's *American Gothic: New Interventions in a National Narrative* (1998), Renée Bergland's *The National Uncanny: Indian Ghosts and American Subjects* (2000), Justin D. Edwards' *Gothic Passages. Racial Ambiguity and the American Gothic* (2003), and John J. Kucich's *Ghostly Communion: Cross-Cultural Spiritualism in Nineteenth-Century American Literature* (2004).

My working definition of the Gothic, as well as the analyses to follow, is especially indebted to and in dialogue with Gothic scholarship that focuses on the Gothic's discursive strategies of racial othering: Judith Halberstam's *Skin Shows: Gothic Horror and the Technology of Monsters*, which configures the Gothic's preference for monstrous otherness as an amalgam of race, class, gender, and sexuality, Howard L. Malchow's *Gothic Images of Race in Nineteenth-Century Britain*, which explores racialized Gothic tropes in the context of European nationalism and imperialism, Kathleen Brogan's *Cultural Haunting: Ghosts and Ethnicity in Recent American Literature* (1999), Edward H. Jacobs' *Accidental Migrations: An Archaeology of Gothic Discourse* (2000), Dani Cavallaro's *The Gothic Vision: Three Centuries of Horror, Terror and Fear* (2002), Andrew Smith, William Hughes and Jonathan Taylor's *Empire and the Gothic: The Politics of the Genre* (2003), and Ruth Bienstock Anolik's *The Gothic Other:*

Racial and Social Constructions in the Literary Imagination (2004), as well as its 2010 follow-up, *Demons of the Body and Mind: Essays on Disability in Gothic Literature*.

Yet, my study differs significantly in two aspects from previous studies that engage critically with the question of race in Gothic fiction, past and present. First, I argue with more and more force for an intrinsic raciality that is discursively sedimented and conventionally encoded in the Gothic's uniquely binary structure, meaning first and foremost the Savage Villain/Civil Hero Gotheme. This approach contrasts emphatically with the traditional approach to the question of race in Gothic fiction, which is summarized by Bienstock Anolik and Howard as

> examin[ing] texts in which Gothic fear is relocated onto the figure of the racial and social Other, the Other who replaces the supernatural ghost or grotesque monster as the code for mystery and danger, becoming, ultimately, as horrifying, threatening and unknowable as the typical Gothic manifestation. (2)

I argue that there is no "typical Gothic manifestation" that would not always already be both racialized and racializing. Whether ghost, monster, or undefined lurking presence, entities of Gothic haunting are intrinsically connected to race and discursive racialization. Second, based on my discussion of earliest Gothic texts, my study carefully differentiates between two types of racializations: the Gothic other and the Gothicized Black abject. Arguing that we must account for a crucial discursive shift form one type of Gothicized savagery to the other—that is, from the Native American Savage Villain to the Africanist Savage Villain as the thingified Black abject—I introduce Sabine Broeck's notion of white abjectorship into the discussion of the Gothic. Broeck explains the discursive process of white abjectorship in this violent ontological repositioning of the Black body as a savage thing, as follows:

> To come into being, the European subject needed its underside, as it were: the crucially integral but invisible part of the human has been his/her *abject*, created in the European mind by way of racialized thingification: the African enslaved, an un-humaned species tied by property rights to the emerging subject so tightly that they could—structurally speaking—never occupy the position of the dialectical Heglian object as other, has thus remained therefore outside the dynamics of the human. ("Legacies" 118, emphasis in the original)

This inclusion of the Gothicized Black abject in the WASP American Gothic must be understood as having a most destructive and lasting impact on the cultural discourse in the United States. Reiteration from the ascribed (or discursively appellated) ontological position of the Gothicized abject, of the thingified Africanist Savage Villain, as I will argue in Part III, is complex, but possible, and inevitably entails the deconstruction of the Savage Villain/Civil Hero Gotheme.

Last but not least, my study also gives answers to most recent developments in the field of Gothic studies, that is, to the efforts in establishing a transnational notion of the Gothic (cf. Monika Elbert and Bridget M. Marshall's 2013 essay collection, *Transnational Gothic*), which broadens the perspective of its conceptual predecessor, the Multicultural Gothic (see for example A. Robert Lee's study of 2009, *Gothic to Multicultural: Idioms of Imagining in American Literary Fiction*). By focusing on the iteration and reiteration of Gothemes, transnationalism becomes visible and negotiable as being inherent in the worldwide exchange of Gothic plots, props, characters, settings, and stereotypes. What is more, my notion of Gotheme helps to understand the truly trans*cultural* agenda writers of the Gothic follow today. While the early Gothic, as soon as it left the shores of Britain behind, can readily be understood as a transnational writing strategy that included traded images of foreign nationality (e.g. European castles, catholic abbeys, aristocratic Princes) within a new nationalist framework (e.g. American wilderness, haunted plantations, Southern gentlemen), its recent American actualizations stand out as intrinsically paradoxical to the utmost extent. Novels like Stephen King's *The Girl Who Loved Tom Gordon* and Toni Morrison's *A Mercy* come from very distinct cultural backgrounds and employ Gothemes differently; however, as we will see, they refer consistently to two shared entities: a shared American Gothic writing tradition and a shared interest (though differently conceptualized) in mythologizing contemporary "Americanness." Gothemes, in this respect, appear to be transculturally exchangeable meaning units that help narrate a contemporary American national experience from manifold and all but commonly shared cultural perspectives. I will analyze in great detail whether and, if applicable, in what way and to what extent this transcultural notion at the heart of the Gothic writing strategy replaces the postcolonial paradigms of writing back and rewriting. While writing about Gothic literatures of peoples that some scholars and activists place into the context of an ongoing colonialization process, moving transcultural Gothemes to the fore will methodologically help us to refrain from predetermining Gothic writing as subversive literature *per se*. While I do not share Wolfgang Welsch's definition of transculturality as being situated outside of power hierarchies (especially between colonizing and colonized peoples), my study is concerned with both the relationship between different (sub-)cultures and literatures of the U.S. today and the intrinsic negotiation within these (sub-)cultures and their literatures. I thus follow Frank Schulze-Engler's analysis of the transcultural and keep my notion of Gotheme open regarding subversiveness and the renegotiation (whether understood as writing back or rewriting) of power hierarchies, that is, regarding what is commonly referred to as "voicing the unvoiced"[24] in Gothic scholarship.

1.3 A Savage Villain/Civil Hero Gotheme?

> "The villain exists as a means by which we can dissociate ourselves from evil; and the easiest way to dissociate ourselves from evil is to limit its definition to that which is easily avoidable." (Balchin 254)

Over the centuries, invaded genres (Gamer 12, 23), cultures, and countries, the Gothic's juxtaposition of villains and heroes has undergone profound changes. Gothic fiction has not only created room for anti-heroes with capacities for failure and a variety of shady dealings; it has also continuously exchanged the violent "freak of nature" (Balchin 236), the villain whom we can hate and judge unquestionably and unerringly, for a complex and lovable (un)human being. No longer the monstrous epitome of the evils of the aristocracy, Catholicism, permissiveness, and industrialization, contemporary Gothic villains like Stephen King's Cujo, Thomas Harris' Hannibal Lecter or Stephenie Meyer's ingratiating duo of Edward Cullen and Jacob Black have arguably undergone a "journey [...] from monster to yuppie" (Tomc 96), ever since "the emergence of the supernatural romance in the 1990s" (Marino-Faza 127).

Despite this observable tendency, the roles of both the hero and the villain within the Gothic plot have been surprisingly consistent. Whether yuppie or monster, all villains function on a basic level as a negative foil for the construction of the hero's and our own humanity, for the guidelines against which the text lets us define normality and healthiness. The need to define ourselves against a negative foil of abnormal "otherness" seems to be a basic individual, social, and cultural need. We create and accept monstrous effigies, not because our society would indeed burst

---

24   This figure of speech is used to capture the Gothic's presumed subversive strategies. Scholars have argued e.g. that the Gothic voices sexual taboos and/or sexual maturing (Alison Milbank); family secrets and hereditary doom (Richard Davenport-Hines), which have been connected to national legacies of slavery and racial discrimination (Allan Lloyd Smith), or to a nation's discourse about multiculturalism and ethnic identity (Kathleen Brogan), that is, also to the anxious encounter with the other (Ruth Bienstock Anolik). Eric Sundquist summarizes that the Gothic utters "the eruption from below of rebellious or unconscious forces and the consequent violation of boundaries, whether racial, sexual, or abstractly moral" (Sundquist 8).

at the seams with real-life manifestations of the pure and unrelieved evil, but because society needs a discourse of singling out dangerously deviant otherness, in order to keep intact its matrix of structural unity and conformity. Hence, in many ways, the villain "is a cancer produced by the tissues of society itself" (Balchin 244). Even the tender-hearted vampire, abstaining from blood and often also sex, be it Meyer's Edward Cullen or Angel from the 1997–2003 television series, *Buffy the Vampire Slayer*, is composed in such a way that he embodies both monstrosity and normality within one endlessly struggling character. The more he tries to subdue his "freak of nature" character traits, the more incapable he appears of ever achieving the status of normality, healthiness, and humanness, and the broader the gap between him and his fully human counterparts becomes.[25]

The explicit occupation with what is villainously deviant and other, or, in other words, suppressed and unvoiced in a particular culture, has granted the Gothic the status of being a radically subversive literature, as it renders visible what the dominant discourse of normality and otherness cloaks; in providing space for the silenced and othered deviants of society, it also sheds light on the mechanisms of power underlying all processes of othering and ostracism. In Balchin's words, "[t]he villain exists as a means by which we can dissociate ourselves from evil; and the easiest way to dissociate ourselves from evil is to limit its definition to that which is easily avoidable" (Balchin 254). To create the Gothicized other, representing a culture's discursively repressed, dark underside, authors from eighteenth-century

---

25   Note the underlying assumption that the character of the vampire can be subsumed under the umbrella term "Gothic villain." This assumption, in turn, rests on two premises: i. vampire fiction is just one variety of the hydra of Gothic fiction, and ii. vampires are villains. Though not self-evidently true, I believe that there are strong arguments in favor of both premises (cf. Chapter Five). For further insights, cf. also Nina Auerbach and/or Jean Gordon and Veronica Hollinger. The vampire is also a standard trope discussed in all major publications on the Gothic.

England onward have indeed relied on the most easily avoidable and yet widely accessible stereotype[26] of evilness, the savage.

While research on the images of savagery generally, and on the tropes of the Nobel Savage and the Evil Savage in British and U.S. American literature in particular, is abundant, the trope of savagery and its intimate connection to the stock-in-trade character of the villain have been widely neglected in Gothic studies and in literary studies *per se*. Gothic fiction constructs both difference and sameness, otherness and normality, in binary opposing pairs (Gothemes) on at least four interconnected levels: first, on the narrative surface level of the plot, which conventionally differentiates between the innocent maiden (also referred to as the "damsel in distress") and her chivalrous savior in the hour of need, on the one hand, and the angst-inducing villain, on the other; secondly, Gothic literature tends to be concerned with markers of social classes, by focusing on the distress and eventual rescue of a young middle-class woman overpowered by an elderly pecunious man of noble port; thirdly, the Gothic always performs gender in stark opposites (passivity/action, piety/passion, incarceration/movement), to either confirm contemporaneous gender discourses or to reiterate them; fourthly, the early Gothic constructs and stages all of the aforementioned dichotomies consistently through racialization strategies, i.e., through the clash of two very white and very civil protagonists with a very dark and very savage villain (indicating either the Native American other or the Black abject).

In the following chapters of my study, I establish these dichotomies in the first five decades of British Gothic literature (from 1764 to 1820, i.e., from *The Castle of Otranto* to *Melmoth the Wanderer*), WASP American Gothic literature (from 1799 to 1852, i.e., from *Edgar Huntly* to *Uncle Tom's Cabin*), and African American literature (from 1789 to 1853); indicating continuity and consistency, I subsequently discuss the contemporary WASP American and African American Gothic novel's reliance on the Savage Villain/Civil Hero Gotheme. The bestselling rise of Gothic fiction and

---

26 A brief note on word choice: I use the term "stereotype" to refer to a sedimented, racially (or sexually) denigrating discourse that may or may not be perceived as still being a discursive "doing," an ongoing practice. My use of "stereotype" ties in with Stuart Hall's (1997/2003) understanding of the term and is, therefore, mainly concerned with the classificatory (discursive) reduction of a people or a person to a simplified and unchanging set of characteristics, which, over time, are perceived as being the natural characteristics of a people and/or a person. Therefore, I have chosen a different path from Gustav Jahoda, who, in his anthropologically motivated study, *Images of Savages. Ancient Roots of Modern Prejudice in Western Culture*, explicitly dismisses the term "stereotype" in favor of "image," which, for Jahoda, "has the advantage of conveying a far richer range of meanings, encompassing not only perceptions and mental representations but also, importantly, feelings" (Jahoda xv). While justified in the context of anthropology and anthropological methodology, "stereotype" is the better fitting notion in the contexts of postcolonial literary and cultural studies.

its heavily racialized characters and plot lines, co-occurs with the cultural necessity of legitimizing and clarifying racial hierarchies at a time when formerly ridged and presumed "natural" hierarchies came under severe attack in the wake of the Haitian Revolution and other slave rebellions, abolitionism, and, controversially, the shift from racial environmentalism to racial essentialism and romantic racialism.[27] By claiming that the early English and early American Gothic's Gothemes generally, and the Savage Villain/Civil Hero Gotheme especially, stage hierarchical dichotomies in overtly racial terms, I place the discourses of race at center stage, both in the texts I analyze and in the historical-cultural context to which I link them; I also add a contrary perspective to scholars of the Gothic who claim that "Gothic fiction [...] has as its most basic premise the need to resolve such duality" (Haggerty 21); the Gothic stages, iterates, and reiterates dichotomic dualities, but it never resolves them.

---

27 In *The Black Image in the White Mind: The Debate on Afro-American Character and Destiny, 1817-1914*, George Frederickson defines a *romantic racialist as someone who* "projected an image of the Negro that could be construed as flattering or laudatory in the context of some currently accepted ideals of human behavior and sensibility" (101f.)

British Origins of the Savage Villain/ Civil Hero Gotheme

2.1 The Villain

The late eighteenth- and early nineteenth-century blueprint for an English Gothic villain could, in fact, be encountered in the racial stereotypes of contemporaneous everyday life: the dark-skinned, black-haired Mediterranean, who would eventually be morphed into the all-black savage creature of the British Empire's colonies. In other words, literary Gothic villainy, from the start, was a physical quality with overtly racial connotations. Matthew Lewis' introduction of the arch-villain, Padre Ambrosio, of his 1796 novel *The Monk*, might function as an illustration:

> He was a Man of noble port and commanding presence. His stature was lofty, and his features uncommonly handsome. His Nose was aquiline, his eyes large black and sparkling, and his dark brows almost joined together. His complexion was of a deep but clear Brown; Study and watching had entirely deprived his cheek of colour. Tranquility reigned upon his smooth unwrinkled forehead […]. (Lewis 18)

One hundred and one years later, Ambrosio's brother from another father, Bram Stoker's Count Dracula, shows features that are identical, to the utmost extent, with the monk's:

> His face was a strong—very strong—aquiline, with high bridge of the thin nose and peculiarly arched nostrils; with lofty domed forehead, and hair growing scantily round the temples, but profusely elsewhere. His eyebrows were very massive, almost meeting over the nose, and with bushy hair that seemed to curl in its own profusion. The mouth, so far as I could see it under the heavy moustache, was fixed and rather cruel-looking, with peculiarly sharp white teeth; these protruded over the lips, whose remarkable ruddiness showed astonishing vitality in a man of his years. For the rest, his ears were pale and at the tops extremely pointed; the chin was broad and strong, and the cheeks firm though thin. The general effect was one of extraordinary pallor. (Stoker 18)

With brown skin, bushy dark hair, and eyebrows so massive that they almost join together above the aquiline nose, the English Gothic's villain is continuously drawn in the racial imagery of the Mediterranean man. What the Gothic essentially added to the stereotypical Mediterranean man of the eighteenth and nineteenth centuries are the factors of age and class: It is the pale, elderly man of noble port (a count, a prince, two monks,[1] and the "ninth Caliph of the race of the Abassides,"[2] to name just five famous (ig)noblemen of the early English Gothic) and classic education that pursues the young, innocent maiden. Even on a visible surface, the villain stands out as racially, socially, and sexually other. He is racially and morally marked from the first encounter onward, and he will not deviate from this initial impression to the end. What Walpole called "[t]he horror of the spectacle" (19), the explicit staging of violence and villainy as visible and witnessable horror events, crucially depends on racial visibility and racial otherness in relation to the reader and to the other characters.

These racial markers become most apparent when the Gothic plot (and, in its course, the villain's power) approaches its climax. When finally reaching the peak of violence and confusion, the moment the villain finally loses his morality and fear of God, there is a slight but significant change of vocabulary used to portray him. As the outraged, loathsome man with piercing black eyes betrays his humanness, his overall features become increasingly racialized, dark, and bulging, until he resembles a "savage, inhumane monster" (Walpole 108)[3]. Lewis' monk follows Manfred's

---

[1] I refer to Lewis' and Ann Radcliffe's monks here. While Radcliffe's *The Italian, or, the Confessional of the Black Penitents* (1797) is commonly understood as a direct reaction to *The Monk* (1796), Radcliffe's different introductory staging of her villainous monk, "a man called father Schedoni; an Italian" (Radcliffe 34), is noteworthy. Having already established Schedoni as a racially connoted (and eponymous) "Italian," Radcliffe can introduce her villain in terms of passionate deviance and, in comparison to Lewis, without further explicit reference to his "Italianess": "Among his associates no one loved him, many disliked him, and more feared him. His figure was striking, but not so from grace; it was tall, and, though extremely thin, his limbs were large and uncouth, and as he stalked along, wrapt in the black garments of his order, there was something terrible in its air; something almost superhuman. His cowl, too, as it threw a shade over the livid paleness of his face, increased its severe character, and gave an effect to his large melancholy eye, which approached to horror. [...] There was something in his physiognomy extremely singular, and that cannot easily be defined. It bore the traces of many passions, which seemed to have fixed the features they no longer animated" (Radcliffe 34-35).

[2] William Beckford's villain is introduced as "Vathek, ninth Caliph of the race of the Abassides, [...] the son of Motassem, and the grandson of Haroun al Raschid" (Beckford 1). The accumulated exoticism of his family's name is only exceeded by his "indulgencies unrestrained: for he did not think, with Caliph Omar Ben Abdalaziz, that it was necessary to make a hell of this world to enjoy paradise in the next" (1).

[3] See also pages 22 and 94.

example and kills Elvira, the maiden's mother, with "a resolution equally desperate and savage" (Lewis 303), before raping and killing the maiden herself with "the most horrible and inhuman" barbarity (391):

> He clasped her to his bosom almost lifeless with terror, and faint with struggling. He stifled her cries with kisses, treated her with the rudeness of an unprincipled Barbarian, proceeded from freedom to freedom, and in the violence of his lustful delirium, wounded and bruised her tender limbs. (383)
>
> [...] Antonia still resisted and He now enforced her silence by means of the most horrible and inhuman. [...] Without allowing himself a moment's reflection, He raised [the dagger], and plunged it twice in the bosom of Antonia! (391)

The Savage Villain in early English Gothic fiction is "characterized by a complete loss of control, a complete usurpation of his rational, human-like qualities" (Derrickson 50); he is an unpredictable and uncontrollable threat. While his belonging to a "dark" race naturally connects him to "that mind which is earthy, sensual, devilish" (Maturin 248), his savagely evil behavior is not devoid of human qualities and considerations: The villain is a human being racially predisposed for extreme feelings of lust, anger, greed, and selfishness. In his inescapable pursuit of satisfaction, the villain falls into a state of "lustful delirium" that, as it is fully devoid of rationality and a civil mindset, was conflated with the stereotypical "savage."[4] Despite his racial predisposition for violence and deviance, however, the villain's fall into savagery is defined as a *temporal* loss of a 'civilized' mindset, as a passionate delirium, not as a natural and, therefore, incorrigible lack thereof.

At this stage of the argument, we have reached a significant discrepancy: If the villain of late eighteenth- and early nineteenth-century British Gothic fiction indeed is racially predisposed for violent outbursts of passion and lust, how can this outburst possibly be temporal? In other words, how can the naturally deviant villain possibly return to a state of rationality and normality? What seems to be a fundamental conflict, however, should rather be considered a fictionalized witness to a crucial point in late eighteenth- and early nineteenth-century British cultural

---

4   The "Savage" and the "Oriental," Ter Ellingson argues, "were the two great ethnographic paradigms developed by European writers during the age of exploration and colonialism; and the symbolic opposition between 'wild' and 'domesticated' peoples, between 'savages' and 'civilization,' was constructed as part of the discourse of European hegemony, projecting cultural inferiority as an ideological ground for political subordination" (Ellingson xiii). The attributions "noble" and "ignoble"/"evil," in turn, can be ascribed to the relationship that the explorers/colonizers presumed to have had with the explored/colonized: The converted and "domesticated" savage must be understood as noble, on the one hand, while the obstructing and resisting savage, on the other hand, is rendered Satanic and evil (cf. Anna Krauthammer 6); the appellation "savage," of course, applies to both racial categories.

history, that is, more precisely, to the transition from one notion of race to another. The Mediterranean Catholic monarch, with temporal passionate outbursts of lust and violence, encapsulates accurately the time period that Ashcroft, Griffiths, and Tiffin have described as "the transition of 'race' from signifying, in its literary sense, a line of descent that a group defined by historical continuity, to its scientific sense of 'race' as a zoologically or biologically defined group" (*Post-Colonial* 182). Early British Gothic depicts "races" that are no longer exclusively rooted in both Greek environmentalism and the Old Testament's theocentric hierarchizations but that start showing an internal hierarchization of whiteness and, thus, the unmistakable characteristics of nineteenth-century racial essentialism. Early Gothic villains such as Manfred of Otranto and Padre Ambrosio foreshadow the mid- and late nineteenth-century "racialist" (Appiah, "Race" 276) division of:

> [...] human beings into a small number of groups, called 'races,' in such a way that all the members of these races shared certain fundamental, biologically heritable, moral and intellectual characteristics with each other that they did not share with members of any other race. The characteristics that each member of a race was supposed to share with every other were sometimes called the *essence* of that race; they were characteristics that were necessary and sufficient, taken together, for someone to be a member of the race. (Appiah, "Race" 276)

The construction of an early Gothic villain intertwines a foreign, Mediterranean setting, a noble yet Catholic ancestry, and a number of stock physiological and behavioral characteristics in mutually conditional and interdependent discourses of racial otherness, understood as both a line of descent defined by historical continuity and as a biologically defined group. Manfred and Ambrosio constantly shimmer between biologically inherent and, therefore, inevitable deviance, and the capability for remorseful rationality. *The Castle of Otranto* and *The Monk* were written years before the publication of Georges Cuvier's influential typology of races (1805) and, decades before, works such as Charles Hamilton Smith's *The Natural History of the Human Species* (1848), Robert Knox's *The Races of Man* (1850), Nott and Gliddon's *Types of Mankind* (1854), and Charles Darwin's *The Origin of Species* (1859) heralded the heyday of scientific racism and Social Darwinism. The racialist mindset, the usage of the notion of race to refer to "biologically or physically distinctive categories of human beings" (Ashcroft, Griffiths, and Tiffin 182), however, both predated and enabled the publication of all the works listed above.

"Humans," as Bill Ashcroft reminds us, "had been categorised in terms of their biological difference from the late 1600s" (312), traceably from the point the French physician François Bernier (1620-1688) categorized human beings based on their facial features and skin colors, thus paving the way toward a hierarchization of peoples (not yet termed "races") based on alleged biological characteristics. It is, however, Immanuel Kant's tremendously popular *Observations on the Feeling of the*

Beautiful and Sublime, first published in 1764 and in the same year that *The Castle of Otranto* was published, which is most often cited as having introduced the German equivalent of the term 'races of mankind' (Kant interchangeably uses "Menschengeschlechter" and "Menschengattungen"), in the sense of physically distinctive categories, particularly with regard to gender, race, and nationality. Recalling our previous analysis of the early British Gothic's villain and its racial construction, it might no longer come as a surprise that Kant, in the fourth section of *Observations* (titled "Of National Characteristics, so far as They Depend upon the Distinct Feeling of the Beautiful and Sublime"), constructs a direct parallel between the 'Negroes of Africa' ("Negers von Afrika"), the 'savages' of North America (die "Wilden"), and 'the barbarians' who 'introduced a certain perverse taste, which is known as the gothic' ("Die Barbaren [...] führten einen gewissen verkehrten Geschmack ein, den man den gotischen nennt," Kant 77). Conceptually connected to each other through his notions of the ignoble 'foolish' ("das Läppische"), 'the exaggerated' ("das Übertriebene"), and 'the adventurous' ("das Abenteuer suchend"), Kant not only reflects in his argument a contemporaneous discourse very much comparable to the racializing and hierarchizing (and, thus, legitimizing) discourses present in early Gothic fiction, but Kant's *Observations* also reflect an early notion of race in flux, i.e., a hierarchizing notion of physical and biological differences that he argues might possibly be accidental and random, depending on the specific tide of historical events, the type of government, or the climate (Kant 58). The early WASP Gothic villain, moreover, reflects the processes of transitioning from one notion of race to the other. While the biological legitimatization discourse already informs the othering of the racially deviant villain, the definitory categories remain unstable and in flux.

In 1820, this instability within the British Gothic is still traceable and most remarkably so in Charles Maturin's composition of the villain, Melmoth the Wanderer. While Maturin introduces "a man of savage appearance," who, when addressed as "villain" applies "a loaded horse-whip to [Stanton's] back and shoulders, till the patient soon fell to the ground convulsed with rage and pain" (Maturin 54), this refers to a very minor character in the plot. Maturin quotes the raciality of the Savage Villain, which was, by 1820, conventionalized, but applies it explicitly only to a racially unmarked, minor character. His villain, in turn, acts "coolly" and "slowly" (582) in the midst of "your vices, your passions, and your weaknesses" (584). This noteworthy deviation from the convention is a reiteration in our established sense of the word. Maturin by no means, however, establishes a civil villain; his construction of Melmoth utilizes the widespread racial myth/trope of the Wandering Jew, thereby establishing a context for the reception of his villain that clearly draws on racial denigration, cardinal passions, and savagery (see Brodkin). If we wanted to add yet another layer to the already rather complex raciality of *Melmoth*, we could hint at Maturin's Irishness and that in "the seventeenth century the English elite first imposed the idea of a less-than-human 'savage' on the 'wild' Irish, who were viewed as wicked, barbarous, and uncivil" (Baker 12, see also Ignatiev).

Despite displaying civil qualities now and then, all villains of the early WASP Gothic tradition, and this, of course, includes Melmoth the Wanderer, are racially marked as the other, and they therefore can and must be punished for their savage passions. This punishment conventionally includes confronting the villain with his deeds and the thus-far undisclosed mysteries surrounding them. Exemplarily, "cast upon a Precipice's brink, the steepest in Sierra Morena" (Lewis 438) and face-to-face with Lucifer, Padre Ambrosio learns "[t]hat Antonia whom you violated, was your sister! That Elvira whom you murdered, gave you birth!" (439). The conventional punishment also, and quite strikingly so, reconstructs the villain in terms of humanness and civilization, thus replacing his former savage behavior with remorse and penitence. Ambrosio asks, "in an hollow trembling voice," for deliverance and reunion with Matilda, while being terror-struck, in the face of the "wildness of the surrounding scenery" (438-439); dropped from the sky onto the rocky wilderness of Andalucía, Ambrosio suffers, immobilized by his broken limbs, for six days, while insects and eagles drink his blood and tear out his live flesh. On the seventh day, "the despairing Monk" is drowned in a swelling stream of water and carried straight to hell and to even "greater torments" (442). "[N]o longer ferocious" (Maturin 600), Melmoth the Wanderer is also cast onto the ridge of a "glowing ocean [...] alive" with agonizing souls (602), before being drowned by "a gigantic outstretched arm [...] blacker than [...] blackness" (602). Manfred of Otranto, overthrown and cast out, renounces his passionate vileness publicly and announces that he will live in seclusion until his death. Caliph Vathek repents too late (though his passions and ambitions are explained as being solely his mother's fault) and is cast into an eternity of torture in the hellfire of the Giaour. The conventional punishment of the villain and the re-inscribing of him into the tight boundaries of civilization bend the traditional English Gothic plot to a moral, yet explicitly violent, ending. The villain is not only killed and removed from society; he is effectively cured of his passionate delirium beforehand—paradoxically, through being tortured until he regains his healthy, civil, and remorseful mind-set.

The conventional punishment of the villain follows the logic of the above-mentioned intertwinement of setting, ancestry, and stock physiological and behavioral characteristics in mutually conditional and interdependent discourses of racial otherness. Following the logic of 'race understood as a line of descent defined by historical continuity,' the villains are removed from their location and time, transplanted to a setting constructed solely for the purpose of staging Biblical retribution in sensational detail. Removed from the old, detrimental soil of Spain and Italy, they can evolve into a different, rational character. Following the logic of 'race understood as a zoologically or biologically defined group,' however, this evolved, now remorseful character cannot possibly be allowed to return to society. While the savagely passionate villain can be forced to repent of his sins (conventionally, murder, incest, and rape), he cannot be reintegrated into the fictional society or plot. The murderous rapist, by nature, is staged as a continuous and unchangeable risk that threatens to attack, racially pollute, and, ultimately, destroy the Gothic's society, by attacking, polluting, and destroying its epitome of integrity, vulnerability, and racial whiteness: the damsel in distress.

I will integrate the damsel in distress into my argument first and then move on to analyze the character of the hero. Taken together, and contrasted with the analysis of the villain I have conducted thus far, I will further trace the early Savage Villain/Civil Hero Gotheme in both racial and political terms.

2.2 The Damsel in Distress

Let me shed more light on the Savage Villain by introducing his "prey" (Lewis 384), the innocent maiden, or damsel in distress, the second of the three best-known stock-in-trade characters of the Gothic. Equipped with the characteristics of a sentimental romance's heroine, the Gothic damsels are depicted as "beautiful, weak, sublime, helpless females crouching on the floor, hiding behind doors, dominated by brutal lascivious males, kidnapped, murdered or worse, their virtue at stake, their beauty their great misfortune" (Aguirre 57). They represent, in other words, the very sentimental helplessness[5] that Mary Wollstonecraft criticizes in her 1792 long essay, *A Vindication of the Rights of Woman: with Strictures on Political and Moral Subjects*:

> Fragile in every sense of the word, they are obliged to look up to man for every comfort. In the most trifling dangers they cling to their support, with parasitical tenacity, piteously demanding succour; and their *natural* protector extends his arm, or lifts up his voice, to guard the lovely trembler—from what? Perhaps the frown of an old cow, or the jump of a mouse; a rat would be a serious danger. In the name of reason, and even common sense, what can save such beings from contempt; even though they be soft and fair? These fears, when not affected,

---

5   "Sentimental helplessness" refers to the popular mid- and late eighteenth-century concepts of Sentimentalism and Sensibility, which had a profound impact on the Gothic novel, as well as on its predecessors, for example, the Graveyard School poetry and Edmund Burke's *A Philosophical Enquiry into the Origin of Our Ideas of the Sublime and Beautiful* (1757). For a discussion on Gothic Sensibility and its possible literary origins, including William Shakespeare's *Hamlet* and John Milton's *Paradise Lost*, cf. Manuel Aguirre; for an inquiry into the linear development of the Sentimental novel to the early Gothic romance, cf. Elizabeth R. Napier's *The Failure of Gothic* (which traces sentimental episodes in Gothic novels) and/or Peter de Voogd (who argues that the Sentimental novel contained Gothic elements from the start and was replaced partly by the Gothic by the end of the eighteenth century).

may be very pretty; but they shew a degree of imbecility that degrades a rational creature in a way women are not aware of—for love and esteem are very distinct things. (Wollstonecraft 153)

The early British Gothic plot indeed reduces its maidens to tremulous pawns in the hand of either the villain or the hero.[6] If we combine the "uncommon degree of 'fine feeling'" (Aguirre 58) with her being "not only of aristocratic, but of stereotypically northern, Teutonic beauty" (Malchow 112), it becomes clear that, in terms of racial and gender stereotyping, the character of the maiden contrasts most visibly with the passionate villain. Lewis, representatively, counterbalances the abovementioned introduction of Ambrosio with the slightly earlier introduction of the fair and pious Antonia with the "mild blue eyes" (Lewis 12):

Her features were hidden by a thick veil; But struggling through the crowd had deranged it sufficiently to discover a neck which for symmetry and beauty might have vied with the Medicean Venus. It was of the most dazzling whiteness, and received additional charms from being shaded by the tresses of her long fair hair, which descended in ringlets to her waist. Her figure was rather below than above middle size: It was light and airy as that of an Hamadryad. Her bosom was carefully veiled. Her dress was white; it was fastened by a blue sash, and just permitted to peep out from under it a little foot of the most delicate proportions. (Lewis 9)[7]

In 1820, it was yet again Charles Maturin's *Melmoth the Wanderer* that brought this excess of innocence and whiteness to an astonishing and highly ambivalent peak. Perceived "face to the earth, in mute admiration" by the child-like, naked, and

---

6   Following Kate Ellis's example (*The Contested Castle: Gothic Novels and the Subversion of Domestic Ideology*, 1989), feminist and gender-oriented scholars of the Gothic have worked on and revised the damsel-in-distress trope excessively. For a condensed overview of the trope and the scholarship it has provoked, see Avril Horner, "Heroine." I refrain from labeling the female character of eighteenth- and nineteenth-century Gothic fiction as a "heroine," as other labels (damsel in distress, innocent maiden in pursuit, etc.) capture her passively reacting role in the plot better. Especially in relation to the actively questing "hero," the designation "heroine" is misleading. Note, however, that this trope has changed significantly in the twentieth and twenty-first centuries, and that the label "heroine" (understood as a replacement for the traditional trope of the Civil Hero) will play a more active role in my analyses of contemporary American Gothic fiction.

7   For the sake of completeness, Radcliffe introduces her maiden, Ellena, correspondingly, except for a clear focus on both Ellena's intelligence and womanly piety: "Her features were of the Grecian outline, and, though they expressed the tranquility of an elegant mind, her dark blue eyes sparkled with intelligence. She was assisting her companion so anxiously, that she did not immediately observe the admiration she had inspired; but the moment her eyes met those of Vivaldi, she became conscious of their effect, and she hastily drew her veil" (Radcliffe 6).

"dark-red tint[ed] [...] natives of the Bengalese islands" (Maturin 309), "the *white* goddess" (310, original emphasis) is introduced as follows:

> The form was that of a female, but such as they had never before beheld, for her skin was perfectly white, (at least in their eyes, who had never seen any but the dark-red tint of the natives of the Bengalese islands). Her drapery [...] consisted only of flowers, whose rich colours and fantastic grouping harmonized well with the peacock's feathers twined among them, and altogether composed a feathery fan of wild drapery, which, in truth, beseemed an "island goddess." Her long hair, of a colour they had never beheld before, pale auburn, flowed to her feet, and was fantastically entwined with the flowers and feathers that formed her dress. [...] On her white bare shoulder a loxia was perched, and round her neck was hung a string of their pearl eggs, so pure and pellucid, that the first sovereign in Europe might have exchanged her richest necklace of pearls for them. (309f.)

Within the sub-plot, "The Tale of the Indians," Immalee (later called Isidora and tied up in the same framing plot line as Goethe's Gretchen) is only constructed as a white, meaning civilized goddess in direct juxtaposition to the Indians' savage, "black goddess Seeva" (303); she is one end of a binary scale of civilization. Immalee behaves like a true lady within the all-enclosing wilderness of the exotic island and covers her nakedness not only pragmatically but with a good understanding of both color arrangements and decorum, up to a point at which her natural beauty and adornment rivals that of European queens. On the other side of the scale, Seeva, the "black goddess," is constructed as follows:

> her hideous idol, with its collar of human skulls, forked tongues darting from its twenty serpent mouths, and seated on a matted coil of adders, [where it] first received the bloody homage of the mutilated limbs and immolated infants of her worshippers. (Maturin 303)

Worshipping Seeva means paying "bloody homage" in the form of "mutilated limbs and immolated infants" (303) and includes performing "a kind of wild dance" (308), while worshipping Immalee requires flowers, prostration, and "chaunted verses in praise of the *white* goddess, and the island sacred to her and to lovers" (310, original emphasis).

Maturin consciously and conventionally uses racial and gender markers as a strategy for positioning his characters and advancing the Gothic plot. The introduction of his maiden, the shining white goddess who reigns culturally and aesthetically supreme, in spite of her confinement on a savage island, reads like both a hyperbolic version of the Victorian ideal of True Womanhood and a good case in point for Nina Auerbach's notion of the iconoclastic trope of the "woman as angel":

> [T]he Victorian angel of the house seems a bizarre object of worship, both in her virtuous femininity and its inherent limitations—she can exist only within families, when masculine angels can exist elsewhere—and in the immobilization the phrase suggests. In contrast to her swooping ancestors, the angel in the house is a violent paradox with overtones of benediction and captivity. Angelic motion had once known no boundaries; the Victorian angel is defined by her boundaries. (Auerbach, *Woman* 71f.)

Maturin's strategy, however, is more complex than that to which Auerbach refers. While he introduces his maiden with explicit reference to her supreme civilized, true womanhood, he augments this goddess with racial markers and lets her stand out as supremely white among the all-encompassing "dark-red" savagery. What makes Maturin's introduction of Immalee so striking is not so much the density and clarity of motifs involved in the gender construction of the "innocent maiden," but, rather, his use of racially overdrawn motifs surrounding a *"white"* character that he, at the same time, racially marks and unmarks. Once Immalee leaves the wilderness of the Bengalese islands behind and is restored to her Madrid family, she is reintroduced as Isidora di Aliaga, daughter of Donna Clara, "a woman of a cold and grave temper, with all the solemnity of a Spaniard, and all the austerity of a bigot" and of "dull and selfish" Don Fernan, who is well known for his "fiery passion and saturnic manners not unusual among Spaniards" (367). Introduced to Spain and reunited with her parents, who are depicted as "Spaniards" and with explicit reference to the racial stereotypes connected to the denigrating term, Maturin renames his damsel first and then reconstructs her, by explicitly killing her former self, that is, the *"white* goddess" Immalee:

> And it was amid such beings that the vivid and susceptible Immalee, the daughter of nature, the gay creature of elements, was doomed to wither away the richly-coloured and exquisitely-scented flower of an existence so ungenially transplanted. Her singular destiny seemed to have removed her from a physical wilderness to place her in a moral one. And, perhaps, her last state was worse than her first. (368)

The damsel's new and only racial identity is that of the Spainard named Isidora di Aliaga, and Immalee "was doomed to wither away" in the wilderness of Spain.

Maturin follows the same logic of constructing a racially signified damsel here that he has in the construction of his villain. Completely removed from time, space, and history, and placed within an exotic wilderness, a notion of 'race understood as a line of descent defined by historical continuity' enables Maturin to construct the epitomic whiteness of Immalee. Following the logic of 'race understood as a zoologically or biologically defined group,' however, this superior being will cease to exist as soon as it is placed within the biological ties of a family of racially marked Spainards. And just like the villain's, Isidora's fate is sealed once the racial predispositions are established; put bluntly, long before encountering the villain, Isidora's tragedy is predetermined by her race and her phylogenetic connection to the Spanish race.

Let me stop here and refrain from jumping headfirst into an analysis of Maturin's *Melmoth*, which would mean departing from my original topic and scope. It has become obvious that within the framework of the traditional, i.e., late eighteenth- and early nineteenth-century British Gothic novel, the "innocent maiden" trope functions only as a contrasting element in direct juxtaposition with elements constructed as being other from it—the other age (villains are disproportionately older than maidens), the other race (Mediterranean, Spaniard, "dark-red" islanders), the other sex (meaning Manfred, Melmoth, Ambrosio, along with their deviant sexual desires, which include rape and incest), and the other class (a count, a prince, two monks, a Caliph). It is the connection of—and the fundamental gulf between—whiteness/civilization and darkness/savagery that structure and control the early English Gothic plot.

2.3 The Hero

The early British strategy of structuring the Gothic plot by placing these opposing pairs at center stage becomes even more apparent when one adds the villain's rival, the chivalrous hero, to the picture. The conventionally "brave, handsome and self-denying hero" (Demoor 173), oftentimes "a young peasant discovered to be the rightful heir to a usurped estate" (Clery 33), complements the maiden and acts as a foil to the villain. Drawn into action by the damsel's distress, the hero, who otherwise shares with the damsel a number of basic characteristics (such as being young, handsome, graceful, humble, morally superior, and racially marked as being white), displays manly bravery, by actively interfering with the villain instead of submissively enduring the hardships with which he is confronted. The hero, we are assured, "fear[s] no man's displeasure [...] when a woman in distress puts herself under [his] protection" (Walpole 54); he "come[s] to bring change and new life by rescuing" her (Milbank 159). While I will not argue against this character positioning of the early Gothic tradition by contemporary scholars of the Gothic (such as Demoor, Clery, and Milbank), which is, by now, itself conventional, I want to shift the focus toward two aspects: the direct juxtaposition of the villain's savagery and the hero's civil virtues within the texts and the racial signification strategies used to establish this juxtaposition in the first place.

Let me first outline the strategy of directly juxtaposing the savagery of the villain with the civil qualities of the hero, by going back to Horace Walpole's *Castle of Otranto*. Walpole introduces his hero, Theodore, "a young peasant, whom rumour had drawn thither from a neighbouring village" (Walpole 20), from the perspective of the enraged villain, Manfred. The young peasant, who presumably dropped an enormous helmet on Manfred's son, is addressed twice as "Villain!" (20, 21), as a "necromancer" and a "monster! sorcerer! 'tis thou hast slain my son!" (21). In the midst of Manfred's enraged accusations, however, Theodore's true nature stands out all the clearer:

> The young peasant himself was still more astonished, not conceiving how he had offended the prince: yet recollecting himself, with a mixture of grace and humility, he disengaged himself from Manfred's gripe, and then, with an obeisance which discovered more jealousy of innocence, than dismay, he asked with respect, of what he was guilty! (20-21)

Theodore displays his civil character, meaning here his rational and humble mindset, surrounded by the "senseless guesses" of "the mob" (20) and faced with a life-threatening encounter with a man of "savage and ill-grounded resolution" (22), who "would have poignarded" (21) him, if he had not been stopped by his friends. This display of heroic civilization, in the face of villainous savagery, permeates the plot of *The Castle of Otranto*: While "the savage Manfred" condemns Theodore to death by beheading, civil Theodore remembers "the charity of [Manfred's] daughter" and "can forget injuries, but never benefits" (94); when Manfred, in a passionate fit, accidentally stabs his own daughter, Theodore wrenches the dagger from the "[s]avage, inhuman monster!" (108), compassionately sparing the villain's life, and tries to stop the victim's bleeding.

All of the above-mentioned early Gothic novels employ Walpole's strategy of continuously juxtaposing villainous savagery with heroic civilization. For the sake of clarity, I will limit my close reading of these other texts to providing one other, quite striking, example from *The Monk*. Just like Walpole, Mathew Lewis introduces his hero, Lorenzo, in direct relation to the villainous savagery of his antagonist, Ambrosio. Lewis, however, constructs this plot-structuring juxtaposition implicitly, by letting Lorenzo renounce beforehand the villainous characteristics that will later be embodied through Ambrosio. After his first encounter with Antonia, Lorenzo defends his musing about her in the following way: "I should be a Villain, could I think of her on any other terms than marriage; and in truth she seems possessed of every quality requisite to make me happy in a Wife" (Lewis 24-25). Lewis thus foreshadows the clash between the abundantly passionate rapist and murderer, the "unprincipled Barbarian" (383), and his moral counterpart, the Civil Hero, who no one "can [...] suspect [...] of such barbarity" (25).

If we, on the above-provided textual basis, tie early English Gothic's fascination with juxtaposing racially overdrawn characters in terms of either savagery or civilization to the two contradictory versions of the myth of the 'savage' Goths, which

I introduced in Chapter 2, a politically motivated and uniquely British national narrative unfolds.

2.4 Gothic Nationalism, or, the Gothic Gothic

In an age of social liberation and political revolution, an age defined by the Enlightenment, the Abolitionist Movement (peaking in the 1807 Slave Trade Act and in the Slavery Abolition Act of 1833), and the beginnings of the Industrial Revolution, as much as by Britain's Revolutionary Wars with its Thirteen American Colonies (1775–1783) and with France (1793-1815), the affirmative Gothic heritage myth of the noble and pristinely parliamentary English (British) nation proliferated (see Chapter 2). It was strategically used as a propaganda tool for legitimizing the presumed moral and political supremacy of British conservatism over the manifold revolutionary barbarians with which Britain found itself confronted. I claim that the attribution "Gothic" (as in the "Gothic" architecture of the Houses of Parliament), with its direct, though ambiguous, relation to the constructed myth(s) of the Goths, is a genuinely political term and that we can excavate "a direct political-fictional correspondence" (Clery 156) between British conservatism under multilateral attack and the rise of early Gothic fiction, which scholars such as Emma Clery and Markman Ellis tend to dismiss.

This already holds true for Horace Walpole's first attribution of "Gothick" to his "Story" of *The Castle of Otranto* (Walpole, title page). If we take into account that Walpole, the Fourth Earl of Oxford, was a lifelong Whig politician and, for many years, a Member of Parliament,[8] the need for a political reading of his explicitly "Gothick" novel becomes even more pressing. Placing *The Castle of Otranto* in the context of the Whig's legitimatization narrative, which constructs the historical Gothic people as England's parliamentary ancestry, Walpole's juxtaposition of an elder, power-abusing prince, in pursuit of an innocent maiden, and a young, courageous peasant, who is established as the rightful heir to the kingdom, indeed reads like a fictionalized eighteenth-century Whig-style pamphlet. Warning the English citizens about the threats of monarchical power abuse and calling for a regulated, parliamentary monarchy, *The Castle of Otranto* truly is a "Gothick" story in the political, that is, mythologized sense of the term.

As in the later Gothic texts by writers such as Lewis, Radcliffe, and Maturin, there is an additional aspect to Walpole's strategic juxtaposition of characters that drops us into the political realm like a trapdoor: It is the elder Mediterranean monarch who pursues his young Mediterranean daughter-in-law and kills an elder Eng-

---

8   While writing and publishing his "Gothick Story," Walpole was an MP for King Lynn, Norfolk, a seat he held until his retirement from the Commons in 1768.

lish princess, before the young English peasant saves not only the day but also Isabella.[9] Conflating names, racial markers, and the setting of the eponymous *Castle of Otranto* that revolves around both medieval and Catholic environments, we could, by now, be tempted to conclude with Robert Miles' argument: "In this contrast between a pleasurable scandalized English reader and the degenerate Catholic Continent, sunk back in priest-ridden Medievalism, we appear to have the makings of English Europhobia" ("Europhobia" 85). In the context of the construction and re-construction of the mythological Goths within a Whig-style national narrative, however, Gothic anti-Catholicism, Medievalism, and displayed Europhobia appear in a different, more specifically, British, light. In 1762, seventeen years after the Jacobite uprising, the Whig politician William Pitt the Elder, 1st Earl of Chatham, stated, "[t]he errors of Rome are rank idolatry, a subversion of all civil as well as religious liberty, and the utter disgrace of reason and of human nature" (188). Human nature, reason, and civil and religious liberty, in other words, cannot be sought in a Europe reigned by the Catholic Church and its firm belief in rank idols. Catholicism, Europe, civil rights, and human nature are conflated by Pitt and, thus, put forward as a negative foil, against which his own English Protestantism is drawn and considered as being a rational, civil, and religious liberty for which human nature calls. Also, we should not forget that Whig politics in general, and William Pitt in particular, sought to define themselves in opposition to what they understood as backward, medieval Tory politics. A rational, civil, and Protestant national narrative, for Pitt, essentially is—and can only be—a Whig narrative.

The early Gothic used racially marked characters, be they Mediterranean or white, to negotiate otherness and belonging within the framework of a national myth of origin. In Walpole's novel, as in all of the early British Gothic novels I have discussed above, the characters function according to a juxtaposition of Mediterranean/Catholic and British (English)/Protestant conflations. The same juxtaposition can also be read as Non-British/legitimately inferior and British (English)/legitimately superior, as it is intimately linked to questions of race, belonging, authority, and, above all, nationalism.

---

9   In *The Castle of Otranto*, the juxtaposition of characters mirrors the juxtaposition of their either Italian or English names. Otranto's castle, that is, the fictional rendering of the real seaport of Otranto in the Province of Lecce in the Apulia region of Italy, is reigned by villainous Prince Manfred, who could well be a descendent of the four marquises of Saluzzo of the same name, or even of Manfred, King of Sicily, himself. Theodore, on the other hand, is a genuinely English rendering from Greek, meaning "God's gift." The female characters also point us into different geographic directions. Matilda might remind us of England's Empress Matilda (also known as Empress Maude), not least due to Shakespeare's Hippolyta in *A Midsummer Night's Dream*. Hippolyta pulls us toward mythological Greece, and Isabella, the maiden in pursuit, transports us back to Italy, bringing us full circle.

In Gothic literature explicitly modeled after Walpole's prototype, but written in the wake of wars and revolutions, that is, after 1775, the need for a national narrative, legitimizing a British Empire under multilateral attack, becomes dominant. The Gothic narrative, literarily and politically, is used to establish a sense of national "belonging" for English, Irish, Welsh, and Scottish citizens, who are not only at war but also in the cultural and social processes of abolishing slavery, industrializing, urbanizing, and transculturizing. Despite profound historical and cultural upheavals, writers of what I would call the second phase of the early Gothic clearly use Walpole's prototypical juxtaposition of the villainous Mediterranean/Catholic and the heroic British (English)/Protestant. As we have seen in great detail, they also use the climactic insertion of "savagery" versus "civilization." For Walpole, who, in 1793, reflects upon the terminology of savagery and barbarity under the direct impact of the French Revolution, second phase writers such as Lewis, Radcliffe, and Maturin must appear to hang on to an old, recently outdated "Dictionary" (Walpole quoted in Ketton-Cremer 305). Having heard of the execution of King Louis XVI, Walpole wrote to Lady Ossory on January 29, 1793:

> Indeed, Madam, I write unwillingly; there is not a word left in my Dictionary that can express what I feel. *Savages, barbarians*, &c., were terms for poor ignorant Indians and Blacks and Hyaenas, or, with some superlative epithets, for Spaniards in Peru and Mexico, for Inquisitors, or for Enthusiasts of every breed in religious wars. It remained for the enlightened eighteenth century to baffle language and invent horrors that can be found in no vocabulary. What tongue could be prepared to paint a Nation that should avow Atheism, profess Assassination, and practice Massacres on Massacres for four years together: and who, as if they had destroyed God as well as their King, and established Incredulity by law, give no symptoms of repentance! These Monsters talk of settling a Constitution—it may be a brief one, and couched in one Law, "Thou shalt reverse every Precept of Morality and Justice, and do all the Wrong thou canst to all Mankind." (Quoted in Ketton-Cremer 305–306, Walpole's emphasis)

What strikes me as most interesting about this quotation is not so much Walpole's introduction of the "monster," to depict both the French revolutionists and, implicitly, Britain's political conservatism; rather, it is his differentiation between "[s]*avages, barbarians*, &c." and "[t|hese Monsters" of the French Revolution that brings us full circle in our discussion of the racialized characters of early British Gothic fiction.

The term "savage" (used synonymously with "barbarians, &c."), in Walpole's letter, is directly related to, even conflated with, race and applies first and foremost to "poor ignorant Indians and Blacks and Hyaenas." Listing "poor ignorant Indians and Blacks" with "Hyaenas" provides a stunningly accurate image of racial hierarchies and proto-scientific configurations at the end of the eighteenth and the beginning of the nineteenth century. Taking the "Spaniards in Peru and Mexico" into account, Walpole's list of savages also summarizes his character composition of "savage Manfred" in *The Castle of Otranto*. Explicitly tying "savagery" to "villainy" in Walpole's early Gothic, in other words, has been influenced by contemporaneous discourses of race and racial hierarchies from the start.

In 1793, faced with the necessity of depicting the abhorred atrocities of the French revolutionists, Walpole deems himself in need of a new vocabulary with which he can put the unspeakable horrors of "Massacres on Massacres" into words. His choice of "Monsters" not only highlights the presumed moral, religious, and political, that is, human degeneration of the French, but it also reinforces the racial differentiation between "savages" and "monsters." Put bluntly, while the French are monstrous revolutionists, they cannot be called "savages," as "savagery" per definition is a racial category and, therefore, applies only to Indians, Blacks, hyaenas, and Southern American (i.e. Mexican und Peruvian) Spaniards. Walpole's struggle for the right terminology (savagery versus monstrosity) at the turn of the century can be understood as a harbinger of British Imperial Gothic fiction,[10] which is the common concept used today to refer to Britain's Gothic/"Gothicized" (Brantlinger, "Imperial" 203) literature from the 1820s until WWI.

Indeed, Walpole's discussion of both savages and the French opens up another, thus far neglected political context of early British Gothic fiction. By focusing on the dichotomic juxtaposition of the Savage Villain and the Civil Hero, we are able to access a politically functionalized discourse of race that clearly stems from colonial encounters with, and hierarchical configurations of, racial otherness. The racialized villains, "vilified because of the skin they wear—and given the skin they wear because they are to be vilified" (Derrickson 44), like their antithetically racialized opponents, are coded culturally and politically, and are utilized within a "Gothic" narrative of British national identity.

Aside from the often-discussed interconnection of early Gothic fiction with the British sentimental romance, early Gothic's racialization strategies, therefore, tie in with a form of writing that consistently intertwined racial othering with sensationalism and very graphic imagery: the British captivity narrative. During (and after) the French and Indian War (1754 to 1763), "Colonial and British authors alike

---

10 To wide critical acclaim, Patrick Brantlinger (2012) has provided a condensed laundry-list definition of Imperial Gothic: "Major themes of imperial Gothic fiction include going native [...]; insanity, which is how going native is often interpreted; reverse invasion or colonisation [...]; racial, civilisational or psychological degeneration [...]; 'sexual anarchy,' as Elaine Showalter (1990) calls it, or anxieties about both feminism and homosexuality [...]; and the possible reality of hauntings and other occult phenomena [...]. Besides evocations of the uncanny and supernatural, imperial Gothic tales utilise a number of conventions drawn from older Gothic romances such as Matthew Lewis's *The Monk* (1796) and Mary Shelly's *Frankenstein* (1818, revised 1831)" (Brantlinger, "Imperial" 204).

debated the conduct of the war, the future of Indian diplomacy, and which white group had placed the British Empire in the present mess" (Bickham 60). In this debate, Native Americans were univocally depicted as evil savages, whose brutality and wildness, according to British writers, was only outrivaled by their continuous siding with France. In his 1759 narrative, *French and Indian Cruelty: Exemplified in the Life and Various Vicissitudes of Fortune, of Peter Williamson*, Scottish-born Williamson, unlike authors of earlier Christian faith-depicting captivity narratives, composes a thoroughly political text that explicitly urges William Pitt to continue the war against France in the American colonies. Williamson intends to exhibit "in a concise manner, a scene of many barbarities, and unheard cruelties, exercised by the savage Indians, instigated by the treacherous French" (Williamson 3). A typical scene of the savage Indians is the depiction of one of their raids—dichotomically constructed in images of savagery/civilization and villainy/innocence with which we are already quite familiar:

> They soon got admittance into the unfortunate man's house, where they immediately without the least remorse, and with more than brutal cruelty scalped the tender parents and unhappy children. Nor could the tears, the shrieks, or the cries of these unhappy victims prevent their horrid massacre: For having thus scalped them, and plundered the house of every thing that was moveable, they set fire to the same, where the poor creatures met their final doom admist the flames, the hellish miscreants standing at the door in their diabolical manner, the piercing cries, ear-rending groans, and parental affectionate soothings, which issued from this horrid sacrifice of an innocent family. (Williamson 17-18)

The direct juxtaposition of savage Indians, on the one hand, and the treacherous French, on the other, reminds us of Walpole's letter. The treacherous French might be the masterminds behind the Indian's actions, but, again, they cannot be called "savage." If we recall the prevalent notion of 'race understood as a line of descent defined by historical continuity,' this clear differentiation foreshadows Walpole's struggle for words: Whether faced with revolutionary monsters or with the treacherous French instigators in the colonies, Walpole and Williamson understand themselves and their British nation as being at war with France. The French in the American Colonies cannot possibly be attributed with savagery, as the term is reserved for the savage Indians living on the exotic American soil; and the French cannot possibly turn into savages themselves, as they cannot be thought of outside of their time and space, that is, outside of their representation of France. Introducing "savage Frenchmen" would have meant creating racially ambivalent, 'Americanized' enemies that would no longer be completely congruent with France.

Perceived in this context, early British Gothic fiction can hardly be reduced to "an epiphenomena of modernity" (Miles, "Review" 119), a construction of a recoverable "past as a lost Golden Age" (Wein 4), or "a type of cautionary tale about what was frequently and unquestioningly labeled 'enlightened' and 'progressive'" (Davison 68) and French. Rather, the early Gothic seems to originate in hierarchically and exclusionary structured discourses of race, belonging, and nationality. Indeed, the terminology it uses strongly suggests a direct correspondence with reactionary captivity narratives starting in the mid-1750s.[11] The staging of dichotomically opposed characters in racialized terms of either their villainous savagery or their heroic, civil virtues creates a visibly marked and genuinely politically active national narrative called forward by a young British nation under multilateral attack.

For early British Gothic writers, there is just one drop of bitterness: While the Gothic revival in architecture became synonymous with British nationalism, the early Gothic novel did not. Rather, it was increasingly viewed with suspicion[12] and, as I discussed in greater detail in Chapter 2, dismissed as a particularly debauched version of sentimental writing for and more and more by women. The nationalistically inspired racial stereotypes and especially the juxtaposition of the racialized Savage Villain and the Civil Hero, however, proved to be extremely successful. Indeed, the Savage Villain/Civil Hero Gotheme became so successful that it quickly crossed the Atlantic, to be utilized within another national narrative—strikingly, one that opposed the British Gothic endeavor.

---

11 Howard L. Malchow later convincingly connects Imperial Gothic texts (such as *Frankenstein*) to the villainous passions and deviant sexuality of the "Negro." He argues that "the threat that white women might be brutalized by over-sexed black men of great strength and size became a cliché of racist writing, ready for appropriation in the creation of Gothic horror and given an extra charge by the recently dramatized and exaggerated stories of the plight of white women in revolutionary Haiti" (Malchow 112).
12 For a survey of contemporaneous reactions, cf. Brandford K. Mudge's "The Man with Two Brains: Gothic Novels, Popular Culture, Literary History."

PART II:
The Savage Villain/Civil Hero Gotheme: WASP Origins and Iterations

Early WASP American Adaptations

> "Doom! Doom! Doom! Something seems to whisper it in the trees of America. Doom!" (D.H. Lawrence, Studies 160)

Without a doubt, early WASP American writers—Charles Brockden Brown, Isaac Mitchell, James Fenimore Cooper, and Edgar Allen Poe, to name just four—imported the bestselling Gothic from Britain and, as is commonly agreed in contemporary Gothic scholarship,[1] adapted it to the peculiar needs and fears of the young American nation. As touched upon in the previous chapters, this adaption is generally viewed as a process of internalization, of bringing the external hauntings and monsters of the British Gothic home, and of rendering the evil of castles, counts, monks, ghosts, and vampires mundane, domestic, and "homely" (Botting, *Gothic* 113ff.). In this chapter, I focus on the Savage Villain/Civil Hero Gotheme, as adapted and functionalized in early WASP American fiction, and offer an alternative reading of the origins of the American Gothic. By stressing the key motif of savagery (as opposed to civilization), it will become clear how and why the American Gothic villain must indeed be understood as the epitome of *externalized* evil and, intrinsically connected to this move, as the crystallization of contemporaneous WASP American discourses of exceptionalism, nationalism, race, and white abjectorship.

3.1 Mock(ing) Villainy

The first step I suggest toward an alternative reading of the early WASP American Gothic is the introduction of a new set of villains to the stage: the 'mock villains.' Mock villains figure prominently in the first five decades of American Gothic fiction writing,[2] that is, from 1799 to 1852, or from Charles Brockden Brown's *Edgar*

---

1 Cf., among many others, Allen L. Smith; Teresa A. Goddu; David Punter; and Glennis Byron.
2 "American Gothic fiction writing" here is used to recall our previously gained understanding of the (American) Gothic as a writing strategy that employs a stable canon of Gothemes, that is, conventionalized motif/trope dichotomies, thereby (re)iterating a racialized discourse of otherness or abjection. Next to analyzing some early Gothic novel classics (such as *Edgar Huntly* and Edgar Allen Poe's *The Narrative of Arthur Gordon Pym, of Nantucket*), we can and

Huntly to Harriet Beecher Stowe's *Uncle Tom's Cabin*, and subsume in one category seemingly diverse characters, such as Brockden Brown's Clithero Edny, Cooper's David Gamut, Poe's Pym as the ghost of Hartman Rogers, and Beecher Stowe's Cassy as the ghost of the attic. The construction, as well as the contemporaneous reading of these characters, essentially depends on the already conventionalized status of the British Gothic's stereotypical characters, settings, props, and plots. Within the early American Gothic plot, these pseudo-villains are established as satirical distractions, as foils of pardonable and justifiable deviance, against which the climactic evil of full-fledged American villainy will stand out as all the more threatening and horrifying. Mocking the British tradition, these inchoate red herrings echo sensationally entertaining external, i.e., physical otherness ("Costume Gothic"[3]), while at the same time they are constantly disclosing their artificiality.

Consider, in this respect, Charles Brockden Brown's introduction of Clithero Edny, the Irish immigrant and "only foreigner among us" (651):

> At this time, the atmosphere was somewhat illuminated by the moon, which, though it had already set, was yet so near the horizon, as to benefit me by its light. The shape of a man, tall and robust, was now distinguished. Repeated and closer scrutiny enabled me to perceive that he was employed in digging the earth. Something like flannel was wrapt round his waist and covered his lower limbs. The rest of his frame was naked. I did not recognize in him any one whom I knew. A figure, robust and strange, and half naked, to be thus employed, at this hour and place, was calculated to rouse up my whole soul. (647)

Dimly lit by the setting moon, the protagonist, Edgar Huntly, reflects upon a truly (British) Gothic scene, complete with a very visibly villainous character, seemingly engaged in digging "a grave" (648). Edgar's pondering on the presumed villain as "calculated" to rise up his "whole soul" reminds us of Brockden Brown's introductory note "To The Public" that contextualizes *Edgar Huntly* as a tale "calling forth the

---

should also readily include texts into our survey that the majority of Gothic scholars have not discussed (yet): James Fenimore Cooper's *The Last of the Mohicans: A Narrative of 1757* and Harriet Beecher Stowe's *Uncle Tom's Cabin*. As we will see in greater detail, the latter texts draw heavily on both British and American Gothic writing conventions.

3   Cathy N. Davidson uses the term "Costume Gothic" to refer to "American Gothics" that draw predominately on the props and setting of the British tradition, up to a point at which the American Costume Gothic "transplant[s], virtually intact, a European castle from Radcliffe's fiction to the wilds of Connecticut" (228). Notably, Davidson differentiates between a group of writers of Costume Gothic fiction (including writers such as Isaac Mitchell and S. S. B. K. Wood) and a group of writers "specializing in subtle psychological analysis" (221), such as Brockden Brown and Poe. She therefore uses the plural and refers to "American Gothics." I claim that the Costume Gothic mode, if we want to keep Davidson's term, is an essential plot feature of the early WASP American Gothic novel and, logically, refers to the early WASP American Gothic in the singular.

passions and engaging the sympathy of the reader," not only by means of what he understands to be widely known "Gothic castles and chimeras," but also by the "perils" for "a native of America" (642). After calling forth and taking into consideration the reader's experiences and expectations of well-known British Gothic conventions, Brockden Brown sets out to rupture these expectations, first by rendering the presumed grave-digging murderer as "nothing but an object of compassion" and of "heart-bursting grief" (648)[4] and, then, by juxtaposing him, his tale, and Edgar's "reflections upon this subject [Clithero's tale and his sudden disappearance]" (721), with the introduction of what will soon turn out to be the new type of villainy suitable "for a native of America": "In the midst of my reflections upon this subject, the idea of the wilderness occurred" (721).

In his most enduringly popular novel, *The Last of the Mohicans*, James Fenimore Cooper also functionalizes a mock villain within his dramatic build-up of a full-fledged and pronouncedly American villain. In a very detailed description covering more than a page, "the ungainly man" (25), later known as David Gamut, is introduced as follows:

> The person of this individual was to the last degree ungainly without being in any particular manner deformed. He had all the bones and joints of other men, without their proportions. [...] His head was large; his shoulders narrow; his arms long and dangling; while his hands were small, if not delicate. His legs and thighs were thin, nearly to emaciation, but of extraordinary length; and his knees would have been considered tremendous, had they not been outdone by the broader foundations on which this false superstructure of blended human orders was so profanely reared. The ill-assorted and injudicious attire of the individual only served to render this awkwardness more conspicuous. [...] (18)

Constructed as "the stranger" (e.g. 26, 27) *per se*, Gamut is physically othered; his body, his inept silk and silver garments, and, not least, his "large, civil cocked hat, like those worn by clergymen within the last thirty years" (18) are established as tokens of a potentially villainous deviancy in British Gothic terms. However, as was true for Clithero Edny, Gamut's physical potential for villainy is qualified quickly and replaced by the introduction of the plot's true villain, "the 'Indian runner" (19) Magua.

---

4 In his 1804 essay, "Novel-Reading," Charles Brockden Brown explains the connection between his novel writing and the moral component of his fiction as follows: "Those who prate about the influence of novels to unfit us for solid and useful reading, are guilty of a double error: for in the first place, a just and powerful picture of human life in which the connection between vice and misery, and between facility and virtue is vividly portrayed, is the most solid and useful reading that a moral and social being [...] can read; and in the second place, the most trivial and trite of these performances are, to readers of certain ages and intellects, the only books they will read." (405)

Instantaneously, Gamut is morphed from a villainous to a merely grotesque character, which, coming up rapidly and unexpectedly behind a group of travelers in the wilderness, now evokes only laughter and amusement—even among the ladies (27).

Clithero and Gamut are typical mock villains of the early American Gothic period, as they are constructed to reflect their literary artificiality and the British literary tradition from which they stem. In the second half of the early American Gothic period, writers such as Edgar Allan Poe and Harriet Beecher Stowe take up the motif of the mock villain and perfect its satirical potential. By letting characters like Pym and Cassy dress up as ghosts, in order to scare their superstitious (and drunk) antagonists, thereby tricking their way out of bondage, both authors explicitly draw on the conventionalized British Gothic as a ready-made supply of shallow scare tactics. When a mock villain enters the stage as a "sudden apparition" (P 66)[5], his combining of "a false stomach," "some bedclothes," "white chalk," and "blood" (P 63), with the "thousand superstitions which are so universally current" (P 66), fully and hyperbolically suffices to let an antagonist "without uttering a syllable, f[a]ll back, stone dead, upon the cabin floor" (P 67). Beecher Stowe's "Authentic Ghost Story" (UTC 479) stretches the mock villainy motif and its profound sense of irony to the extreme, by letting two damsels, Cassy ("unenlightened but [with a] very sincere spirit of piety" UTC 389) and Emmeline (pious, too, but "educated much more intelligently," UTC 389), plot, masquerade, and perform as malicious ghosts,[6] haunting the arch-villain, Simon Legree:

> In vain the doors of the upper entry had been locked: the ghost either carried a duplicate key in its pocket, or availed itself of a ghost's immemorial privilege of coming through the keyhole, and promenaded as before, with a freedom that was alarming. Authorities were somewhat divided, as to the outward form of the spirit, owing to a custom quite prevalent among negroes,—and, for aught we know, among whites, too,—of invariably shutting the eyes, and covering up heads under blankets, petticoats, or whatever else might come in use for a shelter, on these occasions. [...] and, therefore, there were abundance of full-length portraits of the ghost, abundantly sworn and testified to, which [...] agreed with each other in no particular, except the common family peculiarity of the ghost tribe,—the wearing of a *white sheet*. The poor souls were not versed in ancient history, and did not know that Shakespeare had authenticated this costume [...]. (UTC 479-80 emphasis in the original)

---

5   For clarity's sake, the in-text citations from Poe's *The Narrative of Arthur Gordon Pym* are marked "P" and "UTC" refers to Beecher Stowe's *Uncle Tom's Cabin*.
6   Beecher Stowe also writes her characters (and herself) into the literary conventions that structure the nineteenth-century British trope of "the madwoman in the attic" (see Gilbert and Gubar 1979).

If we consider the situation of the American book market in the first 50 years of American Gothic novel publishing in general, and the aforementioned authors' professional efforts within this young market more specifically, this satirical adoption of British Gothic features takes on political implications. With no international copyright laws in place until 1891, American publishing houses were able to publish British classics and current bestsellers for the expense of printing only. In particular, the English romanticists William Wordsworth, Lord Byron, Alfred Tennyson, and others were widely read; Sir Walter Scott, Edward Bulwer-Lytton, and Charles Dickens had become bestselling (though not paid) authors in North America by 1850. American literature and its intrinsic need for self-definition and cultural independence, therefore, were both fueled by and confronted with an overwhelming number of British publications in their home markets. By mocking the British Gothic's villainy, the early American Gothic made its troubled relationship with its British predecessor and prepotent competitor not only explicit but also an issue of satire.

Following Cathy N. Davidson's argument, we can conceptualize the early American (Gothic) novel further as the "chapbook of the nineteenth century" (10), that is,

> a cheap book accessible to those who were not educated at the prestige men's colleges, who were outside the established literary tradition, and who (as both Charles Brockden Brown and Helena Wells noted) for the most part read few books besides novels. Given both the literary insularity of many novel readers and the increasing popularity of the novel, the new genre necessarily became a form of education, especially for women. Novels allowed for a means of entry into a larger literary and intellectual world and a means of access to social and political events from which many readers (particularly women) would have been otherwise largely excluded. The first novels, I would also argue, provided citizens of the time not only with native versions of the single most popular form of literary entertainment in America, but also with literary versions of emerging definitions of America—versions that were, from the first, tinged with ambivalence and duplicity. (Davidson 10)

Against the negative foil of its despised British predecessors, the early American Gothic novel constructs a villain suitable for the young American nation—and for the moral and general education of a continuously growing and otherwise inaccessible readership. The Savage Villain of the American Gothic (as we will see, not to be confused with the British Gothic's villain acting temporarily *like* a savage) indeed pushes Gothic villainy to the next level, terrifyingly, politically, and racially.

3.2 Savage Villainy

The early WASP American Gothic's Savage Villain roams the "infinitely toilsome" (EH 799)[7] American wilderness, which might show "[n]o marks of habitation or culture, no traces of the footsteps of men" (EH 799), but which is the natural habitat of "brown and terrific figures" (EH 790), moving "upon all fours" with "disfigured limbs, pendants from [their] ears and nose, and [their] shorn locks, [the] indubitable indications of a savage" (EH 814). Once trapped in "the heart of the wilderness" (EH 790), which notably conflates the wilderness trope and the presumed savage inhabitants into one powerful metaphor, the white traveler quickly finds himself "haunted by some species of terror or antipathy" (EH 791), well aware of the constantly raiding, torching, women-abducting, and killing "Red-men" (EH 791). Lurking in the dark of the wilderness, the Savage Villain attacks viciously, dishonorably, and, most often, in great numbers:

> It seemed, for near a minute, as if the demons of hell had possessed themselves of the air about them and were venting their savage humors in barbarous sounds. The cries came from no particular direction, though it was evident that they filled the woods, and as the appalled listeners easily imagined, the caverns of the falls, the rocks, the bed of the river, and the upper air. (LM 77)[8]

Constructed as a natural component of the dangerous wilderness, lurking right around the settlement enclosures, the Savage Villain becomes an ever-present threat. Just like the "panther," that is, the other "savage [...] lurking," until the traveler is placed "within the reach of his fangs" (EH 785), the Gothicized Delaware Indians (EH) and Hurons (LM) are, at the same time, rendered an essential aspect of the setting, constricted into one villainous threat. This ever-present threat might be controlled by one individually identifiable and named Savage Villain—such as Old Deb/Queen Mab, Magua/Le Renard Subtil, and Too-wit—but this control is temporary and fragile to the utmost extent. Consider in this respect Cooper's Huron warrior and arch-villain, Magua, who is introduced (in direct contrast to the mock villainy outlined above) as follows:

> The colors of the war paint had blended in dark confusion about his fierce countenance, and rendered his swarthy lineaments still more savage and repulsive than if art had attempted an effect, which had been thus produced by chance. His eye alone, which glistened like a fiery star amid lowering clouds, was to be seen in its state of native wildness. (LM 20)

---

7   "EH" refers to Charles Brockden Brown's *Edgar Huntly*.
8   "LM" refers to James Fenimore Cooper's *The Last of the Mohicans*.

Rather than following the British Gothic convention and introducing his arch-villain as an outstandingly deviant individual, Cooper constructs "the 'Indian runner'" (LM 19) through his "native wildness" and his belonging to the natural, if bleak, environment of "fiery star[s]" and "lowering clouds." Adding his names to the image, Magua/Le Renard Subtil ('The Wily Fox') always refers to a group of presumed treacherous enemies—Huron, as well as French. When Magua attacks, all Hurons attack; when Magua raises "his voice in a long and intelligible whoop, it [is] answered by a spontaneous yell from the mouth of every Indian within hearing sound" (LM 103-4); and when Magua is finally subdued by the questing hero, Hawkeye, and killed, the end of the novel is not brought to a conciliatory ending, but remains hauntingly and characteristically "ajar" (Davidson 230). As the Savage Villain is not one but many (autonomasia), not an individual instantiation of evil deviance but a naturally savage force of the American wilderness (needless to say that Magua cannot repent of his sins but dies in "grim defiance", LM 401), the death of Magua does not and cannot resolve the horrors of the plot: "To tell them this," he [Hawkeye] said, "would be to tell them that the snows come not in winter, or that the sun shines fiercest when the trees are stripped of their leaves" (LM 411).

Before contrasting the differently racialized "B/black"[9] Savage Villains of Edgar Allan Poe and Harriet Beecher Stowe, it is worth conceptualizing the "Indian-type" Savage Villain/Civil Hero Gotheme in more detail for the earlier context of Brockden Brown and Cooper. The Gotheme becomes most readily comprehensible when understood as a discourse situated on the intersection of four intrinsically connected and mutually overlapping structures: the British Gothic plot, the Evil (or Ignoble) Savage motif, the wilderness motif, and the Manifest Destiny legitimatization discourse.

While it is a fair guess to expect the first representations of the encountered New World savagery to already depict horrific, predatory creatures that are one with the demonic wilderness, which the settlers felt they were encountering and that were killing them by the score, the actual depictions are far more affirmative (at first, that is). It is the image of what we have come to call the discursive construct of the "Noble Savage"[10] that travels back from the colonies to the Old World. As a well-known visual example, we might consider the Seal of the Massachusetts Bay Colony, which depicts an Indian man—naked except for a bunch of leaves covering his loins—inviting the English to "Come Over and Help Us." Interweaving

---

9   My contracted term "B/black" indicates the conflation of a typically Gothic black color-coding with the racialization "Black." As we will see in great detail below, this conflated ascription of "B/black" to the SV/CH Gotheme must be understood as a watershed in the American Gothic tradition, as it introduces the Africanist Savage Villain through white abjectorship.
10 For a detailed overview, cf. Ter Ellingson (2001).

legitimatization discourses for the genocide against and the expulsion of the American Indian peoples living in the Massachusetts region and beyond, the seal was created as a tool to draw English people into the colonies. John Canup convincingly argues that finding settlers who were willing to undertake the often deadly adventure of traveling across the ocean, in order to colonize a wild and remote place full of beasts and dangers, was a difficult task indeed. The more the settlers starved to death, died of disease, or were killed in hostilities with the local American Indian people in the early colonies, the more human reinforcement was needed, yet, at the same time, the more reluctant the English people became.

While a thriving and economically successful colony like Massachusetts Bay was continuously dependent on labor reinforcement, the need for substantial reinforcement became all the more pressing, when the local conflicts with American Indian peoples could no longer be communicated across the Atlantic as anything but full-fledged wars (Pequot War, 1634-1638, and King Phillip's War, 1675-1678). The noble, converted or soon-to-be converted, savage offered potential settlers an exotic touch without the danger.

However, there was an intrinsic, evil catch in the depiction of the New World savage. As environmentalists, the English settlers (as well as the prospective settlers) had to think that it was the American environment that had shaped the savage American Indian—the same American environment to which they had been transplanted. Were they to change into savages, too? Or could they turn the American environment into a "New England" that was nourishing and positively stimulating for the English physique and culture? This omnipresent threat of being turned into American Indian savages became overwhelming when the Indians proved to be much more resistant to conversion, the nature much wilder, and the colonies and their settlers much more fragile and immoral than was hoped for and propagated.

Out of the fear of degenerating into Indian savages, into absolute wilderness and immorality, the colonizers drew a line between themselves, the country, and the savages. A new myth accumulated: Long before settling the North American continent, the Indians had been a savage, evil race, led to this remote place on earth by the Devil himself, so that they could worship him unnoticed and undisturbed. The Evil Savage, of course, cannot be converted; just like the hostile wilderness, he needs to be extinguished before God's chosen people can take root in the New Eden to come. The savagery that the settlers experienced among themselves—the everyday immorality and blasphemy that the Puritans punished mercilessly with physical violence and death—was relocated into the Indian tribes. It was through too close contact with the Evil Savage that the pious settlers fell from grace. Wars against the savages were therefore not only justified but inevitable. The colonizers' atrocities, the lying and stealing, the genocide against the American Indian peoples, and the enslavement of survivors were legitimized by the nature of the Evil Savages and their "wild" nature.

Whether noble or ignoble, we must remind ourselves that both attributions to 'savagery' depict the affirmation of the myth (discursive pattern) of the savage and establish the construction of peoples in terms of marginalization, wildness, and primitivity, while confirming the dominant master narrative. And this construction is not just an "exoticization of cultural difference," as Weinstock (43) notes, but an inscription of racial difference and hierarchization. This is why, when dealing with WASP American and British Gothic literature, we have to be very careful about noting a presumed cultural transition from noble to evil savagery. Generally, as Louise K. Barnett argues, "the Indian was by definition [...] a completely ignoble being" (Barnett 87); put bluntly, the Indian, essentially and visibly racialized as being inferior, is in the plot only to be killed by whites. As Manifest Destiny, as well as the frontier myth, two of U.S. America's most powerful self-mythologizing and legitimatization strategies are about WASP men only; the noble Indian also is only—and can only be—a negative foil against the white, civilized, and continuously civilizing glory. Barnett summarizes:

> Although in the aggregate, either as bands raiding the pioneer homesteads or as whole tribes making war on the whites, Indians in the frontier romance usually belong to the bad Indian stereotype, the noble savage concept maintains an uneasy coexistence with the bad Indian image [...] [T]he Indian was by definition a scalper and murderer of whites, a completely ignoble being. To find him otherwise without repudiating their commitment to white civilization, authors had to create a fictive situation which partially antedated white-Indian conflict: in isolation, in his Edenic wilderness, the Indian could be approved of as a noble savage, certainly inferior to whites, but situated to the simple and in some ways attractive life of the forest [...] The easiest way to pay homage to the noble savage without disrupting the plot mechanism was to praise Indian virtue as a phenomenon of the past. (Barnett 86-88)

When "the Indians" were finally subdued and the push of the frontier had reached the Pacific Ocean (a presumed success story that was conceptualized first as being obvious—"manifest"—and certain—"destiny"—by Jacksonian Democrats in the 1840s), the conflation of environmental wilderness and Indian wilderness was sealed in the myth of the frontier, which Patricia Nelson Limerick narrates as follows:

> Europe was crowded; North America was not [...]. In a migration as elemental as a law of physics, Europeans moved from crowded space to open space, where free land restored opportunity and offered a route to independence [...] hardy pioneers struggled until nature was mastered, and then moved on [...] and the result was a new nation and a new national character: the European transmuted into the American [...] pioneers recreated the social contract from scratch, forming

> simple democratic communities whose political health vitalized all of America. Indians, symbolic residents of the wilderness, resisted—in a struggle sometimes noble, but always futile. At the completion of the conquest, that chapter of history was closed. The frontier ended, but the hardiness and independence of the pioneer survived in American character. (322-3)

What the Mediterranean man is for the early British Gothic, the ubiquitous myth of the Evil Savage is for the American Gothic. As we have seen above, the Evil Savage offers the ready-made outlines for an Americanized Gothic villain: a villainous savage born and bred, a wild and vicious predator, a coward who dishonorably lurks among bushes and brings dozens of like-minded friends. A total and utter threat like this needs to be overcome by a true American hero, for the sake of God's divine plan and for one's own survival. If a primitive creature of darkness is established as the adversary, the hero's quest will hardly be plagued and slowed down by ethical questions and restraints. Herein lies the key difference between early British and American Gothics.

The early British Gothic constructed villainy in terms of a passionate delirium that would, for a short period of time, i.e., most often, upon reaching the plot's climax, turn the villain into a character that *acts* savagely, barbarically, and uncontrollably. Early North American writers imported the Gothic and, most notably, kept the motif of savagery, to depict a lack of civilized and pious human qualities within the Gothic villain. What they genuinely added, however, is the 'real savage.' Instead of acting and looking *like* a savage in his uncivil immorality and blasphemy, the villain is blended with eighteenth- and early nineteenth-century America's personification of absolute wilderness: the evil American Indian savage. The alteration of the British villainy motif in early American Gothic writing no doubt created a mass of thrilling texts for a quickly growing and exclusively WASP readership. It is a villain that exists only "as a means by which we can dissociate ourselves from evil" (Balchin 254), and, by conflating the British Gothic's villain with the myth of the Evil Savage, the semantic extension of villainy has, in fact, been narrowed down so far as to exclude the entire WASP readership—villainous savagery is entertaining (and educating) and for the exclusively WASP readership, it is not only "easily avoidable" (Balchin 254) but also racially impossible.

Yet, while the SV/CH Gotheme thrived in the early American Gothic writing, the racialization of the Savage Villain as "Indian" must be understood as a temporary steppingstone in the American adaptation and evolution of the Gotheme only. Although the "Indian" Savage Villain provided a thrilling rendering of American exceptionalism and the promise of Manifest Destiny within the well-known conventions of Gothic literature, its predominance in WASP American Gothic literature was comparatively short. From the 1830s onward, widely-read and influential authors such as Edgar Allan Poe and Harriet Beecher Stowe introduced a re-racialized Savage Villain into WASP American Gothic, a Savage Villain that was no longer "wild" or "primitive," but which was the perfectly horrid image of darkness and of a wilderness that translated not to "primitivism" but to "inhumanity": the Africanist Savage Villain. This new—and, as we will see, utterly persistent—type of Savage Villainy not only depicts a racially othered threat or deviance, but it also functions as an insurmountable insertion of B/blackness as the un-humanized abject. Very much indebted to Toni Morrison's notion of "American Africanism" (developed especially in *Playing in the Dark*) and Sabine Broeck's conceptionalization of "the enslavist white Euro-American abjectorship of the sixteenth to nineteenth century" (Broeck, "Legacies" 109),[11] I will introduce the concept of the Africanist Savage Villain first on the basis of Poe's only completed novel, *The Narrative of Arthur Gordon Pym, of Nantucket* (1838), before broadening my focus to other instantiations of this new type of "un-humaned" (Broeck, "Legacies" 118) arch-villain.

The Narrative of Arthur Gordon Pym, of Nantucket

Poe's narration of the truly eventful journey of Arthur Gordon Pym overflows with conventional Gothic characters, props, settings, and plot lines. Pym, as well as the reader, experiences a variety of Gothic scenes, from repeated live burials to cannibalism, and from a walking corpse to a ghastly ghost ship. Without a doubt, however, the Gothic journey reaches its climax when Pym, onboard the British ship "Jane Guy," lands on the fictional Antarctic island of Tsalal.

Tsalal is "literally swarming" (P 152) with "the most barbarous, subtle, and bloodthirsty wretches that ever contaminated the face of the globe" (P 145)—the "Redmen" (EH 791) of Poe's literary predecessors, however, are no longer enclosed in this group of savage "wretches." In fact, Poe constructs Tsalal's "savages" (P 131) in a way that urged Toni Morrison to analyze Poe, and especially his *Narrative of Arthur Gordon Pym*, as the artificer of "American Africanism" (Morrison, *Playing* 32):

> They were about the ordinary stature of Europeans, but of a more muscular and brawny frame. Their complexion a jet black, with thick and long woolly hair. They were clothed in skins of an unknown black animal, shaggy and silky, and made to fit the body with some degree of skill, the hair being inside, except where turned out about the neck, wrists, and ankles. Their arms consisted principally of clubs, of a dark and apparently very heavy wood. (P 131/2)

---

11   Broeck and other scholars of the "Afro-Pessimist" branch of African American and Black Studies understand this white abjectorship, that is, the practice of discursively unhumanizing, or thingifying, the Black person into the "the African enslaved, an un-humaned species tied by property rights" (Broeck, "Legacies" 118), as the basis for contemporary enslavist practices "of anti-Black racism on both sides of the Atlantic" (Broeck, "Legacies" 109).

Paralleling Poe's previous depiction of the villainous "cook, a negro" (P 36), the savages show the stereotypical racial markers of Africanism—muscular, brawny, with thick and woolly hair, and, most importantly, with jet black skin. Accurately following the American Gothic plot, the savages are blended with the all-black wilderness of the island[12] and function as one wild, villainous body, headed by a named savage, their king, Too-wit. Like the Indian savages of Brockden Brown and Cooper, Poe's Africanist Savage Villain paradoxically is one and many; the ending, therefore, must remain hauntingly "ajar," to borrow Davidson's term once more. Pym and his companion, the noble savage and "most ferocious-looking man" (P 38), Dick Peters ("the son of an Indian woman of the tribe of Upsarokas, who live among the fastnesses of the Black Hills", P 38), only manage to kill a handful of the countless savages and take another one hostage, before escaping the island and their own "inevitable butchery" (P 169) in a canoe; arch-villain Too-wit is not killed in the course of their flight, which makes him a truly exceptional case in the early Gothic tradition.

Of course, neither the narration of Pym's tale nor the novel itself ends with the escape. While imaging three heavily racialized characters—WASP American Pym, "hybrid" Peters (P 54), and the "jet black" savage, now named Nu-Nu—adrift together in a canoe on the Antarctic ocean might be an intriguing closing image for today's readership, Poe constructed a different type of conciliatory ending for his Gothic novel. Leaving the blackness of the island of Tsalal behind, the world surrounding the canoe is more and more drenched in an all-encompassing whiteness; Nu-Nu is paralyzed by his terror of the whiteness and dies as soon as the canoe rushes on through "[t]he gigantic curtain [that] ranged along the whole extent of the southern horizon" (P 174). Behind the curtain, a "shrouded human figure" rises, and with the mentioning of the figure's skin as being "of the perfect whiteness of snow" (P 175), the narrative ceases and is augmented by the closing scholarly note of the frame narrative.

Poe's Africanized version of the Savage Villain takes the racial outlines of early WASP American Gothic villainy, as established by Brockden Brown, Cooper, etc., to the extreme. Rather than merely shifting the racialized color-code from "red" to "black," that is, "Africanizing" the Savage Villain, Poe also introduces the metaphorical connection between this type of racial villainy and contagion ("the most barbarous, subtle, and bloodthirsty wretches that ever *contaminated* the face of the globe", P 145, italics C.L.). What makes the Tsalal savages contagious is the sexual, i.e., also racial, threat they so violently pose. Consider in this respect the metaphor-

---

12 Poe goes to great pains to paint every detail on the island black, including the fish, the birds, the mammals, the stones, the plants, the dwellings of the savages ("the black skin palaces," P 139), etc.

ical staging of the plundering of the ship by "more than a hundred and fifty [...] savages" (P 154) as the raping of a helpless woman:

> In five minutes the 'Jane' was a pitiable scene indeed of havoc and tumultuous outrage. The decks were split open and ripped up, [...] the wretches finally forced her on shore (the cable having been slipped) and delivered her over to the good offices of Too-wit, who, during the whole engagement, had maintained like a skillful general his post of security and reconnaissance among the hills, but, now that the victory was completed to his satisfaction, condescended down with his warriors of the black skin and become a partaker in the spoils. (P 154)

The raping and violent destruction of (the) anthropomorphized and gendered Jane, who/which is the only marker of femininity in the entire novel, also marks the destruction of civilization, the violent tearing open of the fabric of the American society, by the B/black savages. The end of the Jane, that is, the symbolic death of the white woman/mother/moral backbone of society is significantly tied in with the discourse of "racial decline" and "the dreaded race apocalypse" (Diedrich, *Cornelia* 139), surrounding the debate on slavery and foreshadowing the discourse of eugenics, which "entered the public debate toward the end of the 19th century [and decisively shifted the immigrant controversy and] the discourse of nativism from politics to pseudo-science" (Behdad 469). The threating racial contagion embodied by arch-villain Too-wit, all the more when conflated with his tribe of bloodthirsty savages and the peculiarly black wilderness of Tsalal, is rendered an impregnable force that the questing hero cannot overcome (the Jane rendered beyond saving by the sheer number of black rapists) and has to flee. At this moment, the plot of *The Narrative of Arthur Gordon Pym* deviates significantly from Gothic plot conventions (British and American), taking on the literary qualities of a parable.

"Steer[ing] boldly to the southward" (P 170), a white man, a noble savage, and a "jet black" creature flee everything north of the magical curtain stretched "along the whole extent of the southern horizon" (P 174). They leave behind all of the Gothic horrors encountered on the way—the horrible black cook, cannibalism, buried-alive experiences, (walking) corpses, the ghost ship, Too-wit, and Tsalal; the last remnant of these instantiations of B/blackness and Gothic, Nu-Nu, is killed on the threshold to the south. "Embrace[d]" and "receive[d]" (P 175) in the all-encompassing whiteness, the white man and his noble savage companion watch the rise of a gigantic white human figure. A white American and his noble "half-breed Indian" (P 2) companion, i.e., the two pillars of the WASP romanticized construct of American civilization and the legitimacy of colonization, escape the contagious B/black horrors of the north and witness the rise of a white counterforce in the south, which, in Morrison's terms, seems "to function as both antidote for and meditation on the shadow that is companion to this whiteness—a dark and abiding presence that moves the hearts and texts of American literature with fear and longing" (*Playing* 33).

For Poe, the self-proclaimed southern gentleman, the anti-abolitionist, and the professional writer struggling to make a living in Richmond, Virginia, by publishing and writing for the *Southern Literary Messenger*, this ending must indeed have read simultaneously as a biting critique of the north and its anti-slavery politics and the call for a cultural and political future reigned by white southern ideologies, that is, an antidote for the spreading epidemic of the Tsalal. With the creation of a Savage Villain in the bleak Africanized imagery of the racially abject, Poe has pushed the readily flexible and intrinsically racialized American Gothic's Savage Villain/Civil Hero Gotheme right into the legitimatization discourse that nineteenth-century pro-slavery advocates employed. Taking into account that the Gothic novel can be called "the chapbook of the nineteenth century" (Davidson 10), which reaches and educates an otherwise hardly accessible audience, we might want to conclude our reading of *The Narrative of Arthur Gordon Pym, of Nantucket* by quoting Ishmael Reed: "*Poe got it all down. Poe says more in a few stories than all the volumes by historians. Volumes about war. The Civil War. The Spirit War*" (Reed 10, italics in the original).

While Poe depicted the Africanist Savage Villain with striking clarity, I refrain from situating the origin of this revival of evil savagery, enhanced with an unprecedented racial scurrility in *The Narrative of Arthur Gordon Pym, of Nantucket*. Doubtlessly, "*Poe got it all down*" (Reed 10) in fiction, but the genuinely Gothic discourse of a threatening onslaught of an uncontrollable mass of B/black unhuman(ed) savages against white civilization had been of increasing relevancy (especially) for Southern newspapers, journals, and political pamphlets, since "the bloodiest and most shocking insurrection ever recorded [...], the frightful carnage and anarchy" (Dew 6) of Saint Dominique and the Haitian Revolution. When in 1822 and 1831 slave rebellions occurred in South Carolina and Virginia, commentators returned to the Haitian Revolution and to Gothic attributions to describe Denmark Vessey, Nat Turner, and their followers as "banditti" and "horrible [...] monsters" (*The Richmond Enquirer*, 30 August 1831), who willfully caused "the ghastly horrors" (Dew 6) and the "horrid massacre [...] when FIFTY FIVE innocent persons (mostly women and children) fell victims to the most inhuman barbarity" (Warner 38) of "these barbarous villains" (Thomas R. Gray 16) and their "band[s] of savages" (Thomas R. Gray 4). The public discourse, not only but especially in the South and in defense of the institution of slavery, indeed was as "horror-struck at the late tidings" (*The Liberator*, 3 September 1831) as it was invested in a Gothic-tinted sensationalism that increasingly dyed the Savage Villain B/black. Potentially reacting to sensationalistic proslavery texts, such as William Drayton's 1836 *The South Vindicated From the Treason and Fanaticism of the Northern Abolitionists* and James Kirke Paulding's *View of Slavery in the United States* (also 1836), the antislavery discourse in the North likewise employed not only overtly sensationalistic but also Gothicized abject attributions to depict the "plain case" of the institution of slavery, against which "human *nature* [...] has uttered her testimony against [...] with a shriek ever since the monster was begotten" (Weld 7). The employment of Gothic features and conventions in antislavery texts, of course, did not only entail Gothicizing the 'peculiar institution'; it also meant rewriting the, by now, downright fashionable Africanist Savage Villain. In this respect, the Africanist Savage Villain as the Gothicized Black abject is a reflection of the discursive processes of white abjectorship, meaning the discursive "un-humanization" (Broeck, "Legacies" 109) of the Black person to a thingified yet horrifying B/black chattel in an ongoing white "enactment of subjugation" (Hartman, *Scenes* 4), as well as complicit in this enactment. The early WASP American Gothic, therefore, must be understood as one widely influential instantiation of the ongoing discourses of unhumanization that actively and unflinchingly appellate and reposition the Black person as the (Gothicized) abject.

Uncle Tom's Cabin; or, Life Among the Lowly

The last text I will examine in greater detail, within the 'imprinting' phase of the American Gothic, is a novel composed to further the abolitionist cause and, therefore, to diametrically oppose the Africanist Savage Villain: Harriet Beecher Stowe's *Uncle Tom's Cabin; or, Life Among the Lowly* (1852). In *Uncle Tom's Cabin*, Beecher Stowe most prominently blends a wide array of Gothic elements with the writing conventions of the sentimental novel and the abolitionist cause, to depict the full horrors of the slave system for her WASP readership. While British and American Gothic elements can be traced readily throughout the novel, it is Beecher Stowe's complex and racially hierarchized conflations of savage villainy and victimization that render *Uncle Tom's Cabin* a key moment in the development of the American Gothic novel. It is also this network of conflated Gothic attributions that makes it so difficult to answer the most basic question that a Gothic plot's logic poses: Who is the villain?

The most straightforward answer to this question, without a doubt, is "Legree, one of the most revolting villains in nineteenth-century literature" (Otter, "Stowe" 21). In fact, true to early American Gothic conventions, Simon Legree's plantation, where "all was darkness horror" (UTC 409), is set in the wilderness, at the end of "a wild, forsaken road [...] where the wind whisper[s] mournfully" and everything is covered with "funeral black moss" and with "broken stumps and shattered branches [...] rotting in the water" (UTC 389/90). Legree himself, however, is not introduced within this wilderness of dead black bodies, nor is he blended in with it, as the early WASP American Gothic would conventionally demand. Rather strikingly, Beecher Stowe constructs a villain that meticulously follows the early *British* Gothic conventions—except for one crucial aspect: Legree, at least at first, is not yet another embodiment of the villainous Mediterranean man but an exceptionally corrupted and otherwise ordinary WASP man.

Introduced as a "hideous stranger" (UTC 380), "a short, broad, muscular man, in a checked shirt considerably open at the bosom, and pantaloons much worse for dirt and wear, [who] elbowed his way through the crowd, like one who is going actively into business" (UTC 379), Legree's remarkable mix of "gigantic strength" and physical ugliness causes "an immediate and revolting horror at him that increase[s] as he [comes] near" (UTC 380):

> His round, bullet head, large, light-gray eyes, with shaggy, sandy eye-brows, and stiff, wiry, sunburned hair, were rather unprepossessing items, it is to be confessed; his large, coarse mouth was distended with tobacco [...]; his hands were immensely large, hairy, sun-burned, freckled, and very dirty, and garnished with long nails, in a very foul condition. (UTC 380)

No longer utilizing the stereotypical physical characteristics of the Mediterranean man and, yet, also not explicitly referring to his racial 'whiteness,' Beecher Stowe depicts Legree as a villainous "mean, low, brutal fellow" (UTC 387), a "pirate" by trade (UTC 427), and an outstandingly "horrible" instantiation (UTC 388) of "some out-of-the-way specimen" (UTC 386), who ships slaves down south on board "the good steamer Pirate" (UTC 383).

Legree is an "out-of-the-way specim[a]n" of his own race, of white America—North and South—and an outstanding example of what can happen to any man involved in the slave trade. Subsequently conflated with the slave ship "Pirate," his Gothic plantation mansion and, thus, with the economic side of chattel slavery that "with that air of efficiency" objectifies and exploits "the negro, sympathetic and assimilative, after acquiring, [...] just as a chair or a table" (UTC 383), Legree's only lasting physical characteristic is his "glaring greenish-gray eye" that triggers "fascination" in his peers and "horror, fright, and aversion" (all UTC 385) in the black damsels he (sexually) pursues, especially in "Emmeline and the mulatto woman with whom she was confined" (UTC 388). In the course of the novel, the exemplarily greedy Legree is effectively morphed into and conflated with the entire system of slavery. His brutal acts become a mere reflection of the larger evil that has corrupted him. As a matter of fact, his physical features are more and more deleted in the development of the plot and the process of fully conflating Legree with the system of slavery that has created him and what he now represents. At times "perfectly demoniacal in its expression" (UTC 405), at times "aghast" (UTC 470), but always a mirror image of "the deadly character [...] and his despotic power" (UTC 468), Legree's features are now described in emotional, sentimental terms, without reference to his physical characteristics. Upon climax, however, this continuous deletion of the physical features of the villain is reversed, and the depiction of Legree is fully incorporated into the early British Savage Villain/Civil Hero Gotheme:

> "What! ye blasted black beast! tell *me* ye don't think it *right* to do what I tell ye! What have any of you cussed cattle to do with thinking what's right? I'll put a stop to it! Why what do ye think ye are? May be ye think ye'r a gentleman, Master Tom, to be a-telling your master what's right, and what an't! So you pretend it's wrong to flog the gal!"
>
> "I think so, Mas'r," said Tom [...]; "but as to raising my hand agin any one here, I never shall,—I'll die first!"
>
> Tom spoke in a mild voice, but with a decision that could not be mistaken. Legree shook with anger; his greenish eye glared fiercely, and his whiskers seemed to curl with passion; but, like some ferocious beast, that plays with its victim before he devours it, he kept back his strong impulse to proceed to immediate violence, and broke out into bitter raillery. (UTC 406, italics in the original)

Overwhelmed by his passionate hatred for Tom, Legree morphs into an accurate resemblance of the early British Gothic's villain, and his climactic fall into savagery ("*like* some ferocious beast," UTC 406, my emphasis) is defined as a *temporal* loss of a civilized mindset, as a passionate delirium, not as a natural and, therefore, incorrigible lack thereof. For the first and only time in the novel, Beecher Stowe even equips her villain with the stereotypically Mediterranean "whiskers" that "curl with passion," thus foreshadowing the eruption of the violence and savage behavior to follow:

> Tom stood silently. "D'ye hear?" said Legree, stamping, with a roar *like that of an incensed lion*. "Speak!" [...] There was one hesitating pause,—one irresolute, relenting thrill,—and the spirit of evil came back, with seven-fold vehemence; and Legree, foaming with rage, smote his victim to the ground. (UTC 469/70, my emphasis).

From within the legitimizing discourse of chattel slavery (Legree indeed has every legal "*right*" [UTC 406] to the unwavering subjectedness of his systemically thingified slaves as well as to corporal punishment) and the brutal consequences it has for the individual slave, Legree acts as Beecher Stowe's prototypical slave master, whose brutality and savagery are not inbred, racial, and thus unchangeable character traits but, instead, are the bitter consequences of the corrupting force of slavery. In other words, Legree is *not* the Savage Villain of *Uncle Tom's Cabin* but another white victim of the real villainous force in the novel: the overarching system of slavery. Therefore, Legree must be contextualized with other white victims of the corruptive forces of the institution of slavery, including Marie and Ophelia St. Clare (who Beecher Stowe depicts as being led morally astray).

Without a doubt, however, it is the novel's sacrifice of the evangelic Little Eva to the evils of slavery that has the greatest impact on the nineteenth-century reader. Beecher Stowe links Eva's mysterious death explicitly to the Christian doctrine of salvation, to the liberation of "those poor creatures" [i.e. the slaves] and the ending of "all this misery" [i.e. slavery] (UTC 313). On a deeper level, this link between the death of Christianity's must-be First Mother Eva and slavery follows the logic of a dysgenic prophecy of an author who envisions the white mother as the active center and moral backbone of society. Killing Eva means wiping out her future motherhood; it means killing the future of the white American race and, thus, of white American society. This dystopic and dysgenic scenario is explicitly addressed to "you, mothers of America—you who have learned, by the cradles of your children, to love and feel for all mankind" (UTC 505); and, indeed, it must have been both very unsettling for Beecher Stowe's predominately female readership and a very powerful tool for the same reason. With the death of Little Eva, Beecher Stowe, the "Super Mother, an Amazon of domesticity," not only powerfully uses "motherhood as a weapon to destroy slavery" (Frederick 102) but also functionalizes a proto-eugenic discourse of white motherhood and the (endangered) survival of the white race in an antagonistic struggle with the villainous system of slavery. The dire distress of the damsel/mother threatens to destroy white American society via its most intimate relation: the destruction of the WASP family with white motherhood at its core.

By placing the suffering and victimization of white men, women, and children center-stage,[13] *Uncle Tom's Cabin* effectively counteracts its own agenda: Rather than depicting the *"Life Among the Lowly,"* it is a story of life among white America under the yoke of slavery. In effect, Beecher Stowe creates a story that envisions and carries forward a racialized discourse of white (enslavist) superiority that can exist despite and outside of the reality of chattel slavery. This *ex negativo* inscription of white superiority is not only traceable in Beecher Stowe's technique of superposing

---

13   Note that the victimization of a bi-racial ('mulatto') female character, such as Eliza, is not a counter argument to this observation but rather another case in point: Eliza is only positionable in the role of a 'damsel in distress' because, in Beecher Stowe's romantic racialist logic, the high percentage of whiteness in Eliza's blood, her passing for white racialization, grants her at least a percentage of the emotionality a white woman would display. The character of Topsy, in comparison, who is "one of the blackest of her race" (UTC270), functions on an entirely different level of both race constructions and plot logic and cannot possibly be integrated as another Gothic 'damsel.' In polar opposition to Eliza, Topsy's past of brutal abuse and victimization renders her a malicious "sooty gnome" (UTC 274) and a general annoyance. The post-slavery future that Beecher Stowe envisions for both characters, however, is identical: She "sends them packing" (Septo, 142) and back to Africa.

the early British Gothic's villainy with "the abyss of the haunted mind" (Halttunen 126) and the morally rotten foundation of the so-called domestic institution; it also controls the co-existence of the British-inspired Legree with the new, Americanized version of the Savage Villain.

Let me shed more light on this aspect by directly comparing two instances of savage villainy, connected to the symbol of the "dog" in the novel. While Legree, again true to the British plot, will "follow you day in, day out, hanging *like a dog* on your throat—"sucking your blood, bleeding away your life, drop by drop," he is and remains a "man" who can be "know[n]" (all UTC 434, my emphasis). In comparison, Legree's "two principal hands on the plantation" (UTC 393) are introduced in one breath with the plantation's "three or four ferocious looking dogs" (UTC 392) that have "been raised to track niggers" (UTC 393) and which frame perfectly well the following unhumanizing depiction of Sambo and Quimbo:

> Legree had trained them in savageness and brutality as systematically as he had his bull-dogs; and, by long practice in hardness and cruelty, brought their whole nature to about the same range of capacities. [...] As they stood there now by Legree, they seemed an apt illustration of the fact that brutal men are lower even than animals. Their coarse, dark, heavy features; their great eyes, rolling enviously on each other; their barbarous, guttural, half-brute intonation; their dilapidated garments fluttering in the wind,—were all in admirable keeping with the vile and unwholesome character of everything about the place. (UTC 393-94)

Lower than animals and with the heavily racialized features of the Africanist Savage Villain of the early American Gothic, Beecher Stowe's construction of Sambo and Quimbo aims at depicting how "the negro mind has been more crushed and debased than the white," (UTC 393) in a damnable system whose "savage laws" (UTC 253) victimize everyone involved, including the slaveholders and their instrumental Black overseers—"bad as it is for the slave, it is worse, if anything, for the master" (UTC 264). Literary-historically speaking, we can conceptualize the inevitable clash between Legree and Tom as a clash between British Gothic villainy and the docile/heroic epitome of romantic racialism.[14] "The two savage men" (UTC 471), Sambo and Quimbo, on the other hand, function according to the logic of early WASP American Gothic villainy. Like the Savage Villains of Brockden Brown, Cooper, and Poe, Sambo and Quimbo are Savage Villains, one with the wilderness and an insurmountable threat. This, however, should not induce us to read *Uncle Tom's Cabin* as

---

14   The notion "romantic racialism" was introduced into scholarly discourse by George M. Fredrickson in 1971, to terminologically capture the "comparatively benign view of black 'pecularities' [...], a body of thought and imagery about black-white differences that meshed at some points with scientific racial determinism, but which had, in the minds of its adherents at least, very different implications" (101).

just another instantiation of the now racially Africanized Savage Villain. By conflating the wilderness, of which Sambo and Quimbo are a natural extension, with the institution of slavery, Beecher Stowe's novel, self-reflectively and very aware of the implications and opportunities of the early WASP American Gothic, constructs a type of savage villainy that is not only controllable by WASP moral indoctrination but that also—and most significantly—cannot pose a severe threat for white America (present and post-slavery). Sambo and Quimbo, naturally drawn to Christianity, weep and become believers instantaneously, when Tom, Christ-like and reminiscent of Little Eva, dies for "these two souls" (UTC 472). They become (re-)integrated into the logic of Beecher Stowe's romantic racialism and are morphed into "poor disciples [...] with full hearts" (UTC 474), "boys" (UTC 477) "awakened to repentance" (UTC 474) and ready to go back to "poor Africa [...] to make her the highest and noblest in that kingdom which he [God] will set up" (UTC 204). In other words, Sambo and Quimbo's villainous savagery can be understood as the most outspoken accusation against the inhuman and morally deprived system of slavery that infests and victimizes everyone in it, but one that only unhumanizes Black slaves. Simultaneously, this invitation of "Christian men and women of the North" to "*feel right*" and to "*pray!*" (UTC 506, emphasis by Beecher Stowe), via b/Black savagery, does not pose a threat to the white American order as has a convenient and projectable remedy: Upon liberation, the ex-slaves (whether docile or savage) are sent back to Africa.

For Beecher Stowe, the Gothic (British and WASP American) is a promising device for engaging readers emotionally in the cause of abolition; her novel, therefore, constantly shimmers between depicting the horrors of slavery and the risk of transforming these horrors into a narrative effect, similar to that common in the Gothic romance. The horror becomes relocated "from the slave's experience to the white reader's response" (Goddu 134)—real horror turns into entertainment. This problem of authenticity is consciously confronted by African American writers of slave narratives. As we will see in Part III, authors like Frederick Douglass, Harriet Jacobs, and William Wells Brown also make use of Gothic features, but they do so with a twist. Through the Gothic description of the violent whipping of Aunt Hester, for example, Douglass creates an entrance for the reader through "the blood-stained gate" into the "hell of slavery" (Douglass 18). The twist consists in the fact that these Gothic images are not to be read metaphorically but literally. For the sake of authenticity, Douglass has to insist that his autobiography is not fiction and that the Gothic elements depict a reality that far exceeds fictional horrors. The Gothic effect does not dematerialize or aestheticize (Diedrich, *Ausbruch* 58) the evil of slavery but makes it ever-present and literally haunting.

And yet, in spite of the abolitionists' efforts, slavery remains an unspoken topic. As Gothic fear is not so much what is seen but what is sensed beyond sight, most of the torture on Legree's plantation in Beecher Stowe's novel, as well as on Captain

Anthony's plantation in Douglass' slave narrative, takes place out of sight, removed from the emotional life of the protagonists. In fact, the representation of slavery remains an unrealizable task for abolitionist writers. Not only is "slavery [...] too dreadful for the purposes of art" (Beecher Stowe, *Key* 255), as it defies the standards of moral and aesthetic propriety, but it consists of too many stories and horrors. Paradoxically, slavery is made readable, initially by concealing its worst aspects—to protect the white audience, very much in the tradition of the euphemistic notion of the "peculiar institution," a fictionalizing veil is drawn over the realities of slavery.

Let me add a few final remarks to draw my however limited survey of the early WASP American Gothic to a conclusion. Thus far, the Gothic has proven to be a culturally (and geographically) ultra-adaptable, even opportunistic writing strategy. While the early WASP American Gothic can be understood as both an externalized and domesticated adaptation of British Gothic conventions, it is employed in contexts and discourses that are pertinent to the North American context: firstly, the legitimatization of the genocide and expulsion of American Indian peoples in the course of a presumed manifestly destined territorial expansion; and then, with steadily increasing virulence, the legitimatization of racial hierarchies, either in support of chattel slavery and the commodification of the Black body or in support of abolitionism.

It is worth mentioning that racialized and racializing features generally, and the Africanist presence in the SV/CH Gotheme specifically, are not only traceable in nineteenth-century WASP American literature that is directly and explicitly concerned with the issues of slavery, abolitionism, and the ensuing political and cultural conflict between North and South. In Toni Morrison's words: "Even, and especially, when American texts are not 'about' Africanist presences or characters or narrative or idiom, the shadow hovers over in implication, in sign, in line of demarcation" (*Playing* 46/47). Explicitly, the Gothicized Black abject, Carol Margaret Davison notes, "spilled over into cultural productions" in the 1830s and 1840s: "Joseph Holt Ingraham's *Lafitte* (1836) and Henry Clay Lewis' 'A Struggle for Life' (1843), for example, feature bestialized, homicidal, and physically distorted black men who ultimately die violent, ritualistic deaths" ("African American Gothic" 8). By the end of the 1840s, a downright trend toward conflating racial Blackness and savage villainy in American Gothic literature can be asserted. Novels as diverse as Ned Buntline's (Edward Zane Carroll Judson's) *The Mysteries and Miseries of New York* (1848), Louisa May Alcott's *The Inheritance* (1849), and Nathaniel Hawthorne's *The Scarlet Letter* (1850), to name just three, employ the Africanist SV/CH Gotheme in different contexts and to varying degrees.

In Ned Buntline's melodramatic dime novel, the scandalous and uncivilized underbelly of New York City readily accommodates gamblers, child-snatchers, prostitutes, thieves, and murderers. The frequent use of Gothic writing conventions dyes the city and its degenerate population black and, thus, places the blame for the despicable state of New York City on the racial other, i.e. on the b/Black race presumed unfit for American citizenship, ranging "from a hideous pox-marked, one-eyed negro girl, who was so near naked, that the savages, of Africa would have been ashamed of her" (62), over "a black dwarf, a hideous looking wretch" (148) and the "black-muzzled, dark and forbidding" (30) Black Bill, black Moors, black Indians, and black Gypsies, to the villainous Sam Selden "—thief, murderer, wretch, libertine, [and] accomplished [...] in all the phases of villainy—" whose "large, jet-black eyes" betray both his calmness and pale skin, thus allowing a glimpse into a lusting and unabashed "character so black, that if the combined iniquity of Sodom and Gomorrah could be condensed, [...] it would not be half so black, so vile, so devilish, as that heart" (all 181).

Louisa May Alcott's sentimental novel *The Inheritance*, also marks villainous deviance and "mischief" (110) as racial "darkness": The "dark form" (92), "dark face" (110) and "dark smile" (111) of the thief Louis contrast well with the racialization of the beautifully "pale" (4) Italian orphan, that is, the doubly alienated protagonist, Edith Adelon. In 1850, Nathaniel Hawthorne, in his famous novel *The Scarlet Letter*—well known also for its employment of a range of Gothic features combined or blended with "tropes of race, miscegenation, and slavery" (Levine 147, cf. also Person 33 and Grossman 22)—utilizes the Africanist SV/CH Gotheme more sophisticatedly than Alcott. Rather than merely staging deviance and mystery through B/black villainy, Hawthorne freely mixes and dissolves Gothic conventionality—including the Africanist presence in the SV/CH Gotheme. A case in point for this strategy is Hawthorne's construction of Pearl, Hester Prynne's and Arthur Dimmesdale's illegitimate daughter. The child's key characteristics are her "wild, bright, deeply black eyes" (Hawthorne, *The Scarlet Letter* 82) that, in one powerful image, signify both her mother's B/blackness (Hester's "dark and abundant hair" [46] and "deep black eyes" [46/47] as well as "the black scandal of bygone years" [146]) and the "smiling malice," the "fiendlike" evil spirit (86) that possesses the "little imp whose next freak might be to fly up the chimney" (87). If we follow Jean Fagan Yellin's argument and read Pearl's (as well as Hester's) blackness not only as the absence of grace, "as blackened soul" (Yellin 20), but as a racial marker, then "*The Scarlet Letter* reveals the obsessive concern with blacks and blackness, with the presence of a dangerous dark group within society's midst" (ibid.). Instead of following the Gothic script and positioning Pearl as the epitome of endangered innocence and whiteness in the plot, Hawthorne constructs her as a Gothicized miscegenation threat that runs wild in the midst of Puritan society. In the end, Pearl's Gothic side is healed by her shedding tears from her black eyes for her father ("A spell was broken" [233]) and the threat of miscegenation is cast out and relocated to England, where Pearl either lies in "a maiden grave" (238) or is "alive [and] married, and happy, and mindful of her mother" (239).

What I thus consider to be the most striking feature of the early Gothic is not so much its adaptability but the apparent inconvertibility of its racial patterns. In all of the texts, which I have looked at thus far, the highly racialized SV/CH Go-theme motivates and controls the Gothic plot. While Poe's Tsalal savages can, in many respects, be understood as the archetype of Africanist savage villainy and racial denigration, the blueprint (or shall I say "B/blackprint") for Poe's villainous savagery can be traced directly back to early British Gothic's "Mediterranean" savage-like villains. The early Gothic is intrinsically racially structured; its dichotomous Gothemes are both essentially racialized and, when instantiated in a fictional text, essentially racializing.

By now, it is clear that the vehement infusion of race into the WASP American Gothic plot only partially stems from the British Gothic tradition. Like filling gaps in the Gothic formula, WASP American Gothic novels insert the American Indian or Africanist Savage Villain into the already racialized conventionality of the early British Gothic narrative. Political, social, and cultural "agitation over the treatment of African Americans under slavery and freedom, Native Americans in the newly acquired territories and on the frontiers, and European American male and female laborers" (Otter, "Race" 13) filter into both a pseudo-scientific and proto-ethnological race discourse and WASP American consciousness. The early WASP American novels I have analyzed above employ the conflation of the racial savagery with Gothic villainy, consciously and strategically within their political agendas. In a next step, I will focus on contemporary WASP American Gothic novels and analyze their continuous reliance on the Savage Villain/Civil Hero Gotheme. Far from depending on the immediate contexts of territorial expansion, slavery, and the severe political turbulences and socio-cultural changes of the nineteenth century, the racialized and racializing Gotheme still dominates today's WASP American Gothic plots; how and why this stability within the Gothic writing strategy is not only likely but inevitable is the key concern of the following chapter.

Contemporary WASP American Iterations

Even a cursory glance at the contemporary American book market indicates two general trends in the development of the WASP American Gothic in the late twentieth and early twenty-first centuries: First, whether as the fully-fledged Gothic novel or as a novel featuring a significant number of Gothic conventions as part of its overall writing strategy, the WASP American Gothic is still a bestseller and is published in great numbers, not only by traditional publishing houses but just as much as through self-publishing venues and/or in online open access formats. Second, the contemporary WASP American Gothic seems to have lost its teeth in the course of appealing to an ever larger and younger readership. Broadening their readership, increasingly to encompass the literary needs and expectations of teenagers and young adults, the WASP American Gothic apparently has replaced monstrously deviant villains and their many accompanying horrors lurking in the ever-consuming darkness of the Gothic plot with a horde of tame teenage werewolves, sparkling vegetarian vampire beaus, and self-consciously dieting zombies. Yet, this transition from "monster to yuppie" (Tomc 96) might be the most prevalent quality of the contemporary WASP American Gothic, as it has been topping bestseller lists worldwide since the mid-twentieth century, but it is far from being the only development traceable. Next to the tame yuppies, the proliferation of the horror mode in literature and film has developed new types of monstrous deviance and abjection and placed them center-stage on the contemporary Gothic stage. In both current (and most likely interconnected) developments—the transition from monster to yuppie and the renewed proliferation of the monster in the horror branch of Gothic fiction—the Savage Villain/Civil Hero Gotheme is very much alive (or undead) and kicking.

Before offering an in-depth analysis of the SV/CH Gotheme in two contemporary novels, namely in Stephen King's *The Girl Who Loved Tom Gordon* and Karen Russell's *Swamplandia!*, I want to throw some spotlights onto the Savage Villain/Civil Hero Gotheme today and, thus, into the vast territory and marketplace that can be labeled as "the contemporary WASP American Gothic novel." While necessarily limited and incomplete in both scope and validity, this overview survey suggests not just the continuous presence and prevalence of the SV/CH Gotheme in today's

WASP Gothic and Gothicized (i.e., generically hybrid) novels; it also indicates further that the SV/CH Gotheme's racialization must be understood as an intrinsic and unchangeable quality of the Gothic writing strategy per se—so unchangeable indeed that even the significant development of a "yuppie-type" Gothic deviance, since the second half of the twentieth century, has had no traceable impact on the SV/CH Gotheme's racialization.

4.1 Spotlights: The WASP American Gothic Novel Today

When in Stephenie Meyer's hugely successful *Twilight* novel series (2005-2008) vampires struggle with their vegetarian diet, premarital sex, and attractive werewolf rivals in frustrating love triangles, the transition from "monster to yuppie" is both very tangible and comprehensible as the transition of a formerly antagonistic deviance to the position of focalized heroism, that is, from villain to hero. Using the vampire as Civil Hero, he—and the Civil Hero is still predominately male—is re-constructed with attributions associated with civility and heroism. For Meyer, this meant constructing an Anglo-Saxon vampire who goes to high school, who is socially integrated, well-educated and well-mannered, and whose physical deviance is reduced to the super-human strength needed to save his damsel, a thirst for blood, quenchable with a strictly controlled diet of animal blood, and sparkling beautifully and supremely white in bright daylight. The fear, which a vampire like Edward Cullen inspires in a damsel, is the "fear that *he* would be harmed—even as he called to me [Bella, the damsel] with sharp-edged fangs, I feared for *him*" (Meyer, *Twilight* 139; original emphasis).

While Meyer's heroic civil vampire might be the most well-known yuppie-type reiteration of the vampire trope today, it is a direct adaptation of Anne Rice's hugely successful *Vampire Chronicles* (1976-2016). From 1976 onward, Rice's continuous reiteration of the vampire has focused on elevating the predatory, lascivious Gothic villains to the status of "superheroes [...] endowed with immortality, supernatural strength and speed, and even the ability to fly" (Weinstock, "American Vampires" 212f.). Her creation of the archetypal Civil Hero vampire protagonist, Lestat, as "your hero for the duration, a perfect imitation of a blond, blue-eyed, six-foot Anglo-Saxon male" (Rice, *Memnoch* 3), clearly set the tone for the focalized and re-racialized vampire Civil Hero in the contemporary WASP American Gothic branch of vampire fiction. Unlike the conservative, heteronormative perspective developed in Meyer's series, Rice functionalizes her superhero vampire protagonists, mainly to establish and celebrate "queer as the new normal whose progressive attitude toward erotic relationships disregards conventional gender expectations" (Weinstock, "American Vampires" 213), vis-à-vis non-judgmental representations of homosexuality, gender fluidity, and "almost transsexual" episodes (Holmes n.p.).

When authors such as Rice and Meyer re-position and re-racialize the vampire's formerly antagonistic deviance, reiterating him as the WASP Civil Hero, they also refill the vacancy of the villain and, thus, keep intact the Gothic's strictly binary conventionality and plot logic. In the *Twilight* novels, Meyer, for example, differentiates between the good, civil, and heroic vampires of the Cullen family, on the one hand, and the villainous "strange vampire[s]" of the antagonistic Volturi clan (Meyer, *New Moon* 412) on the other. While it is possible to read the traditional, British Gothic vampire's racialization (that is, the Mediterranean Man with fangs) into Meyer's initial construction of uncanny male vampires in "long robes," which are so "pitch-black" that they blend perfectly with a vampire's "jet-black hair," as if the latter "was the hood of his cloak" (*New Moon* 411), her racialization strategy quickly takes on the distinctly WASP American features of the B/black Savage Villain.[1] Consider in this respect the construction of Aro, the head of the Volutri vampire clan and chief antagonist of the *Twilight* series:

> I [Bella] couldn't decide if his [Aro's] face was beautiful or not. I suppose the features were perfect. But he was as different from the vampires beside him as they were from me. His skin was translucently white, like onionskin, and it looked just as delicate—it stood in shocking contrast to the long black hair that framed his face. I felt a strange, horrifying urge to touch his cheek, to see if it was softer than Edward's or Alice's, or if it was powdery, like chalk." (*New Moon* 411)

Meyer constructs Aro's Gothic otherness qua his skin and, more importantly, in overtly racial terms. In the sharp contrast to his "jet-black hair" framing his supposedly "perfect" features, Aro's "translucently white" skin color appears to be of an artificial, misleading quality that effectively taints his beauty and excludes him from "the unnaturally attractive faces that surrounded him" (*New Moon* 411). His skin is far from being naturally "white," like the skin of Edward and his family, but it is "powdery," as if covered with "chalk," and as translucent as an onion whose dark outer skin layers have been peeled. As if staged in the context of a minstrel show, Aro's chalky whiteface performance creates a "shocking contrast" between his claim of (artificial) whiteness and his underlying yet undeniable blackness, causing

---

1 While several critics, including myself, have commented on Meyer's racial bias and her problematic racialization strategies in her *Twilight* series, especially with respect to her portrayal of Native American and Indigenous characters as being either half-naked, over-emotional, and child-like werewolves, or as equally two-dimensional and seminude Amazons, the racialization of the Volturi, and especially of Aro, has not been addressed thus far. For a first introduction to race and racialization in Meyer's *Twilight Saga*, see for example Natalie Wilson ("Civilized Vampires Versus Savage Werewolves: Race and Ethnicity in the Twilight Series," 2010), Alexandra Hidalgo ("Bridges, Nodes, and Bare Life: Race in the 'Twilight' Saga," 2012), and Corinna Lenhardt ("Wendigos, Eye Killers, Skinwalkers: The Myth of the American Indian Vampire and American Indian 'Vampire' Myths," 2016).

the "strange, horrifying urge" in Bella "to touch his cheek." When Bella finally gives in to her "horrifying urge," Aro's skin indeed turns out to be "too strange, too alien and frightening," as it may seem translucently white and "insubstantial-looking," but it really possesses all the qualities of "shale" (*New Moon* 417). In other words, upon touching Aro's skin, the metaphor of onion skin is replaced by the metaphor of shale, and the villain's artificial whiteness is replaced by blackness. In turn, Meyer further specifies Bella's "urge": "I [Bella] was horrified at the thought of allowing him to touch me, and yet also perversely intrigued by the chance to feel his strange skin" (*New Moon* 416). The prospect of the white female teenager, aptly named Bella, being touched by the B/black villain is horrifying and perverse, explicitly not because of Bella being a human female teenager and Aro being a centuries-old male vampire—the reader of the *Twilight* series has come to accept this as the prerequisite for a fantastic romance from book one onward—but because of Aro's "strange skin." The gulf Meyer constructs between Aro and Bella (as well as between Aro and the Cullen vampires) is the gulf between the Africanist Savage Villain on the one side and the white damsel in distress and the Civil Hero on the other. The crossing of this racialized gulf, the physical contact between a B/black man and a white girl, is constructed as a horrific perversity. Only due to Bella's innate supernatural "talent" does this forced physical contact remain without dire consequences for her: Aro may be able to touch Bella's skin, but he cannot touch her soul, read her mind, or torture her with severe pain, as she is completely "immune to [his and other strange vampires'] talents" (*New Moon* 417). Meyer's terminology of innate "talent" only thinly veils the heavily racialized core of her Gothic conceptualization and must be understood as a strategic escape into political correctness. Bella remains unaffected, that is, untouched and untainted by the Savage Villain's assault only because of her superior white race. Her supernatural power, in other words, lies solely in her ability to shield the supremely white race of vampires (which she will give birth to, mother, and defend in the course of the novel) from the racial Blackness that threatens to taint, infect, and destroy it.

In her latest installment of her *Vampire Chronicles*, the 2016 novel *Prince Lestat and the Realms of Atlantis*,[2] Anne Rice is even more explicit in her construction of villainous otherness along the overtly racial lines of the Africanist Savage Villain. She juxtaposes her well-known peace- and culture-loving "tribe" of Anglo-Saxon vampires, "governed by Lestat," with a literally alien race of "non-human thing[s]" (Rice, *Atlantis* 114) that sport a ravenous "desire for the vampiric blood, the vampiric brain" (*Atlantis* 170). These all-but-human creatures are "Replimoids" (*Atlantis* 241),

---

2   *Prince Lestat and the Realms of Atlantis* has not yet found its way into scholarly debates; the few available reviews mainly target Rice's veering "from supernatural into science fiction" (Hand n.p.) and argue that the novel—while still part of her popular vampire series—"could simply be an *aliens-among-us* science fiction novel" (Sweeney n.p.).

an artificially created alien race of superhumanly strong "black-skinned, black-haired non-humans" (*Atlantis* 170) that replicate "like rodents" (*Atlantis* 364), by growing full-sized clones from cut-off body parts. In her fashioning of "the worst challenges [Lestat's tribe] has ever faced" (*Atlantis* xvi), Rice meanders between racialized WASP American Gothic conventionality, (homo)erotic romance, alien abductions, and a thinly-veiled 9/11 allegory.³ However, instead of constructing the alien invaders on a suicide mission along the lines of the stereotypically racialized Arab man, Rice renders them explicitly "what the world calls black people" (*Atlantis* 221), albeit focusing on exoticized Blackness ("they had the special beauty of dark-skinned people, a near polished and sculpted look," *Atlantis* 222). In her plot, this integration of the Africanist Savage Villain has one main function: Rice establishes a connection qua skin color between the threat of the Replimoids and the other villainous characters in the novel, that is, first and foremost Lestat's hereditary enemy and helpmate of the Replimoids, Rhoshamandes. Rhoshamandes is the "cold," "hard and cunning" old vampire with dark "olive skin" (*Atlantis* 18), who "wanders with the mark of Cain on him, that winsome, capricious, heartless blood drinker, with the mark of Cain" (*Atlantis* 64). The mark of Cain—often conflated with the Curse of Ham—is a direct reference to the pseudo-Biblical legitimatization discourse during the Atlantic slave trade that equated black skin color with a presumed moral and ontological inferiority of Black peoples. Far from "erasing what we might call lived or experienced racial differences" in the construction of Rice's vampires (Holmes n.p.), Rhoshamandes and the other "cynical ones, the dark, deeply conservative ones who wanted to know why blood drinkers would bother with anything, presumably, but savaging humans for their blood" (*Atlantis* 44) are marked "B/black" to highlight their savage deviance from Lestat and his civil tribe of white vampires. It is this marked deviance qua skin color that Rice connects continuously to the alien B/blackness of the Replimoids. Taken together, this B/black nexus establishes the conventionally Gothic undercurrent of thrilling uneasiness and impeding doom qua Gothicized racial deviance. If we look more closely, however, Rice creates two different kinds of B/blackness: On the one hand, Rhoshamandes stands in for the type of racialized villainous deviance that, cunning and untrustworthy, marks him

---

3   The black-skinned and black-haired "things" with huge black "almond-shaped eyes" (*Atlantis* 108, 420) have been created and sent to earth by "the Parents" (*Atlantis* 240), to bring down the utopic, prehistoric city of Atalantaya, a city very much "like the city of Manhattan" (*Atlantis* 154), by causing a massive explosion through collective suicide inside its most prestigious tower. When the Replimoids are distracted, through their newly-found love to Amel, Lestat's prehistoric double—"a male, pale skinned as an albino," god-like creature "with substantial red hair and deep blue-green eyes, and very agreeable features" (*Atlantis* 275)—the Parents bomb Atalantaya's towers from outer space and with "the towers melting" and "thousands around [...] splashing and screaming for help when there was no help," the utopic Manhattan falls into the "surging water" (*Atlantis* 318).

as a traitor and discard among the civil Anglo-Saxon vampires. On the other hand, the Replimoids are B/black "things," that is, ontologically abject from the vampire species as much as from human beings. This Gothicized abject, the thingified Savage Villain that multiplies at will, cannot be overcome by Prince Lestat and the other WASP civil vampires; however, as they are the all-but-human "People of the Purpose" only (*Atlantis* 436), they readily adhere to a new purpose given to them by the supremely civil and supremely white ancient proto-vampire and presumed God of the Replimoids, Amel—at least for the time being. Effectively, Rice has constructed a thingified Black race of aliens who—like chattel—are defined solely by their "Purpose" of servitude to both WASP civic vampires and human beings. What renders them "the worst challenges [Lestat's tribe] has ever faced" (*Atlantis* xvi) is the looming uncertainty of whether or not the Replimoids will remain content with their fate or if they will one day learn "what [...] they could do," uniting their forces until they "were all through the streets [... and] cleaving to the buildings" (*Atlantis* 415). The looming threat of the novel is the WASP fear of a mass of Black chattel uprising and overthrowing the WASP hegemony of Prince Lestat and his kin.

Before moving on to two contemporary WASP American Gothic novels that include Gothic writing conventions other than the vampire romance's tropes, plot elements, and character ensemble, I want to add a rare instance of an ultra-conservative and at times overtly racist generic vampire novel to my overview sketch, namely Michael Romkey's *American Gothic* (2004).[4] Romkey's novel differentiates starkly between villainous female vampires and civil male vampires on the basis of race and racialization. In *American Gothic*, the protagonist, Union soldier and soon-to-be-vampire fledgling, Nathaniel Peregrine, stumbles through New Orleans's French Quarter in the midst of the Civil War. In "one of the city's more notorious haunts," the "Quadroon Ballroom," where "Mulatto mothers would bring their free quadroon daughters [...] and auction them to rich men not to serve as slaves but mistresses" in "perversely ritualized" arrangements that often result in "bastard children," the protagonist notes that something about "the most beautiful café au lait women" (Romkey 42)[5] feels off, sending a shiver "through [his] body" (43). In the "madness threatening to smother him in a boiling chaos of delusion" (43), one of the "*femmes de couleur*" stands out as "smaller than the other women, with a complexion so white and perfect that she might have been made of porcelain" (43). In a "world made up of dualities: day and night; white and black; inside and out; love and hate; good and evil" (75), the too white and "far too innocent looking" (199) "little Creole girl-woman" (73), Delphine Allard, unsettles the stark (racial) dualities

---

4   There is no secondary literature on Michael Romkey's novel available yet, nor has the book been reviewed in the press.
5   All following page references in this paragraph refer to Romkey's *American Gothic*.

with her mixed-raced being. Indeed, Romkey constructs the racial contamination of the blood through miscegenation as the very root of her vampirism. In his dualistic world of Black and white races, Delphine will indiscriminately "dilute the purebred African racial lines" of early twentieth-century Haitians, the presumably all-white Union soldiers and their accompanying prostitutes and drug dealers in the nineteenth-century South, as well as members of the contemporary Goth gang "Ravening Brood" (211). It must be noted that Romkey's overtly racialized—or racist—construction of the vampire intersects with gender stereotypes connected to the respective racializations: While Delphine Allard, one of the lascivious Creole vampire "jezebels" (48) must give in to the "animal passion" (59) so essential to her "secret race" (57) and "tear savagely into" the necks of her victims (208), the white male Peregrine, who is turned into a vampire by Delphine, upon solving her "bloody mystery" (57), learns to control his passions up to the point at which he puts "himself at [a white female teenager's] service" (293). In sum, Romkey disguises *American Gothic* as a historic (Southern) Gothic romance (at least over two-thirds of the novel), while engaging in decidedly problematic, racist, and misogynistic reconstructions and misrepresentations of U.S. American history. His usage of a female Africanist Savage Villain, in the role of the Creole vampires' chief "demoness" (292) and contaminating temptress, is both remarkably ignorant and highly consistent with the WASP American Gothic tradition's continuous employment of the B/black Gothicized abject.

John Langan's 2016 small-press genre publication, *The Fisherman*,[6] is also constructed around the contaminating B/blackness of an Africanist Savage Villain. In his novel, which oscillates between Gothic conventionality, perpetuating fishing myths, and loosely adapted (and re-colorized) motifs of Herman Melville's *Moby Dick*, Langan constructs a truly evil "great beast" and "monster" (Langan 237)[7] as a B/black "Leviathan [who] is swimming in that water" (134) of the "black ocean" (e.g. 134, 138, 154, 203, 237, 242) "whose waves were as black as [...] ink" (2, also 203, 228), and whose "black currents" are actually "[d]ark shapes darting around" (243) "like a swarm of insects" (31). By establishing clear references to the Middle Passage and the millions of dead black bodies buried on the ground of the Black Atlantic—and by completely eclipsing white collective responsibility and guilt—Langan constructs an all-encompassing B/blackness that pushes onto the shores of white America, threatening and contaminating white female innocence and WASP core families wherever it touches them. Far from being confined to the "oddly dark"

---

6   While *The Fisherman* has been hailed as a "superb new novel," with a "rolling, unpredictable flow [and] a distinctive rhythm," in Terrence Rafferty's review for the *New York Times* (n.p.), and subsequently won the Bram Stoker Award in the category of "Horror Novel of the Year 2016," it has not received scholarly or broader critical attention yet.

7   All following page references in this paragraph refer to Langan's *The Fisherman*.

water (138), the black Leviathan is "bigger, much bigger" (31), a "black ocean" of "great muscles flexing and releasing, and there's no doubt [it] is alive" (145). Whatever—and whoever—is touched by the "dark ocean [that] is leaking through" (138) and "surrender[s] to the blackness" that arises all around "in a tide" (245) is irrevocably blackened and "transformed" (32, 226). Langan, for example, paints trees black "as if they'd been shaped out of night itself" (30) and refers to "black light" (139) and "the black, muddy ground" (203). Most significantly, however, he constructs wives, mothers, and daughters, who, with skin as "pale as the flesh of a lily" (218) and beautiful and innocent "like [...] Snow White" (117), are poisoned and contaminated by the black Leviathan's black waters and transformed into undead "savage figure[s]" (235) of half-female and half-fish zombie "nymph[s]" (222), with wounds "smeared" with "black, viscous liquid" (32). When such a tainted "walking dead woman" (87) is attacked, the formerly female "thing" (221) will bleed "[b]lack blood—literally black blood" (81) and either attack its mourning husband or father, with a "mouth jammed with teeth like steak knives" (208), or seduce and have sex with him (220/221). Represented by the statue of a "headless" and "pregnant, enormously so" mother (224), a tribe of savage zombie fish nymphs rises "stone cold [and] damp" (80) from the black Leviathan's fleshy currents, turning formerly well-kept family homes into blackness-infested deathtraps:

> The walls, ceiling, floor, all of the room he's entered is dark, furred with dense, black mold. It's impossible to tell where the windows are. The room is full of gray, diffuse light. Mold envelopes what must have been a steamer trunk. It joins a trio of chairs along the opposite wall. It transforms a small table into an enormous toadstool. The only thing in the room clear of mold is the woman standing in the middle of it, at the center of a large puddle of dark water. (124)

Qua contaminating white wives and daughters, the B/black Leviathan has infested the core of WASP American civilization: The family home has been turned into a blackness-infested, molding "thicket" (141), that is, into wilderness controlled by the Africanist Savage Villain.

This contamination is constructed in both sexual and racial terms: The B/black Leviathan's black waters rise like the tide, enter the "limp, passive" white women's bodies (31), and turn them into headless "hodgepodge monster" nymphs (124) bathed in "gray, diffuse light" (124). In other words, *The Fisherman* functionalizes the Africanist Savage Villain for a twenty-first-century version of threatening male Blackness and racial miscegenation as the antithesis to (racially and culturally purely white) family and civilization. Confronted with a B/black Savage Villain as all-encompassing as the Black Atlantic, a "handsome prince" will not do "to ride in and save our daughter" (117); what will do, according to Langan's narrative logic, is "her father and his books" (118), plus "their neighbors in Woodstock" (121). Civil heroism, in other words, is defined as white righteous men (radiant "as if someone were focusing a white light on" them, 140), equipped with artifacts of rationality and culture (books) and "carrying axes they've burrowed from work" (122). At the end of their heroic battle with the thicket of black wilderness and sensual ex-wife nymphs, these men are able to retrieve one of their abducted daughters, but they must learn that the B/black Leviathan itself cannot be overcome. Effectively rewriting the Middle Passage and the Black Atlantic as ciphers for Black invasion and an all-encompassing threat of Blackness to the white race, Langan insists that a B/black ocean of "rows and rows of people float[ing]" (262) and its seductive "underspeech—the speech of the Fisherman's creatures" (167) cannot be silenced for good. The only option left to the WASP male characters, living in a thus invaded country, is to keep the B/black contamination at bay, by living in civil, whites-only neighborhoods of homes with "[f]ather, mother, and two girls" (253) and under the immediate protection of "the Sheriff's deputies," who will pull up "in their boat to offer [white men faced with zombie fish nymphs] the choice of rescue" (262).

The last novel in this overview sketch is Dave Eggers's 2013 bestseller, *The Circle*, a dystopian science fiction novel that functionalizes a number of Gothemes and Gothic elements in its dramatization of a powerful global technology company that successively promotes, enables, and controls the total transparency of information, governments, and individuals. Narrated form the perspective of Mae Holland—info-tech newbie, willing accomplice and villain in the making—the novel initially juxtaposes the "gulag" (Eggers 4)[8], the "abyss" (8), and the "chaotic mess [...] [o]utside the walls of the Circle," where all is "noise and struggle, failure and filth" (30) with the perfect "utopia" (30) of "great peace" (324) and "no friction" (370), i.e., the "good, clean and right" (392) enclosure of the Circle's company campus. Using a number of Gothic props and settings, however, Eggers undermines this utopia from the start and creates a revealing undercurrent in the Circle's propagandistic claims to progress, transparency, and "unrestrained Manifest Destiny" (368): Entering through the CEO's "enormous door, which seemed and likely was medieval, something that would have kept barbarians at bay" and passing a "pair of giant gargoyle knockers" (22), we enter a Gothic setting ripe with "secret chamber[s]" (27), "labyrinth[s]" (217), "shadowy stairwell[s]" (211), dark hallway[s]" (319) and "dimly lit corridor[s]" (218). From here, we are led to a variety of Gothic *mise-en-scènes*, spanning from "a feast raided by animals or Vikings" (32), to "a strange combination of manmade tunnel and actual cave [...] where stalagmites and stalactites gave the tunnel the look of a mouth full of uneven teeth" (222), and a grotesque aquarium displaying the "brutal force" and "quick and savage movement" (475) of the Circle itself, bringing us thus eye-to-eye with the "bizarre creature, ghostlike, vaguely menacing and never still" (307), "[t]he fucking shark that eats the world" (480). Eggers, in other words, constructs a Gothicized ivory tower, by using, as John

---

8   All following page references in this paragraph refer to Eggers's *The Circle*.

Masterson argues, "the campus as a fortified chronotope against the maddening swarm of human life beyond. [...] The idea of a swarming contagion of other bodies to be held at bay, symbolized by clean seats or fortified compounds, is extended into a realm where borders separating first and third worlds are disconcertingly porous" (735). In this Gothic setting with "quasi-eugenic undertones" (Masterson 735), Eggers racially positions his protagonist from the beginning:

> Mae—her wide mouth, her thin lips, her olive skin, her black hair, [...] her high cheekbones gave her a look of severity, her brown eyes not smiling, only small and cold, ready for war. Since the photo—she was eighteen then, angry and unsure—Mae had gained much-needed weight, her face had softened and curves appeared, curves that brought the attention of men of myriad ages and motives" (5)

In the WASP American Gothic script, Mae fits the description of the standard villain. She is racialized as a dark-skinned, dark-haired, and dark-eyed angry woman, nicknamed "*Black Lightning*" by her co-workers (9); she can twist "her mouth into a smile" (8) but is betrayed by her "brown eyes not smiling, only small and cold, ready for war" (5). Over the years, Mae's body has softened and become more appealing, but her "angry and unsure" personality has not changed. Throughout the book, her descent into villainy/ascent to the top of the Circle is driven by her anger and uncertainty, constructed by Eggers in terms of "a fathomless blackness spreading under her" (333), "an unbearable hiss" (334) coming through "this black rip, this loud tear within her, a few times a week" (196). While Mae rationalizes the "black rip" in her mind as "the madness of not knowing" (465) that can be worked through and eventually killed (412), with the help of the transparency-enabling devices of the Circle, Eggers connects Mae's "spreading blackness" to her race-based hatred and violence. Truly villainous, "*Black Lightning*" is in pursuit of a "very cute, dimpled and long-lashed, with hair so blond it could only be real" (13) damsel in distress, Annie. Time and again, Mae's villainy is connected to her envy for Annie's presumably superior Anglo-Saxon heritage:

> Annie's family line went back to the *Mayflower*, her ancestors having settled this country, and their ancestors having owned some vast swath of England. Their blood was blue all the way back, it seemed to the invention of the wheel. In fact, if anyone's bloodline *had* invented the wheel, it would have been Annie's. It would make absolute and perfect sense and would surprise no one. (360)

Annie's blue blood, her "lineage, her head star, the varied and ancient advantages she enjoyed, were keeping Mae second" (409) and spawning a race-based envy that would effectively destroy Annie and help a "very hungry, very evil empire" (401) succeed. Indeed, the fall of whiteness—the elimination of Annie's "little entitled blond head" (360) and the presumably wheel-inventing civilization she represents so perfectly—is constructed as the ultimate threat of a technological and racial pseudo-"Enlightenment" (59): Qua the Circle's newest invention, "PastPerfect" (349), the *"evil in DNA"* (443) can be accessed until the "rough patches" (428) and "weird stuff" (436) in Annie's and everyone's "bloodline" (428) will uncover the "blackhearted people" (428), parading as the blue-blooded masters of civilization.

With the demise of white Annie (she ends up in a coma and catatonically awaits Mae's latest inventions, a mind-reading program) and the ascent of B/black Mae to the Circle's "face" and "ambassador" (481), all "sense of perspective, and [...] humanity" is lost (368) and "a new species, omnivorous and blind [...]" (307) rises, as the perfect "embodiment of predatory instinct" (314). The Africanist Savage Villain, once more composed of one (Mae) and many (the Circle), has obtained an easy victory, not least because of the apparent lack of intervening forces. By mistaking Mae as a damsel in distress that needs saving, the novel's two Civil Heroes—Kalden (a.k.a. Ty) from within the Circle and Mercer from the world outside—fail miserably. Kalden becomes the *"Unidentified Freaky Man"* (171) and his secrecy and "invisibility" are (mis)understood as being "intentional and even aggressive" (172) by Mae; "[p]oor Mercer's" "directionless blather" (368) about evil empires and unrestrained Manifest Destiny aspirations discredit him as "a very disturbed, antisocial young man" (462). In the end, Kalden/Ty is imprisoned on the Circle's campus and Mercer is pushed into suicide by a tech-savvy mob, acting on the newly established lynch law ("Lynch her!," in reference to Fiona Highbridge, an assumed "kid-killer" 451). In other words, by Gothicizing the uncontrolled, "omnivorous and blind" advancement of (digital) technology in *The Circle*, Eggers has iterated the SV/CH Gotheme and composed a dystopian narrative based as much on technology as on racialization. Backed by a mass of willing accomplices around the globe, the end of civilization is reigned in by the elimination of WASP racial supremacy and the concurrent rise of the Africanist Savage Villain. The tragic and frustrating inadequacy of the Civil Hero(es) in the novel gives rise to the novel's critical and satirical potential: The Circle is a fictionalized conglomerate of present-day Google and Facebook and a dystopian brave new world of morally (and culturally?) unrestrained technological progress. "Google's motto, 'Don't be evil,'" Betsy Morais argues in her review of *The Circle* for *The New Yorker*, "is upended in Eggers's telling: these companies may not have started out as the clubhouses of moustache-twirling villains, but, he writes, in a return to Orwell, 'We're closing the circle around everyone—it's a totalitarian nightmare.'" In the end, we should add, the moustache-twirling villain would have been a manageable task, even for such frustratingly ineffective Civil Heroes as Kalden/Ty and Mercer; it is the Africanist Savage Villain and the worldwide mob of lynching consumers that complete the dystopian Circle.

A spotlights chapter offers the unique opportunity to read and compare texts that appear to share little to no commonalities with one another but their use of Gothic writing strategies. Yet, through the Gothic, most of the novels discussed above create surprisingly assimilable visions of a racially coded apocalypse. *The Circle*, *Prince Lestat and the Realms of Atlantis*, and *The Fisherman* most clearly culminate in white civilization's defeat, the Africanist SV's ultimate victory. While Longan's novel is very explicit in its discursive deletion of slavery and the slave trade and its (re-)writing of white guilt as victimization, all texts position Blackness as the root of evil and white civilization's apocalyptic downfall. Blackness is imagined as a contaminating, over-fertile power against which whiteness knows no defense. Given that all novels in this however limited survey were written and/or published during the Obama presidency, they can and must be connected to the racial paranoia discourses and the anti-Black hate crimes so prevalent at the time. The inflation of Black church arson all over the U.S., the internet's flooding with images of a White House contaminated by the Black family in residence, and other equally violent hate crimes triggered by politicized anti-Black sentiments (that doubtlessly culminated in the 2016 election of a man unapologetically racist) must be seen as the discursive habitat for these novels. They prove, with great clarity, that the Obama-age "myth of a postracial America" (Norwood) was just that, a myth created by and for WASP people.

In the following two subchapters, I will provide a much more detailed reading of the Savage Villain/Civil Hero Gotheme in two WASP American Gothic novels. Examining Stephen King's *The Girl Who Loved Tom Gordon* (1999) and Karen Russell's *Swamplandia!* (2011) in their entirety—instead of continuing to present examples and spotlights from various works—will allow me to explore in depth how these novels construct, functionalize, and embed the SV/CH Gotheme in their overall writing strategies. While my (however limited) overview indicates a continuing prevalence of the Africanist Savage Villain in the contemporary WASP American Gothic, only a close reading of the Gotheme in contemporary novels can really argue for or against the assumption of an unchanged, conventionally fixed and racially highly-problematic writing strategy at the core of the WASP American Gothic.

4.2 Shirley Temple, Sidney Poitier, and the Africanist Savage Villain Walk into the Woods…: Stephen King's *The Girl Who Loved Tom Gordon*

> "There is nothing, absolutely nothing, calculated to raise the goose-flesh on the back of an audience more than that of a white girl in relation to Negroes." (Shirley Temple Black, Autobiography 90)

Who would be more eligible to start off an in-depth discussion of contemporary WASP American Gothic novels than Stephen King, the "Bestsellasaurus Rex" (Collings 210) who has dominated the global book market for Gothic and horror fiction since the late 1970s? Aware of the many possible choices among King's vast text corpus, I want to focus mainly on his 1999 novel *The Girl Who Loved Tom Gordon*. This award-winning coming-of-age narrative intertwines the conventions of the U.S. baseball novel with a Gothic plot and character ensemble that, to a striking extent, resemble early nineteenth-century WASP American Gothic writing strategies. In the context of my ongoing survey of the WASP American Gothic, past and present, King's novel offers the opportunity to test the presumed intrinsic raciality of the Gothic, vis-à-vis the author's knowledge of these problematic conventions in Gothic texts, as well as in his own writing. Though fully aware of the manifold allegations of constructing and iterating both noncredible stereotypical female characters and the heavily racialized motif of the "Magical Negro" in his fiction (and films), King composes a novel that fully iterates the Savage Villain/Civil Hero Gotheme by juxtaposing a Shirley Temple-like damsel—accompanied by the re-instantiation of the "Ebony Saint" Hollywood stereotype/motif—to an omnipresent B/black threat. King's novel therefore not only thwarts its innovative potential and adds grist to the mill of his critics; it also effectively re-inscribes a desexualized, Christian-conservative notion of womanhood, in addition to racial constructions of Blackness reminiscent of mid-twentieth-century post-minstrel character depictions. It goes without saying that this constellation is rendered ever more problematic when King's version of an Africanist Savage Villain is included in the picture.

When looking into the research directly concerned with *The Girl Who Loved Tom Gordon*,[9] this strong emphasis on the construction of race and raciality might seem odd. In his 2002 article, "Childhood and Media Literacy in *The Girl Who Loved Tom Gordon*," Michael A. Arnzen argues that King constructed the protagonist Trisha as a "child born into a commodity culture so saturated by media and the cult of celebrity that she must learn how to survive the forest of signs" (9), thereby connecting the novel to other popular turn of the millennium texts and films (e.g., *The Blair Witch Project*) that "enjoy tossing the modern civilians of consumer culture back into their uncivilized past, leading to both a psychological and cultural form of regression" (8). For Arnzen, Trisha's process of growing up and survival is

---

9   Note that, despite favorable reviews upon publication (cf. Ted Anthony, "King's 'Unplanned' Offspring is Readers' Joy," Erik Lundegaard, "*The Girl Who Loved Tom Gordon*," and Dorman T. Shindler, "Baseball Tied to Wilderness Survival," all published in April 1999) and its *New York Times* bestseller number one listing (May 2, 1999), *The Girl Who Loved Tom Gordon* has not yet received broad scholarly attention and, thus, can be understood as a case in point for Tom Hansen's general observation about King scholarship (or the lack thereof): "In spite of (or more likely because) his prolific productivity, precious little attention has been paid to King by critics" (Hansen 290).

a matter of media literacy, i.e., of learning to master the signs and implications of an omnipresent consumer culture. Further highlighting the importance of Trisha's ongoing consumption of radio broadcasts with her Walkman, Frances Gray briefly looks into Trisha's role as a listener on the intersection where "information meets imagination" (250) in the 2006 anthology, *More Than a Music Box: Radio Cultures and Communities in a Multi-Media World*. In the most recent discussion of the novel, Matthew M. Holman adds to Arnzen's argument of psychological regression, offering a psychological reading (based on Freud's notion of the "id" and Julia Kristeva's "abject") of the cold voice of pop culture, adulthood, and panic that Trisha dubs the "tough tootsie." Only after having mastered the tough tootsie voice, grown and toughened "Trisha [can] ultimately stand up to the God of the Lost" (82).

It is worth mentioning that neither Arnzen nor Holman, despite their focus on the young female protagonist's coming-of-age development, connects their analyses of *The Girl Who Loved Tom Gordon* to the branch of critical King scholarship explicitly concerned with King's depiction of women specifically and his construction gender roles more generally. Following Carol Senf's lead, we can imagine gender-focused King critics on a spectrum ranging from "King's fiction is clearly misogynist" to readers who "observe that King's woman characters are weak—though they do not necessarily agree on the causes of this weakness" (Senf 92). On one end of the spectrum (King's texts are misogynist), we can position, for example, the essays collected in Theresa Thompson's (ed.) baseline study, *Imagining the Worst: Stephen King and the Representation of Women*, which problematizes, from various gender and/or feminist perspectives, King's apparent inability to portray female characters beyond the one-dimensional Gothic damsel or the nurturing helpmate. In the words of Robin Wood: "In the King World women are wives and mothers, and ideally they are much in need of male protection (if they don't realize it there is something wrong with them)" (305). In King's fiction, the rare occurrences of strong, independent female characters are instantaneously conflated with deviance, antagonism, and villainy. All of King's female characters, whether portrayed as likable or as antagonistic, are understood as lacking "the emotional dimensions so apparent in his children and men" (Pharr 20).

In his often-quoted 1983 interview with Eric Norden for the *Playboy* magazine, Stephen King signals his awareness of gender and feminism-based criticism and admits his "problem with women in [his] books" (Norden, "Playboy Interview" 234). He states:

> Yes, unfortunately, I think it is probably the most justifiable of all those [criticisms] leveled against me. [...] And when I think I'm free of the charge that most male American writers depict women as either nebbishes or bitch-goddess destroyers, I create someone like Carrie—who starts out as a nebbish victim and

then *becomes* a bitch goddess, destroying an entire town in an explosion of hormonal rage. I recognize the problems but can't yet rectify them. (Norden 234)

Oblivious to the irony of Norden and King's discussion of gender stereotyping in a medium like the *Playboy*, critics like Tony Magistrale have used King's interview statements to attest the author a gender sensibility akin to feminism: "[...] the feminist-inspired fictions that King produced during the nineties did much to redress the charge that he was restricted in his ability to create real female characters as is the genre for which King is best known" (139). *The Girl Who Loved Tom Gordon* (1999), if we follow Magistrale's defense, would conclude, maybe even spearhead, this "feminist-inspired" repositioning of King. In his short analysis of the novel, Magistrale himself, however, does not elaborate on this presumed link between the newly "feminist-inspired" writing and King's 1999 version of a damsel in distress, Trisha.

Instead, Magistrale is mainly concerned with highlighting the role of the Red Sox baseball team and, especially, of African American star closer Tom Gordon; however, it is a minor aspect within his analysis of *The Girl Who Loved Tom Gordon* that will be of the utmost importance for my own reading of King's novel(s): Magistrale is the first to connect King's Tom Gordon character to the recent criticism of King's forthright rule of basing black-white relationships on the racial stereotype of the "Magical Negro." While he is both aware of the manifold examples of the Magical Negro in King's fiction (he lists *The Shining*, *The Talisman*, *The Stand*, and *The Green Mile*)[10] and at least of some of the critical controversies they have provoked, Magistrale's discussion of the character Tom Gordon is solely in accord with the few critics who give King "credit for creating strong African American characters" (McAleer 97), incorruptible by an "exposure to evil" and with a sheer endless "capacity to love" (Figliola 56). Magistrale even concludes, by attempting to apologize for King's vast usage of the racial motif: "As a Mainer, King's exposure to blacks has been necessarily limited" (Magistrale 38).

Most critics aware of the problematic cluster of Magical Negroes, or "MAAF" ("Magical African American Friends," as Heather J. Hicks [27] names the motif), in King's fiction, however, come to less forgiving conclusions. Indeed, the articles on King's Magical Negroes by Heather J. Hicks (2003), Nnedi Okorafor-Mbachu (2004), Sarah Nilsen (2005), Brian Kent (2008), Matthew W. Hughey (2009), and Linda Williams (2015), among others, have made King's continuous lapse into depicting a "latently racist character" (Hughey 544) in his fiction a buzz topic within King scholarship.

---

10 Magistrale's list is surprisingly short, given the fact that King's novels, short stories, and film adaptations have become inextricably linked to the Magical Negro motif, so much indeed "that the *Wikipedia* entry for the 'Magical Negro' lists his characters as emblematic of this stereotype" (Nilsen 132).

> The MN ["Magical Negro," C.L.] has become a stock character that often appears as a lower class, uneducated black person who possesses supernatural or magical powers. These powers are used to save and transform disheveled, uncultured, lost, or broken whites (almost exclusively white men) into competent, successful, and content people within the context of the American myth of redemption and salvation. (Hughey 544)[11]

King's usage of the Magical Negro and the charges of racism in his fiction first entered the scholarly as well as the public debate with the release of the 1999 film adaption of his novel *The Green Mile* (1996). In her watershed article, "In Hollywood, Racist Stereotypes Can Still Earn Oscar Nominations," Tania Modleski discusses *The Green Mile* as a film that enables "white people to indulge their most prurient and fearful imaginings about African Americans and have their dread symbolically exorcised, all the while allowing them to feel good about a black man's dying to preserve the status quo" (n.p.). Also referring to *The Green Mile*, Spike Lee, addressing students at Yale University in 2001, was even more explicit: "I gotta sit down; I get mad just thinking about it. [...] They're still doing the same old thing ... recycling the noble savage and the happy slave" (Gonzalez n.p.). Linda Williams links this longevity of the Magical Negro (as the fictional cross between "the noble savage and the happy slave") in fiction and film to Harriet Beecher Stowe's *Uncle Tom's Cabin* and to the ensuing Tom and anti-Tom myths in the late nineteenth- and early twentieth-century United States. "The first magical negro, strictly speaking, was Uncle Tom," Williams ("Why" n.p.) argues and further explains:

> Figures like Richard Wright's Bigger Thomas, Alex Haley's Kunte Kinte, and blaxploitation's anti-heroes Superfly, Shaft and Sweetback were hypermasculine and "bad" precisely to counter the saintliness of the emasculated Tom, even at the risk of playing into the hands of the even more racist "anti-Tom" myth that has continued to have some kind of valence in American culture since Dixon's *The Clansman* transmuted into Griffith's *The Birth of a Nation*. (Williams, "Why" n.p.)

While the link Williams establishes between *Uncle Tom's Cabin*, the Tom and anti-Tom myths, and the (contemporary) racial melodrama will be of great importance for my reading of King's *The Girl Who Loved Tom Gordon*, my analysis differs from her (and Magistrale's) argument with respect to a key point: I argue that Tom Gordon

---

11 Note that the "Magical Negro," its characteristics, and instantiations are typically discussed in the academic field of Film Studies. Literary and Cultural Studies have not fully claimed the term (nor closely related terms such as "MAAF" or "Numinous Negro" [Brookhiser 32]) yet. The extensive discussion of film adaptations of Stephen King novels, however, is paving the way for scholars, such as Tony Magistrale, Nnedi Okorafor-Mbachu, and myself, to discuss King's fiction itself, by referring to the Magical Negro as a concept/motif active in different types of media.

does not represent just another instantiation of the Magical Negro but, rather, of an "Ebony Saint" conflated with the Gothic writing conventions of the Civil Hero. Note, however, that the link between King's depiction of an African American character and *Uncle Tom's Cabin* remains untouched: Tom Gordon's namesake, Uncle Tom, also cannot be labeled a "Magical Negro," but instead must be seen as the archetype of the Ebony Saint, which, however, does not eradicate the demeaning qualities of either racialized character.

The characters Sidney Poitier portrayed, especially in films like *The Defiant Ones* (1958), *The Heat of the Night* and *To Sir, With Love* (both 1967), but also as early as 1950 in his major film debut, *No Way Out*, are often referenced as "typifying the new Hollywood stereotype of the 1960s" (Verney 81), which film historian Daniel Leab dubbed "the ebony saint" (Leab 163). The Ebony Saint character conventionally is male, middle or lower middle class,

> and invariably intelligent, dignified and non-violent, often despite extreme provocation. Possessing no obvious personality flaws, he had a tolerance and understanding of the racist misconceptions of the whites who shared his environment. Saintliness had an added connotation in that the character usually had no visible sex life or desire to have one. (Verney 81)

While close to the Magical Negro motif, the Ebony Saint has no mystical, supernatural powers but is rather exclusively defined by his saintly, unflinching and unconditional love for the white protagonist he accompanies. The saintly characters Sidney Poitier portrayed in the mid-twentieth century debunk the myth of the dancing, musical, and happy black man that the Shirley Temple/Bill "Bojangles" Robinson films staged in the early twentieth century and, thus, replace comedy with drama and tap-dancing, with a notion of black suffering directly reminiscent of *Uncle Tom's Cabin*. Stressing this (melo)dramatic stance of Poitier's characters, K. Anthony Appiah asks, does

> the Saint draw[s] on the tradition of the superior virtue of the oppressed? Is there, in fact, somewhere in the Saint's background a theodicy that draws on the Christian notion that suffering is ennobling? So that the black person who represents undeserved suffering in the American imagination can also, therefore, represent moral nobility? Does the Saint exist to address the guilt of white audiences, afraid that black people are angry at them, wanting to be forgiven, seeking a black person who is not only admirable and lovable, but who loves white people back? (Appiah, "No Bad" 83)

Appiah's questions echo those that the African American playwright Clifford Mason posed about the popularity of "the same old Sidney Poitier syndrome"[12] (Mason n.p.) in *The New York Times* in 1967:

> And why do they love him [Sidney Poitier] so? Because he's a good actor? Partly. Because he's worked hard to get where he is? Maybe. Because he stands for a proud, black image, something all of us who are non-white have needed in this country for a long, long time? Nooooo. (Mason n.p.)

King himself—again, in the *Playboy*—has shown awareness for both his shortcomings in depicting non-stereotypical black characters in his fiction and for the controversies these texts have evoked since the late 1970s. Reflecting on the manifold criticism leveled against his writing, King reflects: "Both Hallorann, the cook in *The Shining*, and Mother Abagail in *The Stand* are cardboard caricatures of superblack heroes, viewed through rose-tinted glasses of white-liberal guilt" (Norden, 234). Again, King "recognize[s] the problems but can't yet rectify them" (Norden 234). Thus, for *The Girl Who Loved Tom Gordon*, we might take up Appiah's and Mason's inquisitive stances and ask: Why does the novel need a fictionalized Tom Gordon? Because he is so civil and heroic? Partly. Because Tom Gordon is the perfect role model for WASP girls? Maybe. Because he stands for an authentic Black image, something King's fiction has been lacking for a long, long time? Nooooo.

The Damsel, Tom Gordon, and the Civil Hero

When read in direct comparison to early WASP American Gothic novels, *The Girl Who Loved Tom Gordon* allows the 200 years between Charles Brockden Brown and Stephen King to fade into insignificance. With a high degree of precision, King's coming-of-age novel copies and blends structural plot elements of WASP American Gothic archetypes and thereby constructs the epitome of an innocent damsel in peril and en route from wilderness to civilization, from childhood to womanhood: The alienated nine-year-old Trisha McFarland becomes lost in the increasingly uncanny wilderness of the Maine-New Hampshire branch of the Appalachian Trail. Trisha constantly shimmers between compositional elements derived from the Gothic damsel and the literary *heilsgeschichte*, a conventional device that has controlled not only the quest of the protagonist, structuring the WASP American Gothic plot

---

12   Explained by Mason as "a good guy in a totally white world, with no wife, no sweetheart, no woman to love or kiss, helping the white man solve the white man's problem" and, with regard to both Poitier and Uncle Tom, further specified/denigrated as "a showcase nigger, who is given a clean suit and complete purity of motivation so that, like a mistreated puppy, he has all the sympathy on his side and all those mean whites are just so many Simon Legrees" (n.p.).

since Charles Brockden Brown's *Edgar Huntly*, but also that of innumerable protagonists in a multitude of text types since the mid-nineteenth century.

Trisha's original state, at the beginning of the novel, is defined by both civilization and alienation. Having recently experienced the divorce of her parents, she lives in Maine with her older brother Pete and her mother Quilla.[13] Inwardly, Trisha feels either like the "weak glue," (TG 8)[14] holding the torn family together, or like Marvel's "The Invisible Girl" (TG 17, 18); outwardly, she acts "like a contestant on a TV game show, all but peeing in her pants at the thought of winning a set of waterless cookware" (TG 8). Indeed, I understand her often remarked upon "oh-wow-it's-waterless-cookware" voice (TG 10, 14) as the perfect blend of contemporary suburban civilization and alienation, in the face of a breakdown of traditional core family structures. This original state is ruptured when Quilla, Pete, and Trisha go on one of their obligatory weekend trips, and Trisha, trying to avoid a fierce argument between her mother and her brother, leaves the beaten track of the Maine branch of the Appalachian Trail, stepping right into the Gothic wilderness.

Equipped with "a half-loaded knapsack" (TG 19) stuffed with artifacts of civilization (all in all, Trisha brings a rain poncho, a hardboiled egg, a tuna sandwich, some celery sticks, a small bag of chips, a bottle of water, a bottle of Surge lemonade, Twinkies, a Walkman, a Gameboy, and her Red Sox cap into the woods), the lost girl enters into a nightmarish world "of revulsion and horror" (TG 24) that is "full of everything you [don't] like, everything you [are] afraid of and instinctively loath, everything that [tries] to overwhelm you with nasty, no-brain panic" (TG 25). Trisha's entire quest, aimed at returning home but leading her deeper and deeper into the wilderness first, is marked by privation and sickness, frequent physical injuries, and constant fear, lapsing her into uncontrollable, "primitive" panic (TG 67); Trisha goes "[f]rom town girl to cave girl in one easy step" (TG 67).

King goes to great lengths and into great detail to portray Trisha's declension from youth and innocence into primitivism, wildness, and wilderness. What is more, he constructs this degeneration in overtly racial terms:

> [Trisha] applied mud for five minutes, finishing with a couple of careful dabs to the eyelids, then bent over to look at her reflection. What she saw in the relatively still water by the bank was a minstrel-show mudgirl by moonlight. Her face was a pasty gray, like a face of a vase pulled out of some archeological dig. Above it her hair stood up in a filthy spout. Her eyes were wide and wet and frightened.

---

13   Note that Mama Killa, Hispanicized "Quilla," according to Inca mythology is the goddess of the moon and the overseer of marriage and the well-being of women. We will see later how King connects her failing as wife and mother to Trisha's quest and her subsequent re-positioning within the family.

14   For clarity's sake, the in-text citations for Stephen King's *The Girl Who Loved Tom Gordon* are marked "TG."

> [...] Speaking to the face in the water, Trisha intoned: "*Then* Little Black Sambo said, 'Please, tigers, do not take my fine new clothes.'" (TG 94)

In a parody of adult femininity (that is, of a woman applying make-up), Trisha goes from white, clean suburb-girl to "minstrel-show mudgirl," and from innocent Shirley to the wild child minstrel archetype, Topsy, in the course of roughly ninety pages. That the nine-year-old girl envisions herself not only in the role of Topsy but also as "Little Black Sambo," the child-protagonist of Helen Bannerman's 1899 children's book *The Story of Little Black Sambo* (out of print, due to manifold allegations of racism since the 1940s), is not only implausible but in itself very problematic. By explicitly evoking male (Sambo) and female (Topsy) minstrel characters in the construction of Trisha, gender is effectively deleted from the episode and replaced by a pointed emphasis on race. Just as the minstrel tradition's derogatory motif of the "pickaninny" overwrites gender and individuality with race and homogeneity, King connects Trisha to Sambo/Topsy/pickaninny, to indicate his protagonist's degeneration to the wild child, a degeneration that King envisions in terms of racial decline. This decline, however, is rather playful. Trisha struggles with losing her grip of civilization, but she never becomes Topsy or Little Black Sambo; King never explicitly, syntactically or metaphorically contests her whiteness, by leaving the level of masquerade, of the "minstrel-show," to fully conflate her with either character. Rather, Trisha's minstrel episode marks both her nadir of primitivism and the negation of her (adult) white femininity. "As with all black performances, the performance is never about black people and black culture but rather about constructions of whiteness" (Hébert 185), as Kimberly G. Hébert states in her study of the minstrel tradition. In King's 1999 novel, the inclusion of a minstrel scene and characters also serves to reinforce King's construction of what will most not be Sambo/Topsy/pickaninny: the white and civil female Trisha McFarland. The minstrel also serves as King's introduction of Ebony Saint Tom Gordon.

Tom Gordon starts out as the "pretty good-looking" (TG 11) heartthrob of Red Sox fan Trisha, as "the handsomest man alive, and if he ever touched her hand she'd faint," and if he "ever kissed her, even on the cheek, [...] she'd probable die" (TG 11). King connects Trisha's constant daydreaming about Tom Gordon with her need to escape her broken home and the ever-present feeling of alienation, on the one hand, and with her budding sexuality on the other. However, when Trisha, lost in the woods, conjures up the familiar fantasy of Tom Gordon after her "minstrel-show," King has erased all sexual connotations from the picture. No longer dreaming about touching or kissing "the handsomest man alive," Trisha now passes "the time of day with Tom Gordon," chattering "away quite naturally, telling him which landmark she was heading for next, explaining to him that a fire had probably caused this swamp" (TG 123), until she "actually [sees] Tom Gordon for the first time" (TG 150). Running a fever and badly shaken by nausea and cramps, Trisha faces

Tom Gordon, standing "there in the moonlight, as clear as the cuts on her arm, as real as the nausea in her throat and belly" (TG 151). In a truly Gothic scene, Tom Gordon's perfect and content "stillness waiting for a sign" (TG 151) convinces the damsel to calm down, too, to "cool[...] and focus[...]" until the "shivers ease[...], then stop[...] entirely" (TG 152), allowing her to fall asleep calmly. It is utter weakness, a white child in peril and in pain and sickness, that calls forward the Ebony Saint. And it is the complete deletion of Tom Gordon's potentially dangerous B/blackness in the whitening moonlight that finally legitimizes the contact between a white girl and a Black man, within a tentative context marked by desexualization, whiteness, and a complete lack of physicality.

The thus legitimized relationship between Trisha and Tom Gordon, at this point of the narrative, resembles, to a striking extent, the "culturally tenuous relationship" (Greaves 178) of 1930s Shirley Temple and Bill Robinson films. The spectacle of an African American man arm-in-arm with a white female child "would almost certainly never have been permitted outside of innocuous and seemingly harmless depictions of screen song-and-dance routines" (Greaves 178). However, what should not be forgotten in this context is the fact that "[t]he same little girl who spent most of her film career in the arms and laps of white men never got closer to Robinson than a handshake" (duCille 17f.). While the 1935 film *The Little Colonel*—featuring the famous staircase scene of Shirley Temple and Bill Robinson tap-dancing up the stairs and toward the little girls bedroom—"was approved without eliminations by the Production Code Administration and various state and municipal boards" (Hatch 79), there are also documented reports "of their song-and-dance scenes being eliminated when screened in certain Southern towns" (Greaves 178). "Dazzling as the duet was for most Depression audiences, the sight of a black male and a white female holding hands—and heading for the bedroom, no less—imitated a relation so taboo that the dance sequence had to be cut from the film when played in southern cities" (duCille 17). It is the same racial taboo that controls King's construction of Tom Gordon.

The complete lack of physicality foreshadows Tom's ultimate unsuitability to fulfill the Gothic role of the Civil Hero and to ultimately save Trisha from the wilderness. While for King this aspect is presumably due to the imaginary quality of Tom, it also falls completely into the tradition of the Ebony Saint character and its associated tabooing of a (sexual/physical) relationship between a Black man and a white woman—let alone a white girl. I strongly believe that this implication in King's novel is not a coincidence but a plot-structuring device. Upon its climax—i.e. at the moment when the Civil Hero should step up and face (and overcome) the villain—Tom Gordon disappears and is replaced by a white male *Deus ex Machina* in a Red Sox T-shirt. Moving like "she'd learned on TV, watching Gordon" (TG 251) and using her Walkman, which "no longer felt like a Walkman [but] like a baseball" (TG 248), as "a weapon" (TG 251), Trisha pitches what in baseball broadcaster jargon is called "the heartbreaker, the serious bent cheese" (TG 251) and throws the "bear-thing" (TG 251) off balance, long enough for the *Deus ex Machina* ("*It's God's nature to come on in the bottom of the ninth*, Tom had told her" [TG 246, King's emphasis]) to step in and fire his gun. Travis Herrick chases the "fucking BEAR" (TG 254) away, "pick[s] her up" (TG 255), and carries her in his arms back to civilization, to the hospital, and to her family. In other words, it needs a white man with a gun, the very epitome of a racially white masculinity narrative, to save the damsel in distress. The gun must be read as "a cultural symbol of masculinity" (Cox 141) that signifies "being a good American" (Kohn 17), vis-à-vis the "male responsibility as fathers and husbands" (Kohn 106) to protect the family. The Ebony Saint Tom Gordon, who qua his race has been constructed as standing outside the realms of physical contact, interaction, and gun ownership, is now replaced completely by the white Civil Hero and relegated back into the realm of dreams and religious inspiration. Once more, King's Ebony Saint follows in the footsteps of Harriet Beecher Stowe's construction of characters such as Uncle Tom, Topsy, and the Harris family: Once the African American characters have fulfilled their function of supporting and fostering the construction and development of white characters, they are readily deleted from the plot. While Uncle Tom dies and Topsy and the Harris family are removed to Africa, Tom Gordon morphs back to being a girl's fantasy.

Let me point out that this renewed Ebony Saint fantasy is problematic in respects other than race and racialization as well. Tom Gordon accompanies and helps an increasingly frail Trisha to regain composure, on her quest through the wilderness and toward civilization. All the while, Tom is a dignified, faithful, asexual, and guiding entity that Trisha comes to accept as her very real "fulltime companion" (TG 204), who "no longer seem[s] especially miraculous" (TG 217) in the woods. He guides her toward civilization, by pointing out "a post" (TG 211), "a gate" (TG 213), "another post, girl" (217), and finally "an old woods road" (TG 219); most of all, however, he teaches her that "it's God's nature to come in on the bottom of the ninth" (first mentioned TG 185). True to the Ebony Saint character, Tom introduces (a baseball-tinted) religious faith into Trisha's quest, until the hostile wilderness, like the Red Sox stadium, seems "like a church congregation about to sing a hymn" (TG 81). He helps Trisha overcome manifold obstacles in her journey from a childhood of alienated passivity toward agency and survival; eventually, he inspires and motivates a form of ideal womanhood that Douglas E. Winter has fittingly termed "frontier Christianity" (58). Upon realizing that "[s]he was lost but would be found" (TG 85), and in good Gothic tradition, Trisha eventually faces the wilderness' archvillain, the God of the Lost—only to fall into the role of the damsel in distress and right into the comforting arms of a white man with a gun, who carries her back into civilization and into the midst of a recently reformed nuclear family.

Sick and too weak to speak, Trisha wakes up in a hospital bed, ready to face the other antagonist of her life, the alcoholism that has destroyed her father and their family ties. The prodigal daughter, who has found religious faith in a wilderness church of Tom Gordon, now saves her alcoholic father by tapping

> the visor of her cap, she point[s] her right index finger up to the ceiling. The smile which lit his face from the eyes down was the sweetest, truest thing she had ever seen. If there was a path, it was there. Trisha closed her eyes on his understanding and floated away into sleep. Game over. (TG 261–262)

Aside from the heavily racialized Ebony Saint character, this ending of the novel is problematic in at least two other respects. First, and this is the only criticism it has provoked thus far, King has constructed "a somewhat dangerous childhood fantasy—whose moral lesson is that if you run away, you can repair a broken home" (Arnzen 11). Secondly, and more importantly, at the point of arrival and belonging, the protagonist's white female identity is seemingly constructed as depending on the resurrection of the WASP nuclear family. On a closer look, however, this nuclear family is fully defined by the father, while Trisha's mother and brother are virtually absent from the closing hospital scene. Coming of age and womanhood are tied to the father at the center of the nuclear family and, thus, are firmly (re-)integrated into a patriarchal value system. Coming-of-age for Trisha means having passed through a process of religious education, physical hardship, desexualization, and racial purification, to a point where she can fill the vacant center of the traditional nuclear family, which her father's absence and her mother's inability to create a nurturing home have left. Tom Gordon, the Ebony Saint who temporarily replaces Trisha's absent father in her spiritual education, and the arch-villain of the wilderness have been overcome and left behind, in favor of white femininity and a WASP patriarchal family idyll. Instead of feeling like the "weak glue" (TG 8), holding the family together, Trisha has now become the moral and religious backbone of the reunited family, which, in King's fictional world, is the strongest glue imaginable. The infusion of the Ebony Saint into the Gothic plot, without a doubt, is the most fitting helpmate for this problematic salvation narrative.

The "Velvety-dark, Brown or Maybe Black" Thing in the Black Woods: King's Africanist Savage Villain

Following the conventions of WASP American Gothic further, King intensifies his white protagonist's quest, by introducing the Africanist Savage Villain as the unhumaned and sexualized conflation of B/blackness and wilderness.

The God of the Lost's "human feature" contains "arms," a "head," an "eye," and "a smiling mouth," partially hidden under a "black robe," and its hood (TG 170). Yet, "the creature" (TG 170, 249), "the thing" (TG 245, 246) is also always a "they," a loose assembly of countless wasps, of predatory claws that constantly shape-shift and that might hunt you down and feed on you as mosquitoes do, as wasps, as "a gazillion flies" (TG 127), as the biggest "fucking BEAR" (TG 254) in the history of the Appalachian Trail, or as "the lord of dark places, the emperor of understairs, every kid's worst nightmare" (TG 187). Note how King meanders between labels and names assigned to the Savage Villain. Aside from "the God of the Lost," Trisha most frequently refers to the Savage Villain as "the wasp-priest" (first TG 171). With this label, King not only summarizes the one-yet-many paradoxical natures traditionally inherent in the villainous embodiment of the wilderness, but he also reconnects his villain to the traditional British Gothic and its obsession with uncanny "black-robe[s]" (TG 170) and lascivious clerics. Thus, his Savage Villain indeed becomes the drawing-board version of "every kid's worst nightmare" (TG 187), a conflation of the key attributes of conventional (British and WASP American) Gothic villainy. Utilizing the traditional WASP Savage Villain, King lets his protagonist synthetize one named villain out of the innumerable hardships she faces, in a wilderness that has gone from "the woods in a Disney cartoon" (TG 64) to a nightmarish "yellowish and tallow" darkness of "things long drowned" (TG 122), and from a late twentieth-century hiking trip to a bleak survival scenario.

Indeed, King's God of the Lost is not only a conflated image of Gothic wilderness but one of B/blackness directly reminiscent of the B/black wilderness that Tsalal Arthur Gordon Pym finds himself in. From the very beginning of Trisha's journey onward, King paints the wilderness black. Trisha is entrapped in "a black orbiting universe of bugs" (TG 116), of "black moths" (TG 200), "black butterflies" (TG 210), "shining black mud" (TG 116), "black earth" (TG 188), "black water" (TG 122, 127), and of "black eyes" (TG 125), watching and pursuing her constantly. The omnipresent black wilderness smears Trisha's clothes, dyes her shoes and socks black but leaves her "white skin" (TG 121) untainted. The racial overtones in this color-coded construction of wilderness versus civilization, of the threatening annihilation of innocent whiteness in the realms of savage B/blackness, are palpable and, indeed, very close to the construction of the Island of Tsalal in Poe's *Pym*. Consider, in this respect, the direct foreshadowing of Trisha's encounter with the one embodiment of the black wilderness, the Savage Villain, when she is faced with a "fat black snake" early on in her journey:

> She looked down and saw a fat black snake slithering through the leaves. For a moment every thought in her mind disappeared into a silent white explosion of revulsion and horror. Her skin turned to ice and her throat closed. She could not even think the single word *snake* but only feel it, coldly pulsing under her warm hand. Trisha shrieked and tired to bolt to her feet, forgetting that she wasn't yet in the clear. A stump of branch thick as an amputated forearm poked agonizingly into the small of her back. She went flat on her stomach again and wriggled out from under the tree as fast as she could, probably looking a bit like a snake herself. The nasty thing was gone, but her terror lingered. (TG 24)

The color-coding of this episode is clearly racialized and racializing: The "black snake" causes a "white explosion of revulsion and horror;" upon touching the "nasty thing," its coldness sinks into Trisha's white "skin" and turns the girl "a bit [into] a snake herself." As if a textbook case of the Gothicized abject, King constructs an unhumaned, thingified B/blackness, which—despite being a "nasty thing" only—can infect the white girl via skin contact, rendering her "a bit like a snake." We already know how this first contact with a B/black terror- and revulsion-inspiring body will develop: Trisha will go from civil city girl to minstrel showgirl, from Shirley to "a bit like" Topsy. What must be noted in this foreshadowing scene, too, is the sexual connotation of a white girl who, crawling over the ground, feels "something move under her," notices a "fat black snake slithering through the leaves," and feels "the nasty thing," "coldly pulsing under her warm hand" (TG 24). King creates a claustrophobic Gothic scene in which a white female child is preyed upon by a B/black sexual predator, who lurks in waiting to attack and force himself on her. When the "nasty thing" is "gone," it is never gone for good but only out of sight. Trisha already is surrounded by the "[g]ross-gross-gross" (TG 120) predatory B/blackness of the "woods [that are] full of them." Still meandering between B/black terror and white revulsion and disgust, King again starts to oscillate between the personal pronoun "it" and "they" ("What if *they* were poisonous? What if the woods were full of them?" [TG 25, emphasis in the original]), to refer to "[t]he nasty thing," already implying the omnipresent racial threat of the one-but-many Africanist Savage Villains.

King constructs the Africanist Savage Villain as inspiring a claustrophobic feeling of being watched by a B/black (sexual) predator, by "something with slumped shoulders [...] with black eyes and great cocked ears like horns" (TG 225) that will "draw a circle around" you, to mark you as "property" (TG 227), and that might look like "a fully grown North American black bear" (TG 244), but that clearly "wasn't a bear" (245); "[i]t wasn't human; nor did she think it was an animal" (TG 225). What it is, though, is the B/black thing: It is "[t]he thing that wasn't a bear," "[t]he thing that looked like a bear," the "thing," the "creature," "it" that never loses its "velvety-dark, brown or maybe black" appearance (TG 165), its "black eyes, big and inhuman" (TG 228), its "tan muzzle" (TG 245). King's Africanist Savage Villain might display randomly "the face of teachers and friends [...], the face of parents and brothers," the face of the rapist, "of the man who might come and offer you a ride" (TG 250); yet, its essential otherness is never blurred or complicated. The God of the Lost, "the figure in the middle" of the wilderness, "[is] black" (TG 167), that is, a racially contained, abject evil. Given the stability and racial irreconcilability of the Savage Villain, white Trisha, even during her wildest episodes, never risks becoming one with the surrounding B/black wilderness.

This Gothicized abject has two profound impacts on the text. First, it is, just like the appearance of Tom Gordon, dependent on the white damsel's failing health: The weaker Trisha gets, the more real and the more savage the God of the Lost becomes. Second, Trisha might see herself confronted with "a double row of huge, green-stained teeth" (TG 245), but the villain she faces is actually the most toothless evil entity in King's fictional world. Without any physical contact or real interaction, it is the epitome of distress and pursuit that a white Gothic damsel might be subjected to. The omnipresent threat of the B/black un-humaned predatory thing, pursuing the female white child, is very palpable and constitutes the claustrophobic undercurrent of the novel. At the same time, King's construction of the Africanist Savage Villain takes the complete lack of Black physicality of the Ebony Saint to the extreme. In the end, the Savage Villain is a racialized pseudo-evil, a both sickness-induced and sickness-inducing nightmare that can be overcome by a nine-year-old white girl, throwing a Walkman, and a white hippie firing a warning shot. Thus, it is first and foremost a racialized negative foil against the development and the coming-of-age of the white protagonist. Trisha's victory over the B/black savage wilderness both reflects and concludes her development from a sexual pubescent wild child to a desexualized white frontier Christian, thus rendering her "a woman instead of a child" (TG 200). This white woman has matured, by successfully dodging and mastering the two virulent B/black threats to her sexuality: the saintly Black lover figure and the savage Black (sexual) predator.

This victorious conclusion of her quest toward white womanhood and familial belonging is staged by King as a clash of wilderness versus civilization and of B/blackness versus baseball narrative. And this is the point where the underlying WASP discursive practice of unhumanization and thingification of the Black person into an abject becomes once more clearly palpable. In order to re-create the ideal WASP American core family with the white frontier Christian woman at its center, King constructs the white female coming-of-age narrative as a discursive battle with the Africanist Savage Villain. It is also a discursive standoff between "a white man's game by design" (Bryant, "Don't Expect" n.p.)[15] and its frequent narrative associations with WASP American civilization, quite fittingly since baseball is the sport that is broadly known as WASP America's national pastime and "national religion" (famously coined by Morris R. Cohen in 1919) and a Blackness discursively rendered as an unhumanized abject. The defeat of the "bear-thing" (TG 247) and the survival of Trisha, that is, also the superiority of the WASP values and cultural systems over the threatening Black body, are never really at stake and contested; they are racially predetermined and contained.

---

15 The Boston Red Sox have a long history of racism and of being recognized as a "racist franchise" (Bryant, *Shut Out* 113). Noteworthy is that the Boston Red Sox were the last major league baseball team to integrate their roster. The first African American infielder (Pumpsie Green) was admitted into the roster as late as 1959 and "[e]ven after signing Pumpsie Green, Boston's pace of integration was painfully slow. Black players in Boston faced hostility and racism in doses unexpected from a city known for its abolitionist roots" (Grigsby 92).

The utilization of the baseball motif, within the discursive battle against an omnipresent threat of B/blackness and for the re-creation of King's version of a WASP family idyll, can also be traced on a meta-fictional level. King structures the reading experience parallel to the way the protagonist structures her reality—as a baseball game. *The Girl Who Loved Tom Gordon* stages the transformation of Trisha (from alienated girl via the wild child to a desexualized, Christian-conservative notion of womanhood) not in chapters, but in innings, and "the reading process, as spectator sport, echoes the themes and issues of the book" (Arnzen 11). Not just another instance of "King's children [...] who must cling to their youthful idealism and romantic innocence [...] under fierce attack in his fiction from the oppressive forces of societal institutions" (Figliola 146), this meta-fictional stance is directed at a target audience of young adults and wavers itself between educational impetus and quasi-religious conversion.

By motivating the plot through the Savage Villain/Civil Hero Gotheme, King's novel also teaches a "subaudible" (e.g., TG 169) lesson of racial denigration and white abjectorship. For Trisha's quest toward familial belonging and civilization, as well as for his construction of a popular Gothicized baseball novel for a young readership, King relies on traditional WASP Gothic conventions and fully iterates their racial qualities. *The Girl Who Loved Tom Gordon* centers upon the protagonist's quest, accompanied and nurtured by the Ebony Saint Tom Gordon, toward civilization and the ultimate battle with the embodiment of wilderness and Africanized savagery. Constructed with the stability and racial irreconcilability of the WASP Gothic's Savage Villain but exposed as an ultimately toothless B/black "thing," King's Africanist Savage Villain functions as the "abnormal [...] allowed center stage solely as a foil to the cultural order, which will ultimately be vindicated by the end of the fiction" (Carroll 199).

Throughout his novel, King iterates racial denigration (think of the Ebony Saint, Little Black Sambo, Topsy, and the references to "the Indians" [TG 5, 7, 254]) and matter-of-factly instantiates white abjectorship and the hegemonic power structures underlying the dire race hierarchies in the United States. I, therefore, strongly argue against approaches to King's representations of race that romanticize King as being "naturally" drawn to the "racial stereotypes of eighteenth- and nineteenth-century American literature [that] held much appeal for a writer who identifie[s] himself, artistically and politically, with outsiders" (Figliola 145). In an enticing coming-of-age narrative for young adults, King iterates and reinforces racial stereotypes and discourses of racial denigration, hierarchization, and exclusion. King's fictional defense, his "feminist-inspired" account of a strong girl accompanied by a real- yet larger-than-life black character,[16] is thus thrown into reverse, there-

---

16   King, in his "Author's Postscript" to *The Girl Who Loved Tom Gordon*, assures us that "[t]here is a real Tom Gordon, who does indeed pitch in the closer's role for the Boston Red Sox" and who

by fueling the arguments of critics such as Spike Lee, Sarah Nilsen, and Nnedi Okorafor-Mbachu.

By now, we can tie this type of criticism to King's reliance on the Savage Villain/Civil Hero Gotheme, that is, more generally speaking, to the writing conventions of the late eighteenth- and early nineteenth-century WASP American Gothic. By iterating the Gotheme for his constructions of the damsel, hero, and villain, King also iterates the racialized denigration and white abjectorship conventional to it. *The Girl Who Loved Tom Gordon* might have been set out as King's reaction to allegations of racism and misogyny, but it/he effectively adds fictional representation strategies often connected to Shirley Temple (gender/age/innocence) and to Sidney Poitier (race/gender/Ebony Saint), to a Poesque instantiation of the Africanist Savage Villain/Civil Hero Gotheme, within a coming-of-age narrative, targeting a young WASP readership. Instead of taking a step forward, King therefore took two steps backward.

At this point in my survey, the outstanding consistency of conventional early WASP American Gothic writing strategies in contemporary WASP American fiction is noteworthy, but it might be dismissed as a single author's inability—or unwillingness—to produce texts that go beyond the Gothic's sensationally dreadful entertainment value, without reflecting on and reinforcing racism. In the following discussion of Karen Russell's 2011 novel, *Swamplandia!*, the question of whether the consistency of the racialized WASP American Gothic writing strategies is indeed conventional and, thus, potentially changeable, or whether these strategies are essential to the Gothic and, much like the rules to a game, definitory and invariable, moves center-stage.

4.3 "Monster: Half Woman and Half Invention"—Karen Russell's *Swamplandia!*

In many respects, surprisingly close to *The Girl Who Loved Tom Gordon*, Karen Russell's Pulitzer Prize-nominated 2011 debut novel *Swamplandia!* also sends young adults on perilous journeys, straight into the Gothic wilderness of contemporary America. Just as King, Russell closely adheres to Gothic writing conventions and completely iterates the Savage Villain/Civil Hero Gotheme; unlike *The Girl Who Loved Tom Gordon*, however, *Swamplandia!* instantiates a self-reflective meta-perspective

---

"recorded forty-four saves to lead the American League" in 1998 (TG 263). Hereby, King might circumscribe the fallacy of creating yet another Magical Negro character, but it does not protect him from fictionalizing Tom Gordon, to a point where he blends with the characters that Sidney Poitier portrayed in mid-twentieth-century Hollywood productions.

that sets out to qualify the WASP American Gothic's biases within a feminist coming-of-age narrative. Reading Russell's novel with a focus on the iteration of the SV/CH Gotheme, the subversive potential and the limits of this writing strategy become most apparent: *Swamplandia!* exploits the Gothic's tilted and gendered power balance, to create a powerful feminist message "in the face of post-feminist myths of equality" (Graham 589), and, at the same time and for the same end, it reinforces discourses of race and the Black abject linked to the SV/CH Gotheme.

Set in the eponymous "Number One Gator-Themed Park and Swamp Café" (S 5)[17] in the Florida Everglades, *Swamplandia!* centers upon the Bigtree family moving in and out of crises. Following the death of Hilola Bigtree, beloved matriarch, star alligator wrestler, and tourist magnet, and faced with financial ruin, the male family members move to mainland Florida, in order to find new means of income, while the two girls, namely the thirteen-year-old protagonist Ava and her older sister Osceola, remain alone in the now desolated theme park. One after the other, the girls follow two Gothicized men (the apparitions of a long-deceased dredge worker and the dubious Bird Man) into the wilderness of the Everglades and into the brutality of the dominating patriarchy.

In his 2012 article, "Absurdist Narratives in the Sunshine State: Comic, Criminal, Folkloric, and Fantastic Escapades in the Swamps and Suburbs of Florida," Jason Marc Harris first notices *Swamplandia!*'s manifold meta-fictional moves and discusses the motifs, genres, and rhetoric strategies of folklore that are in opposition to "fakelore" (Harris 57) in Russell's novel. Significantly stretching Harris' line of argument, Lori Cornelius ("Into the Swamp: An Examination of Folk Narrative Structures and Storylines in Karen Russell's *Swamplandia!*") conflates local Floridian folklore with the Grimm brothers' fairy tales, outlining consistencies with "Little Red Riding Hood," "Snow White," and "Hansel and Gretel."

Rather than emphasizing the meta-fictional and intertextual moves, Robert Ziegler, Michael K. Walonen, Tammy Powley, and Caren Irr place *Swamplandia!*'s setting center-stage and contextualize the wilderness of the Ten Thousand Islands' water and mangroves labyrinth with the "terra incognita of the psyche," reminiscent of Joseph Conrad and James Dickey (Ziegler 8); the motif of the theme park as a meaningful site where late capitalism "can be confronted—intellectually at the very least" (Walonen 269); stereotypical images of Florida past and present (Powley); or, with the genre of the New Green Novel which, placed at the intersection of the Anglophone political novel and literary nature writing, is used by Irr, to analyze the gendered settings of *Swamplandia!* (i.e. the opposition of the male, hyper-capitalist "World of Darkness" theme park and the female, family-run tourist trap "Swamplandia"). Adding to the importance of the setting in *Swamplandia!*, Sarah Graham,

---

17 All in-text quotations and references marked "S" refer to Karen Russell's *Swamplandia!*.

in "Unfair Ground: Girlhood and Theme Parks in Contemporary Fiction," also argues that the gendered theme parks of *Swamplandia!* function as microcosms of American society, as they reproduce the heteronormativity of gender and sexuality imposed on young adults today. By showing how Russell constructs heteronormativity as being irresistible for her protagonist, Graham argues that the novel points to the continuing importance of feminism in presumed post-feminist times (Graham 589). Last but not least, by including *Swamplandia!* into his brief outlook of contemporary American environmental Gothic novels, i.e. of recent novels that stand "at the nexus between […] two literary modes," the American Gothic and environmental literature, Matthew Wynn Sivils is the first scholar to notice, if not analyze, the novel's adherence to Gothic writing conventions. Following Sivils' lead, in addition to drawing on Graham's feminism thesis and placing Russell's iteration of the SV/CH Gotheme center-stage in my reading of *Swamplandia!*, I can unlock the novel's complex negotiations of Gothicized gender and race depictions. More specifically, I suggest imagining the SV/CH Gotheme in *Swamplandia!* as a tree split into two main branches: (i.) a Gothicized gender branch and (ii.) a Gothicized race branch.

 i. The Gothicized gender branch grows out of the novel's precise copying of the Gothic's conventional "damsel in distress" motif. Indeed, over the course of the novel, Russell constructs three damsels with different chances at survival.

 Osceola, the protagonist's older but "weak" sister (S 194), "was born snowy—not a weak chamomile blond but pure frost, with eyes that vibrated between maroon and violet" and looks "like the doomed sibling you see in those Wild West daguerreotypes," the one who makes you think, "*Oh God, take the picture quick; that kid is not long for this world*" (S 6, Russell's emphasis). Thus, when the very white and "very beautiful" (S 26) Ossie starts contacting and dating ghosts who "enter her," "moving through her, rolling into her hips," and make her "do a jerky puppet dance under her blankets" (S 34), until she longs for "a place called the underworld" (S 20), no member of the mourning Bigtree family is surprised or concerned. When Ossie, however, falls in love with Louis Thanksgiving, a long deceased "dredgeman from Clarinda, Iowa" (S 88), and runs off with him to get married in the swamps of the Everglades, the mood changes "in a finger snap" (127), and Ava sets out to find her. Consistent with the Gothic plot, Ossie is not found and saved by Ava, but by her brother, "Kiwi Bigtree, World Hero" (207), and his flight instructor, Mr. Pelkins. For constructing Ossie as a damsel in distress, tempted into "a small nocse" (S 301) by a ghost, Russell utilizes the early WASP American Gothic fake villain motif—villainous Louis turns out to be the very definition of "the most good-natured boy" (S 106), who has "no problems with any man alive, black, white, or Indian" (S 105)—to set into motion the real pursuit of the novel's main damsel, thirteen-year-old Ava Bigtree.

Ava, "World Champion Alligator Wrestler, [...] strong as ten men, ferocious," is used to playing "the hero" (S 177, note the masculine noun), and when she starts her quest to retrieve her sister from the death-grip of her ghostly fiancé and from the perilous swamp, the reader, just as Ava herself, is tempted into envisioning her as the Gothic's Civil Hero, ready to step in and save the day. Upon understanding that Ava's and the reader's association of and interaction with the standard motif of the questing hero "ha[s] been a big hoax" (S 271) and set "a green trap for us" (S 261), the protagonist is put most violently into the damsel's place: She is raped by the Savage Villain, the Bird Man. Adventurous "Ava Bigtree of the Bigtree Wrestling Dynasty" (S 63) is brutally forced into womanhood (her embarrassment and disgust "grow acutest in that one spot: [...] *Your legs are still hairy, he'll think you're a kid*," S 262, original emphasis) and subdued into passivity, rendering "a string you could pluck, 'A-va'" (S 263). Following the motif's convention, Ava escapes the villain, but only to be chased by him through "the most treacherous part of the swamp" (S 271), until he is once more "grinning at [her]" (S 304). After escaping a second time, Ava is finally rescued by two hunters, Harry and Trumbull, a two-headed *deus ex machina* that looks "a little like Superman, or Superman's sort of squirrelly twin" (S 307).

The third damsel in distress in *Swamplandia!* is Kiwi Bigtree. While this might not only sound counterintuitive but also contradictory to my description of him, as the savior of damsel Osceola above, we need to take into account that Kiwi starts his quest and rise in The World of Darkness theme park not as "Kiwi Bigtree, World Hero" (207) but as the frequently picked-on "Margaret or Margie" (S 62, short for "Margaret Mead," S 61), who earns "$5.75 an hour to work as part of an army of teenage janitors" (S 62) and who requires "[w]omen's size medium!" (S 67) to cover his "girlish hips" (S 220). Russell sets Kiwi on a journey, ironically paralleling the journeys of Ossie and Ava, by means of over-the-top allusions to the Gothic's damsel fate. Kiwi, for example, feels constantly intimidated by the "squeal of mainland girls' laughter—a wolf pack howling for blood on an open glacier would have been less terrifying, the bellow of a thousand Seths would be a lullaby" (S 165). He learns mainland behavior by "snipers tutor[ing him] on the limits of the prison yard" (S 70), and he might very well be "slated for death in a midnight raid" (S 65). Unlike his sisters, whose fates, in many respects, "underline the dangers of complacency inspired by the illusion of empowerment" (Graham 602), Kiwi can quickly attain masculinity and agency. Moving up in the World of Darkness hierarchy, he is promoted to lifeguarding first and, after having saved a girl's life, then to pilot training. When the flightless bird "Kiwi" finally takes to the sky, he triumphantly rescues his sister not only from the swamp but also from her likely death, thus sealing his status as hero, angel, and man. Kiwi's metamorphosis from damsel to hero, while his sisters are most violently put into the damsel's place, highlight, in Graham's words, "the disparity in the experience of growing up" (Graham 604). While Kiwi finds support and elevation in his strife for self-realization and agency, Ava and Ossie find themselves disempowered, traumatized, and on antidepressant drugs.

While the growing-up of the three teenagers in *Swamplandia!* indeed takes place on the "unfair ground" (Graham 589) that is typical for the Gothic plot and character structure, this tilted hierarchy is not the novel's final note. The gender branch of the SV/CH Gotheme provides a fictionalized water-level report of gender equality and female empowerment myths, thereby blossoming into a powerful feminist warning message, in times of a "stalled revolution" defined by the continuous "resurgence" of traditional Western gender ideologies (Walter 9, 11).

By the end of her quest, and in the very last paragraph of the novel, Ava effectively leaves the damsel's role behind and starts her lifelong quest as an adult woman: "[T]he show really must go on. Our Seths are still thrashing inside us in an endless loop" (S 316). If we understand Russell's "Seths" as being a blend of alligators, wrestling show, and godlike masculinity,[18] we can read Ava's continuous battle with her internalized Seths as a battle of resistance against the patriarchally tinted gender ideologies that aim at disempowering and silencing her. Even more, we can understand *Swamplandia!* as Ava's first-person autobiographical testimony of her otherwise silenced quest ("*No, I don't have to tell a soul about this*, I promised myself," S 263) that she throws at us, with the same vigor that she throws her red Seth at the Bird Man. On a meta-fictional level, Russell's novel of active resistance to patriarchal ideologies is pitched at her readership and into the U.S. book market to claim and add a female voice among a literary environment of what Deborah O'Keefe calls "good girl messages" (O'Keefe 4) and what I have termed "frontier Christianity" in *The Girl Who Loved Tom Gordon* above. Russell lays open and deconstructs the fictionalization of conservative moral instructions that aim at fostering an agreed-upon standard for female behavior.

ii. The three paralleled Gothicized quests for adult identity and agency are also quests into family history and identity. When integrated, however, into the broader context of WASP American Gothic writing strategies, we can decode how Russell encodes this family history and, thus, the departure point for the Bigtree children, exclusively in racial terms. The "family, the Bigtree tribe of the Ten Thousand Islands" (S 5) has "not a drop of Seminole or Miccosukee blood" (S 5) in its veins, but, clad in "buckskin vests, cloth headbands, great blue heron feathers, great white heron feathers, chubby beads hanging of [their] foreheads and [their] hair in braids, gator 'fang' necklaces" (S 5), the self-proclaimed tribe members are their "own Indians" in "Indian" costumes. The fake identity, originally created as a means of economic survival by grandfather Sawtooth, also known as "Ernest Schedrach, the

---

18   Seth (or Set) is the name of an ancient Egyptian god. "In myth, Seth takes the form of many different animals, such as bulls, pigs, hippopotami, wild asses, crocodiles, and panthers, to carry out destructive acts" (Pinch 162).

white son of a white coal miner in Ohio" (S 24), has become part of the family's lived identity. It determines the name choices for the father, known only as "Chief Bigtree," and of Osceola, who "is named for a Seminole chieftain" (S190), meaning either for the actual early nineteenth-century Seminole leader, or for the manifold adaptations of the historic figure, especially in the twentieth century. *Swamplandia!* positions the faking of "Indian" identity and history for economic reasons as the epitome of alienation and political incorrectness, and it is a fair guess to expect a novel that is conscious of the problematic cultural appropriations, behind the widespread and highly topical "going Indian" phenomenon,[19] to reiterate the traditionally racialized SV/CH Gotheme in a way that consciously renegotiates race and racial denigration.

In fact, the hints at this reiteration process are manifold. Let us consider, for example, the description of the uncanny dredge's first appearance: "This is a pretty boring massacre," said my sister. "When is lunch?" I was stirring the bucket of vitreous poisons when I looked up and saw the shape: something black, liquefying and resolving behind the reddish grain of pines. [...] I thought it might be a house of some kind" (S 77). Everything in this brief passage deserves the label "American Gothic": the fake but foreshadowing "massacre," the sudden rupture in the girls' play, caused by seeing "a shape" constructed in the typical black and red color-coding we have discussed in great detail above, the possibility of a haunted house in the middle of the pine forest. Quickly, however, Ossie realizes that "[i]t's a boat after all, Ava..." (S 77), and the Gothicized encounter is qualified as a girlish fantasy only.

Read in the context of the SV/CH Gotheme, this passage triggers at least three questions: Does Ava's Gothic fantasy, fueled by "the galloping da-dum, ba-dum of the Tennyson and Edgar Allan Poe poems that [she] had once memorized" (S 265), include the racialized color code? In other words, does Russell qualify and reiterate the racialized convention as a persistent but childish fantasy? Or, does this passage rather iterate the well-known color-coding, for the sake of creating the entertaining chill factor the Gothic is known and loved for, without reflecting on the racialized conventions it therefore employs? To answer these questions, let me consider the climax of *Swamplandia!*, which is also the peak of the self-reflexive qualification of Gothicized narrative elements within the narrative: Russell's successive construction and deconstruction of the Savage Villain.

Constructed as the fascinating but ultimately dreadful chimera of bird and man, i.e., of wilderness and patriarchy, the Bird Man is first introduced as blended into the swamp's wilderness:

---

19   Cf. *Going Indian: Cultural Appropriation in Recent North American Literature* (2012) by Judit Ágnes Kádár.

> When I looked up again I saw something high in the trees: two shoes. Two burgundy boot toes [...], when tracked backward with my flashlight beam, sprouted two thin legs. Above these I found a feathered torso, and added to this a puffy white face which—compared to the boots and the patchwork outfit—looked almost ordinary. The man was blinking violently down at me, caught in the light, his pale lips twisted in a grimace. [...] "Jesus, kid, get that out of my face." (S 128)

Russell's writing strategy here is very close to the strategy employed when introducing the potentially haunted dredge. The tension built, by means of Gothic writing conventions (a damsel on her own, the sudden detection of being watched in the dark, an uncanny and not-quite-human onlooker), is ruptured and qualified by the man's addressing of Ava and his outspoken normalcy. Instead of focusing on his sudden and fantastic appearance any further, Ava apologizes, and the Gothic is deleted from the following contextualization of the Bird Man as a paid for, "avian pied piper[...], or aerial fumigator[...]" (S 129), who might be able to lure the girl, with the "rainbow sound" (S 129) of his bird call, yet he no longer frightens either her or us. Upon climax, it is the apparent normalcy of the Bird Man, the realization "that the Bird Man could be anybody" (S 244), that he is clad in a "crazy person's disguise" (S 246), only to cover up his most horrible nature that effectively triggers Ava's flight—"[t]he Bird Man is just a man, honey" (S 264, original emphasis). By bringing the blend of a bird and a man and of wilderness and patriarchy full circle here, it is tempting to integrate Ava's traumatic encounter with the pedophilic Bird Man into our discussion of the gender branch of the SV/CH Gotheme. However, this move alone would not suffice to account for the manifold and explicit racialized ascriptions that Russell has included in her construction of the Savage Villain.

The racialization of Russell's Bird Man shimmers in unison with Ava's changing perception of him. Ava notices his "puffy white face" (S 128) and his beak- or blade-like nose (S 148) and that the Bird Man's "unwashed and wobbly" (S 244) appearance remains mostly hidden under his black hat and the "heavy, tussocked coat" of black feathers (S 129). At first, this renders him, in her eyes, "a gypsy" (S 129), i.e., it firmly situates him in a framework of racist stereotypes connected to the Romani people.[20] Russell, however, revokes and qualifies this initial ascription

---

20   The racial stereotypes connected to the Romani (or Roma) people today have been traced back to Victorian and modern British literature, where "gypsies" with "sinister occult and criminal tendencies" (Bardi 65) are closely connected to thievery, child abduction, and murder (MacKay 35); the English Renaissance and baroque theatre also employ "elements of outlandish charm and elements which depict (the Romani people) as the lowest of social outcasts," as blended with "magic and charms," and as "juggling and cozening" (Pugliatti 293,294,295). Even more, as Celia Esplugas (152 ff.) informs us, the Romani people are depicted as provocative, sexually available, gaudy, exotic, and mysterious, in a vast variety of European cultural productions (e.g. opera, literature, and popular music).

quickly: "This Bird Man was not what I'd expected a Bird Man to be; for starters, he was very kind. He did not conform to any of the common stereotypes of his profession: redneck exterminators, mangrove gypsies, backwoods ornithologists, black magicians, feathered druids, scam artists" (S 132). As if ticking ascriptions of this list, Ava subsequently connects the Bird Man to "War Chief Osceola" and the curse of the "still haunted swamp": "If the Great Spirit will show me how, I will make the white man red with blood; and then blacken him in the sun and rain … and the buzzard live upon his flesh" (S 191). Accompanying the Bird Man into this Gothicized version of a "'real' Indian's" curse (S 191) and into the swamp, in search of the "underworld"—the "gateway to the world of the ghosts," fittingly a fantastic "Indian landmark" (S 119)—means entering the wilderness of "the Black Woods" (S 150), where not only the trees are of "a dark variety" (S 196), but this part of the swamp is also the home of the B/black "island bogeyman" (S 287), Mama Weeds, the "female monster" (S 287), who might have "started life as a real woman, Midnight Drouet, a light-skinned black seamstress descended from freed slaves who lived in the Ten Thousand Islands" (S 287), but who now haunts "the most treacherous part of the swamp" (S 271) to avenge her murder.

Like Russell's construction of the Bird Man, Mama Weeds is a blend of gender and wilderness; and very much like the racialized ascriptions of the Savage Villain, Mama Weeds is blended into the treacherous swamp by means of Gothic racialization. Let us consider the following passage of Ava's "battle with Mama Weeds" (S 291), keeping in mind both Russell's strategy of successively calling up and deconstructing Gothic conventions and the question of whether the utilized racialization of the conventions used is effectively deconstructed as well:

> Our eyes met. I looked up, still swaying from my fistfuls of the stolen dress. What I saw inside them was all landscape: no pupil or colored hoop of iris but the great swamp—the islands, the saw-grass prairies. Long grasses seemed to push onward for miles inside the depths of her eyes. Inside each oval I saw a world of saw grass and no people. Believe me—I know how that must sound. But I stood there and I watched as feathery clouds blew from her left eye behind the bridge of her nose and appeared again in her right socket. I saw a nothing that rolled forward forcefully forever. There was nobody in the ether of either white sky. I heard the wind on the pond all around us, a deep clay smell rising from her skin. When she blinked again, her eyes looked black and oily, ordinary. For years I've wondered if this person I met was only a woman. (S 290)

The duel composition of Mama Weeds as both an extended, "grabb[ing]" (S 290) arm of the Gothic wilderness and a Black "nobody," who's empty B/blackness in the depths of her eyes is reminiscent of "no people" and no humanity, must be read as an epitome of racialized WASP American Gothic writing strategies and can easily be placed into the tradition of Africanized villainous savagery and the

Gothicized abject. While the Gothic effect again is quickly drained from the picture and Mama Weeds rendered "ordinary" and "only a woman," the racialization (again) of the character remains: "[H]er eyes looked black and oily," which is apparently not only "ordinary" for Black women but reconnects her most visibly to the black "oily feathers" (S 147, 207) of the Bird Man's odd attire.

By reading the peculiar setting of the Black Woods, together with its two chief instantiations of Gothic villainy—Mama Weeds and the rapist Bird Man—a much more static racialization of savage villainy in *Swamplandia!* becomes visible. Villainy in Russel's novel is B/black. In most parts of the novel, the Africanist presence hovers over the plot "in implication, in sign, in line of demarcation" (Morrison *Playing* 46/47); at times, it hides readily behind a "puffy white face," before coming powerfully to the fore with Mama Weeds, or when the Bird Man is re-imagined as looking "like a huge crow intelligently attacking a piece of metal," as if he stepped out of a nineteenth-century Jim Crow caricature. While the Bird Man is demystified as "*just a man*" (S 264) when he rapes Ava, the act itself is related to "the black-and-white palette" (S 260) of the Gothic's racial binary: "The man" is accompanied by "the black millions" surrounding Ava, quickly turning her world "into a black kaleidoscope" (S 261), while Ava's thoughts run in circles around her weakness ("like a tourist girl"), pain, and the "very very white" stars of her memory (S 263). Upon her flight, the predatory Bird Man, one with the Black Woods he so readily navigates, pursues Ava, whose whiteness in the treacherous black wilderness lets her stand out like an "albino Seth in the wild" (S 269), thereby rendering her fair prey to the B/black villainous forces surrounding her. This Africanized villainy is never qualified or rendered a matter of perspective in the novel. Rather, it is constructed as the key source of horror, disgust, and claustrophobic entrapment that the protagonist must endure and survive, until the civil "heroes" (S 307) finally save her and return her to white civilization, that is, to blushing rangers, other white supermen, to "Kiwi, Ossie, and an older white couple" (S 309).

In sum, *Swamplandia!* iterates the WASP American Gothic's SV/CH Gotheme within a feminist coming-of-age narrative. It also iterates the Gotheme's heavily racialized structure and, thus, positions itself as a counter-narrative not only into a patriarchal canon of "good girl messages" (O'Keefe 4) but also into a literary history of racial denigration and outspoken racism. Unlike the gendered conventionality of the Gothic, this aspect of the iteration process happens outside of Russell's metafictional stance and, thus, dodges reflection.

Taking this reading of *Swamplandia!* even one step further, I claim that the restricted and highly subjective perspective of the first-person narrator and protagonist, Ava, cannot qualify the racialized Gothic ascriptions. Even if one would argue affirmatively that the Bird Man, Mama Weeds, and the underworldish wilderness are only Gothicized in the imagination of a thirteen-year-old girl, who enjoys spending her days "mossed inside the Library Boat," reading and memorizing "Frankenstein" (S 23) and "Tennyson and Edgar Allan Poe" (S 266), the iteration still persists, and the racialization of the SV/CH Gotheme is contemporized and engraved further into the WASP American Gothic tradition. In *Swamplandia!*, the monsters and their victims are half men or "half woman and half invention" (S 283), half white and half B/black; they are also half patriarchal discourses of gender and half Gothicized discourses of race. The fact that the racialized Gothic is an "invention" and a continuous fictionalized doing does not render it less harmful; rather, the continuous iteration and re-"invention" of traded stereotypes and racialized conventions connected to the SV/CH Gotheme further racial denigration and hierarchization in contemporary (U.S.) culture and society.

4.4 Gothic Continuities and a Necessary Intervention (Interim Results)

Let me summarize my main findings thus far. I have looked at the SV/CH Gotheme, British and WASP American, past and present, and its manifold staging of a clash of two extremely white and civil characters with a very dark and savage villain. The bestselling rise of early Gothic fiction and its heavily racialized characters and plot lines, I have argued, co-occurs with the cultural necessity of legitimizing and clarifying racial hierarchies: at a time when, in the two colonial empires, formerly rigid and presumed "natural" hierarchies came under severe attack, in the wake of the Haitian Revolution and other, equally terrifying slave rebellions, abolitionism, and, controversially, with the shift from racial environmentalism to racial essentialism and its early twin, romantic racialism. By claiming that the early British and early American Gothic's Gothemes generally, and the SV/CH Gotheme especially, stage hierarchical dichotomies in overtly racial terms, I have placed the discourses of race center stage, both in the texts I have analyzed and in the eighteenth- and nineteenth-century historical-cultural context, to which I have linked them.

By focusing on the SV/CH Gotheme, I have also offered an alternative reading of the origins of the American Gothic. By stressing the key motif of savagery (as opposed to civilization), I have argued that the early WASP American Gothic must be understood as both an externalized and domesticated adaptation of British Gothic conventions. Also, adaptation means employment in contexts and discourses that are very much peculiar to the North American context: the legitimatization of the genocide and expulsion of American Indian peoples, in the course of the manifestly destined territorial expansion, and the legitimatization of racial hierarchies, either in support of chattel slavery and the commodification of the Black body, or in support of abolitionism.

However, what I have considered to be the most striking feature of the early Gothic is not so much its cultural (and geographical) adaptability but the apparent inconvertibility of its racial patterns. In all of the texts that I have looked at thus far, the highly racialized SV/CH Gotheme motivates and controls the Gothic plot. The early Gothic is intrinsically racially structured; its dichotomous Gothemes are both essentially racialized and, when instantiated in a fictional text, essentially racializing. This also holds true for the exemplary contemporary WASP American Gothic novels I have surveyed and/or analyzed in detail above. Far from depending on the immediate contexts of territorial expansion, slavery, and the severe political turbulences and socio-cultural changes of the nineteenth century, the racialized and racializing Gotheme still dominates the contemporary WASP American Gothic book market today.

The continuous consistency of conventional early WASP American Gothic writing strategies in WASP American fiction is definitely outstanding and clearly answers one part of our earlier question concerning the unity of the (American) Gothic: There is indeed *one* WASP American Gothic with clear-cut patterns, and it has not changed significantly since the late eighteenth century. Another question, however, seems far more pressing now: Are these racialized WASP American Gothic patterns—and, first and foremost, the SV/CH Gotheme—indeed conventional and, thus, potentially changeable, or are they essential to the Gothic and, much like the rules of chess, definitory and invariable? I believe these questions are of the utmost importance not only to Gothic scholarship but to contemporary American Studies *per se*.

Let me exploit the game metaphor a little further. If the Gothic writing strategy (WASP American as well as early British) indeed dichotomically structures a plot, according to the ascribed, racially coded capacities of the white hero and his B/black savage antagonist—i.e., according to the SV/CH Gotheme—it follows that the racialized character's capacities and powers (or the lack thereof) constitute his/her structural position in the plot, prior to his/her actions. Just as prior to a game of chess, we know which antagonistic black and white pieces (characters) can be moved around on which board (plot) and according to which rules (conventions):

> The spatial and temporal capacities of the queen (where she is located and where she can move, as well as how she can move) articulate an irreconcilable asymmetry of power between her and a rook or a pawn, for example. Vest the rook with the powers of the queen (before the game begins, of course) and it is not the outcome of the game that is jeopardy so much as the integrity of the paradigm itself—it is no longer chess but something else. (Wilderson III, *Red, White & Black* 8)

The fact that Frank Wilderson III's chess analogy can be blended into my analysis of the Gothic readily contextualizes the issue now at hand: My analysis of the continuously racialized and racializing SV/CH Gotheme in WASP American literature ties in (to a certain extent) with the Afro-Pessimistic criticism of Saidiya Hartman,

Hortense Spillers, Frank Wilderson III, Jared Sexton, and others, who argue "that the race line continues to be the foundational socio-political fault line in the United States" (Weier 419). In a time marked by "a discourse of race and racial history proclaiming a new era," a presumed post-racial era, "marked by America's conquest of racism, and Barack Obama's election to the United States presidency [as the presumed] smoking gun of racism's defeat" (West 439), Afro-Pessimism first strove to describe and explain the continuing prevalence of racial discrimination and everyday instances of anti-blackness in American culture and society. Instead of falling for the post-racial utopia—a utopia that has been unmasked as mere blindness by the 2016 presidential election and Donald Trump's inauguration as the 45th President of the United States—Afro-Pessimism's core axiom posits that black life is really the "afterlife of slavery" and that no amount of "letting go" or "post-racial" utopianism will slip the yoke (Hartman, *Scenes* 6). Equating the WASP racial discourses of contemporary blackness with the legitimizing racial discourses, surrounding and supporting chattel slavery—thus, stating a continuous and unchanging strategic invisibilization of black humanity within U.S. civil society—Afro-Pessimism intends to separate the structural positions of American Indians, Latin Americans, Asian Americans and other ethnic groups (all presumed "junior partners" of WASP civil society: Wilderson III, *The Black Liberation Army* 13) from the special position of the Black person. No longer is Blackness considered one of civil society's discursive positions among others (traditionally, academia focuses on the tripartite matrix of race, class, and gender); rather, Afro-Pessimists think of black people as structurally excluded, as "the necessary foundation for the articulation of the latter positions" (Weier 421). On Wilderson III's chessboard, this special position of the black person would be outside of the board, structurally excluded from the game proper, but—much like a table, a chattel—both sustaining and facilitating the game of civil society.

My analysis, just as the education it is based on and the academic framework it is produced in, in many respects, belongs to what Afro-Pessimists criticize as "the avant-garde of white supremacy" (Weier 424) and makes no claims toward writing or furthering the writing of a Black "grammar of suffering" (Wilderson III, *Red* 56) outside of the standard concepts of contemporary American Studies. Nevertheless, I am convinced that the outstanding consistency of racialized writing strategies, in mainstream WASP American Gothic literature, fuels the urgency of Afro-Pessimistic claims. The innumerous echoings and iterations of the Africanist Savage Villain and his ongoing battle with—and ultimately inescapable surrender to—the white heroic forces of civil society expose the paradigm of a post-racial U.S. society and culture as being a utopian ideal, with no traceable effect on the problematic SV/CH Gotheme so active within WASP mainstream literature. In this respect, WASP American Gothic fiction is one form of the structural violence inscribed in what Wilderson calls "the rubric of antagonism (an irreconcilable struggle between entities, or positions, the resolution of which is not dialectical but entails the obliteration of one of the positions)" (*Red* 5). Recent bestsellers like King's *The Girl Who Loved Tom Gordon* and Russell's *Swamplandia!* show unequivocally how persistent and appealing racialized Gothic dichotomies still are. When these exemplary novels are read together with the many novels encountered as spotlights in my overview of the contemporary WASP American Gothic novel, "an amazing continuity" becomes palpable that "belies the hypostatized discontinuities and epochal shifts installed by categories like slavery and freedom etc." (Hartman, *Scenes* 7). All texts discussed thus far functionalize the Africanist presence, the "fabricated brew of darkness, otherness, alarm, and desire" (Morrison, *Playing* 38), in contemporary WASP American Gothic texts, by continuing to conflate blackness and Blackness, savage villainy and the Black body in an "enactment of subjugation" (Hartman, *Scenes* 4).

In the following part of my study, I will look at how African American writers (past and present) make use of the Gothic writing strategy as a means of critically reiterating, in a discourse-altering way, the underlying racial stereotypes, while, at the same time, writing themselves into mainstream American literary consciousness. Only after understanding the functionalization of the SV/CH Gotheme by African American authors today, can I answer the two decisive questions:

1. Is the Gothic intrinsically racialized and racializing, or can the central SV/CH Gotheme be reiterated outside of the boundaries of race—that is, is an intradiscursive emergence of "unthought" possible/desirable?
2. Can we continue to speak of an "American Gothic" outside of the close confinements of the WASP American Gothic? Or, do we need to drop the notion, in favor of a multiplicity of Gothics such as "WASP American Gothic," "African American Gothic," or even "Morrisonian Gothic"?

PART III:
"You say I am wilderness. I am" — Black Origins and African American Reiterations

Innovation and Resistance: The SV/CH Gotheme in Black Writing, 1789 to 1861

> "This is precisely the time when artists go to work. There is no time for despair, no place for self-pity, no need for silence, no room for fear. We speak, we write, we do language. That is how civilizations heal." (Toni Morrison, "No Place" n.p.)

> "Fuck it, he thought. You have to learn how to swim sometime. He opened the door and walked into the sea of the dead." (Colson Whitehead, Zone One 259)

In many respects, this third part of my study on Black/African American[1] Gothic writing strategies, past and present, starts out as the structural twin of the previous part's discussion of the Gothic writing strategies by WASP American authors. We will first engage with early examples of Gothic strategies in Black texts, also in the transnational and transcultural context of the Black Atlantic. This will enable us to connect the nineteenth-century WASP American Gothic's invention of the Africanist Savage Villain—Edgar Allan Poe's contagious Tsalal savages functioned as archetypal representatives in Chapter 4.2—to contemporaneous Black and African American writing and rewriting strategies. Only then can we evaluate the implications that the continuous WASP iteration and the African American reiteration of the Savage Villain/Civil Hero Gotheme have for both contemporary North American culture and for the (theoretical and political) intervention, which has been launched under the label of Afro-Pessimism. Far from being a merely reactive writing against

---

1   Note on terminology: In my study, I refer to people of African descent as "Black" and "African American." However, "African American" implies residence in the United States, while "Black" functions as a larger umbrella term, referring to individuals throughout the Black Atlantic and the African diaspora. Especially in the context of early Black writing and early slave narratives, the term "Black" helps to capture the fluidity and movement of Black identities and texts throughout the Black Atlantic.

racialization and racial discrimination, Black and African American authors have also utilized the Gothic's ultra-adaptability and rewritten and re-contextualized its conventions since 1789. The implications this strategically reiterated—even reinvented—employment of Gothic writing conventions has for the umbrella concept of an "American Gothic" will be touched on, before being discussed in detail in my concluding Chapter 8.

My comparative perspective is not only called forward by both my ongoing testing of the assumed intrinsically racialized and racializing SV/CH Gotheme and the question of whether it specifically, and the Gothic more generally, can be reiterated outside the boundaries of race. Rather, it is also necessitated by the Afro-Pessimistic claim to Black exceptionalism, to a specificity of anti-Black racism, inherent structurally and ontologically in the dominant WASP discourses of Black identity, culture, space, race, and humanity. Equating the WASP racial discourses of contemporary Blackness with the legitimizing racial discourses surrounding and supporting chattel slavery, Afro-Pessimism separates the structural and ontological positions of American Indians, Latin Americans, Asian Americans, and all other ethnic groups (all presumed "junior partners" of WASP civil society: Wilderson III, *The Black Liberation Army* 13) from the special position of the Black 'non-person.' Afro-Pessimism thus states a continuous and unchanging strategic invisibilization of Black humanity within U.S. civil society. In this respect, this chapter is a crucial part in an ongoing negotiation of two decisive questions in my study: If the white Gothic traditions—as my analysis of early British and early and contemporary WASP American novels suggests—are intrinsically racialized and racializing, does the same hold true for Black/African American Gothic texts, past and present? Is there even such a thing as an African American Gothic text, or are African American authors merely reacting to, writing against, and renegotiating white Gothic conventionality, including (potentially) conventional racialization? And, finally, if the continuous racialization and denigration of the Black body in (WASP) American Gothic fiction fuel the arguments of Afro-Pessimism, does the continuous creative battle of African American authors against, and maybe even outside, the Gothic conventionality of racial denigration give rise to a however restricted optimism?

In a first step toward answering these questions, I will put to the test the well-established hypothesis that claims that the African American Gothic writing tradition started roughly in 1845 (that is, when Frederick Douglass framed aspects of his horrifying experiences in Gothic terms),[2] as both a writing back against raci-

---

2   With her 2014 article, "The African American Slave Narrative and the Gothic," Teresa A. Goddu is the first to acknowledge an earlier point of origin and introduces James Williams' 1838 slave narrative, *The Narrative of James Williams, an American Slave*, as a possible point of origin of African American Gothic.

al slavery and discourses of WASP dominance and a rewriting of WASP American Gothic conventionality. The African American Gothic, as I hinted at above and will outline in detail in the following subchapter, started much earlier; so early indeed that it predates Charles Brockden Brown's presumably first American Gothic novel, *Edgar Huntly*, by ten years, thus turning upside down the traditional answer to the American Gothic's chicken or egg causality. Hence, this chapter not only analyzes the parallel development of WASP American Gothic iteration and African American Gothic reiteration strategies since 1845, via the SV/CH Gotheme, but it also establishes an alternative point of origin for the American Gothic—outside the WASP tradition—in the Black Atlantic, that is, in Olaudah Equiano's 1789 *The Interesting Narrative of the Life of Olaudah Equiano, or Gustavus Vassa, the African. Written by Himself*.

5.1 The Interesting Narrative of the Life of Olaudah Equiano, or Gustavus Vassa, the African, Written by Himself

"I was now persuaded that I had gotten into a world of bad spirits, and that they were going to kill me. Their complexions too differing so much from ours, their long hair, and the language they spoke, which was very different from any I had ever heard, united to confirm me in this belief. Indeed, such were the horrors of my views and fears at the moment, that, if ten thousand worlds had been my own, I would have freely parted with them all to have exchanged my condition with that of the meanest slave in my own country. When I looked round the ship too, and saw a large furnace of copper boiling, and a multitude of black people of every description chained together, every one of their countenances expressing dejection and sorrow, I no longer doubted my fate, and, quite overpowered with horror and anguish, I fell motionless on the deck and fainted." (Equiano, The Interesting Narrative 55)

Positioning *The Interesting Narrative of the Life of Olaudah Equiano* at the beginning of my discussion of Gothic writing strategies in early African American texts is both consequent and unusual. It is consequent when understanding Equiano's[3] 1789 text

---

3   Note that I always cite the author by the name "Olaudah Equiano" and not by one of his slave names ("Gustavas Vassa" being the third of these slave names). In *Black Imagination and the Middle Passage*, Maria Diedrich, Henry Louis Gates, Jr., and Carl Pedersen have found a most intriguing way to mark the difference between both names: "Olaudah Equiano—a name representing the African 'I am,' in which past, present, and future are one, the 'I am' of an African self that could soar even through firmly rooted. [...] Gustavus Vassa—a name representing the Atlantic diaspora that threatened to wipe out the self, an unnaming and chaining down that signified the end of participation in history" (17).

as the "prototype"[4] for all African American slave narratives, as Henry Louis Gates, Jr. (*The Classic* 8) has called it. This line of thought can dismiss seemingly incompatible characteristics between *The Interesting Narrative* and African American slave narratives and novels. Indeed, Equiano's place of publication (London), the primary addressees (the British Parliament and public), the book market needs that the text adheres to, and also Equiano's self-identification as African[5] "make it difficult to claim Vassa [Equiano] and his work as specifically black American" (Reid-Pharr 138). The dispute over Equiano's nationality, or his primary affiliation to a national literary canon, has been summarized by David Kazanjian (47) as the opposition between an "Afro-American" camp (as, for example, represented by Houston A. Baker, Jr. [1984]) and an "Afro-English" camp (William L. Andrews [1986] and others). Both perspectives today, that is, post-Gilroy, seem outdated and too limited in their nationalist frameworks. If we understand Equiano and his *Narrative* as being both formed by and representative of the Black Atlantic, suspending the possibility of a more than superficial association with a country of origin, the ambiguity, fluidity, and indeterminacy of person and text can be (de-)localized in a transnational

---

4   Equiano's *Narrative* is not the first English slave narrative we know of (currently James Albert Ukawsaw Gronniosaw's "as-told-to account" [Carretta, "The Emergence" 52], *A Narrative of the Most Remarkable Particulars in the Life of James Albert Ukawsaw Gronniosaw, an African Prince, as Related by Himself* [published 1772], is understood to be the first). However, while Ukawsaw Gronniosaw's account introduces some themes, features, and motifs that will become conventional in the early nineteenth century (e.g. the white testimony and legitimatization, or the "I was born" opening sentence), it is Equiano's text that prototypically introduces the breadth of the genre's conventions. This becomes very clear when looking at the use of Gothic features in both early narratives: While in Ukawsaw Gronniosaw's text no Gothic features are discernable, Equiano's *Narrative* already functionalizes an array of Gothic conventions, a practice that will become conventional in the nineteenth-century African American slave narrative.

5   The question of Equiano's birthplace has triggered a debate about fact and fiction in his memoir in the late twentieth century. In 1999, Vincent Carretta, editing a new version of Equiano's memoir, found two archival records that led him to question Equiano's account of being born an Igbo (an area that is now Nigeria). In his 2005 biography, Carretta claims that Equiano may have been born in South Carolina rather than Africa and further states: "Equiano was certainly African by descent. The circumstantial evidence that Equiano was also African American by birth and African-British by choice is compelling but not absolutely conclusive. Although the circumstantial evidence is not equivalent to proof, anyone dealing with Equiano's life and art must consider it" (Carretta, *Equiano* xvi). Should Carretta's circumstantial evidence ever tilt the debate toward depriving Equiano's text of its iconic status as autobiography, I will gladly side with Cathy N. Davidson and "proclaim him the Father of the American Novel" ("Olaudah" 25) instead. Equiano's immense literary accomplishment in the immediate context of the "great charnel house of the country" (Rutman and Rutman 44), i.e. in the low country of South Carolina, under the South Carolina Slave Code, does by no means pale in comparison to a first-hand account of the Middle Passage.

frame, rather than in the United States or in England. Also, we should not forget that "black texts, particularly slave narratives, had from the beginning to conform to the demands of eighteenth- and nineteenth-century reading publics" (Reid-Pharr 139) and that Equiano's text marks the beginning of a "transatlantic antislavery print culture" (Gould, "Early Print" 48), in which a large number of Black texts, also by American-born authors, were published in London, before returning to North America in print. This, indeed, is a literature of and "about movement—geographical, ontological, and rhetorical" (Gould, "Early Print" 39).

Equiano's narrative, in many respects, sets the standards for the genre of the African American slave narrative in the United States and, more importantly for us, for the use of Gothic writing strategies within. Published for a book market that experienced bestselling success after bestselling success, by publishing Gothic romance authors such as Horace Walpole, Clara Reeve, Ann Radcliffe, and Matthew Gregory Lewis, it is not surprising that Equiano would turn to adapting and reiterating Gothic props, settings, and character types, in order to inspire in his readers "a sense of compassion for the miseries which the Slave Trade" entails (TIN 7)[6]. If we are looking for the advent of the Savage Villain/Civil Hero Gotheme in Black literature, *The Interesting Narrative*—not despite but because of its transnational fluidity—is the place to start.

I want to briefly point out that Equiano's *Narrative* is not the earliest Black text we know of today; however, the earlier writings by Briton Hammon, Jupiter Hammon, and James Albert Ukawsaw Gronniosaw, while fascinating texts and of the utmost importance for the development of the African American literature in their own right, do not employ Gothic writing strategies. While Briton Hammon's and Jupiter Hammon's (apparently no relation) texts were recorded and published a few years before Horace Walpole's *Castle of Otranto*, only Gronniosaw's 1772 *A Narrative of the Most Remarkable Particulars in the Life of James Albert Ukawsaw Gronniosaw, an African Prince, as Related by Himself* could at least be potentially viewed as utilizing Gothic features. Scenes like the following, however, make clear that Gronniosaw's narrative strategy follows a different logic:

> One day I had just clean'd the knives for dinner, when one of the maids took one to cut bread and butter with; I was very angry with her, and called upon God to damn her; when this old black man told me I must not say so. I ask'd him why? He replied there was a wicked man call'd the Devil, that liv'd in hell, and would take all that said these words, and put them in the fire and burn them.—This terrified me greatly, and I was entirely broke of swearing.—Soon after this, as I was placing the china for tea, my mistress came into the room

---

6   In-text citations marked "TIN" refer to Equiano's *The Interesting Narrative of Olaudah Equiano, or Gustavus Vassa, the African, Written by Himself*.

just as the maid had been cleaning it; the girl had unfortunately sprinkled the wainscot with the mop; at which my mistress was angry; the girl very foolishly answer'd her again, which made her worse, and she call'd upon God to damn her.—I was vastly concern'd to hear this, as she was a fine young lady, and very good to me, insomuch that I could not help speaking to her, "Madam, says I, you must not say so," Why, says she? Because there is a black man call'd the Devil that lives in hell, and he will put you in the fire and burn you, and I shall be very sorry for that. Who told you this replied my lady? Old Ned, says I. Very well was all her answer; but she told my master of it, and he order'd that old Ned should be tyed up and whipp'd, and was never suffer'd to come into the kitchen with the rest of the servants afterwards.—My mistress was not angry with me, but rather diverted with my simplicity and, by way of talk, She repeated what I had said, to many of her acquaintance that visited her; among the rest, Mr. Freelandhouse, a very gracious, good Minister, heard it, and he took a great deal of notice of me, and desired my master to part with me to him. (Gronniosaw 11-12)

Obviously, Gronniosaw's *Narrative* "introduced a number of the conventions, motifs, and themes found in subsequent works" (Carretta, "The Emergence" 97); above, for example, we encounter the themes/motifs of spiritual conversion, the prohibition of educating slaves, the spiritual superiority of a slave, in contrast to his/her master/mistress, the whipping of a slave, and the selling of a slave. Note, however, that Gronniosaw's description of these aspects is stated in a matter-of-fact "simplicity," devoid of Gothic features or other markers of fictionalization.[7] This, of course, must by no means be misread as a deficiency or as indicating a lack of literary merit. Black authors of slave narratives had to strategically position their texts as testimonies, as factual and truthful accounts of witnessing, in order to reach their target audiences and political aims. Any indicator of fictionalization would have created leverage for pro-slavery critics and advocates.

Compare in this respect the 1785 *Narrative of the Lord's Wonderful Dealing with John Marrant, a Black*. The freeborn Black author and minister Marrant employs a comparable narrative strategy of religious conversion and spiritual superiority, while blending in the plot elements of a captivity narrative. Marrant, however, also refrains from employing any sensational or Gothic features and strategies, even when describing the gruesome details of Indian captivity and torture practices. To

---

7   The only exception to this style is Gronniosaw's relaying of his encounter with the wicked man/black man "call'd the Devil," which, while greatly terrifying and life-changing for him, is an encounter with the Bible rather than with Gothic villainy. His subtle substitution of "wicked" with "black," while potentially a slip of his white amanuensis, is possibly connected to biblical conflations of blackness, with a lack of morality, as well as to eighteenth-century depictions of demons and the devil as being black. See Robert Earl Hood's *Begrimed and Black: Christian Traditions on Blacks and Blackness*, especially pages 84-85.

the missionary Marrant, the Cherokee "dungeon" is not and cannot be a Gothic prison, but his "chapel" and the "near prospect of death" evoke "hope for a speedy deliverance from the body," not terror (Marrant 22). Rather than following the logic of the slave narrative, Marrant's *Narrative* must be read as adhering to the conventions of the Protestant conversion narrative. Self-representing as a true and virtuous Christian man, Marrant dramatizes the miraculous adventures and the spontaneously answered prayers, to inspire his predominately white Protestant readership. Rhetorically, then, Marrant avoids "the sensational qualities of much of eighteenth-century captivity [and Gothic] writing, thereby implicitly challenging contemporary stereotypes associating blackness with unregulated passions [i.e., villainous savagery]" (Carretta and Gould 7).

Coming back to Equiano, my positioning of *The Interesting Narrative* at the beginning of my discussion of Gothic writing strategies in early African American texts is nevertheless quite unusual. As a rule, the scholarship concerned with Gothic elements and/or strategies in African American writing (past and present) does not include Equiano's text, but it canonically begins with Douglass's 1845 slave narrative. Even book-length studies concerned with early African American Gothic and/or Gothic features in slave narratives[8] mention Equiano's text, if at all, merely in passing and *en route* to Douglass and his presumably first employment of Gothic features. I believe this reluctance to analyze *The Interesting Narrative* within the framework of Gothic conventionality has to do with the text's diasporic fluidity, on the one hand, and the Gothic scholarship's obsession with localization/placing texts within ostensibly stable categories, such as "British Gothic," "English Gothic," "American Gothic," "Canadian Gothic," "Australian Gothic," "Southern Gothic," or "New England Gothic," on the other. For me, *The Interesting Narrative*'s innovative application and reiteration of British Gothic elements lead to a rethinking of the subsequent African American Gothic writing strategies. Also, it will bring us one step closer to understanding the opportunities and limitations of the umbrella term "American Gothic."

The Interesting Narrative can best be described as well-structured chaos. Its plot structure is ruptured continuously; indeterminacy motivates all character and plot development arches; the protagonist's quest remains teleologically incomplete; salvation is beyond reach, even beyond imagination. This structural chaos is reflected by the many allusions Equiano makes to a multiplicity of literary genres and traditions. Davidson summarizes:

---

8   See, for example, Kari J. Winter's *Subjects of Slavery, Agents of Change: Women and Power in Gothic Novels and Slave Narratives, 1790-1865* (1992); Justin D. Edwards's *Gothic Passages: Racial Ambiguity and the American Gothic* (2003); A. Robert Lee's *Gothic to Multicultural: Idioms of Imagining in American Literary Fiction* (2009); Maisha L. Wester's *African American Gothic: Screams from Shadowed Places* (2012).

> The text combines (in unequal parts) slave narrative, sea yarn, military adventure, ethnographic reportage, historical fiction, travelogue, picaresque saga, sentimental novel, allegory, tall tale, pastoral origins myth, gothic romance, conversion tale, and abolitionist tract, with different features coming to the fore at different times, and mood vacillating accordingly. (Davidson "Olauhda" 19)

Yet, this chaos, this meandering between innumerable plot episodes and generic conventions[9] best depicts the chaotic, continuously ruptured and indeterminate state that the Black person (whether enslaved or free) found himself/herself in at a time and in a multiplicity of places when black skin color is equal to enslavement. Thus, *The Interesting Narrative* structurally reflects both Equiano's transcultural and transnational meandering and his vulnerability to white power. That Equiano is being subjected to white dominance and arbitrariness, time and time again, is neither preconditioned nor limited to his being a slave, but it is solely due to the equation of having black skin color with being a slave. Hence, like an "existential rug-pull" (Davidson, "Olaudah" 20), white characters consistently functionalize Equiano's Blackness and turn a promising friendship, a quiet sea journey, and a paycheck, at the blink of an eye, into a horrific scene of exploitation, enslavement, and brutalization.

Strikingly, one rare instance of consistency in the text is Equiano's version of the Savage Villain/Civil Hero Gotheme. Just as in contemporaneous British Gothic texts, Equiano creates villainy from "the appellation of savages and brutes rather than of Christians and men" (TIN 109). Legitimized and controlled by the system of slavery, his white villains act *like* savages in their "wild, wicked, and mad career[s]" (TIN 216), without ever being categorically conflated with savagery. With this appellation of villainous savagery as the *temporal* loss of a civil and ethical (Christian) mindset, Equiano's adherence to British Gothic features in *The Interesting Narrative* ceases. Reiterating the British Gothic and significantly foreshadowing the WASP American Gothic, *The Interesting Narrative* constructs villainy in terms of both antonomasia (a singled-out, named white character represents a great number of equally villainous people/the system of slavery itself) and racialized villainy.

Creating a typically Gothic perspective of "us victims" against "they villains," through narrative voice and racialization, Equiano renders the white characters the

---

9   Vincent Carretta rightly argues that "[c]ategorizing black writers by genre is as difficult as classifying them by national affiliation" and, therefore, the multigeneric texts by first-generation authors of African descent "should be read and assessed on their own historical terms, rather than as anticipating later generic expectations and conventions" (Carretta, "The Emergence" 54). In my reading of *The Interesting Narrative*, I trace the early British Gothic as an intertext for Equiano's text and, understanding the importance of the text for the African American slave narratives to be composed in the first half of the nineteenth century, I note innovations that will later become conventional African American Gothic writing strategies.

Gothicized other. "Their complexions [...] differing so much from ours, their long hair, and the language they spoke, which was very different" confirm: Equiano has arrived in "a world of bad spirits" (TIN 55), where the "iron muzzle, thumb-screws, &c. are so well known, as not to need a description, and [are] sometimes applied for the slightest faults," where it "is not uncommon, after a flogging, to make slaves go on their knees, and thank their owners," and where "they make husbands flog their own wives" (TIN 107). While Equiano readily distinguishes "a multitude of black people of every description [...], every one of their countenances expressing dejection and sorrow," he constructs the white other as a homogenous group that uniformly displays savage villainy, that is, as "those white men with horrible looks, red faces, and long hair" (TIN 55), who might very well turn out to be cannibals.

Rendering "the Europeans as a homogeneous, indistinguishable 'other,' deprived of individual qualities," as Jesús Benito and Ana María Manzanas convincingly claim (49), is a crucial step in creating "an ironic counterpoint [that] subverts the categories the Europeans established in their encounters with the unenlightened or uncivilized" (48). Benito and Manzanas go on to argue that, in the course of the *Narrative*, Equiano would erase "the insurmountable difference—of kind—between white (spirits) and black (men)," until the only difference left is "a quantitative differentiation because white men are superior" (50). In contrast to this last argument, I claim that the villainous white other—the many treacherous, unreliable slave-owners and profiteers of the slave trade, the *"Christian master"* (TIN 106, italics Equiano) in all disguises—remains a constant throughout the otherwise continuously crisscrossing and meandering text. Doubtlessly appealing to and culturally assimilating the English Gentleman ideal, thereby aspiring to be culturally "white" instead of a spirit-believing young African, it is Equiano who changes and develops in his *Narrative*, not the villainous forces that obstruct his journey, never ceasing to rob him of a much-deserved state of arrival (in freedom) or belonging (in terms of cultural, social, and legal citizenship).

Slavery and its representatives can no longer be mistaken as spirits; rather, the European and WASP American people involved in slavery, in the "tortures, murder, and every other imaginable barbarity and iniquity practised upon the poor slaves with impunity," in the business of "neck-yokes, collars, chains, hand-cuffs, leg-bolts, drags, thumb-screws, iron-muzzles, and coffins; cats, scourges, and other instruments of torture" (TIN 234), are very real indeed. What happens here is not so much the evening out of ontological difference, but the evening out of the risk of rendering the villain(s) and his (their) atrocious acts "a Gothic conceit, thereby denaturing it as a real, historical horror" (Bodziock 256). For nineteenth-century African American slave narratives, Teresa A. Goddu has called this intrinsic catch in framing the experiences of slavery as simultaneously "real" and "Gothic," a "double bind: the difficulty of representing a Gothic history through Gothic conventions without collapsing the distinctions between fact and fiction, event and effect" ("The

African American Slave Narrative" 137). That this double bind can already be found in Equiano's 1789 text is outstanding and, once more, stresses *The Interesting Narrative*'s importance for the (African) American Gothic tradition.

If we now turn to the other side of the Savage Villain/Civil Hero Gotheme, meaning the white Civil Hero stepping in to save the white damsel in distress from the harm that the villainous racial other embodies, another strategic deviation from the early British Gothic conventionality becomes apparent. In a world of Black damsels and white villains, Equiano effectively suspends the heroic intervention of civilization and ethics from the text, relegating it into the future and the hands of the English parliament and public. Consider, in these respects, the following archetypal passage of the *Narrative*:

> Another negro man was half hanged, and then burnt, for attempting to poison a cruel overseer. Thus by repeated cruelties are the wretched first urged to despair, and then murdered, because they still retain so much of human nature about them as to wish to put an end to their misery, and retaliate on their tyrants! These overseers are indeed for the most part persons of the worst character of any denomination of men in the West Indies. Unfortunately, many humane gentlemen, by not residing on their estates, are obliged to leave the management of them in the hands of these human butchers, who cut and mangle the slaves in a shocking manner on the most trifling occasions, and altogether treat them in every respect like brutes. They pay no regard to the situation of pregnant women, nor the least attention to the lodging of the field-negroes. Their huts, which ought to be well covered, and the place dry where they take their little repose, are often open sheds, built in damp places; so that, when the poor creatures return tired from the toils of the field, they contract many disorders, from being exposed to the damp air in this uncomfortable state, while they are heated and their pores are open. This neglect certainly conspires with many others to cause a decrease in the births as well as in the lives of the grown negroes. (TIN 105)

Equiano's writing strategy here, and throughout his text, can be described as listing and concurrently juxtaposing a number of de-individualized appellations with markers of chattel slavery. More specifically, Equiano juxtaposes the white villainy of cruel overseers/tyrants/persons of the worst character/human butchers to the black victimhood of the negro man/the wretched/pregnant women/field-negroes/poor creatures. Adding the brutality of chattel slavery to this dichotomous picture, Equiano lists the systemic "repeated cruelties" of hanging, burning, cutting, mangling, and murdering the latter group of people "in a shocking manner." He refrains from assigning names and/or characteristics to the few individual slaves (the negro man, the wretched), and, most often, he uses plural constructions for depicting a generalized fate and joint plight of all slaves. The "shocking manner" is also never made explicit, and the many forms of torture and hardship are either merely listed as "so well known" aspects of chattel slavery that do "not need a description" (TIN 107), or they are hinted at implicitly and between the lines (the "pregnant women" indicate rape, and the "decrease in the [...] lives of grown negroes" hints at the mass murder of enslaved Black people, especially in the dire context of plantation slavery). Equiano's insistence on a shared knowledge of the systemic atrocities of slavery replaces the early British Gothic's focus on a specific "horror of the spectacle" (see Chapter 3) with a brutal history of ignorance and opportunistic acceptance. This strategy should not be confused with the veil that Harriet Beecher Stowe would draw over an institution "too dreadful for the purposes of art" (Beecher Stowe, *Key* 255), roughly sixty years later: She spares the arts as well as her readers, while the gaps in Equiano's *Narrative* hold the reader to account for the gap between knowing and doing.

Note how Equiano, in the passage quoted, excludes—and excuses—the "many humane gentlemen" from the horrors of the slave trade. Pressed by more immediate business needs, these gentlemen have to delegate the management of their plantations to their employees, who happen to be human butchers. Instead of blaming the plantation owners and traders, and thus the wealthy and powerful individuals behind the slave industry, Equiano opens up a third category, next to human butchers and poor creatures: the humane, namely English gentlemen. These humane gentlemen in the compromising slave business are place holders for the "Lords and Gentlemen" of the "Lords Spiritual and Temporal, and the Commons of the Parliament of Great Britain" (TIN 7), to whom the *Narrative* is primarily addressed.

It is in this circle of primary addressees that Equiano re-positions the Civil Hero. It is a suspended, or potential, civil heroism that combines gentlemanly humanism with the political power over "thousands [who] in consequence of [the parliamentarians'] determination, are to look for Happiness or Misery!" (TIN 8). True to the early British Gothic plot, the atrocious villainy must be counterbalanced by a force of civilization and humanism, by a heroic invention. In the *Interesting Narrative*, the Civil Hero is suspended from the plot, not because the plot would lack a civil and courageous hero or horrific events, thereby necessitating a heroic intervention from the forces of civilization, but, rather, in a reality where civilization equals chattel slavery, the Civil Hero cannot be Black, no matter how civil and heroic he is. He will need white allies, meaning the British political and clerical elite. By rendering himself an ineffective Civil Hero, Equiano places the savage villainy of the slavery system center stage—a total and inescapable evil that cannot be counterbalanced by neither his nor other correcting forces of humane civilization. Thus, the Gothic reality of Black existence is stressed to the utmost extent. What is more, by suspending (instead of deleting) the Civil Hero from the plot, Equiano has also created a very immediate stimulus for acting on "the question of Abolition" (TIN 7).

Let me shed more light on these aspects, by tracing the suspended Civil Hero in the *Narrative*. While courageous, even heroic, deeds can be found readily in the plot, especially by Equiano himself, these deeds and events at first lack consequences and therefore fail as interventions. Consider in this respect the following scene of Equiano being threatened "by two white men":

> I was beset by two white men, who meant to play their usual tricks with me in the way of kidnapping. [...] but I told them to be still and keep off, for I had seen those tricks played upon other free blacks, and they must not think to serve me so. At this they paused a little, and one said to the other—it will not do; and the other answered that I talked too good English. I replied, I believed I did; and I had also with me a revengeful stick equal to the occasion; and my mind was likewise good. Happily, however, it was not used; and, after we had talked together a little in this manner, the rogues left me. (TIN 159)

Faced with the threat of kidnapping and renewed enslavement, Equiano takes a stand and confronts the "rouges," as a British gentleman would: eloquently, courageously, calmly, and equipped with a walking stick. He is neither attacked nor kidnapped but reclaims control over the situation, driving the two hostile white men off. This episode, without a doubt, marks Equiano as a civil and heroic British gentleman. Using blatant irony, Equiano positions himself as being (rhetorically, culturally, physically, and morally) superior, while, at the same time, he highlights his (free) Black identity. Indeed, I would suggest reading the verbal exchange between the outspoken gentleman Equiano and the intimidated, dim-witted white rouges as one of many examples of Signifyin'[10] in the *Narrative*. In this passage, Signifyin', through irony and boasting, certainly stresses Equiano's superiority and status on the diegetic and extradiegetic levels of the *Narrative*. But, there is more to it. By claiming and appropriating the superior British gentleman ideal for himself—a concept racialized as exclusively white—Equiano positions himself not only as the Civil Hero but as a Black British Civil Hero.

---

10 Signifyin' is a form of Black (vernacular) wordplay, a Black mode of double-voicedness, that Henry Louis Gates Jr. defines as the "trope for repetition and revision, indeed [the] trope of chiasmus, repeating and reversing simultaneously [...], as the slave's trope, the trope of tropes," which "are subsumed several other rhetorical tropes, including metaphor, metonymy, synecdoche, and irony" (Gates, *The Signifying Monkey* 52). In *The Signifying Monkey*, Gates traces and analyzes Equiano's Signifyin' practices, mainly through the tropes of chiasmus (cf. 153) and the Talking Book (154). Elaine B. Richardson points out many other instances of Signifyin' in the *Narrative* and states that, from the chosen title to the conversion narrative, "Equiano litters the text with Black-styled signifyin' references" (45). In the scene quoted above, Equiano's Signifyin' blends irony with an indulgence "in considerable boasting," a narrative strategy "that can be traced to African oral traditions and to black American folk tales and literature" (Costanzo 18).

However, very clear boundaries and limitations have been set to the concept of a Black Civil Hero. His civil superiority over the rouges does not impact the plot positively and/or lastingly. The next "rouge," yet another "white man" (TIN 171/170) conning Equiano out of his money, waits just around the corner; Equiano will be robbed, beaten, kidnapped, and tortured, before, by chance, "be[ing] admitted to partake in the blessings of your Majesty's happy government" (TIN 232, note the ironic stance again)—only to find himself re-instantiated in the position of "[t]he oppressed Ethiopian" (TIN 232). In other words, *The Interesting Narrative* seems to construct a painfully ineffective Black Civil Hero on a repetitively frustrating and futile quest.

On the one hand, the suspended, or potential, civil heroism from the Savage Villain/Civil Hero Gotheme allows Equiano to strategically position the British political and clerical elite in the plot, without having to unmask them as the powerful and rich originators and profiteers of the atrocious system of the transatlantic slavery trade and American chattel slavery. With the explicit educational impetus "to become better and wiser, and learn 'to do justly, to love mercy, and to walk humbly before God'" (TIN 236), the plot's blank space of civil, humane intervention necessitates a response by the British addressees and broader readership.[11] The abolition of the villainous system of slavery becomes the ultimate duty of the British parliament and the public's civil heroes and is the only hope for the countless people of the Black Atlantic who are subjected to this system, due to skin color. In this respect, the British decision in "the question of Abolition" (TIN 3) is also a decision for either expelling or feeding the Gothic quality of Black reality in slavery and of taking to heart, or throwing away, "the jewels of instruction" (TIN 236) that Equiano's *Narrative* simultaneously stages and offers.

On the other hand, we must not forget that, through his self-construction as a British gentleman vis-à-vis his civil and superior characteristics and behavior, Equiano re-focuses his narrative indictment. While disempowered in the system of slavery, Equiano is never a voiceless, passive victim, that is, never a damsel, though in dire distress. Through stressing education, articulation, civilization, and gentlemanly humanity, Equiano constructs himself as a human(e) agent in a Gothic system that strives to delete the very possibilities of Black humanity and agency. In contrast to the countless nameless and voiceless slaves/victims in his *Narrative*, he embodies both the exceptional success story of an educated Black man's plight from slavery to Englishman and the promise that, given the abolition of slavery, all Black people will finally live up to their civil and genteel natures. Equiano's implication of a necessary British intervention, therefore, is not so much a re-instantiation of

---

11   Equiano strategically addresses the *Narrative* to the British parliament and clergy, well aware of the fact that the English Antislavery Society published the text in the form of inexpensive pamphlets for the broad public.

a white heroic savior by/for a victim of slavery but a loud call for white allies. It is the call for justice of one gentleman to another and simultaneously the most annihilating condemnation of the perverted crimes committed by white rogues against British gentlemen, thereby deeming slavery as inhuman(e).

Equiano's reiterated and reinvented Gothic writing strategies can thus be positioned in the mid- to late eighteenth-century philosophical (and political) debates "about the very meanings of 'race' and 'humanity'" (Gould 46). In Part I, I outlined the shift of the concept of race, from signifying any group of people bound by both a shared history and geography toward a proto-essentialist assumption of race, as a blend of religious teaching (e.g., the monogenist belief in one humanity traceable to Adam and Eve), physiological ideas regarding bodily fluids and temperaments, and environmentalism (as the proto-biological explanation for physical difference with geographic environments). With Philip Gould,

> we can say that Black print literature emerged at a time when the belief in the singular nature of the human race [...] still prevailed. [And when] progressive-minded British and American thinkers publicly defended the humanity of Africans—as many abolitionists did for Wheatley in the face of Jefferson's critiques—they did so generally by marshaling biblical and environmentalist arguments. (47)

Equiano's Gothic account of slavery connects sentimental concepts of sympathy (for the slaves) and condemnation (for the system of slavery and its many advocates) with race and humanity: White *"Christian* masters" and slave drivers are confronted with the enormous gulf between their humanity and their systematic acting like savages and brutes. It is this discrepancy, the gulf between an uncontested humanity and the savagery systemic to chattel slavery, that Equiano constructs as being condemnable. His Black characters, in contrast, evoke sympathy, by being the civil and human(e) victims of this savage and inhumane system. The renegotiated racial color-coding of Equiano's *Narrative* (white villains and Black victims) thus appeals, in a strategically sophisticated manner, directly to his white readership's own image of (their) civil humanity, thereby calling for a sympathetic identification across color-lines, on the basis of a shared humanity. This sympathetic identification must be understood as an especially potent strategy, Phillip Gould states, because it "at once appealed the white readers' understanding of their own civilized humanity while simultaneously allowing them sufficient distance to safely witness the crimes of slavery" (43).

In summary, Equiano's *Narrative* not only significantly exploits and intervenes in the (British) Gothic's racialization, by creating white villains with the attributions of savage barbarism, but Equiano also broadens the concept of villainy altogether and uses it, long before Harriet Beecher Stowe and Frederick Douglass did, to unmask the villainous system of slavery that grows individual white villains, like the

Hydra of Lerna (re-)grows heads. What is more, with an educational and politically activating impetus, Equiano suspends the Civil Hero from the Savage Villain/Civil Hero Gotheme, creating a gap in the *Narrative* that—given the institution of slavery—must be filled by the British elites and their active furthering of the abolition of slavery. This carefully constructed gap, while stressing the continuous disempowerment that the Black person is subjected to, never bows to slavery's systemic deletion of Black humanity and agency: Equiano calls for allies, not for saviors. Both Equiano's artistically masterful balancing of the double bind (fictionalizing slavery via the Gothic, but only to depict the Gothic reality) and his reinvention of the British Gothic writing strategy become cornerstones in the development of other Black Gothic texts. Thus, *The Interesting Narrative*'s Gothic strategies should not be understood as a mere haunting back, a quality Goddu ("The African American Slave Narrative" 76) has reductively attested to the African American slave narratives from 1838 onward, but as a strategic combination of reiteration and reinvention of a heavily racialized haunting in the context of the Black Atlantic. Equiano's text marks the point of origin for a Black Gothic writing tradition that, at least for the North American context during the first decades of Gothic writing, we can imagine as having developed parallel to the early WASP American tradition. Although my project is not aimed at establishing a speculative account of "who influenced whom" but at theoretically contextualizing and explaining contemporary authors' iteration and reiteration practices, I indeed argue that Equiano's *Narrative* must be understood as the archetypal Black Gothic text. Let me hijack Henry Louis Gates Jr.'s argument here:

> Equiano's *Narrative* was so richly structured that it became the prototype of the nineteenth-century slave narrative, best exemplified in the works of Frederick Douglass, William Wells Brown, and Harriet Jacobs. It was Equiano whose text served to create a model that other ex-slaves would imitate. […] Equiano's strategies of self-presentation and rhetorical representation heavily informed, if not determined, the shape of black narrative before 1865. [His] two-volume work was exceptionally popular. Eight editions were printed in Great Britain during the author's lifetime, and a first American edition appeared in New York in 1791. By 1837, another eight editions had appeared, including an abridgement in 1829. Three of these editions were published together with Phillis Wheatley's *Poems*. Dutch and German translations were published in 1790 and 1791. (*The Signifying Monkey* 152-153)

Equiano's *Narrative* was so well known and so widely available that a direct impact on African American pre-Civil War texts—also in terms of Gothic reiteration strategies—could be expected.

The presumed parallel development, however, clashes with the WASP American Gothic's invention of the Africanist Savage Villain. From this point onward, as I will discuss in the following, African American texts have incorporated two Gothic traditions: the Black Gothic conventions, derived and perfected from Equiano's archetype, as well as from (in reaction to) the WASP American Gothic, with its new and incomparably vile racial denigration of Black peoples.

My shift of focus to African American texts—at least to a certain extent—contains the risk of highlighting, maybe even localizing, the Black/African American slave narrative tradition(s) outside the Black Atlantic. I not only silence the texts of the Black Atlantic that precede those by James Williams, Frederick Douglass, and others, as well as those that succeed *The Interesting Narrative*, but I also silence the dialogue corresponding to this complex network of texts and voices. While the focus of my project does not permit a detailed discussion of the fascinating Gothic writing strategies in texts such as Mary Prince's *The History of Mary Prince, a West Indian Slave* and Juan Francisco Manzano's *Poems by a Slave in the Island of Cuba, Recently Liberated [...], with the History of the Early Life of the Negro Poet, Written By Himself [...]*, I will, however, consider and position the Gothic strategies of African American authors as individual voices, in the complex transnational and transcultural network of the Black Atlantic, limiting myself to only highlighting specific consistencies or differences when they are helpful for my more focused argument.

5.2 Gothic/Slavery: African American Slave Narratives

> "Cruelty is contagious in uncivilized communities." (Jacobs 52)

Much has been written about the strategic employment of Gothic conventions in nineteenth-century African American slave narratives. Even though the studies of Theresa Goddu, Kari Winter, Carol M. Davison, Maisha L. Wester, and Janina Nordius, to name just five currently important research perspectives, differ greatly in terms of method and text corpus, they do share a key hypothesis: "Although presented as autobiographies, slave narratives often drew on tropes and conventions borrowed from Gothic romances to drive home the very real horror of the events described" (Nordius 631). In fact, the question of Gothic features in African American slave narratives has reached a consensus within the field of Gothic Studies that can best be described as the proposition of "a structural affinity between the discourse of slavery and the conventions of the Gothic" (Goddu, "The African American Slave Narrative" 72). Authors like Frederick Douglass, William Wells Brown, and Harriet Jacobs employ Gothic features to varying degrees, but it is assumed that they do so with a twist. "Represented as a house of bondage replete with evil villains and helpless victims, vexed bloodlines and stolen birthrights, brutal punishments and spectacular suffering, cruel tyranny and horrifying terror, slavery reads as a Gothic romance" (ibid.); the twist, then, consists in the fact that this Gothic imagery in African American slave narratives is not to be read metaphorically but literally. For the sake of authenticity, authors of slave narratives had to confirm that their narratives stated lived experiences and facts, not fiction, and that the Gothic elements employed depicted a "dark reality of evil" (Williams 19) that far exceeded fictional horrors. Only an authentic testimony of the real horrors of slavery would enable a white readership to experience, witness, and empathize—an empathic "obliteration of otherness" (Boyarin 86)—thereby furthering the abolitionist cause.[12]

Note that this consensus rests on two underlying assumptions. First, the slave's story, as Laura Doyle and Theresa Goddu argue, was an "already-framed" (Doyle 255), Gothicized and "overwritten" (Doyle 256) discourse, which was "possessed by whites" from the start (Doyle 255). Second, the African American Gothic can be best described as a reversal of traditional, meaning British and WASP American Gothic, conventions.

The first assumption highlights how Gothic conventions in African American slave narratives must be read in conjunction with the "white envelope" (the authorizing and legitimizing preface and certifying appendix), as one aspect of "the framework that made the slave's story intelligible" (Goddu, "The African American Slave Narrative" 73) for an overwhelmingly white audience. This line of reasoning is not limited to Gothic features in slave narratives; rather, African American writers, writing for a nearly exclusively white book market, faced a "basic but formidable challenge" (Ernest 97), for "while white abolitionists were eager to privilege the authenticity of Black writers' descriptions of slavery, it was only insofar as their descriptions confirmed what white readers had actually accepted as true" (Smith Foster 82). Like a self-fulfilling prophecy, as Dwight A. McBride argues, the abolitionist discourse repeats and trades itself through every new witness account: "Any testimony that is to be successful—by which I mean in this context, that is to have political efficacy for the cause of abolitionism—must address itself [...] to the very discourse that creates, allows, and enables the situation for the slave to be able to speak to us at all. It must recognize the codes and terms that animate abolitionist discourse" (172). In other words: "Before the slave ever speaks, we know the slave; we know what his or her experience is, and we know how to read that experience" (5). It must be understood, however, how intricate and political the doubly-bound text production really was. The Gothic—one of the most popular fictional

---

12 From the perspective of the Afro-Pessimism branch of contemporary Black Studies, Saidiya Hartman points out "the difficulty and slipperiness of empathy" (*Scenes* 18) and white witnessing. She argues that the white suffering for the slave essentially involves a "violence of identification," as it "fails to expand the space of the [Black] other but merely places the self in its stead" (20).

writing strategies in the early and mid-nineteenth century—has the potential to easily turn the account of an individual biography into a de-particularized, generic Gothic romance for entertainment purposes. For Southern proslavery advocates, this reliance on traditionally fictional conventions and features was a golden opportunity for disparaging slave narratives as opprobrious lies, written and told by dangerously radical abolitionists.

The hypothesis of a direct, mimetic reflection of the Gothic reality of slavery in African American slave narratives is also at the center of arguments of the second underlying assumption. What is added here is the idea that early African American Gothic texts produce, as Jerrold E. Hogle argues, "cultural transformations so distinctive that they end up using the Gothic tradition to turn it on its head" ("Teaching" 215). In sum, the (early) African American Gothic is understood as turning the traditional Gothic's racial color-coding of villains and victims upside-down, while maintaining intelligibility and accessibility for its predominately white audience.

In my following discussion of the SV/CH Gotheme in African American slave narratives, I will test both underlying assumptions and renegotiate the consensus outlined above. By focusing on the strategic employment of the SV/CH Gotheme, I will trace the racialization of African American Gothic writing strategies, as motivated by both the Black Atlantic/Equiano tradition and the rise of the Africanist Savage Villain in WASP American discourse and fiction. Understanding the necessity of the double bind inherent in these texts, i.e. the complex balancing of Gothic and autobiographical writing strategies, I will continue working with spotlights and start by discussing the construction of villainy, before adding the damsel and the hero to the gloomy picture. The slave narratives I include in my analysis are James William's controversial 1838 *Narrative of James Williams, An American Slave*, Frederick Douglass' famous *The Narrative of the Life of Frederick Douglass, an American Slave, Written by Himself* (1845), William Wells Brown's *Narrative of William W. Brown, a Fugitive Slave, Written by Himself* (1847), and Harriet Jacobs' 1861 *Incidents in the Life of a Slave Girl*. Chapter 4.1.3 will then transfer the discussion to the SV/CH Gotheme in early African American novels, namely in *Clotel; or the President's Daughter* and *The Bondwoman's Narrative*, which arguably "realizes the possibilities of the slave narrative as a gothic work to the fullest extent" (Wester 56). Taken together, these two subchapters will contextualize my discussion of contemporary African American Gothic novels, be they neo-slave narratives, vampire romances, or post-apocalyptic zombie novels.

Savage Villainy

In his groundbreaking essay of 1984, "'I Was Born': Slave Narratives, Their Status as Autobiography and as Literature," James Olney argues that the "overwhelming sameness" (46) of slave narratives is due to their adhering to a rigid conventionality that was "so early and so firmly established that one can imagine a sort of master outline drawn from the great narratives and guiding the lesser ones" (50). At the same time, every slave narrative that we know today is a unique and highly individual piece of literature; a literature that may not be primarily interested in depicting "the intellectual, emotional, moral growth of the [individual] narrator" (51), but which knows and employs a variety of highly individual rhetorical strategies to take on the institution of slavery. While the construction and functionalization of Gothic villainy in African American slave narratives can indeed be positioned on the side of conventionality—Savage Villains in African American slave narratives are unequivocally white and come in numbers—the Savage Villain/Civil Hero Gotheme as a whole shows a great potential for variation and reiteration outside the boundaries of what Hogle has called turning "the Gothic tradition [...] on its head" ("Teaching" 215). Before tackling variation, however, let me describe the status quo of Gothic villainy in the slave narratives of James Williams, Frederick Douglass, William Wells Brown, and Harriet Jacobs.[13]

Master George, Captain Anthony, Captain Auld, Captain Braut, Major Freeland, Dr. Flint, Mr. Crop, Mr. Severe, Mr. Gore, Mr. Covey, Mr. Cook, Mr. Page, Mr. Conant, Huckstep, Ludlow, Plummer, or McKinney—the countless masters, overseers, slave drivers, slave traders, slave catchers, and their "Northern tools" (Jacobs 216) are the many, yet hauntingly similar white faces of savage villainy. The white villain is "a miserable drunkard, a profane swearer, and a savage monster," (Douglass 20) who "take[s] pleasure in manifesting his fiendish barbarity" (Douglass 25). He is a "vile

---

13   Of the many possible texts, the slave narratives by Williams, Douglass, Brown, and Jacobs have been selected for two main reasons. First, all four slave narratives are very well-known and well-researched (including from the perspective of Gothic Studies), which enables me to focus most narrowly on the SV/CH Gotheme, without aspiring to reinvent the wheel. Second, the Gothic writing strategy plays a key role in both the narratives themselves and in the (contemporaneous and/or contemporary) reception of them: Douglass' *Narrative* and his depiction of the whipping of Aunt Hester have become the archetypal reference for Gothic features in slave narratives; Harriet Jacobs' *Incidents* is often discussed as the female companion piece to Douglass' Gothic. William Wells Brown's *Narrative* has been read in opposition to Douglass' "highly self-conscious rhetorical flourishes" and as a "decidedly understated, restrained, almost deadpan manner of recounting his life" (Andrews "Introduction," 5). This, however, by no means implicates an un-Gothicized slave narrative, as we will see. Lastly, triggered by Southern proslavery advocates who attacked Williams' *Narrative* as "a specimen of the most horrible calumnies and unmitigated falsehoods that ever disgraced the press of an enlightened public" (Birney and Tappan 71), the ensuing controversy mainly targeted his amanuensis, Gothic writer John Greenleaf Whittier, who clearly frames Williams' texts as "a Gothic tale" (Goddu, "The African American Slave Narrative," 75). Williams, the Southern critics were certain, had been "made to say" falsehoods embedded in a Gothic romance, in order to advance the politics of "gulling the public" (Birney and Tappan 71).

monster" (Jacobs 30), a "demon" (Williams 38), a "despicable creature[...]" (Brown, *Narrative* 66), "a tiger" (Jacobs 43, Douglass 68), and "a snake" (Douglass 69). He orders "the women to pull up the clothes, in Alabama style [...] and then whip them for not complying," all the while "cursing and swearing, laughing and telling stories full of obscenity and blasphemy" (Williams 28f.). "He [is] a cruel man," who, at times, "whip[s] a woman, causing the blood to run half an hour at the time; and this, too, in the midst of her crying children, pleading for their mother's release" (Douglass 25); who, at other times, makes "base offers" and "vile proposals," who "threats" and "bribes" "his prey" into (sexual) obedience (Brown, *Narrative* 45). White Savage Villains come in "swarms" (Brown, *Narrative* 44), "like buzzards around a carrion" (Brown, *Narrative* 65), and their cruelty is as fatal and "contagious" (Jacobs 52) as "a plague" (Jacobs 20).

This construction of savage villainy as being white and standing-in for the institution of slavery directly reflects Equiano's strategic inversions, pointing toward an ensuing African American Gothic conventionality. There are, however, two significant (and interconnected) alterations to the Savage Villain that are unique to the genre and period of the African American slave narratives studied here: Firstly, savage villainy has taken on "contagious" qualities (Jacobs 52); it is "a plague" (Jacobs 20), rampant in "uncivilized communities" (Jacobs 52). Secondly, it has spread and infected white middle and upper class women already, creating an entire branch of white *female* Savage Villains—a first in the Gothic writing tradition.

We have encountered the concept of contagious savagery before: Poe's Africanist Savage Villains, the pitch-black savages of the island of Tsalal, who sexually and racially contaminate "the face of the globe" (P 145), up to a point where images of miscegenation and racial decline culminate in an apocalyptic vision of the violent destruction of civilization. It goes without saying that "civilization" for Poe and his peers is racially coded as "white only." For Harriet Jacobs, "uncivilized communities" are white slaveholding or proslavery communities in the South that—due to the sickening and degenerating effects of the institution of slavery—decline racially into a contaminated and contaminating state of uncivilization and savagery. The "white man [who] claimed to have given to America, specifically the Blacks who were brought as slaves, civilization" (Guerrera 96) is depicted as degenerating into an uncivilized state of cruelty and unreason: "Murder was so common on his plantation that he [Mr. Litch] feared to be alone after nightfall. He might have believed in ghosts" (Jacobs 52). By connecting the white Savage Villain with a narrative of white racial decline and contamination, Jacobs effectively adds a radically new dimension to her pro-abolition argument: In the face of the spreading contamination and the white racial decline, the self-preservation of the white race and of white civilization necessitates the abolition of slavery. Jacob's strategy of framing the institution of slavery as an uncontrollably contaminating threat that triggers racial decline directly connects the abolitionist cause to virulent discourses of miscegenation and racial purity, thereby foreshadowing eugenic discourses of the late nineteenth and twentieth centuries. As long as the institution of slavery exists, any white person might be befallen by the "plague" (Jacobs 20)—even white middle and upper class women.

Consider in this respect the introduction, or awakening, of the female Savage Villain, "the wife of master George" (Williams 23), in James Williams' *Narrative*:

> [...] the slightest disregard of her commands—and sometimes even the neglect to anticipate her wishes, on the part of the servants; was sufficient to awake her. The inanimate and delicate beauty then changed into a stormy virago. Her black eyes flawed and sparkled with a snaky fierceness, her full lips compressed, and her brows bent and darkened. Her very voice, soft and sweet when speaking to her husband, and exquisitely fine and melodious, when accompanying her guitar, was at such times, shrill, keen, and loud. [...] If the young ladies remonstrated with her, she met them with a perfect torrent of invective and abuse. [...] She said she had gone down in the night to the cell under her father's house, and whipped the slaves confined there with her own hands. (Williams 23)

What is performed in this passage is the loss of idealized white femininity—the erasure of the True Woman—in the face of slavery's contagious qualities. The "wife of master George" (itself an inferior appellation), we learn, "commands" a household, is an "inanimate and delicate beauty," speaks in a "soft and sweet" voice with her husband, and performs music for him "exquisitely" (23). In other words: The pious, pure, submissive, and domestic wife is constructed as if she was a textbook example for Barbara Welter's conceptualization of the nineteenth-century "Cult of True Womanhood." These qualities, however, disappear instantaneously when the institution of slavery and its stark power asymmetry animate and awaken her into an active state of "snaky fierceness" and unfeminine ugliness. By subsequently turning all idealized qualities of True Womanhood upside-down, the wife is rendered a passionate, shrill, abusive, foul-mouthed, and physically violent "virago" (23), "half woman, and half fiend" (24).

What is more, and here matters become complicated: The erasure of femininity and the awakening of the "virago" in Williams' slave narrative completely follow the structural and racial logic of the *early British* Gothic's introduction of the temporary villain who acts and looks like a savage, out of passion and the loss of reason. The white female villain becomes racially visible, is "darkened," and her "black eyes" sparkle, as if she stepped out of Walpole's *The Castle of Otranto*. Should we read this surprising inclusion of the early British Gothic's racialization strategies in an African American slave narrative as a performance of the degeneration narrative discussed above, that is, as an instantiation of white racial and social/cultural decline? Teresa A. Goddu also notices this problematic repetition of "the Gothic's negative association of blackness with evil in this description" and finds that "Williams both demonizes the slaveholder in the Gothic's terms of racial difference and reinforces his culture's association of dread and menace with the racialized other" (Goddu, "The African American Slave Narrative" 77). Why would he do this? My answer is that Williams did not frame female villainy as the B/black racial other; rather, his amanuensis John Greenleaf Whittier did. Compare, in this respect, the "first appearance" of a "terrible" woman in Whittier's 1833 Gothic short story, "The Opium Eater":

> It was the face of one of the fabled *furies*: the *demon glared in the eye*, the nostril was dilated, the pale *lip compressed, and the brow bent and darkened*; yet above all, and mingled with all, the supremacy of human beauty was manifest, as if the dream of Eastern superstition had been realized, and a fierce and foul spirit had sought out and animated into a fiendish existence some beautiful sleeper of the grave. (Whittier n.p., italics C.L.)

By ignoring the negative and strategically harmful implications the racialization of his Gothicized fury/virago would have, when instantiated in a slave narrative, Whittier imposed his stock-in-trade rendering of female villainy on Williams' *Narrative*. Following the early British Gothic's strategy of racially visualizing the passionate deviancy of an otherwise white villain, Whittier dyes his deviant female virago racially Black. Instantiated in Williams' slave narrative, this conflation of demonic evil/passionate deviance with racial Blackness significantly ruptures the abolitionist quest for Black resistance and liberation. As the association of B/blackness and evil "resonates throughout the text," it is all the more difficult "for Williams to validate slave resistance without invoking the threat of slave rebellion" (Goddu, "The African American Slave Narrative" 77).

While the female white Savage Villain itself, i.e., the erasure of the True Woman vis-à-vis the plague-like qualities of the institution of slavery, can be found in all slave narratives in my corpus, Douglass, Brown, and Jacobs refrain from employing the early British Gothic's racialization strategies. In an almost identical imagery with Williams, Douglass, for example, constructs Mrs. Auld as follows:

> The fatal poison of irresponsible power was already in her hands, and soon commenced its infernal work. That cheerful eye, under the influence of slavery, soon became red with rage; that voice, made all of sweet accord, changed to one of harsh and horrid discord; and that angelic face gave place to that of a demon. (Douglass 45)

Douglass connects the fall of the True Woman to the poisoning and possessive qualities of the evil entity of slavery. Mrs. Auld's appearance, however, is neither "darkened" nor dyed black; rather, she turns "red with rage," in the overtly passionate and infernal state of "irresponsible power." She is and remains racially white. The same holds true, to add a final example, for Jacob's depiction of Mrs. Wade, who, fallen from her initial state of "the Angel in the House," has turned her house into a living "hell":

> At no hour of the day was there a cessation of the lash on her premises. Her labors began with the dawn, and did not cease till long after nightfall. The barn was her particular place of torture. There she lashed the slaves with the might of a man. An old slave of hers once said to me, "It is hell in missis's house. 'Pears I can never get out. Day and night I prays to die." (Jacobs 53)

In all instances of female villainy, the impact of slavery is depicted as having deteriorated a white woman's femininity: her morality, virtue, sympathy, and beauty. If we take into account that, in the rapidly changing world of the early and mid-nineteenth century, "men were charged with the task of creating and expanding an industrialized civilization from a wilderness, [while] a True Woman was expected to serve as the protectress of religion and civilized society" (Cruea 188), the threat slavery poses becomes clear: The system of slavery contaminates/poisons the very heart of the American nation. If the True Woman falls, her father, husband, brothers, and sons will follow; and if the pillar of moral strength and virtue she represents crumbles, the American nation resting on it will fall, too. Thus, we encounter poisoned, sickened, and possessed white women in slave narratives, who no longer guide their male family members toward morality and virtue, but who, instead, created an environment for "vile monster[s]" (Jacobs 30), "savage monster[s]" (Douglass 20), and "fiends who bear the shape of men" (Jacobs 30). By pairing "equally mean and cruel" (Douglass 61) male and female white Savage Villains, African American slave narratives strategically conflate discourses of racial and moral decline into one powerful Gothic image aimed at the core of the WASP American self-conception. The word choices framing and motivating this image—sickness, poison, possession, drunkenness—qualify the construction of white savage villainy for the predominately white readership: The white Savage Villains are the products of the system of slavery. Their savagery and ungodly behavior is not an intrinsic quality of their race (as the early WASP American Gothic constructs of Savage Villainy) but results from the systemic and ever-present "brutalizing effects of slavery" (Douglass 56). In other words, the racial degeneration and decline process can be reversed, if the contaminating plague, the institution of slavery, is eradicated.

Fair Damsels in Distress and Black Civil Heroism

The significant other Gothic feature that seems turned "on its head" (Hogle, "Teaching" 215) in African American slave narratives is the racialization of the traditionally exclusively white damsel in distress. Douglass's reversal of conventional racialization in his depiction of the stripping and whipping of his Aunt Hester by Captain Anthony is by far the most known and often quoted example of a Black

Gothic damsel in slave narratives.[14] Aunt Hester, however, is but one example of a downright onslaught of distressed damsels: Douglass narrates as equally "horrible exhibition[s]" the fates of Henrietta and Mary ("of all the mangled and emaciated creatures [Douglass] ever looked upon, these two were the most so," 46), of his "poor old grandmother" (57), of "Henny" (65), Caroline (70), and "a woman slave, whose name I [Douglass] have forgotten" (82). Williams recalls the many "delicate young women," the "faint and exhausted [...] Virginia ladies" (31), Sarah and Hannah (40-42), and big Sarah (43). Brown includes his memory of "every groan and cry of [his] poor mother" (28), of Patsy (33), "poor Delphia" (41), "poor Cynthia" (45), Lavinia (69), and a trembling mother and her crying child (46). Jacobs' damsels include "a young slave girl dying soon after giving birth" (16), a mother in anguish, leading "seven children to the auction-block" (18), beaten and whipped "little ones" and their mothers equally "crushed by the lash" (96-97), Fanny (175), and, most forcefully, herself as Linda Brent.

In the wake of the Dred Scott decision, slave breeding, and systemic hypodescent, it is a fair assumption that all the female characters listed above (as well as their children "who follow the condition of the mother," Jacobs 46) are contemporaneously considered to be racially Black only. The Gothic reiteration strategy of African American authors of slave narratives, however, is far more complex than turning the traditional racialization of the damsel upside down. In fact, in my text corpus, racial markers that indicate a reversed color-coding are missing in every single depiction of a Gothic damsel. Instead, it is the "perfectly white, with straight light hair and blue eyes" (Brown, *Narrative* 37) damsel that makes her reappearance

---

14   Not least because of the innumerous quotations and repetitions of the Aunt Hester scene in literary scholarship, it must be noted that many critics have argued that Douglass's text appears to voyeuristically participate in the Gothic scene, by positioning the reader (as well as the contemporary critic) "like the child who hides in the closet, as an unseen witness to this abject event" (Giles 785). David van Leer argues that this voyeuristic consumption of violence equals a "subtle form of pornography" (132); Deborah McDowell adds that Douglass's text is complicit with the "record of black women's abuse" ("In the First Place" 203)—any recirculation of the scene would also recirculate and, thus, reinstantiate the violence inflicted on the Black woman's body. For Gothic scholarship, and for my reading of Douglass's *Narrative* and the SV/CH Gotheme, this scene introduces the text's key Gothic personnel: The powerful but savage villain (Captain Anthony/system of slavery), the damsel in dire distress (Hester as the first of many similar characters and scenes), and the future Civil Hero (Douglass). From this perspective, spectatorship and voyeurism are controlled and doubly bound: The Gothic invites voyeurism vis-à-vis the spectacle of (sexually connoted) excess, but Douglass counterbalances these tendencies with a rhetoric that assures the reader of the factual reality of this "most terrible spectacle" (Douglass 21). Thus, he ends the Hester scene by assuring the reader that—while most terrifying because "all new to [him]"—it is just one "of the scenes that often occurred on the plantation" (22).

on a very different Gothic stage. Consider in this respect the following two passages, in which two damsels, in the hands of two white Savage Villains, are introduced, first by Douglass and then by Brown:

> While I lived with my master in St. Michael's, there was a white young man, a Mr. Wilson [...]. I have seen him tie up a lame young woman, and whip her with a heavy cowskin upon her naked shoulders, causing the warm red blood to drip [...]. Master would keep this lacerated young woman tied up in this horrid situation four or five hours at a time. I have known him to tie her up early in the morning, and whip her before breakfast, leave her, go to his store, return at dinner, and whip her again, cutting her in the places already made raw with his cruel lash. The secret of master's cruelty toward "Henny" is found in the fact of her being almost helpless. (Douglass 64-65)

> Poor Cynthia! In knew her well. She was a quadroon, and one of the most beautiful women I ever saw. She was a native of St. Louis, and bore an irreproachable character for virtue and propriety of conduct. [...] I [Brown] heard him [Mr. Walker] make his base offers, and her reject them. He told her that if she would accept his vile proposals, he would take her back with him to St. Louis, and establish her as his housekeeper on his farm. But if she persisted in rejecting them, he would sell her as a field hand on the worst plantation on the river. Neither threats nor bribes prevailed, however, and he retired, disappointed in his prey. (Brown 45)

Douglass's strategy here and elsewhere in his *Narrative* consists in juxtaposing an explicitly "white" male ("man"/"Mr."/"master") villain and his female prey, whose attributions may include "lame," "young," "lacerated," "almost helpless," and semi-naked but contain no racialized features. Instead of including markers of the damsel's race, Douglass focuses on gender, that is, on the contrast between a "white young man" and a "young woman" and on the damsel's utter helplessness in this forced relationship. Douglass reflects the damsel's complete passivity syntactically: While the white villain actively ties her up, whips her, leaves her, whips her again, and cuts her, the woman he calls "Henny" (note the quotation marks indicating that "Henny" is the master's name for the woman) is forced to passively endure the violence inflicted on her, due to "her being almost helpless" (note the gerund in the passive voice).

In direct comparison to the construction of "Henny," Brown's strategy appears to be different, as he explicitly marks his damsel's race as "quadroon," that is, as multiracial with one-fourth Black ancestry. At a time defined by a "new intensity of white racial exclusiveness" (Williamson, *New People* 24) and the proliferation of pseudo-scientific racial taxonomy, these categories served two main functions. First, in principle, "these categories identified the precise nature of a person's lineage," while, in practice, they "were typically determined by reputation or physical appearance, with light skin serving as a proxy for mixed ancestry" (Hochschild and Weaver 162). Second, these subcategories did not influence an individual status as belonging to the "Negro" race or the clear demarcation of the white and Black races that chattel slavery depended on; rather, "[b]y classifying the mulatto as a Negro, [white colonists, plantation owners, and profiteers were] in effect denying that intermixture had occurred at all" (Jordan 200). Still, these "distinctions had deep symbolic and substantive impact; most saliently here, they created inequalities within as well as across groups" of enslaved peoples (Hochschild and Weaver 163). Slaves found themselves hierarchized, according to color codes that subjected lighter-skinned "Negros" to "more 'favorable' and privileged positions on plantations" (Busey 121) and darker-skinned slaves to toilsome field labor.[15]

Most clearly, Brown's depiction of a female "quadroon" in distress invokes the established tradition of "tragic mulatto" or "quadroon" fiction. More specifically, Brown draws on the well-known trope of the "tragic mulatta" here, without explicitly including—or without having to include—the trope's standard characteristics, narrative lines and plot points. "The literary tragic mulatta is sometimes enslaved, sometimes free, but always doomed by her racial liminality, which denies her a niche in a rigidly bi-racial world" (Clark 260). Since her literary birth in Lydia Maria Child's 1842 short story, "The Quadroons," the "tragic mulatta" trope had quickly grown in popularity in WASP American literature and culture, "becoming a favorite of those who were warning against intermarriage, performers of blackface minstrelsy, and indifferent white readers identifying with the more flattering characteristics" (Carter 58). For abolitionist writers, Black or white, the "tragic mulatta" trope tapped into both sentimental conventions and readerly expectations, facilitating the identification of a predominately white middle class female readership with enslaved Black female characters across otherwise uncrossable color lines. While Brown will set out to critically and creatively renegotiate the trope in his 1853 novel *Clotel; or, The President's Daughter*, his construction of "poor Cynthia" in his *Narrative* closely follows the conventions underlying the "tragic mulatta" trope. Through this, Brown could completely (re-)focus on gender and Cynthia's white femininity: She is a most beautiful woman, indeed a virtuous and incorruptible True Woman. Only due to the reality of slavery and the constantly preying white Savage Villain will poor Cynthia fall and be "established [...] as [Mr. Walker's] mistress" (Brown 45). In a bold political move, Brown explicitly marks Cynthia's body "as the result of miscegenation and her present position notes the continuance of the transgression" (Wester 43); yet, Cynthia's femininity (including her later motherhood) and moral

---

15　The hierarchization of and stratification between "full Blacks" and "mulattos," via color codes, led to intraracial division and class discrimination, two "of many ugly legacies of slavery and plantation politics" that continue to haunt the United States today (Busey 120).

superiority over her lascivious master and rapist remain rhetorically unquestioned and morally unquestionable.

In sum, when it comes to constructing damsels in distress, the slave narratives written (or narrated) by the male authors discussed in my text corpus uniformly highlight (a WASP American ideal of) femininity. True Womanhood—and, by implication, racial whiteness—lies at the core of these constructions, whether the slave narratives directly link the damsel to racial whiteness, or whether they omit an explicit racialization. It is, however, worth noting how strategically innovative and important this focus on gender really is: The Cult of True Womanhood, to borrow Barbara Welter's 1966 terminology once more, i.e., the essentially WASP, middle and upper class ideal of femininity and religiously inspired womanhood, makes its reappearance in African American slave narratives. By constructing white True Women as Gothic damsels in the white brutal hands of the savage system of slavery, Williams, Douglass, and Brown creatively and powerfully appropriate both the Gothic tradition and the Cult of True Womanhood. Female African American slaves also have the potential to be True Women; what corrupts them is their being subjected to the savage and villainous system of the institution of slavery. Through this construction of the damsel, Douglass, Brown, and Williams uncouple the damsel's physical and sexual abuse from her moral integrity and innocence. In other words, the strategic uncoupling of the abused female Black body from moral integrity is negotiated vis-à-vis the Savage Villain.

Placed in polar opposition to the damsel's retained/re-established femininity, the Savage Villain, whether embodied in the multiplicity of lascivious male characters or abstracted as the patriarchal system of slavery, loses his claim of—and affiliation to—the characteristics and privileges of idealized white American manhood. Once the Savage Villain succeeds in his evil schemes, meaning most often, once he has tortured and raped his helpless victim, the authors of slave narratives rhetorically deconstruct his masculinity. Signifying on the contemporaneous masculinity ideal of the Genteel Patriarch, the "Christian gentleman," whose manhood was defined along the lines of "property ownership and a benevolent patriarchal authority at home" (Kimmel 16), the corrupted patriarchs are morphed into superstitious, anxious, and, thus, feminized boys. The plantation owner Mr. Litch "feared to be alone after nightfall. He might have believed in ghosts" (Jacobs 52); James Williams recalls Mr. Huckstep, a rapist and murderer who now fears to be "haunted" by one of his brutally murdered slaves (32).[16] And with bitter irony, Dou-

---

16   In Chapter 4, we encountered a fictionalized version of the superstitious villain, Harriet Beecher Stowe's Simon Legree. Especially in Legree's interaction with Cassy, Beecher Stowe links his "superstitious excitability" (UTC 454) of being haunted by the ghosts of murdered slaves to both his godless character and well-deserved ridicule. In the wake of Cassy's "fires of fiercer passions" (UTC 456) and under her pseudo-Gothic spell, Legree is feminized, rendered

glass also deconstructs the "Christian gentleman"—and with him the possibility of white American manhood within the institution of slavery:

> Finally, my benevolent master, to use his own words, "set her ["Henny"] adrift to take care of herself." Here was a recently-converted man, holding on upon the mother, and at the same time turning out her helpless child, to starve and die! Master Thomas was one of the many pious slaveholders who hold slaves for the very charitable purpose of taking care of them. (Douglass 65)

Douglass not only uses the ideal of the Genteel Patriarch to depict the corrupting forces of institutionalized violence, but he also unmasks the masculinity ideal of the Genteel Patriarch itself, as a corrupting ideology that is as fake as the Christian piety of his Master Thomas. By depicting how Savage Villains deem themselves Christian patriarchs and philanthropists, Douglass ridicules their masculinity as much as he shatters the claim of Southern white men as being both gentlemen and Christians.

At a first glance, Harriet Jacobs employs a different—though not less potent—strategy in her construction and positioning of the damsel in distress, as she recouples the damsel's/True Woman's moral integrity with her physical inviolacy in *Incidents in the Life of a Slave Girl*. Composed explicitly "to arouse the women of the North to a realizing sense of the condition of two millions of women at the South" (Jacobs 3), Jacobs constructs her plight through the "deep, and dark, and foul [...] pit of abominations" (Jacobs 4) as a Gothic damsel's authentic(ated) testimony. Ever since Teresa A. Goddu's 1997 seminal study on "Jacob's refashioning of the gothic mode" (*Gothic America* 141), *Incidents* has been discussed as a cornerstone text for the development of a female African American Gothic writing tradition. Largely based on the analysis of *Incidents*, in relation to the genre of women's sentimental domestic fiction,[17] scholars such as Goddu, Kari J. Winter, Jennifer Rae Greeson, and Georgia Kreiger especially highlight Jacobs' self-positioning as "the victim of a gothic plot," while simultaneously insisting "on her ability to haunt back" (Goddu 147), in a "conceptual framework through which the sexual order of Southern slavery could be made intelligible—and intolerable—for Northern readers" (Greeson 279). In the face of the excellent scholarship already available on the construction of Jacobs/Brent as a Gothic damsel, I want to focus on an

---

anxious, submissive, and paranoid, until the perfectly gendered paradox happens: "the man fell down in a swoon" (UTC 481).

17 The texts most often cited to contextualize Jacobs' uses of and divergence from nineteenth-century sentimental fiction are Hazel V. Carby's 1987 *Reconstruction Womanhood: The Emergence of the Afro-American Woman Novelist*, P. Gabrielle Foreman's "The Spoken and the Silenced in *Incidents in the Life of a Slave Girl*" (1990), Franny Nudelman's "*Harriet Jacobs and the Sentimental Politics of Female Suffering* (1992), and Joanne Dobson's "Reclaiming Sentimental Literature" (1997).

outstandingly innovative, yet largely unnoticed (or uncommented on), use of the trope in *Incidents*: Jacob's insertion of a Black *male* damsel. This strategic move, I argue, is both the logical conclusion of the feminization of the Savage Villain and a striking example of Jacobs' Signifyin' on Harriet Beecher Stowe's *Uncle Tom's Cabin*.

Very late in her slave narrative, in Chapter 40 "The Fugitive Slave Law," Jacobs includes, as "one of [her] Southern reminiscences," the story of "a slave named Luke" (Jacobs 214). Luke's young white master Henry, who fell "prey to the vices growing out of the 'patriarchal institution'" at an early age, returns from completing his education in the North, with his "greatly increased" "despotic habits" and the unmistakable signs of syphilis: "He was brought home, deprived of the use of his limbs, by excessive dissipation," in "his head the strangest freaks of despotism" (Jacobs 241). Jacobs masterfully constructs the villainous master as the epitome of a white man incurably and fatally infected by the despotism of the "patriarchal institution"[18] of slavery (fittingly, by implying a sexually transmitted disease), while simultaneously rendering him a helplessly "degraded wreck of manhood," who must be "tended like an infant" and who is "entirely dependent on Luke's care" (Jacobs 214). Of course, Henry's physical "helplessness" by no means eradicates his power. Rather, the feminized, infant-like Henry can rely on the "patriarchal institution" to send another powerful "strong arm[ed]" white man, the town constable, as a replacement for the weak "arm of his [Luke's] tyrant" (ibid.).

Luke, on the other hand, is constructed as a nursing caregiver, tending to an infant-like and sick young master like a mother or a maid would be expected to do. In this already feminized role, Luke is further subjected to "the strangest freaks of despotism," some of which "were of a nature too filthy to be repeated" (Jacobs 214). Luke is frequently whipped, while kneeling bare-backed "beside the couch," and he often is forced to serve Henry bare-bottomed, "not allowed to wear any thing but his shirt" (ibid.). Comparable to a female Gothic damsel in slave narratives, Jacobs constructs "poor Luke" as being "chained to the bedside" of a lascivious male Savage Villain in "the black pit" of slavery (Jacobs 215). "In language that characteristically reveals as it also conceals," *Incidents* exposes the male-on-male abuse "to which male narrators rarely admit" (Foreman 22). Jacobs' resolve "that knowledge should be increased" (Jacobs 214) about all "freaks of despotism" is one of the rare and remarkable instances of documenting the sexual assault on an enslaved Black man,

---

18   The notion of slavery as the "patriarchal institution" was widespread in the nineteenth-century South; it idealizes and legitimizes slavery as an institution, "where authority was vested in a patriarchal head of household who presides over a small society of women, children and slaves. According to custom and law, he was responsible for providing his 'dependents' with protection and economic security, and they returned his beneficence with their submission, respect, and grateful love" (Tracy 141).

despite the given multiplicity of social and cultural restraints and barriers.[19] Due to the elucidatory work by scholars such as Robert Richmond Ellis, Martha Hordes, and Thomas A. Foster, we know that "enslaved black men were sexually assaulted by both white men and white women" and that the "sexual assault of enslaved men took a wide variety of forms, including outright physical penetrative assault, forced reproduction, sexual coercion and manipulation, and psychic abuse" (Foster 447).

Jacobs positions her testimonial account of a feminized and sexually abused Black man in her chapter on the Fugitive Slave Law. By stressing the systemic violence involved, via positioning a Black man as a feminized damsel in distress, she can strategically contextualize the newly established (i.e. following the passing of the Fugitive Slave Act) "reign of terror," of "the 'dominant race'" in the North, as an invasion of Southern infectious and contagious savagery and sodomy (Jacobs 213). In her epitomic positioning of a Black male damsel in the Southern hotbed of sin, Jacobs constructs slavery as a tangible threat that viscously attacks all aspects of Northern social and cultural norms and ideals—easily ranging from religion, sexuality, and gender norms to sanity, sobriety, and cleanliness. One part of Jacobs' strategy is that she effectively eradicates the white master's manhood and replaces it with a symbolic tableau of infancy, helplessness, and epidemic contagion, protected and glossed over only by slavery's systemic but completely artificial power imbalance. In a second strategic step, Jacobs deletes the Black male damsel from her narrative, by carefully reinstating and centralizing Luke's manhood and agency: Having escaped from Henry's deathbed with "money nuff to bring him to de Free States," Luke successfully "tuk car fur dat" (Jacobs 215) and tricked his way out of bondage, torture, and impecuniosity. In direct speech and Black vernacular, Jacobs lets Luke relate his own journey toward freedom and the Canadian border, ultimately relaying that Luke should not be considered a thief, as he "had a *right* to that money, as a portion of his unpaid wages" (216, italics Jacobs). The Black man, in other words, has outdone "dem cussed whites" and restored the power balance for and by himself, before starting a free life in "Canada forthwith" (ibid.).

It is especially this elaborate re-masculinization of the Black body that facilitates a re-reading of the Henry/Luke episode as an instance of Black Signifyin' on Harriet Beecher Stowe's *Uncle Tom's Cabin*. In Chapter 23 of *Uncle Tom's Cabin*, the reader is introduced to Henrique, the "noble, dark-eyed, princely boy" (UTC 301), who "value[s] himself on his gentlemanly adroitness in all manners of gallantry"

---

19   It is also worthwhile to turn this argument on its head: "Given the variety of social and cultural barriers to documenting the sexual abuse of enslaved black men, however, it would be an error to assume that the pattern of surviving sources reflects the historical practice of abuse." Indeed, Thomas A. Foster goes on to argue, "the unlikelihood that cases would have been documented at all suggests that it would be safe to say that, regardless of location and time period, no enslaved man would have been safe from the threat of sexual abuse" (447/448).

(UTC 303) but whose abusiveness and passionate brutality render him the perfect counter-image to "the spirituelle graces of his cousin Evangeline" (UTC 302). Before he is "sen[t] [...] North for his education, where obedience is more fashionable, and where he will associate more with equals, and less with dependents" (UTC 307), Henrique encounters Little Eva. True to the logic of *Uncle Tom's Cabin*, the angel-like Eva converts young Henrique into a quasi-religious epiphany to "love poor Dodo [his equally young slave] and be kind to him" (UTC 309). This conversion narrative effectively counterbalances the chapter's discussion of the possibility of a French Revolution-like slave rebellion (UTC 305). Rather than dwelling on the Dodo's "white blood in his veins [...] and the sparkle in his eye" (UTC 302) and the deadly threat this infusion of "Anglo-Saxon blood" poses, "[i]f ever the San Domingo hour comes" (UTC 306), the education and upbringing of Dodo fade into the background, while the necessity of a "Christian-like" moral education of the white male characters is highlighted (UTC 307). Dodo, as Eva so pleasingly—and so confined within the boundaries of Romantic Racialism—compliments, is and remains an utterly docile, "good boy" (UTC 304).

In *Incidents in the Life of a Slave Girl*, Jacobs' depicts an older Henry upon his return from his education in the North. In her signifyin' reiteration, Henry is no longer a dark counter-image, to be converted by the faith of an angel, but the perfect representation of the norm. His mind, morality, race, and gender—his very being—are constructed as both contaminated and contaminating. He is beyond healing, beyond conversion and reversal, and, instead, a transgenerational threat, grown-up in the South and migrating and sprawling freely across the Nation and its women. His degenerate character, his violence and abusiveness remain unquestioned and backed by the patriarchal institution of slavery. In Henry's very own "reign of terror" (Jacobs 213), of sexual abuse and violence, an intervening force of morality and Christianity is neither existing nor imaginable. Slavery has corrupted and contaminated the white race to a point of no return. Thus, instead of relying on a white savior figure, Jacobs gives back agency and a voice to the abused and feminized slave damsel. She envisions a grown-up version of Dodo, a versatile and articulate trickster, who frees himself and escapes to the North. Jacobs ends her version of the Henrique/Henry episode with Luke, living unheard of in Canada ever since his escape. Though a man rather than a docile boy, Luke lives a quiet life in freedom. The subtext here is that free Black manhood is possible and by no means equals slave insurrection and rebellion. Luke, in other words, has managed to escape uncontaminated; in turn, Henry's contaminating plague stands out all the more as racially white. Slavery is constructed as a white plague that drives the white race to the fringe of extinction. As a matter of fact, the North of the United States also remains threatened by the disease of slavery, as long as the Fugitive Slave Act triggers "cupidity and mean servility" in "noble heart[s]" and "brave heart[s]," turning upstanding Northerners into "Northern tools" and "bloodhounds" for the South (Jacobs 216).

One could be tempted to argue that this unresolved, or uncured, Gothic reality of slavery would keep Jacobs/Brent trapped in the position of the Damsel in Distress, despite her acquired freedom. Her "dream of [her] life is not yet realized," and she cannot end her story as a sentimental heroine would, "in the usual way, with marriage" (Jacobs 224). However, Jacobs' narrative does not end with denying a sentimental(ized) closure. It ends with the pain of "the dreary years I passed in bondage" and the memory of her grandmother, which creates "light, fleecy clouds floating over a dark and troubled sea" (Jacobs 225); it ends, therefore, with endurance, family relations, and the power of bearing witness. Jacobs might not be able to "completely exorcise the demons of slavery" (Goddu, *Gothic America* 152), but she certainly bids the Gothic damsel farewell.

The conventional, traditional ending, meaning early British or WASP American Gothic romance, of course, would envision a very different ending to Jacobs' and the three other slave narratives discussed here. The traditional Gothic plot ends with the destruction of the villain and the eradication of passionate deviance and B/black evil from the norm of (white) civilization; the sole active force behind this intervention and repatriation narrative is the Civil Hero. Before Equiano, this Gothic plot convention must have seemed virtually incompatible with the African American slave narrative's conventional and politically motivated open ending, which refuses closure and a self-positioning of the narrator in an autobiographical state of arrival and belonging, as long as slavery is not abolished and all slaves are liberated. Post Equiano, we know that a Gothicized narrative can combine a questing Black Civil Hero (accompanied by white allies) with a politically motivated openness of the plot. In the African American slave narratives discussed in this subchapter, the reiteration of the Civil Hero is taken one crucial step further: Black civil heroism is not only possible, but it can be emancipated from a white frame of reference, i.e., from white fears of the Africanist Savage Villain, Nat Turner-style uprisings, and fully-fledged slave rebellions, just as much as it can be emancipated from an overemphasis on white allies and support systems.

Civil Heroes in African American slave narratives share the same initial position as the many damsels in distress: Despite their intelligent, articulated, civil, and humane nature, they are enslaved and debased as chattel, continuously subjected to a variety of systemic violence, abuse, and denigration. What sets damsels and civil heroes most clearly apart is the ability to become an active force in the narrative. While Gothic damsels, per definition, must remain passive when in distress, the Civil Hero, per definition, must rebel actively against the system of slavery and its many white Savage Villains. In Williams', Douglass', and Brown's narratives, the Civil Hero's humane nature lets him strike "a tree instead of the woman," when forced to act as an overseer (Williams 43); his intelligence lets him understand early in his life that "the pathway from slavery to freedom" (Douglass 45) is self-education, reading, and the mastery of the master's language and rhetoric; and he can be a guileful and deceptive trickster who has "a *right* to" outwit (Jacobs 216) his master, to ensure his survival and the advancement of his interests (cf. Brown 62). The Civil Hero, in other words, functions as a lens with which the narrators focus their self-construction and self-positioning in diametrical opposition to the savage villainy of the institution of slavery in their narratives. Part of this self-construction and self-positioning as Civil Hero is the initial failure, in the face of a seemingly insurmountable evil system, made of innumerable Savage Villains. Having to witness damsels "tortured, and to hear their cries, and not be able to render them assistance," (Brown 28), initially, the Civil Hero "ceases to be a man" (Douglass 98).

To a certain extent, this also holds true for Jacobs' *Incidents*. In her slave narrative—and within the strict barriers of contemporaneous femininity—Jacobs constructs herself as both a damsel and a heroine. It is worth noting that the conflation of heroine and victim in the Gothic plot has been described as a key characteristic of the British Female Gothic by Ellen Moers, Diane Hoeveler, Alison Milbank, and others. While the British Female Gothic, which is understood to originate in Ann Radcliffe's satirical Gothic romances, employs female protagonists as persecuted heroines, it would however be overly simplified to conclude that *Incidents* "draws on the female Gothic [...] and forges parallels between African American female slaves and white women confined to the British domestic sphere" (Davison, "African American Gothic" 8). White upper class women in the British patriarchal society are not and cannot be the adequate point of reference for a Black female slave subjected to American chattel slavery. A strategic appeal to a WASP American upper and middle class female readership, well-versed in Gothic romances, however, seems likely and a more suitable reference frame. Thus, equipped with "a woman's pride, and a mother's love," as well as "a determined will" (Jacobs 95), Jacobs sets out to battle the system of slavery, not by violence or direct confrontation but by choosing her own Gothic scenes of distress. Rather than being raped by Dr. Flint, Jacobs chooses a different white man as sex partner and father for her children, and, rather than seeing her children and herself sold into plantation slavery, she chooses to be buried alive "in that little dismal hole, almost deprived of light and air, and with no space to move [her] limbs, for nearly seven years" (Jacobs 166). Jacobs' resistant passivity allows her, to a certain extent, to stay within the strict boundaries of femininity[20] and womanhood, while advancing her and her children's escape from slavery.

The resistant passivity of the damsel heroine in *Incidents* must not be confused with the oftentimes non-violent resistance of the male Civil Hero. Williams disobeys orders before escaping into the night unseen; Brown tricks and guiles his masters before succeeding to escape; and Douglass's two-hour fist-fight with Covey might have been both "the crime of raising [his] hand against a white man" and "a glorious resurrection" of his "own manhood" from "the tomb of slavery" (78), but Covey's "most unbounded reputation for being a first-rate overseer and negro-breaker" remains as untarnished as the system behind which Covey remains unchanged. A violent slave insurrection, the ever-present threat of "the San Domingo hour" (UTC 306) that would transcend a manly one-on-one fist-fight, is rendered virtually impossible by the "civil" nature of the narratives' construction of Black heroism. Rather than envisioning the instigation of a slave uprising that would overthrow the system of slavery violently—a new Nat Turner—Williams, Douglass, Brown, and Jacobs effectively turn Gothic heroism into Black civil activism. Once in the North, the Civil Hero (and the damsel heroine) joins "the anti-slavery movement," "embrace[s] the temperance cause," teaches, lectures, and "devote[s] [his/her] time to the cause of [his/her] enslaved countrymen" (Brown 80). The strict focus on *civil* resistance by educated former slaves not only ties in with William Lloyd Garrison's and the American Anti-Slavery Society's "principles of non-resistance (non-violence and non-voting)" (Stauffer 208) but also counters the quickly spreading image of the monstrous Africanist Savage Villain post Nat Turner. In polar opposition to the preying, raping, and murdering Africanist Savage Villain, slave narratives inscribe a non-violent resistance of civil Black men and women that relies solely on moral suasion and verbal discussions, replacing the traditional Gothic's violent stand-off between good and evil, between Civil Hero and Savage Villain. The final battle against the evil of slavery is thus suspended from the individual narratives and transferred into the non-violent abolitionist movement of the American Anti-Slavery Society. The savage hydra of slavery cannot be battled and overcome by a single person—this, too, was a lesson drawn from the Nat Turner insurrection—it needs a civil counter-force that comes in equal strength and numbers. Thus, this reiteration of the Gothic Civil Hero (completing the reiteration of

---

20 Jacobs' active and strategic choosing of Mr. Sands over Dr. Flint's vile proposals poses a significant threat to her femininity and social acceptability, as she willingly gives up her purity in an extramarital relationship with a white man. Jacobs, aware of the harmful implications this biographical aspect might have when encountered by her predominately WASP female readership, defends herself by stressing the damsel motif to the utmost extent: "I want to keep myself pure; and, under most adverse circumstances, 'I tried hard to preserve my self-respect; but I was struggling alone in the powerful grasp of the demon Slavery; and the monster proved too strong for me" (60).

the SV/CH Gotheme as a whole) directly motivates the white reader to abolitionist action; all the while, it renders the aimed-at liberation of all enslaved Black people not only a humane cause but an unthreatening necessity.

Closely connected to the calling of the readership to abolitionist action are the function and position of white allies in the Gothic strategy of African American slave narratives. Equiano could position himself as an English gentleman, on one level with the British elite, because racial monogenism (one origin for all human races) was still prevalent in his time; a Black English gentleman was as exotic for the British public as it was for the *Interesting Narrative*'s white readership, but it was in the realm of possibility. Williams, Douglass, Brown, and Jacobs face a reality of racial otherness and abjection largely based on polygenism (all races have separate origins) and the first proto-scientific attempts to change race from a taxonomic to an essential, i.e., biological concept. They also write in the close vicinity of the WASP American Gothic and its dark champion, the Africanist Savage Villain. Self-positioning on one level with (potential) white allies, if possible at all, would in these respects be even more challenging than for Equiano.

Williams, Douglass, Brown, and Jacobs all include white allies as individual characters in their narratives. They teach, transport, hide, or connect the Civil Hero on his quest to freedom and upon arrival in the North. Rhetorically, these white helpers are constructed as outstandingly humane individuals, hardly ever as groups or representatives of a larger authority (the only exception are the Quakers). Out of "sympathy and kindness" (Williams 63), as "angel[s] of mercy" (Brown 79), with "vigilance, kindness, and perseverance" (Douglass 106), these named white men and women treat a fugitive slave "as an equal" (Brown 76) and "as kindly as if I had been one of their own children" (Brown 77). The former slaves, in turn, vow to "never forget" (Douglass 106) their helpers and praise their noble and sympathetic characters euphorically: "The noble heart! The brave heart! The tears are in my eyes while I write of her [Mrs. Bruce]. May the God of the helpless reward her for her sympathy with my persecuted people!" (Jacobs 217). Often placed in direct opposition to the vile forces of slavery, waiting to re-enslave the Civil Hero, these individuals function as role models and offer room for identification for the reader. Without giving away telltale details of the network enabling the escape from slavery, for example of the Underground Railroad or the names of Quakers involved in the hiding and transportation of fugitives, these white allies stand in for the effectiveness of individual sympathetic actions, in the face of the overwhelming evil of slavery.

In the slave narratives discussed here, two strategies stand out that directly negotiate the problem of white savior versus ally, or white superiority versus racial equality. Firstly, the Civil Hero has "long since made up [his] mind" that he trusts himself "in the hands of any man, white or colored" and that, in the corrupting system of slavery, the "slave's friend" can only be "the North Star!" (Brown 73). In the reality of the chattel slavery and at a time when "the slightest manifestation of humanity toward a colored person was denounced as abolitionism," entailing "frightful liabilities," hardly any person had the "degree of courage" (Douglass 97) necessary to intervene in the systemic violence of the institution of slavery. The likelihood of finding an ally in this situation is deemed almost impossible, as everyone surrounding the Civil Hero is depicted as morally corrupt, recreant, and a potential danger to the escape and the life of the slave. Thus, it is the civility and morality of the Black Civil Hero in slavery-infested America that makes creating alliances, based on equality, virtually impossible, in the South and outstandingly rare in the North.

Secondly, white allies are not only, and quite frequently not, the Civil Hero's most important support system. Unlike Equiano's *Interesting Narrative*, African American slave narratives depict a range of non-white allies, from the slave's close and extended family (cf. Jacobs), to many instances of "a free colored man, whose name I [Douglass] deem it imprudent to name" (Douglass 84); the Black fortuneteller "Uncle Frank" who convinces Brown that it is his fate to "*be free!*" (71); the free Black friends who cordially welcome the fugitive "as one rise from the dead" (Williams 61), and even "Indian women" "in the Creek country" who offer food and shelter "with a great deal of kindness," even if located "not far distant" from the plantation (Williams 56). Prioritizing the importance of a Black network of family, friends, and allies, supporting the Civil Hero's escape from slavery, is especially prevalent and noteworthy. While the stress on outstandingly courageous and humane white allies ties in well with the abolitionist movement in general and the activation of the primary readership in particular, the depiction of Black networks follows a different logic. Borrowing a title phrase from John Sekora, I argue that the Black Civil Hero and his active establishment of, and reliance on, a Black support network should be understood as a "Black message," within the "white envelope" of the slave narrative's conventionalized appeal to a mostly white readership. Black networks highlight the survival and utmost importance of African American communities within—and in spite of—the negating and destructive forces of slavery. While families are torn apart and marriages and friendships are systemically corrupted, alternative Black networks thrive and are fundamental to the survival of the Civil Hero. This message is aimed as much at contemporaneous Black readers (and listeners) as it is at later generations of Black readers. With a transgenerational stance, the necessity of bearing witness is projected together with a most powerful statement of African American identity, community, and survival, in the face of the overwhelmingly destructive, white supremacist institution of chattel slavery. For the white readership, this Black support system, based on the shared experiences of white racism and slavery and on the shared (political and ethical) ideals of freedom and liberty, also stands in polar opposition to the popular phantom of the Africanist Savage Villain. Black networks and alliances function on the same principles of kindness and shared humanity as those of white abolitionist alliances, and they are by no means to be feared as real-life versions of a Poesque B/black swarm of savages.

From a broader perspective, the reiterated SC/CH Gotheme in slave narratives takes part in expressing

> the burdens of those who were less-than-citizens in a nation to which they contributed so much. Either directly or indirectly, the writing was meant to bear witness to the cultural literacy, moral strength, and viable independence of free black communities. Even while acknowledging their commitments to abolition, the fight was to break the bonds of being slave-classed. (Blockett 131)

By the mid-nineteenth century, civil heroism, which Equiano strategically suspended from his *Interesting Narrative* in 1789, had been centralized in slave narratives in the form of a Black Civil Hero protagonist. By emancipating the Civil Hero from white frameworks, i.e., by both distancing the character from exclusively white support systems as well as juxtaposing his civility and the Africanist Savage Villain, narrators and authors like Williams, Douglass, Brown, and Jacobs complete a politically-charged and highly strategic reiteration of the SV/CH Gotheme. Rather than using an upside-down version of the bestselling Anglo-American Gothic for writing themselves into the nineteenth-century literary marketplace, Williams, Douglass, Brown, and Jacobs understood the Gothic as a helpful yet highly racialized and thus problematic writing that had to be functionalized and adapted strategically and creatively, to promote their political convictions and the abolitionist cause. The reiterated Gothic writing strategy in African American slave narratives, therefore, marks one key component in the development of African American literature:

> Indeed, in their increasingly strategic approaches to autobiographical writing, black abolitionists opened the way for the development of African-American fiction and, over time, the African-American novel—in part because, through fiction, African-American writers could represent more fully the numerous contexts, concerns, and pressures that shaped African-American life and that were necessarily part of any comprehensive approach to antislavery activism and social reform. (Ernest 100)

If we further include William L. Andrews' concept of "the novelized autobiography" (*To Tell a Free Story* 265), we can conclude for now that one aspect in the very complex and multilayered African American turn toward the novel began in the reiteration of the Gothic—and especially of the SV/CH Gotheme—in African American slave narratives.

5.3 Early African American Novels: *Clotel* and *The Bondwoman's Narrative*

> "I seldom gave way to imaginary terror. I found enough in the stern realities of life to disquiet and perplex, without going beyond the boundaries of time to meet new sources of apprehension." (Crafts, The Bondswoman's Narrative 136)

> "Slavery has never been represented; Slavery never can be represented." (Brown, "A Lecture Delivered before the Female Anti-Slavery Society of Salem" 104)

By the middle of the nineteenth century, African American literature had started to turn to the novel as a form of artistic expression. Still targeting mostly white (and female) audiences in Great Britain and/or the United States, early African American novels were "meant to bear witness to the cultural literacy, moral strength, and viable independence of free [B]lack communities. Even while acknowledging their commitments to abolition, the fight was to break the bonds of being slave-classed" (Blockett 131). The urge and need to claim a distinct Black voice, culture, and history, that is, to represent Black humanity and agency, must be understood as in dire tension with the systemic implications of American chattel slavery and its devastating and (as we know today) utterly long-reaching effects on the thingification of the Black subject via white abjectorship, to borrow Sabine Broeck's terminology once more. The self-positioning of Black agencies and voices in the grand narrative of the United States of America from within chattel slavery indeed was "an urgent and direct challenge to the state of the union" (Blockett 131). Firmly rooted in the Black slave narrative and the white popular novel (and especially in the domestic or sentimental romance and Gothic novels), novelists such as William Wells Brown, Hannah Crafts, and Harriet E. Wilson explored and paved new creative ways for the very possibility of African American artistic self-expression that exceed the conventions and standards of both roots. Authoring verisimilar (though not verifiable)[21] fiction about African American humanity and life under chattel slavery for a mostly white target audience not only necessitates a broad knowledge

---

21 For more details on the meaningful difference between slave narrators' strategic insistence on verifiability and novelists' focus on verisimilitude, see Havard ("Slavery and the Emergence" 87).

of African American cultural traditions, WASP American literary history and writing conventions, and acceptable strategies for establishing the veracity of the fictional account vis-à-vis "proslavery charges of dishonest exaggeration" (Havard 87), but it also requires an understanding of the British and/or U.S. book markets and the intricate intertwinement of financial and political interests. Having observed the impact that bestselling WASP fiction—first and foremost Harriet Beecher Stowe's *Uncle Tom's Cabin*—had on the slavery debates, early African American novelists with outstanding creative and political agency "refused to grant Stowe and other white abolitionists the sole right to tell the story of slavery in novel form" (Havard 88).

While the African American turn toward the novel is a highly complex process, we have already singled out one key element of the fictionalization playbook: the strategic and politically charged reiteration of the Gothic—and especially of the racialized and racializing Savage Villain/Civil Hero Gotheme—in African American slave narratives. Indeed, among the specific criticisms leveled against early African American novels, today as much as in the nineteenth century, "are its appropriation of white narrative techniques" (Frye, "The Case against Whiteness" 527), which are predominately defined as the formulaic "woman's fiction" and/or as the bestselling subgenre of "woman's fiction": the Gothic romance. However, the early African American novels that we know today differ greatly from one another—also with respect to the degree to which they have been Gothicized—through either the iterative inclusion or the reiteration of white Gothic writing conventions and intertexts. All known authors of the early African American novels employed, to varying degrees, Gothic writing strategies in their negotiation, for example, of the debates on slavery, Black citizenship, and the white literary canon; nevertheless, as Mulvey contends, their writing must be understood as developing independently from one another and as representing a fresh start each time:

> Critical silence meant that William Wells Brown and Martin Delany were not reviewed in the white press. Racial isolation meant that Frank Webb in London, Harriet E. Wilson in New England, and Hannah Crafts in New Jersey could have no impact on their contemporaries. Silence and isolation prevented normal writerly exchanges of example, inspiration, and competition. Modern readers can bring titles together and see patterns and influences, but there is a sense in which all of these titles stand apart. Each one represents a fresh start. (Mulvey, "Freeing the Voice" 29)

In this subchapter, I discuss two such "fresh starts" with respect to their different and yet distinctly African American employment of Gothic writing strategies: William Wells Brown's *Clotel; or, the President's Daughter* (1853) and Hannah Crafts's *The Bondwoman's Narrative* (c. 1850s). Taken together, these novels offer a unique glimpse into the creative adaptability and strategic versatility of the Gothic. At the same time, the analysis will help in extracting and emphasizing once more the evolution of the one common denominator: the Savage Villain/Civil Hero Gotheme and its intrinsic raciality.

Clotel; or, the President's Daughter

William Wells Brown's 1853 version of Clotel—a novel that was revised, adapted to different audiences, and reissued at least three times—is an excellent starting point for an analysis of early African American Gothic writing strategies in the novel form. The ways in which Brown either utilizes or deletes Gothic sub-plots from the different editions of his novel indicate his highly strategic and sophisticated usage of the Gothic's ultra-adaptability to writerly needs and readerly expectations. According to the current state of research, *Clotel* is understood to be the first African American novel; the text's outstanding hybridity, which expertly "mingles popular history, abolitionist propaganda, and personal experience with a complex plotted melodrama" (Bradford Warner 12), is used as a prototype for reading how early African American novelists bridge the gap between fictionalizing "personal or public history" and the inclusion of "actual documents or factual history" (Bradford Warner 12). The fact that *Clotel* is a "notoriously hybrid text" (Havard 91) has been utilized either to dismiss the novel as inchoate and inferior to WASP American novels in the past[22] or to highlight the stylistic ingenuity of William Wells Brown;[23] it has not been considered to better understand Brown's usage of—and subsequent erasure of—Gothic features in the novel(s). By focusing my analysis first on Brown's Chapter XXIII, "Truth Stranger than Fiction" (1853), I will show how Brown carefully and strategically intertwines the SV/CH Gotheme with a true onslaught of non-Gothic paratexts, that is, of often verbatim quotes and excerpts from at least

---

22   Dismissals include Vernon Loggins, *The Negro Author: His Developments in America* (NY: Columbia UP, 1931, p.166) and Arthur Davis, "Introduction" to *Clotel; or, the President's Daughter: A Narrative of Slave Life in the United States*, by William Wells Brown (NY: Collier Books, 1970, p. xv).

23   To give just two recent examples of a positive re-evaluation of Brown's "expropriative practices" (Sanborn, "People Will Pay" 65) in *Resistance and Reformation in Nineteenth-Century African American Literature: Brown, Wilson, Jacobs, Delany, Douglass, and Harper,* John Ernest argues that Brown acts like an editor who places a number of genres and narratives into tension, until his reader understands how this hybridity- and ambivalence-infused tension reflects the conflicts of the democratic slaveholding nation at large. John C. Havard argues that *Clotel* is a "national novel," according to Benedict Anderson's and Jonathan Culler's theorization, i.e., a novel that documents the contemporaneous nation, by capturing the diverse "actions of people who, while unknown to each other personally, simultaneously act their part in a national story" (Havard 92).

seven distinct literary and extra-literary sources.[24] As we will see, the infusion of the SV/CH Gotheme frames and motivates his usage of intertexts and is both self-reflective (as the chapter title already implies) and specifically geared toward the reading expectations of his white British target audience. Once Brown leaves the British readership and book market behind, addressing the North American literary scene and reading public, his writing strategies change, and the self-reflective Gothic sub-plot is erased from both the chapter and the novel. This means that, in all the later versions of the novel, starting with *Miralda* (1860-1861), the Gothic "Jane episode," specifically her imprisonment in the "forest prison," her attempted escape, and the yellow fever frame narrative are omitted completely from the novel, and the respective chapter is renamed "The Law and Its Victim." This revision showcases, with striking clarity, Brown's strategic usage of the Gothic: As soon as Brown refocuses on a North American readership—which will not only include but explicitly target a Black readership in his 1864 version, *Clotelle: A Tale of the Southern States* (part of the dime novel series "Books for the Campfire"), and especially in his 1867 update, *Clotelle; or, the Colored Heroine*—he thoroughly replaces the romanticized "mulatta"-damsel of the WASP literary tradition with the agency of (now fully) Black characters and heroines. In "The Law and Its Victim," victimhood is no longer conventionally occupied by the "tragic mulatta" of the WASP romance or the early Black/African American Gothic; nor is agency/villainy constructed as white and male. Rather, Brown highlights the system of slavery, more specifically, the abstract agency of "the law" as the actively destructive force in his revised chapter. Following the logic of a self-fulfilling prophecy, Brown also ironically re-constructs victimhood as both white and male: The victim of this episode is now Mr. Morton, the unsuspecting heir to Dr. Morton's estate and debts and the horrified uncle of Jane and Alreka, who is reduced to inaction by the law of the land.

Only in *Clotel* does Brown include a brief but explicitly Gothic sub-plot that narrates the fate of Althesa's (Clotel's sister and the daughter of Currer and Thomas Jefferson) two daughters, Ellen and Jane. Ellen commits suicide quickly after being "bartered away like cattle in Smithfield market" (*Clotel* 174), a dramatic episode that Brown relates in fewer than nine lines, while her younger sister's fate is constructed as an intricate Gothic romance. At the New Orleans slave market, Jane, too, is sold

---

24 Aside from the Lord Byron epitaph ("Canto X" from *Don Juan* [1819-1824]), Geoffrey Sanborn lists for Chapter XXIII the following paratexts: John Reilly Beard's *The Life of Toussaint L'Ouverture, the Negro Patriot of Hayti* (1853), Harriet Martineau's *Society in America* (volume 2, 1837), Lydia Maria Child's "The Quadroons" (1842), "The Woes of Slavery" (*Pennsylvania Freeman*, 18 November 1852), "A Peep into an Italian Interior" (*Chambers' Edinburgh Journal*, April 16, 1852), and "Story of a Slave Mother" (*Pennsylvania Freeman*, November 18, 1852). See http://www.geoffreysanborn.com/clotel (last accessed September 2, 2017) for the extended full-text version of the appendices of his 2016 publication, *Plagiarama! William Wells Brown and the Aesthetic of Attractions*.

to "an unprincipled profligate," whose appearance at the auction block spells the "impending doom" (*Clotel* 175), to which the "young lad[y]" (*Clotel* 174) will be subjected from now on. Up to this point, Brown closely follows the plot of Child's "The Quadroons," whereas his take on the Jane episode starts to deviate. In the tradition of the early British Gothic—yet firmly situated on American soil—the nameless profligate imprisons Jane "in something closely resembling a castle overlooking the Mississippi River" (Siân S. Roberts 150), a "forest prison" located in a "most singular spot" (*Clotel* 175):

> This was a most singular spot, remote, in a dense forest spreading over the summit of a cliff that rose abruptly to a great height above the sea; but so grand in its situation, in the desolate sublimity which reigned around, in the reverential murmur of the waves that washed its base, that, though picturesque, it was a forest prison. Here the young lady saw no one [... and the] smiles with which the young man met her were indignantly spurned. (*Clotel* 175)

Reminiscent of the incongruous transplantation of a British Gothic castle to Connecticut in Isaac Mitchell's 1811 Gothic romance, *The Asylum; Or, Alonzo and Melissa*, Brown likewise employs a genuine prop of the early British Gothic. This artificial transplantation is indeed a self-reflexive inclusion of a quasi-verbatim copied intertext: Brown borrows this passage from an 1852 journal article, "A Peep into an Italian Interior," and subsequently Gothicizes the picturesque description of an Italian resort. Brown adds "a dense forest" to the setting, which effectively Americanizes the remote location, by rendering it a part of the American wilderness. Brown thus transforms the Italian resort into a "forest prison" on American soil. His self-reflexive and marked-as-artificial play with British Gothic conventionality reaches its climax when Brown introduces Jane's lover and potential Civil Hero. Whereas in "The Quadroons" Jane's lover is an Englishman, Brown inserts Volney Lapuc, a Frenchman, into the plot. As Fabi argues, the "choice of this name is revealing of the attention that Brown, in writing his novel, devoted even to minute details" ("Explanatory Notes" 273). Rather than restricting the name Volney to the historical persona of Constantin-Francois Chassebeuf de Boisgirais (1757-1820), better known as Volney, and his support "of the cultural and artistic achievements of blacks" (Fabi, "Explanatory Notes" 273), however, we can also follow Siân S. Roberts's line of argumentation and understand "Volney" as an alliterative allusion "to such Radcliffean heroes as Vivaldi or Valencourt" (151). Adhering very closely to the British Gothic romance, Brown constructs a moonlit rescue mission, with Volney arriving at the remote castle on horseback, with a love letter and a rope ladder in hand, to liberate the damsel from her lascivious oppressor. This kind "of romance conventionally concludes with a happy marriage in a disenchanted world voided of tyrannical injustice and supernatural elements" (Roberts 151); for Brown, this is the very point at which the utility of Gothic intertextuality stops dead, unmasked as a completely artificial and—at least for the fictionalization of a female slave's fate—completely unsuitable happy ending. In an almost comical manner, Volney, "the enthusiastic lover, with his arms extended," waits at the bottom of the castle tower to "receive his mistress," only to be casually shot dead by Jane's owner, returning from his nightly "hunting excursion" (*Clotel* 176). At the very climax of the traditional Gothic plot, Brown renders the Gothic sub-plot as ineffectual as its notion of civil heroism and returns to the "intense melancholy" (*Clotel* 176) of Child's short story. The heartbroken Jane is unceremoniously buried "at night at the back of the garden by the Negroes" (*Clotel* 176).

Let me unpack Brown's reiterative usage of the SV/CH Gotheme in this brief episode. The "young Southerner" and "unprincipled profligate," who buys Jane as a sex slave for his remote Gothic mansion, functions as the nameless stand-in for the countless perpetrators of the "thousand wrongs and woes" (*Clotel* 177) committed in the name and under the protection of the institution of slavery. Being just one head of the hydra of slavery, he doubtlessly represents "the inhumanity and barbarity" (*Clotel* 59) of the WASP slave-holding society of the South. However, Brown also reiterates the villainous "cruel master" (*Clotel* 176) to a certain extent. When confronted with Jane's "heart-piercing [...] sadness" (*Clotel* 176), his lascivious passion is gradually replaced by compassion, until the villain is merged with the prisoner of the Byronian epitaph: "He's as far/From the enjoyment of the earth and air/Who watches o'er the chains, as they who wear" (*Clotel* 172). The compassionate "cruel master" (*Clotel* 176) by no means unhinges the SV/CH Gotheme. Rather, Brown renders the compassion a hollow and ineffective emotion of a representative of a system that is all "bitter and dreadful," which knows "no help," "no sympathy," and "no hope" (*Clotel* 177). Under the temporarily compassionate gaze of the villain, "the poor girl die[s] of a broken heart" (*Clotel* 176) and is buried with no one—not even the temporarily compassionate villain—weeping at her grave. Villainy in this episode is white and systemic: It causes the utmost "agony" and "intense melancholy" of help- and hopelessness, while being legitimized by "the laws of the Southern States" (*Clotel* 177). In other words, by placing a dashing Southerner into the footsteps (and the castle) of well-known British Gothic villains, and without the implication of specific persons or social ranks, Brown, true to his announcement in his preface to the 1853 version of *Clotel*, strikes slavery to the core, "by revealing not just the iniquity of slaveholding's minor villains" (Havard 87) but also of those who "move in a higher circle" (*Clotel* 4). Brown concludes:

> If the incidents set forth in the following pages should add anything new to the information already given to the Public through similar publications, and should thereby aid in bringing British influence to bear upon American slavery, the main object for which this work was written will have been accomplished. (ibid.)

Truth, in this brief episode, is indeed not only "stranger than fiction" but also much crueler and more inevitable than Brown's British readership would have expected from a Gothic romance. From today's perspective, Brown's in-depth exploration of the systemic implications of chattel slavery on the Black subject anticipates, in stunning clarity and detail, the conceptual main pillars of both Afro-Pessimism and Sabine Broeck's notion of white abjectorship. At the same time, Brown's reiterated Gothic unmasks the systemic villainy of the institution of chattel slavery, which obscures white agency and responsibility behind a multilayered mask made of contemporaneous race theory, cultural production, legal and political discourse. Brown's construction of villainy in *Clotel* thus both directly reflects and weighs in on the systemic workings of "white abjectorship and un-humanization of Black being" (Broeck, "Legacies" 109). By reiterating the Gothic villain and its highly racialized logic, Brown gives a white face to the system that produces slaves qua their presumed racially (and legally) inevitable "slavishness" (ibid.).

As a consequence of this re-reading of Gothic villainy as systemic enslavism, the trope of the damsel in distress must also be reiterated by Brown. While we have encountered all-but-white True Women before, Brown's "mulattas' are so light-skinned that they readily (and strategically) pass for white. In effect, Brown unsettles—even deconstructs—the contemporaneous biological essentialism, by depicting race and racialization as an arbitrary attribution of status, vis-à-vis an equally arbitrary codification of skin color. Fabi summarizes:

> Foreshadowing late-twentieth-century deconstructionist discourses on "race" as a cultural construct and a social fiction rather than a biological fact, Brown shows the permeability of racial boundaries, the unreadability of "race" (and gender, for that matter), and the precariousness and contingency of those very definitions of blackness and whiteness in which social institutions like slavery (as well as the right to first-class citizenship in the American nation as a whole) found their supposed legitimation. (Fabi, "Introduction" xiii)

The central importance that the permeability of race has for Brown's construction of the SV/CH Gotheme, outside the strict boundaries of racial essentialism, is highlighted by the fact that he frames his Gothic episode by an—in many ways equally Gothic—account of the yellow fever outbreak in New Orleans in 1831. After a gruesome medical account of the decomposition of the infected body and mind, Brown concludes:

> On an average, more than 400 died daily. In the midst of disorder and confusion, death heaped victims on victims. Friend followed friend in quick succession. The sick were avoided for fear of contagion, and for the same reason the dead were left unburied. Nearly 2000 bodies lay uncovered in the burial-ground [...]. The Negro, whose home is in a hot climate, was not proof against the disease. (Clotel 173)

In this passage, as much as in the medical account of the infected body, Brown extensively and often borrows verbatim from John R. Beard's *The Life of Toussaint L'Ouverture, the Negro Patriot of Hayti* (1853). For the Jane episode, two aspects in this frame are of immediate importance for Brown's reiteration of the Gotheme. Firstly, other than Beard and the majority of late eighteenth- and early nineteenth-century accounts and commentaries on yellow fever,[25] Brown insists that the Black population is not immune to the disease. "This specific change to his source material suggests," Roberts claims, "that Brown consciously sets out to dismiss the racist logic of autochthony and immunity" (158). What categorizes human beings into various races cannot be inherent in their biological make-up; the yellow fever outbreak becomes the great leveler of races. Thus, by unsettling the presumed "natural" boundaries between the races on the level of biology and highlighting the arbitrary codification of skin color, vis-à-vis the status as either slave or citizen, chattel or human being, Brown's damsel in distress morphs into a liminal category. Rather than adhering to the qualities and functionality of the tragic mulatta—and thus to "The Quadroons" intertext—Jane understands and manipulates the system of slavery and its intricate and corrupting forces. Jane is experienced and/or knowledgeable enough not to trust another "slave [...] to drug his master's wine" (Child 139), as the betrayed Xarifa does in "The Quadroons;" she dares "not trust the old Negress with her secret, for fear that it might reach her master" (*Clotel* 176). Despite being enslaved and imprisoned, Jane, in a clear act of Black female agency, uses her liminality strategically to plot her escape. Her death, "far from being the inevitable result of [her] personal mixed-race status [is] clearly connected with [her] search for freedom and take[s] on explicitly political connotations" (Fabi, "Introduction" xiv).

To take this argument even one step further, we can understand Jane's failure to escape, in the arms of a traditional Civil Hero, as a dismissal of the paternalistic view on slaves and slavery, as derived from their presumed (biological) inferiority and childlike docility. Jane plots her escape strategically and fails only because she relies on a white, ineffectual Civil Hero. In fact, she does not even need his rope ladder: Her torn and knotted bed sheets are enough for her to leave her prison

---

25   Beard uses the Black slaves' immunity to the disease to highlight their benevolent humanity, charity, and discipline, when faced with the diminishing strength of an increasingly panicky and morally degenerating white society (*The Life of Toussaint* 218). Matthew Carey (*A Short Account of the Malignant Fever, lately Prevalent in Philadelphia; with a Statement of the Proceedings that Took Place on the Subject in Different Parts of the United States*, 1793) and Benjamin Rush (*Letters of Benjamin Rush*) speculate that the yellow fever outbreak in Philadelphia originated in the West Indies and that the Black population was immune to the disease. A fictionalized account of the same racialized assumption can be found, for example, in Charles Brockden Brown's 1799 novel *Arthur Mervyn*, in which Black characters function as healthy undertakers and nurses in an otherwise infected and infectious environment.

behind. Leaving the boundaries of the Gothic behind most clearly, Brown envisions Jane's escape not only as an act of Black female agency but as an act of self-liberation.

This strategic and rebellious potential in the damsel is also implicitly introduced by Brown in the yellow fever frame narrative. The yellow fever epidemic, which Brown describes as heaving bodies upon bodies, until nearly 2000 bodies lie rotting on the ground, did not occur in New Orleans but in Saint-Domingue. By including Bread's *The Life of Toussaint L'Ouverture*, Brown places his reiterated, self-liberating Gothic damsel (and *Clotel* as a whole) in the larger context of Black rebellion and revolutionary history. Brown is even more specific. He writes, "[i]n the summer of 1831, the people of New Orleans were visited by one of these epidemics [i.e., the yellow fever, C.L.]" (*Clotel* 172). Brown, however, has carefully constructed and hidden a trapdoor here that, when uncovered, lets us enter into another realm of signifying and protest: When we consult the historical records of yellow fever causalities in New Orleans in 1831, we do not encounter "nearly 2000 bodies" but an officially recorded number of two deaths related to the disease.[26] I claim that Brown's reference to the year 1831 is not a historical date related to the yellow fever epidemic but, rather, a metaphorical reference to the most dramatic and incisive event of the same year: the slave rebellion led by Nat Turner in Virginia (August 21 to 23, 1831). Just as yellow fever can be understood to be the great, deadly leveler of races, so the Nat Turner-led slave rebellion killed white and Black people alike, plantation owners and their families, as well as the rebellious slaves (who themselves set out to avenge the torture and death of millions of Black slaves). The infection, which caused the fatal "disorder [that] began in the brain" (*Clotel* 172), until death heaps victim on victim, is slavery: "Thus carnage was added to carnage, and the blood of the whites flowed to avenge the blood of the blacks. These were the ravages of slavery" (*Clotel* 181).

While we have already encountered the metaphorical coupling of slavery and contagion in *Incidents of a Slave Girl*, Brown's reference to Black rebellion and past slave insurrections is an important and striking addition, especially because it is not used to morally judge either the white or the Black population. Rather, rebellion and death are the inevitable consequences of life in the system of chattel slavery. In Brown's use of the yellow fever epidemic, as an allegorical comment on slavery, the tension between Brown's urge to represent Black agency, on the one hand, and his intent to explore to the fullest (and in stunning anticipation of today's Afro-Pessimistic concepts) the systemic implications of American chattel slavery, on the other, is very tangible. Systemically reduced to a thing, a chattel, an abject, Black

---

26 See Louisiana Division/New Orleans Public Library, "Yellow Fever Deaths in New Orleans, 1817-1905" (http://nutrias.org/facts/feverdeaths.htm; last accessed September 26, 2017).

humanity and agency is rendered ontologically impossible within the white system. Liberation, the cure for the disease of slavery, thus, cannot be expected to come from the white agents—be they willing or unsuspecting accomplices—of the system; rather, Brown's solution to the tension between Black agency and white abjectorship is Black self-liberation.

This can best be seen in Brown's construction of the Civil Hero. While Jane, as has been outlined above, certainly is rebellious for a "mulatta" damsel in distress, Brown especially utilizes the reference to Nat Turner and the history of Black rebellion and resistance in his reiteration of the Civil Hero. I have argued above that the Civil Hero in "Truth Stanger Than Fiction" is so incongruently transplanted from the traditional British Gothic romance into the context of American chattel slavery that he is rendered a completely ineffectual and even comical prop, in a maze of horror and hardship. Brown places the Civil Hero at the intersection of "The Quadroons" and his reiterated Gothic villainy and ironically bedizens him with the qualities of a hopelessly romantic Don Quixote, who is defeated and rendered useless by the common reality of slavery in the southern states. In fact, the dismissal of the traditional Civil Hero is so absolute that it leaves a blank in the text that Brown thrice makes explicit: "no help can relieve, no sympathy can mitigate, and no hope can cheer" (*Clotel* 177). In other words, all the chief qualities of the Civil Hero—being the savior in the hour of need, the voice of sympathy for the inconsolable, and the ray of hope for the doomed—are negated and banished from the episode. However, if we include the yellow fever frame narrative once more into our reading, this blank in the text becomes not just comprehensible but also replenished. In a way that directly reflects the replacement of the white Civil Hero with Black Civil Heroism and support systems in slave narratives, Brown inserts "a vocal protagonist new to the American novel: the slave community" (Fabi, "Introduction" xvi). In "Truth Stranger than Fiction," Brown envisions Jane's resistance against the villain's lust and power, as being linked to the slave rebellions in Saint-Domingue and Virginia. While far from being the focal point of the novel (Jane, too, is a minor, secondary character), it is the excessive proliferation of secondary Black characters that poses a threat to the institution of slavery:

> Their ethos of resistance, knowledge of American political, religious, and institutional hypocrisy, and sense of belonging to a community (not only because they are communally oppressed, but because they are united by a common history and shared cultural values) effectively qualify them as a veritable nation within the nation, as another African American author, Sutton Griggs, would put it a few years later in his novel Imperium in Imperio (1890). (Fabi, "Introduction" xvi)

In deleting white Civil Heroism from the plot, Brown elevates Black resistance to the point at which it becomes the only viable option for intervention. In reiterating the Gothic, he not only depicts, documents, and celebrates this resisting Black community and culture that have developed, despite conditions of extreme and brutal captivity, but he also practices and actively furthers it with the very writing of *Clotel*. When we perceive all four versions of *Clotel* as a progressive unity, Brown's reiterative Gothic writing strategy forms an important stepping stone toward Black heroism and liberation:

> [...] Brown adjusts his narrative in subsequent editions, all published in America, to meet and influence the cultural expectations and beliefs of changing audiences, transforming once heroic white characters as Henry and Georgiana into impotent, ineffective abolitionists, and the once marginal African American slaves Jerome and Miralda into heroes. In the fourth and final edition of the novel, published after the Civil War, Brown offers a revolutionary vision of America, one in which—guided by a heroine—African Americans verbally and physically battle to help create and shape a new republic. (Stampone 76)

Jane, we could argue, will finally liberate herself and leave the castle behind; envisioning her as the fair damsel in Gothicized sub-plots is no longer strategically reasonable or necessary.

The Bondwoman's Narrative

Hannah Crafts's (possibly autobiographical) novel *The Bondwoman's Narrative*, has triggered a massive scholarly response and a renewed interest in early African American Gothic writing, since its publication by Henry Louis Gates, Jr. in 2002.[27] In his detailed introduction to the novel, Gates states that indeed one of his first impressions of *The Bondwoman's Narrative*, upon reading the manuscript for the first time, was that it presents "an unusual amalgam of conventions from gothic novels,

---

27   Literary scholars, among them Maisha L. Wester (*African American Gothic*), Teresa A. Goddu ("American Gothic"), Russ Castronovo ("The Art of Ghost-Writing: Memory, Materiality, and Slave Aesthetics"), Karen Sánchez-Eppler ("Gothic Liberties and Fugitive Novels: *The Bondwoman's Narrative* and the Fiction of Race"), John C. Havard ("Slavery and the Emergence of the African American Novel"), and Robert S. Levine ("Trappe(d): Race and Genealogical Haunting in *The Bondwoman's Narrative*"), all highlight that Crafts's novel shows considerable influence from the era's gothic fiction—especially from Horace Walpole's *The Castle of Otranto* and Charles Dickens's *Bleak House*. While it is generally accepted that "Crafts trained in the same school of self-education as Douglass and Brown and was influenced by what she read, as they were" (Mulvey, "Freeing the Voice" 21), scholars disagree about the level or quality of her adaptation. In a nutshell, what could be dismissed as "sentimental fiction, made worse by untutored storytelling skills" (Havard 94) could also indicate the necessary transgression of the stereotypical Gothic from within the context of American chattel slavery, as Crafts's take on the Gothic "is not that gothic after all but is rather a critical aesthetic response to the everyday horrors of slavery" (Castronovo 195).

sentimental novels, and the slave narratives" (*The Bondwoman's Narrative* xxxiv). "Gothic effects ooze and seep throughout *The Bondwoman's Narrative*," so seconds Russ Castronovo Gates's impression ("The Art of Ghost-Writing" 206), and, in fact, the novel abundantly uses the props and settings that nineteenth-century readers (both British and American) would readily identify as "Gothic." Gothic mansions, already "exceedingly aristocratic and antique for a New World setting" (Gates, *The Bondwoman's Narrative* 254), are further augmented with secret rooms, mysterious passageways, and communicative portraits; lascivious villains pursue innocent damsels; and blood and torture are as much a part of everyday life as are human skeletons, haunting ghosts, and dreadful curses.

In my study, I read *The Bondwoman's Narrative* as an important stepping stone for understanding the development of the Savage Villain/Civil Hero Gotheme in African American literature. In many respects, close to Brown's *Clotel*, by accomplishing a "fresh start" (Mulvey, "Freeing the Voice" 29) while drawing critically and creatively on a number of Anglo-American fictional and non-fictional intertexts, *The Bondwoman's Narrative*'s utilization of the SV/CH Gotheme differs significantly from *Clotel* and the slave narratives discussed above. Rather than reiterating the Gotheme's raciality and its intrinsic abjection of Blackness, vis-à-vis the Savage Villain, Crafts iterates, with great precision, the British Gothic's racialized villainy. She even goes so far as to include the fully-fledged Africanist Savage Villain as the uncontrollable horde of dreaded sexual predators, that is, the "promiscuous crowds of dirty, obscene and degraded objects" (TBN 213).[28] With an artistic rationality to write herself into the Anglo-American literary canon and—more importantly—into the contemporaneous ideology of WASP Americanness, Crafts utilizes the Gothic's ultra-adaptability in ways that contrast profoundly with *Clotel*, yet the SV/CH Gotheme, for Crafts as much as for Brown, is the strategic literary weapon of choice. In the following, I will unpack Crafts's use of the SV/CH Gotheme, by closely reading and contrasting the two key Gothic episodes of the novel: the Lindendale episode, which frames Crafts's introduction of both Mr. Trappe and Lindendale's new mistress, and the North Carolina episode, which confronts Hannah with "the brutes" living "in [the] utter darkness" of the slave huts (TBN 206).

What I refer to as "the Lindendale episode" spans from the latter half of the first chapter to the end of the second chapter of *The Bondwoman's Narrative*, thereby forming the Gothic undercurrent of the plot. The slave protagonist, Hannah, narrates the preparations for a bridal party at "the ancient mansion of Lindendale" (TBN 13), describing how she is sent on an errand through the mansion. Instead of completing her errand and heeding the order of the housekeeper not to "loiter in the rooms" (TBN 15), Hannah ends up in the mansion's portrait gallery. Triggered by the portrait of Sir Clifford de Vincent under "the shadows of the linden" (TBN 17)

---

28   In-text citations marked "TBN" refer to *The Bondwoman's Narrative*.

and the eerily picking-up wind, "shrieking like a maniac" (TBN 20), Hannah recalls the "history of that tree" (TBN 20), "the legend of the Linden" (TBN 25). The legend, which Crafts refers back to throughout the novel, describes in dire detail the torture and subsequent death of an elderly house servant and nurse, Rose, and her white "little dog," which had an uncannily "strong resemblance to [...] a child" (TBN 21). The narration of the legend ceases with the relation of Rose's curse ("In sunshine and in shadow, by day and by night I will brood over this tree, and weigh down its branches, and when death, or sickness, or misfortunes is to befall the family ye may listen for ye will assuredly hear the creaking of its limbs" [TBN 25]), and Hannah returns to the party preparations. In a parallel construction of characters and props, Crafts now introduces a mysterious "small brown woman" as the new mistress of Lindendale (TBN 27), "and following close behind her like her shadow" (TBN 29), the "rusty seedy old-fashioned gentleman" (TBN 28), dressed "in black" (TBN 29). The wind picks up once more, the linden branches moan and shriek, and the painting of Sir Clifford falls to the floor.

When read in direct comparison to *Clotel*, the Gothicized composition of the Lindendale episode seems close to Brown's reiteration strategy. Villainy is white and blended with the system of slavery, both structurally and intertextually: Sir Clifford de Vincent, "a nobleman of power and influence of the old world" (TBN 16), has turned into a "stern old man [and] hard master to his slaves" (TBN 20), on "the shores of the Old Dominion" (TBN 16). He cruelly and regularly tortures his slaves "within the full sight and hearing of their agonies," while "drink[ing] wine, or coolly discuss[ing] the politics of the day with some acquaintance, pausing perhaps in the midst of a sentence to give directions to the executioner, or order some mitigation of the torture only to prolong it" (TBN 21). Crafts's construction of villainy closely follows the early British Gothic traditions, up to the point at which Sir Clifford, overwhelmed by rage and passion, turns into the savage-like villain, with "features distorted and his whole frame seeming to dilate with intensity of passion" (TBN 23). Here, much like the constructions of white villainy by Brown, Douglass, and Jacobs (and other than Williams's/Whittier's account of white female villainy), Crafts carefully deletes the early British Gothic's racialization upon climax. Sir Clifford is and remains white; his passionate deviance, for example, neither darkens his brow nor turns his eyes black. Rather, through Sir Clifford's briefly related biography, as well as the British Gothic convention employed in the construction of his character, Crafts directly connects "the old world" and "the Old Dominion," in terms of the villainous agency and atrocities committed, "with appalling indifference" (TBN 23), within the institution of slavery. Instead of embodying abolitionism and the hope for transatlantic political intervention, the British nobleman—unflinchingly addressed as "Sir" Clifford—becomes the perpetrator of the "direst act of cruelty" and "the deepest horror" (TBN 21) and, thus, not only unmasks the British involvement in and profiteering of American slavery but renders the British elite an active force of torture and death on American soil. In direct opposition to Brown's first version of *Clotel*, the British elite are introduced as part of the horror and not as the chief agent in a hoped-for solution.

This construction is paralleled by Crafts's introduction of the arch villain, Mr. Trappe. Mr. Trappe, as scholars such as Gates, Wester, Goddu, and Sánchez-Eppler have argued, is an adaptation (or reiteration) of Charles Dickens's mysterious villain in *Bleak House* (1853), Mr. Tulkinghorn. While the outer appearances, racial markers (including the "great black eyes so keen and piercing" [TBN 28]), and function in the plot remain almost unchanged, Crafts equips Mr. Trappe with clear motivations (in the context of Lindendale, Crafts adds to Trappe's general greediness for money, a keen desire for revenge, for having been spurned by the new mistress). More importantly even, Trappe has a much more concrete power than Tulkinghorn: the complete power over his prey's body and soul. Indeed, in her revision of Dickens, "Crafts may be suggesting that [...] slavery provided conditions in which excavating family secrets could result in a woman bred for refinement being declared a slave" (Havard 95)—a familiar plot line from *Clotel*. Thus, Crafts's Mr. Trappe must be understood as a context-appropriate reiteration of a canonical British villain. However, while Sir Clifford constantly shimmers between old world and Old Dominion, between England and Virginia, Mr. Trappe is firmly rooted in the North American context: "The mistress is haunted by, and Trappe haunts as a result of, knowledge of a secret that cannot be revealed because of the institution, which haunts, therefore, more by what it evokes for the future than by what it summons from the past" (Wald 225).

In the Lindendale episode, Crafts balances her parallel construction of two white villains with an equally parallel construction of two damsels in distress, Rose and the new Lindendale mistress. Though both damsels are racialized as "mulattas," their fates are not just "tragic" but, taken together, marked as the very epitome of hope- and helplessness. Painfully suspended from the linden tree, in the course of torture lasting six days, "poor old Rose" (TBN 22) and her "little dog, white and shaggy," who—with the eyes "of a child" and the singular beauty and innocence of whiteness and "helplessness" (TBN 21)—directly stands in for her youngest daughter, are reduced to "wasted and decayed" flesh (TBN 24), to "the helpless object[s] of his [Sir Clifford's] wrath" (TBN 25). Neither the tears nor the prayers of Sir Clifford's wife, nor the "near frantic" entreaties by his son (TBN 24), can avert Rose's fate. A Civil Hero, the other slaves, divine intervention, and any other savior in the hour of need are missing from the scene. Even Rose's curse, the climactic Gothic nod toward retribution and revenge, turns out to be the empty threat of a helpless old woman: The curse foreshadows the novel's plot, as it fully embodies the workings of the institution of slavery, but, other than in the traditional Gothic plot, it is neither a supernatural nor any sort of actively intervening force. Whenever the creaking and moaning linden branches are tied to the plot, for example, to the ill-fated marriage of the current master of Lindendale or to Mr. Trappe's eventual demise, the narrator directly and explicitly blames the institution of slavery rather than the curse. When Lindendale is finally dismantled, its ancient portraits are auctioned off as if they were slaves (cf. Sánchez-Eppler 270), the linden tree is chopped down, and Mr. Trappe is killed by the sons of his next, all-but-white, damsel: The workings of the institution of slavery are to blame every time. Slavery, it turns out, is intrinsically doomed. In Maisha L. Wester's words:

> No slave uprising burns the plantation to the ground; no slave ever lifts a hand against the plantation's master. The very institution under which the family prospers dooms the family to suffering. Furthermore, the destruction's passive-aggressive form presses the fact that this is not an individual offense. The only villain in this plot is Trappe, a pawn and representative of the slave system, prospering from its rules and information. A nonviolent harbinger of destruction, Trappe likewise repeats the text's message of systematic social ruin. (Wester 58)

For Rose, however, this means that even her final act of resistance against Sir Clifford and the system that he represents remains ineffective, further stressing the damsel's complete and utter helplessness. The true curse at work in the novel is not Rose's final words but the institution of slavery, which legally, systematically, and ontologically eliminates the very possibility of Black agency and resistance.

The deletion of any possibility of supernatural retribution or intervention, as a marker of complete helplessness and the elimination of Black agency, is also taken up as a means for constructing the nameless new mistress of Lindendale. When the mysterious and "indefinable" (TBN 27) bride, "sweep[ing] gracefully along in her bridal robes"—of course still pursued like "her shadow" by "the old gentleman in black"—stops to "examine beneath a broad chandelier the portrait of Sir Clifford," the "image regards her with its dull leaden stare" (TBN 29). When the music and dancing adjourn momentarily, the painting crashes to the floor. For avid readers of Gothic romances, portraits coming to life are a common prop relating directly back to Walpole's *The Castle of Otranto*. In *The Castle of Otranto*, the damsel Isabella, already "half-dead with fright and horror" (25), is pursued by her villainous father-in-law, Manfred. At the very moment when Manfred moves "to seize the princess" (26), "the portrait of his grandfather" comes alive, steps out of his frame, and saves Isabella, by first leading the startled Manfred in the wrong direction and thereafter locking him in a chamber. Donald Ringe argues convincingly that Walpole's supernatural elements are motivated by the need to restore the order "to a world in which a usurper has broken the natural line of descent and seized possessions that are not rightfully his" (Ringe, *American Gothic* 19); the "infernal spectre" (Walpole 26) of the walking painting thus serves to "reveal the truth of the usurpation, to identify the legitimate heir, and to help him restore his rightful position in society" (Ringe 19). In Crafts's adaptation of the trope, the portrait indeed "repeats the supernatural rebellion against an unlawful presence/marriage in the ancestral line" (Wester 58); rather than protecting the damsel from distress and leading Mr. Trappe astray, the painting of Sir Clifford rebels loudly against the prospect of having a slave—and her blood—in the family tree. Again, Crafts highlights the damsel's utter helplessness. This time, however, she also includes the peculiar institution's long history as a damnatory superstructure that works across generations, as if it were as hereditary as the slave status. From beyond the grave, the white ancestor rises to protect the white family line, while the "mulatta" damsel is doomed from beyond the grave by her dead mother's Blackness. In this systemically fixed power hierarchy, the damsel stands without the ghost of a chance before Mr. Trappe, who in turn can approach her legitimately and non-violently and claim her not only as his prey but as his chattel. "The greatest curse of slavery," Hannah exclaims in North Carolina, "is it's [sic] hereditary character" (TBN 205).

I want to pause here for a moment and analyze Crafts's reiterative elimination of supernatural interventions from a slightly different angle. Just as Rose's curse is not translated into a plot-influencing event, so is the communicative portrait of Sir Clifford subsequently explained, by the "corrupting canker over the polished surface of the metal that supported it, and crumbled the wall against which it hung" (TBN 30). If we read this deletion of the Gothic from the episode, in conjunction with Hannah's creative animation of the painting in the Lindendale gallery earlier, Crafts seems to build up a self-reflective commentary on the process of writing, the agency of authorship, and the self-introduction into the WASP American literary canon. Gazing at the ancient paintings and musing over their stories, Hannah changes "the pale pure features" into "smiles and dimples," adding "a gracious expression" or relaxing the "haughty aspect[s]" (TBN 16/17); somewhat bored with her results, she starts morphing the paintings into "some fearful tragedy" (TBN 17). The portrait of her master "change[s] from its usually kind and placid expression to one of wrath and gloom," and "the calm brow" becomes "wrinkled with passion, the lips turgid with malevolence" (TBN 17). Hannah, standing in the gallery and morphing the painting in her mind, as well as before the reader's eyes, is effectively portrayed as the author of the traditional Gothic villain.

> [...] I seemed suddenly to have grown old, to have entered a new world of thoughts, and feelings and sentiments. I was not a slave with these pictured memorials of the past. They could not enforce drudgery, or condemn me on account of my color to a life of servitude. As their companion I could think and speculate. In their presence my mind seemed to run riotous and exult in its freedom as a rational being, and one destined for something higher and better than this world can afford. (TBN 17/18)

Through Hannah's reiteration, the epitomic instantiation of ancestral power and white dominance, of authority and entitlement of the many masters of Lindendale, is rendered mutable. At the same time, she enters "a new world" of "pictured memorial of the past," the world of art and literature, that is, of the WASP cultural canon. As a rational being—creatively and culturally on par with her white "companion[s]"—Hannah becomes the very manifestation of "artistic agency, her authorship becomes a figure of her liberation" (Wald, "Hannah crafts" 219). Reconnecting this liberating authorship and Crafts's Gothic writing strategy, Karen Sánchez-Eppler argues that

> [i]f young Hannah sees in these pictures "companions" rather than owners, she does so through a complex process of interpretation and denial that rejects the artistic and ancestral intentions behind such portraiture, refusing to view them as signs of lineage possession, and power. So, too, in writing this scene Crafts adopts and alters the conventions of gothic fiction, for generic norms hold the act of viewing an ancestral portrait as testimony to the inescapable tentacles of the past, in inevitable entrapment of blood ("Gothic Liberties and Fugitive Novels" 257).

I want to take this argument one step further and claim that Crafts's subsequent elimination of the traditional Gothic writing convention from the portraits, as well as from the Lindendale episode as a whole, self-reflectively creates the "rational being" outside the racialized boundaries of her "color." Throughout the novel, Crafts intertwines Blackness with superstition ("I am superstitious, I confess it; people of my race and color usually are" [TBN 27]); the elimination of Gothic superstition, supernatural curses, walking paintings, and other forms of supernatural intervention must thus be read as claiming for herself a position among the WASP "companions," as writing herself into authorship and, more importantly, into white, rational Americanness.

This strategic repositioning of Hannah (and, qua her authorship, of herself) becomes most visible when Crafts forcefully writes herself into the contemporaneous American novel and, as a matter of fact, confronts her protagonist with the Africanist Savage Villain. When Hannah arrives in North Carolina at "Mr. Wheeler's fine plantation [...] near Wilmington," (TBN 203) Crafts goes to great lengths to construct her protagonist as a well-cultivated and sophisticated woman, with an expert eye for esthetics and garden design. Strolling through her master's Edenic garden, Hannah is "fairly charmed," while "admiring" the "lime trees," "the orange trees [...] dropping with fruit," the "peach trees," "the purple clusters of grapes," the "great heaps of marrows, glowing pods, and luscious melons," the vegetables, the herbs, the roses, and the "world of pinks" (TBN 204). Never leaving this image of abundance and esthetic pleasure, Hannah depicts plantation slavery as the "cotton field with the snowy fleece bursting richly from the pod" and the "large plantation of rice" that is beautifully "sweeping down to the river's edge" (TBN 204). Hannah's beautifying ecstasy is contrasted powerfully with the promiscuous "swarm of misery,

[the] crowds of foul existence" (TBN 204), with the "old and ruinous," the "decay," the "dust," and the "rubbish" of the slave huts (TBN 205). Constructing herself in direct opposition to the plantation slaves, Hannah muses:

> [...] Isn't it a strange state to be like them. To shuffle up and down the lanes unfamiliar with the flowers, and in utter darkness as to the meaning of Nature's various hieroglyphical symbols, so abundant on the trees, the skies, in the leaves of grass, and everywhere. [...] It must be strange to live in a world of civilization, and elegance, and refinement, and yet know nothing about either, yet that is the way with multitudes and with none more than the slaves. (TBN 206/207)

Hannah is the positive against this negative foil of "utter darkness," ignorance, and savagery. Excluded rhetorically from "them," she is the civilized, elegant, and refined representative of the "habitation of their master" (TBN 204). This self-fashioning, as being culturally and racially superior to the field slaves, is, as Gates (TBN 293) and Wester (62) argue, an especially stark differentiation between house slaves and field slaves, along the lines of degrees of Blackness and hierarchized class allocation. As a baseline assumption rather common in slave narratives as well as in white literature, Crafts's construction of intraracial class distinctions is taken to the extreme, once Hannah is "with all [...] force" degraded and exiled by her villainous mistress's "perfect fury" and "in language unsuitable for a lady" (TBN 209) to "[t]hose brutalized creatures in the cabins" (TBN 210). Thus reduced to the class of field slaves, she feels "doomed to association with the vile, foul, filthy inhabitants of the huts, and condemned to receive one of them for [her] husband [her] soul actually revolted with horror unspeakable" (TBN 211). Part of her "horror unspeakable" clearly stems from having "been brought down to their level," to the "filth and impurity of every kind," and to the "dozen women and children [...] sitting on the ground, or coiled on piles of rags and straw in the corner," until they engage in their nighttime "rough and rumble" mass brawl (TBN 215).

However, her horror is caused most significantly by being forced "into a crime against nature" (TBN 213), specifically into a sexual relationship (and subsequent marriage) with Bill, the hyperbolic personification of the "promiscuous crowds of dirty, obscene and degraded objects" (TBN 213). Fair Hannah, with bleeding and blistering fingers "unused to such employment" in field work, grows "faint with the unwonted exertion" and "too weak and weary, too dispirited and overcome to offer resistance" (TBN 214), while "with a hedious [sic] grin," Bill advances to "take her to [his] cabin" (TBN 214). Luckily for Hannah, Bill is caught-up in a mass brawl and she can escape his promiscuous lust. Crafts's juxtaposition of Hannah and the Africanist Savage Villain clearly works along racial lines: The fair and not just maladjusted but completely alienated Hannah is pursued by the Black "grossly sensual and repulsive" (TBN 214) horde of rapists and savage creatures. Indeed, Hannah is so whitened against the negative foil of the Africanist Savage Villain that a forced sexual encounter between her and Bill would indeed, in the logic of the novel, be "a crime against nature," namely miscegenation. Rather than living with the constant threat of being raped by her white master, Crafts's nightmare scenario for her protagonist consists exclusively of the introduction of the Black savage rapist, who would once and for all seal her fate as being "no better than the blackest wench," despite her "pretty airs and [her] white face" (TBN 210). As if to prove how grotesquely wrong Mrs. Wheeler's ascription of Blackness to Hannah is, the protagonist, in the manner of a True Woman, "weep[s], and pray[s], and meditate[s]" (TBN 210) over her fate and the Biblical teachings, while the "black wenches" in the slave huts—male and female, young and old—engage in a brutal mass brawl. The racial threat becomes tangible: Should Hannah be degraded to their level once and for all, her offspring would be one of promiscuous Bill's many children, that is, one of the kicking, yelling, and clawing (TBN 215) savages. Hannah not so much passes for white; at this point in *The Bondwoman's Narrative*, she is constructed as racially white. This becomes clear when Crafts relates Hannah's escape. Rather than narrating Hannah's passing-for-white scheme, she focuses exclusively on her passing for male: Hannah cuts her hair and dresses in "a suit of male apparel" (TBN 216), her whiteness, most essential to this escape plan, goes without saying.

It is of the utmost importance to note that this construction of a juxtaposition of a white damsel with the Africanist Savage Villain in *The Bondwoman's Narrative* is framed by, or has its roots in, the white literary tradition—and this interracial intertextuality is marked as such by Crafts. In her introduction of the nauseating slave huts, as containing "a swarm of misery" and "crowds of foul existence," as the natural habitation of the Africanist Savage Villain, she copies almost verbatim from Charles Dickens's *Bleak House*:

> Now, these tumbling tenements contain, by night, a swarm of misery. As on the ruined human wretch vermin parasites appear, so these ruined shelters have bred a crowd of foul existence that crawls in and out of the gaps in walls and broads; and coils itself to sleep, in maggot numbers, where the rain drips in; and comes and goes, fetching and carrying fever [...]. (Dickens, *Bleak House* 135)

In *Bleak House*, this passage introduces the rundown "Tom-all-Alone" dwellings of Jo and his equally poor and uneducated peers. Timothy Carens argues that Dickens created a setting here "in which the 'condition of England' belies the presumed distinction between the 'civilized' imperial metropole and the 'savage' periphery," up to the point at which the equally run-down and ignorant inhabitant Jo "collapses the privileged distinction between the 'native' Britons and the African 'native'" (Carens 121, 134). Could we build a similar case for Crafts's usage of Dickens as an intertext? Could Hannah's degradation to "the foul existence" in the slave huts, on the periphery of the Edenic garden, so much unbalance the hierarchy between master and slave along presumed color lines, as to collapse the racialized distinction and even the legitimization of the institution of slavery? This would position the racial politics of *The Bondswoman's Narrative* on one level with Brown's *Clotel* and its unsettling of biological essentialism in favor of a more fluid, socially and politically inspired notion of race. However, I believe that *The Bondwoman's Narrative* does not allow for such an affirmative reading. While it would help to explain, or rather excuse, Hannah's extreme "revulsion at blackness" at this late point in the novel, which indeed seems to be "out of proportion," especially "when compared to Hannah's seeming obliviousness to the threat posed to her body by her white masters" (Levine, "Trappe(d)" 291), such a reading cannot be brought in line with the novel's ending. Stylized as a return to the Edenic garden of the plantation, "freedom and happiness" (TBN 245) in the free state are imagined as "a tiny white cottage half-shaded in summer by rose-vines and honeysuckle appears at the foot of a sloping green. In front there is such an exquisite flower-garden, and behind such a dainty orchard of choice fruits that it does one good to think of it" (TBN 246).

Crafts effectively re-establishes and thus affirms the intraracial hierarchy, which Mrs. Wheeler had grotesquely and only momentarily stripped from Hannah. Living in her own version of a contemporaneous True Woman's paradise, Hannah has her mother, a husband, friends, and children (of the school she has founded) gathered around her, to live in their midst a life marked by religious piety, community education, sophisticated conversations, writing, exquisite gardening, and sewing. This ending stands in stark contrast to the endings of slave narratives, as well as to the ending of *Clotel*. Rather than aiming at a furthering of the abolitionist cause, that is, rather than reconnecting Hannah's fate with the need for a "common salvation" that would abolish the "distinction between the bond and the free" (*Clotel* 209), Crafts re-establishes Hannah in her initial position as an intellectually, culturally, and racially superior white True Woman. Thus, the concluding chapter reads like an "untroubled celebration of black uplift, 'goodness,' and 'undeviating happiness' [TBN 246], and interracial harmony reads more like a white abolitionist fantasy than an affirmation of black community" (Levine, "Trappe(d)" 292).

Borrowing her introduction of the Africanist Savage Villain from Dickens is thus not so much a borrowing of Dickens's sociopolitical criticism but a self-reflective and self-confident positioning of Crafts as an author. Very close to Hannah's construction of an author in the Lindendale episode, Crafts uses Dickens's *Bleak House* to write herself not only into the white literary and cultural canon but equally so into white American identity. This includes—indeed, must include, if we accept Toni Morrison's argument—the self-definition of white Americanness against the negative foil of the Africanist presence. In this respect, Hannah becomes a white American woman at the very moment she is attacked by the Africanist Savage Villain. Writing Hannah into the ideologies of WASP female Americanness, in other words, means writing her out of (American) Africanism. Crafts's juxtaposition of

Hannah with the Africanist Savage Villain thus iterates closely the nineteenth-century WASP American Gothic plot and especially its racial (even racist) agenda.

One last aspect must be included in this iterative strategy of Crafts's crafting of white Americanness, qua writing, qua education, and qua sophistication: the Civil Hero. Civil heroism, as has been especially hinted at in my analysis of the Lindendale episode, is a curious blank space in *The Bondwoman's Narrative*. Crafts resolves this absence in a completely different way from Brown; she underlines the utter helplessness of the damsels on the Lindendale plantation, as much as Hannah's "horror unspeakable" in North Carolina. Rather than including the Black community and/or Black agency as an actively intervening force in the plot, Crafts effectively crushes this mere option. When Hannah escapes Mr. Wheeler's plantation and its Africanist Savage Villain in particular, she meets "a black man" (TBN 222), Jacob, and his dying sister. While Jacob would have all the qualities to be a Civil Hero, as he is a strong man who gathers food, builds a shelter, and helps to alleviate the "toilsome journey" (TBN 230) to the free North, his Blackness renders him unfit for the role: "Jacob and myself traveled many days together, but strange to say he had not penetrated my disguise. He learned to love me, however, as a younger brother, and his society and gentle care greatly relieved the difficulties of our toilsome journey" (TBN 230). Crafts apparently does not trust the "gentle care" of the Black man enough to let him travel alone with a fair/white woman. Rather than creating an effective counterbalance to "the fear and loathing of blackness expressed by Hannah (and Crafts) in Bill's cabin" (Levine, "Trappe(d)" 292), the continuous necessity of passing-for-male attire renders Jacob a potentially uncontrollable sexual threat on par with Bill. As a matter of fact, he not only cannot be the Civil Hero who saves Hannah, but he also cannot be permitted in her life once she is revealed to be female. Hence, Jacob is shot and dies as soon as the duo encounters the first "of these dangerous spots" (TBN 232). Crafts quickly replaces him with her version of a *deus ex machina*, her white "old friend, Aunt Hetty" (TBN 233). Standing in for the many "friends of the slave in the free state," who are "just as good as kind and hospitable as [Hannah] had always heard they were" (TBN 244), Hetty's "superior feasibility" secures Hannah's survival, enabling her journey north "in an expeditious manner" (TBN 236). Civil Heroism in the novel therefore reads like an abolitionist's pamphlet, in which the Black race, due to the individual actions of courageous and pious white women, is uplifted and liberated. Wherever these women, as the upholders of moral superiority and justice, are missing—that is, in places such as the Lindendale plantation and Mr. Wheeler's plantation in North Carolina—the slaves are inescapably subjected to a dire state of utter help- and friendlessness. White True Women, the most likely target audience for her novel (had Crafts ever had the option to publish her manuscript), are stylized as both the sole saviors in this hour of need and the ideal white Americanness, into which Crafts aims to write herself:

"Child" she [Aunt Hetty] said "I was thinking of our Saviour's words to Peter where he commands the latter to 'feed his lambs,' I will dispense to you such knowledge as I possess. Come to me each day. I will teach you to read in the hope and trust that you will thereby be made better in this world and that to come." (TBN 7)

It is not least this narrative of Black racial uplift, qua white heroism, that sets *The Bondwoman's Narrative* most visibly apart from Brown's *Clotel*. The hyperbolic iteration of the Africanist Savage Villain in Crafts's narrative of becoming white, vis-à-vis education and cultural sophistication, indicates very well the SV/CH Gotheme's ultra-adaptability to different strategic needs and literary contexts. As Crafts suggests in her introduction, and as Brown titles his Chapter 26, the truth of slavery is indeed "stranger than fiction," and its representation within fiction and outside the conventional boundaries of more established writing traditions than the African American novel both necessitates and furthers an adaptable yet clearly race-based writing convention, such as the SV/CH Gotheme.

African American Gothic Today: Black Tradition and Reiterative Practices

> "I, too, live in the time of slavery, by which I mean I am living in the future created by it." (Saidiya Hartman, Lose 133)

If I were to draw only one conclusion from my previous in-depth reading of early Black and African American Gothic texts, I would state: The early Gothic was far from being the prerogative of solely WASP American authors; before authors such as Charles Brockden Brown, James Fenimore Cooper, and Edgar Allan Poe established the WASP American Gothic's persistent conventionality, Olaudah Equiano already had created a uniquely Black reiteration of the nascent British Gothic from the oftentimes nightmarish surges of the eighteenth-century Black Atlantic. This finding counters the majority of scholarship that firmly positions the American Gothic "as a white invention" (Lorenzo 57) and, hence, discusses the African American Gothic in terms of a secondary, or reactionary, development on the American soil. The "frequency with which the terms 'appropriation' and 'subversion' appear when we deal with African American gothic" (Lorenzo 57)—up to the point where scholarship claims an African American "anti-gothic" (Smethurst 29)—indeed is telling. As I have shown in detail above, the early African American Gothic novel balances a uniquely Black Gothic writing strategy and conventionality (traceable back to Equiano and the African American slave narrators) with a reiterative practice of responding to—and resisting—the early WASP Gothic's rampant racism. In this respect, the early African American Gothic is as far from being "anti-gothic" as it is from being readily subsumable under the term "American Gothic."

In the remaining subchapters, dedicated to African American Gothic literature, I will pinpoint this balancing of Black tradition and ongoing reiterative practice in contemporary African American Gothic novels. For this end, I will survey the SV/CH Gotheme in a necessarily limited selection of contemporary African American Gothic novels, before providing in-depth readings of two novels, namely of Tony Morrison's *A Mercy* and Colson Whitehead's *Zone One*. Largely following the structure of Chapter 5, I provide an overview of the contemporary African American Gothic marketplace, by including a range of male- and female-authored novels, some of which fall into the category of fully-fledged genre novels, while some are generic hybrids; in an effort to describe the African American Gothic novel today as comprehensibly as possible, I will discuss current bestsellers, published by major publishing houses, next to lesser-known independent publications.

In line with my previous analyses of Black and African American Gothic writing strategies, I will pay special attention to the iterative or reiterative functionalization—and possible deconstruction—of the racialized and racializing Savage Villain/Civil Hero Gotheme. My key concern will be to position the SV/CH Gotheme in the unflinching African American challenge of WASP ideological assumptions and racism, vis-à-vis and through the Gothic writing strategy. If the continuous racialization and abjection of B/blackness in WASP American Gothic fiction fuel the arguments of Afro-Pessimism, does the continuous creative battle of African American authors from within, against, and maybe even outside the Gothic conventionality of racial denigration give rise to a however restricted optimism?

6.1 Spotlights: The African American Gothic Novel Today

The first novel in my tour de force of the contemporary African American Gothic marketplace is Octavia E. Butler's *Fledgling* (2005), a vampire novel that creatively reiterates the WASP American vampire trope, both by rewriting the racial dimension of the vampire and its prey within the SV/CH Gotheme and by firmly positioning itself within the African American Gothic tradition generally and, particularly, in the footsteps of Jewelle Gomez's *The Gilda Stories* (1991). While vampires and their unquenchable thirst for the blood and life of the innocent are stock characters of the European and WASP American Gothic traditions, at least since the enduring success of nineteenth-century bloodsuckers such as Joseph Sheridan Le Fanu's Carmilla, Bram Stoker's Count Dracula, or Edgar Allan Poe's Ligeia, they did not emerge in African American literature until the advent of neo-slave narratives in the late twentieth century (cf. Robinson 61). Doubtlessly, Toni Morrison's *Beloved*, which features at least two clear-cut allusions to the vampire trope,[1] and Jewelle Gomez's fully-fledged Black queer vampire novel *The Gilda Stories*, can be understood as early representations of a nascent literary tradition of Black vampire fiction in the United States. Morrison and Gomez, just as more recently as L.A. Banks and Octavia Butler, claim and inscribe themselves and their unique perspectives into one of

---

1 Morrison draws heavily on the vampire trope for the construction of *Beloved*'s ravenous feeding on Sethe's guilt and of the Ku Klux Klan as a "dragon [...] desperately thirsty for black blood" (Morrison, *Beloved* 79); as Cedric G. Bryant points out, the dragon can be read as a direct reference to Stoker's *Dracula*, as "Dracula" literally means "son of the dragon" (546).

the most vibrant subgenres of Gothic fiction and, thus, "construct an inclusive vision of those traditionally absent from literary discourses in general and sf, horror, and especially vampire tales in particular" (Jones 154). Often in direct, intertextual, and co-creating conversation with one another, these texts "utilize complex literary expressions to repeatedly [and jointly, C.L.] question the ideological constructions underlying hegemonic and patriarchal societal structures" (Löffler 117); in this respect, in African American fiction, the vampire trope has evolved into "a powerful tool for protesting social injustice and renegotiating conventional power hierarchies in general" (ibid.). In *Fledgling*, Octavia Butler confronts the intersectionality of anti-Black racism and patriarchal sexism in the United States, by transgressively writing Black feminism, racial hybridity, and interracial symbiosis into a powerful narrative of Black female resistance and futurity.

Butler's protagonist, Shori, a fifty-three-year-old human-Ina hybrid (who looks like a ten-year-old Black girl), is the result of a genetic experiment targeting the creation of a superior race of vampires, by combining the Caucasian vampire species of the Ina with the genome of an African American human woman. We learn that the vampires we know from literature and film are really distorted representations of Ina, a matriarchal species who lives in a mutually beneficial symbiosis with humans, within seemingly utopian communes unrestrained by gender, class, age, or race issues. Shori's hybridized DNA successfully eradicates some of the weaknesses of the Ina species—while pure-blooded Ina burn in the sunlight and involuntarily fall asleep during daytime, Shori can endure exposure to sunlight, more or less unscathed, and stay awake during the day. In sum, in Butler's protagonist, we see a self-reflective reiteration of the contemporary (that is, á la Anne Rice and Stephenie Meyer) WASP American vampire's gender, race, and age, to the point that Theodora, one of Shori's human symbionts, will wonder: "According to what I've read you're supposed to be a tall, handsome, fully grown white man. Just my luck. But you must be a vampire" (*Fledgling* 97).

Offering a clear-cut alternative to the often ultra-conservative and misogynous WASP male vampires, so dominant in the contemporary mainstream Gothic, Butler's reiteration is also firmly weaved into the vampiric world of Jewelle Gomez's *The Gilda Stories*. Especially influential for *Fledgling* is Gomez's innovative replacement of the conventional juxtaposition of vampire and prey with the construction of a Black lesbian vampire, governed not by her impulses and unquenchable thirst but by a rational and ethical "notion of benevolent vampirism" (Young, "Performing the Abyss" 213), that is, an "egalitarian ethics of exchange [... through which] Gomez not only challenges traditional vampire mythology but also offers an epistemological shift concerning the ethics of intimacy and family in the face of dystopia and apocalypse" (Morris 151). While *The Gilda Stories* confronts its vampiric protagonist with an external apocalyptic reality of chattel slavery (in both the mid-nineteenth century and a dystopian future), *Fledgling* negotiates Black female agency, resistance, and futurity in the face of the Ina's own greatest, existence-threatening weakness: racism. The male branch of the Silk family, who, we are assured, are an honorable Ina clan, murders all of Shori's immediate male and female kin and comes very close to murdering her, too. For the Silks, Shori is the personified threat of miscegenation, a biological weapon leveled at the destruction of the superior Ina race: Since Shori is "dark-skinned [... and] Ina mixed with some human or maybe human mixed with a little Ina" (*Fledgling* 179), the Silks see and appellate her at various times as "a clever dog" (*Fledgling* 244), a "[d]irty little nigger bitch," and a [g]oddamn mongrel cub" (*Fledgling* 179) whose tainted DNA might "give us [the Ina] all" fur and tails (*Fledgling* 306). In stark contrast to the Ina's self-understanding as living outside of race-based ontologies completely—"[h]uman racism meant nothing to the Ina because human races meant nothing to them" (*Fledgling* 154)—Shori's multiracial liminality uncovers that, while the Ina might not care about human races, they do care very much about the Ina race. Thus, having to defend their mass-murdering spree against Shori's family, during the "Council of the Seven" (*Fledgling* 197), the Silks try to discursively delete both Shori's victimhood and their own guilt, by discursively reinstantiating her in the position of the animalistic Africanist Savage Villain, whose very presence aggressively and sexually endangers the racial purity (qua contamination and racial degeneration), in addition to the social/cultural unity of Ina society and civilization (qua Shori's ontological status as slave):

> You want your sons to mate with this person. You want them to get black, human children from her. Here in the United States, even most humans will look down on them. When I came to this country, such people were kept as property, as slaves. (*Fledgling* 278)

More and more hate speech and provocations are leveled against Shori by the Silks and their allies, in order to discursively create the Africanist Savage Villain that would "not only [...] look unusual with [her] dark skin, but to be out of [her] mind with pain, grief, and anger, to be a pitiable, dangerous, crazed thing" (*Fledgling* 271). Butler's Ina, in the words of Ali Brox, "do not embody the fears and anxieties of the society they infiltrate; rather, Butler shifts the monstrosity from the figure to the social ills themselves" (396). Through her reiteration of the vampire, Butler strips the Silks of their traditional, vampiric monstrosity, while, at the same time, highlighting a monstrosity far more perilous and contagious than vampirism: white abjectorship and the anti-Black racism so prevalent in WASP American Gothic (vampire) literature particularly and the U.S. society generally. By dissolving the conventional Gothic binaries between vampire and prey, villain and damsel, Butler can inscribe a biting social commentary on the WASP American society, in which the manifold discursive and systemic workings of anti-Black racism and white abjectorship work unacknowledged yet penetratingly toward the enslavement and social death of Black people. Following the argument of Lin Knutson, we might understand

Shori as "an agent of change, [who] exposes the structural racism and violence that operates silently beneath Ina society" (231); beyond this exposure and temporary truce, however, *Fledgling* allows for only a little optimism. Despite Shori's complete and successful refusal to let herself be discursively appellated and repositioned as the Africanist Savage Villain by the Silks abjectorship, four of the eleven families present in the trial support the Silk's anti-miscegenation discourse, as well as their racist violence, and refuse to accept Shori as the rational, self-controlled, and culturally literate "treasure" of (*Fledgling* 220) and "damn good ally" for (*Fledgling* 316) the Ina community.

The little optimism that *Fledgling* allows for therefore comes not so much from imagining some sort of Ina learning curve toward racial equality and future hybridization to happen, once Shori "come[s] of age" and mates with Ina and/or human men (*Fledgling* 86); rather, the novel encourages an optimistic outlook (of sorts) on the human community of symbionts, and especially on Shori's self-selected family of people of diverse ethnicities, genders, ages, sexual orientations. While the Ina fight fiercely over a verdict for the murderous Silk family and Shori's ontological status, the human symbionts are unaffected by the debate, in their unflinching und unbiased love for Shori, and stay "outside roasting meat over contained fires—barbeque pits—and eating and drinking too much" (234), all the while celebrating jointly, peacefully, and often sexually across all races, genders, ages, sexual orientations, and Ina family-relations. In this Woodstock-like utopian atmosphere that is common among the Ina's symbionts, racism, homophobia, and other kinds of bigotry are non-existent, even jealousy among symbionts sharing one Ina is a passing passion, bound to subside in the all-encompassing atmosphere of love and peace. That this atmosphere is both evoked and controlled mainly by the drug-like quality of Shori's saliva—and not, say, by the humans' intrinsic goodness and morality—satirically points (once more) toward the self-reflective limitations of Butler's optimism in *Fledgling* and for the WASP U.S. society's eradication of violent race relations and white abjectorship. What remains unquestioned in this only quasi-utopian perspective of the novel, however, is Shori's survival against all odds and her futurity as a liminal but well-loved (and well-nourished) character. In the end, Shori has successfully reclaimed and reconstructed her gendered, racial, and Ina identity from the brink of social and biological death. For the Gothic-savvy reader, this means facing an "alternative social world that seems, at first, alien and then [...] force[s] us to consider the nature of our own lives with a new, anxious eye. It's a pain in the neck, but impossible to resist" (Charles n.p.).

Let me add a note on Black vampires here. While African American authors have started to claim and reiterate the vampire subgenre of Gothic fiction since the 1980s, not all vampires in African American fiction have been re-racialized and turned Black like Gomez's Gilda, Butler's Shori, or Due Tananarive's "African immortals" of her acclaimed novel series of the same name (1998-2011). A good case in point for the unflinching yet re-evaluated presence of white vampires in African American fiction are L. A. Banks's two novel series of Gothicized erotic literature, *Vampire Huntress Legend* (2003-2009) and *Crimson Moon* (2007-2010). The twelve novels of the *Vampire Huntress Legend* series introduce an African American vampire huntress, Damali Richards, whose natural "scent is like a drug [,] an aphrodisiac [that] makes them [male vampires, C.L.] go nuts" and forces them "to choose to kill her or take her" (Banks, *Minion* 142). Damali faces a multiplicity of supernatural evils (including the conventional vampire) and, except for her race and her more explicit sex drive, largely resembles the character Buffy of the popular 1997-2003 U.S. American TV series, *Buffy the Vampire Slayer* (created by Joss Whedon). The *Crimson Moon* series focuses on Black/Native American hybrid werewolves, their passionate love lives, and their battle against a drug-peddling ring run by demon-infected werewolves, werewolf-blood addicted humans, ghosts, corrupt military personal, and money-laundering and cartel-running vampires. The latter resemble the stereotypical European and WASP American vampire trope to the utmost extent:

> She [werewolf Sasha] watched merriment shimmer in his [vampire baron Geoff] big blue irises that were a color so intense it made her feel as if they were being swallowed by the sea. He was handsome to a flaw, she had to admit that much. He had a full, lush mouth and his strong chin was marred only by a tiny cleft that added character to his stunning profile. Silken brunette waves created an onyx fall over his shoulders. Even in his relaxed linen tourist suit with a collarless shirt to match, his bearing still had Old World Europe firmly stamped on it. [...] his smile faded, giving way to a more intense desire. (Banks, *Bad Blood* 19)

Despite his overall attractiveness, Banks uses the conventional, that is, "Old World Europe[an]" vampire, mainly as a marker of an archaic sense of white privilege and power that painfully reminds the Black protagonist Sasha "of those privileged pricks who had made her life a living hell when she was in high school" (Banks, *Bad Blood* 22). Feeling thus excluded from and appalled by "the beautiful people, alive or dead" (ibid.), Sasha does not "go home with one of [the] undeads" (Banks, *Bad Blood* 24) but seeks out a male werewolf instead, first Shogun, a "massive and strong" and "nicely muscular [...] dark, intense [...] and too damn pretty" Asian werewolf (ibid.) and, finally, Max Hunter, her larger-than-life Black/Native American shadow wolf mate, ideal sex partner, and perfect Civil Hero to lean on and be carried home by after a fierce battle. While firmly situated in the erotic literature branch of the Gothic, L.A. Banks's re-evaluation and inversion of the British and WASP Gothic's racialized aesthetic and fetishization of whiteness must be understood as an important reiterative intervention, vis-à-vis the racialized and racializing qualities of the Gothic writing strategy. The conventional white vampire trope, in other words, can also be a very effective discursive tool against racism and white abjectorship, when in the hands and stories of a Black genre author like L. A. Banks.

The next novel in my overview is *The Killing Moon*, the 2012 opening volume to N. K. Jemisin's *Dreamblood* novel series.[2] *The Killing Moon* is a world-building epic fantasy novel, with some allusions to the vampire trope, and, more importantly, a full reiteration of the WASP American SV/CH Gotheme: "Set in a mythical never-was Egyptian-and-Nubian influenced past" (Horáková n.p.), with a cast consisting almost exclusively of Black characters, Jemisin completely reverses the WASP American SV/CH Gotheme's raciality. Given the novel's complex world-building, a brief summary is necessary, in order to introduce some of Jemisin's many epic concepts and ancient Egyptian-style neologisms. Set in the mythical city-state of Gujaareh, the Hetawa temple is dedicated to Gujaareh's sole goddess, Hananja, goddess of dreams, and the Hetawa priests harvest ("Gather"), in her name, the people's dreams to create dream-magic that heals wounds, cures ailments, and stimulates like a most potent drug. Aside from easing the dying into the paradisiac dream realms of Hananja, the Gatherers are also sent to kill those judged corrupt before Gujaareh's only law—peace. When Gatherer Ehiru is ordered to kill a Bromarte, a corrupt barbarian from the northern outlands, his Gathering goes sinfully wrong, and the Bromarte dies, to suffer eternally in agony and horror. Shaken, Ehiru goes into seclusion, until he and his young servant-caste apprentice, Nijiri, receive urgent orders to kill Sunandi Jeh Kalawe, the deemed corrupt ambassador from the neighboring city-state of Kisua. Instead of letting herself be "Gathered" by the two Hetawa priests, Sunandi confronts Ehiru and Nijiri with a vast conspiracy that she has been uncovering in Gujaareh's highest circles, involving war, murder, monsters, and the divinely chosen Prince of the Sunset Throne, Eninket, Ehiru's brother. Sunandi suspects the Hetawa temple to be at the very center of the conspiracy, as people are murdered by a Reaper, an insane abomination of a Gatherer, who feeds vampire-like on the dreamblood of the innocent, only to satisfy his own inhumane lust. It is, however, the Prince himself who has created the Reaper and corrupted the Hetawa for his own ends: conquering the continent with the help of the "ax-mad barbarians" (TKM 59)[3] of the North and an insatiable Reaper, who not only can kill thousands of enemies telepathically but also feed the Prince's secret addiction to dreamblood. In the end, Ehiru, having turned from Gatherer to Reaper himself, and Nijiri can stop the Prince but not the war; Ehiru dies peacefully in the hands of his former apprentice, and Nijiri helps to rebuild the Hetawa temple and its healing mission in the midst of invasion and destruction.

---

2   Unfortunately, the novel (series) has not yet received any scholarly attention and only very few critical reviews have been published as of today, a shortcoming that my brief analysis of the novel can draw attention to but hardly remedy.
3   Citations marked "TKM" refer to Jemisin's *The Killing Moon*.

In Jemisin's re-racialized version of the SV/CH Gotheme, the novel's Savage Villain, Eninket, the Prince of Gujaareh, stands out from the beginning as "[t]he strange man" (TKM 71) whose overall appearance is regal, "smooth and youthful [... with a] thicket of long rope-braids" (TKM 70) that frame "a face that was fine-planed and flawless, apart from the misfortune of his coloring" (TKM 21). It is this misfortunate coloring of the Prince's too fair skin and eyes, his color "like polished amber from the tall forests across the see," that deems him racially "improper for a nobleman," because, at some point, his "royal lineage" must have been "diluted by northerners" (TKM 24), that is, by the white-skinned and "piggish"- looking (TKM 11) "barbarians who scorned all civilized folk as soft and decadent cowards" (TKM 381). In this construction of racial hybridity, as a problematic mixture of Black civil blood and "northernblooded" savagery (TKM 168), the character's Black side initially "firmly control[s]" his white side's "roughness [... and] lust" (TKM 24); all the while, "his golden eyes hungry as a lion's" (TKM 25) function as an unflinching reminder of his destructively liminal and predatorily animalistic nature. While a certain level of violence is perfectly acceptable for the Prince (for example, his slaughtering of hundreds of his "siblings and their mothers," as well as his father in his succession to the throne, TKM 90), his type of evil is deemed inexcusable and a "much greater sickness" (TKM 184) than even the abomination of the Reaper, "the most contagious of diseases, so virulent that no herb, surgery, or dream-humor could cure it" (TKM 262). Interestingly, the Prince's corrupting and evil disease spreads not by his bodily fluids, not by bacteria or viruses, but discursively. The Prince whispers into the ear of Una-une, turning the former elite Gatherer into his Reaper, a passively enduring beast on a leash (TKM 372). Highlighting Una-une's infection with the Prince's evil, the Reaper is also re-racialized, and the perfectly B/black Gatherer's eyes are turned into "the color of pitted iron surrounded by bloodshot whites" (TKM 236); the pride of the Hetawa is rendered a "slack-jawed apparition" (TKM 346), which, "like a moth" (TKM 349), is drawn to the Prince's golden appearance and thus attacks the Prince's enemies, "quick as a dust snake" (TKM 386). In all these similes, Blackness is depicted as dusted, grayed, faded-out and is replaced by a fairer, that is, whiter color-coding. Like Ehiru, "even the Reaper" is a "most pitiful victim[...]" of the Savage Villain's contagious sickness (TKM 295). Upon climax, Jemisin finally makes explicit what this discursively transmitted sickness actually consists of. The Prince, wanting to turn Ehiru into another Reaper, whispers into his brother's ear:

> "They will come here, Ehiru. Infect us with their savagery and chaos, destroy our peace—Her peace—forever." The voice moved closer to his ear, whispering warning over distant screams of pain and rage and his own ravening lust. "Stop them, little brother. Take them. Take them all now, and share them with me." [...] Stretching out his hands and mind, Ehiru took hold of over twenty thousand lives, and began to Reap. (TKM 376)

The Prince's contagious sickness, the disease corrupting Gujaareh, is racism. And indeed, we can trace the corrupting impact of racism back to the beginning of the novel and to Ehiru's initial fall from grace: Ehiru has "perverted the Bromarte's Gathering because [...] he had disliked the man already—without cause, simply because he was a barbarian. And then he had allowed that prejudice to overwhelm his sense of duty" (TKM 226). Contagious racism, discursively and seductively whispered from one ear to the other, is thus the core of Gujaareh's downfall. This perspective forces us to reconsider the function of the Sunset Prince's racialization. Jemisin's Savage Villain is not racially hybrid, because she would only invert the WASP Gotheme following the logic of an African American "anti-gothic" in Smethurst's sense (29); rather, by coding rampant racism as racially white and depicting the novel's Savage Villain as equally infected by its corrupting effects, as her protagonist, Jemisin also re-inscribes race and racism forcefully, that is, visually and discursively, into the SV/CH Gotheme. Thus, she lays open the racialized and racializing core of the Gotheme, all the while turning the tables and writing Black characters not just into an otherwise typically WASP-dominated genre of epic fantasy fiction but setting Blackness as the norm, from which whiteness/white racism is abjected.

The civil Black norm in the novel is established through an inverted but otherwise very conventional reiteration of the Civil Hero: Nijiri. Nijiri sets out as a "fine-looking boy" of the servant-caste (TKM 72), and apprentice to the Hetawa, but quickly advances to Ehiru's life-savior, frequent dreamblood donor, and fiercely loyal friend (even lover), in the hour of greatest need. In fighting physically and manly against the pursuers of innocent damsels, he goes from the "little killer" (TKM 279) to a full-fledged Civil Hero: "The face is hardened, turning as cold as his mentor's. 'Stay with me,' he told her. [...] I'll protect you both" (TKM 279). Finally, Nijiri reaches "a new maturity;" by Gathering Ehiru's tithe, he lets go of his "frustrated restlessness" and "the anger that had always churned beneath his calm façade," (TKM 402) becoming a Gatherer at peace with himself and his duty for the Hetawa. What makes Nijiri such an interesting Civil Hero, therefore, is not so much his racial deviation from the conventional script—that is, his being a Black Civil Hero—but his function of counterbalancing the corrupting forces of the Savage Villain, that is, white racism. Taken together, Jemisin's reiterated SV/CH Gotheme lays open both the rampant white racism that corrupts even the seemingly most utopian societies—it is only a very small step from *The Killing Moon*'s strong and prosperous 'One Nation Under Hananja' (cf. TKM 165) to the United States, during the Obama administration and with the so-called "post-racial" debate in full swing—and the invisibilization of Black characters, beyond the racialized boundaries of villainy in speculative (fantasy/Gothic) fiction. At the same time, the novel constructs a countering strategy, by centering exclusively on Black fantastic myths, on Black characters, and on African American political, social, and cultural perspectives as "building-blocks" for the "non-traditional (read: non-feudal European societies)" (Herstig and Wybrew n.p.)—that is, non-WASP epic fantasy storytelling and non-WASP mythologies:

> This genre [epic fantasy, C.L.] is rooted in the epic—and the truth s that there are plenty of epics out there which feature people like me. Sundiata's badass mother. Dihya, warrior queen of the Amazighs. The Rain Queens. The Mino Warriors. Hatshepsut's reign. Everything Harriet Tubman ever did. And more, so much more, just within the African components of my heritage. I haven't even begun to explore the non-African stuff. So given all these myths, all these examinations possible... how can I *not* imagine more? How can I not envision an epic set somewhere other than medieval England, about someone other than an awkward white boy? How can I not use every building-block of my history and heritage and imagination when I make shit up? (Jemisin, "Dreaming Awake" n.p.)

At first glance, Victor LaValle's take on the Black fantastic narrative in his recent bestseller novel *The Changeling* (2017), could not differ more from Jemisin's all-Black world-building epic. Instead of creating a narrative with "the building-blocks" of Black heritage and history, LaValle negotiates an old European tradition (well-documented since the late Middle Ages) of changeling stories, that is, stories centering on the uncanny replacement of a stolen human baby by a demon/devil/incubus changeling that resembles the stolen baby just enough to fool the parents—at least initially (cf. Munro 251). On closer inspection, however, LaValle's version of a changeling story is only the backdrop against which he can construct a contemporary and outspokenly political African American art fairy tale (*Kunstmärchen*). LaValle's protagonist Apollo will learn that "[a] bad fairy tale has some simple goddamn moral. A great fairy tale tells the truth" (TC 244); by looking closely at LaValle's reiterative employment of the SV/CH Gotheme, we can outline some of these truth-telling efforts, especially with regard to the anxieties and inevitable strains of Black parenthood and what it means to be—and to survive as—a Black man (and father of a Black son) in the United States generally and during the Trump administration particularly.

In many respects, *The Changeling* is the novel that, in my overview of the contemporary African American Gothic, comes closest to what Smethurst conceptualizes as "anti-gothic" (29), that is, by completely turning the SV/CH Gotheme's intrinsic raciality on its head, LaValle creates an inverted Gothic with a clear political stance. His inversion, indeed, goes so far as to include the WASP American Gothic's trope and plot element that I named "mock villainy" in Chapter 4.1, that is, LaValle establishes inchoate pseudo-villains as red herrings and foils of pardonable and justifiable deviance, against which the climactic evil of full-fledged savage villainy will stand out as all the more threatening and horrifying. In the hands of LaValle, mock villainy is stripped of its often satirical potential, thereby becoming a very effective tool both for misleading the protagonist (and the reader) toward the edge of misogyny and foreshadowing the all-encompassing atrocity and evil to come. LaValle's reiterated mock villains are all women, more specifically, mothers who have killed their babies. Together with the Black protagonist, Apollo Kagwa, we suffer through a first-hand experience of the horrific transition from mother, wife, and "soulmate to supervillain" (Truitt n.p.): Apollo wakes up in his kitchen, chained to a steam pipe, while his six-month-old baby boy, Brian, is shrieking in the nursery. Ever more desperate to get up and tend to his baby, Apollo repeatedly burns his exposed neck, "like a pork cutlet pressed against a hot skillet," unable to accept that he must remain seated, "in one position, exactly straight, to keep himself from being choked or burned" (TC 121).[4] When "[t]he monster" finally steps out of the darkness of the doorway and reveals itself, Apollo is face-to-face with what seems to be a veritable Gothic villain:

> The monster's hair was long and hung over its face. The locks were ratty and dry. It slumped as it moved forward, which only made it seem more ghoulish. It stepped into the kitchen, brushed past him. So close. Only inches. The chair underneath him rose, and its legs banged against the floor. Despite the chains around his shins, the ones around his wrists, he would've crashed this little man, this thug, with so much force that it would've gone through the fridge. But that bike lock wasn't playing. (TC 124)

Yet, this ghoulish monster, this little man, this thug that will beat him with a claw hammer, until his cheekbone breaks, and make him listen to the yelps and screams of his infant being killed with boiling water, is Emma Valentine, Apollo's wife and baby Brian's mother. Certain that "[i]t's not a baby" (TC 128), Emma leaves her dead baby and severely wounded husband behind, escaping to a secret community of "Wise Ones," "Witches," and their children on a remote island, "cloaked" by "a shadow darker than even the night sky," in New York's East River (TC 223). Driven by a murderous need for revenge, "the god Apollo" (TC 229) and his new friend, William Wheeler, enter the perfectly camouflaged community of Callisto and her followers, only to be subdued, ridiculed, and imprisoned immediately ("[t]hose four women beat the dog shit out of Apollo Kagwa," TC 230). While he is walked over to the makeshift prison, Apollo's notion of the villainous witches starts to crumble:

> He imagined all those women and children tucked into some dark, airless bunker and wondered at the idea that they'd fled because of him. This didn't make him feel powerful. Instead it gave him a different perspective on what had just happened. A strange man showed up in the middle of the night screaming that he

---

4   In-text citations marked "TC" refer to *The Changeling* by Victor LaValle.

was a god, demanding vengeance on his wife. Why wouldn't these women and children be terrified? (TC 236)

From this turning point onward, LaValle quickly and fully deconstructs the novel's mock villainy, to the point at which the women and their children—including Emma Valentine—are revealed to be the Damsels in Distress, trapped and pursued in an "ugly fairy tale" by male "monsters," who will outdo all notions of villainy and evil that the novel has thus far pondered (TC 259). At the same time, LaValle uncovers *The Changeling*'s Savage Villain: William Wheeler, whose "true name" is "Kinder Garten," and who has gathered an army of "ten thousand men," online and offline, uniting them under his name—"We are Kinder Garten. Ten thousand men with one name" (TC 277). True to a veritable Savage Villain, Kinder Garten is one yet many; he snarls, hisses, and crawls; his "nails looked as ragged as claws" (TC 277); and he slowly morphs into "a figure [...], not a man but a shape" (277), that commands an army and has enough "artillery fire" to burn the female safe haven to the ground (TC 279). Kinder Garten, Apollo uncovers, are also the Internet trolls who have not only ridiculed and viciously taunted his dead son on Social Media platforms ("Dinner plans tonight. A meal inspired by Baby Brian. [...] *Boiled Vegetables!*," TC 277) but also preyed on his family, ever since Apollo posted the first pictures of his son online: "Vampires can't come into your house unless you invite them. Posting online is like leaving your front door open and telling any creature of the night it can enter" (TC 222). In a fantastic bridging of story lines and genres, LaValle lets the Internet troll(s), Kinder Garten, prey on children online and steal them from their families, by exchanging them for a changeling, only to sacrifice the children to an ancient real-life troll, with an eye "as large as a manhole cover," (TC 418) that happens to live in a cave of Forest Park in Queens. Kinder Garten's motives are twofold: While the online trolls, assembled under the name "Kinder Garten," primarily want to satisfy their voyeuristic lust, by getting "to watch the troll eat [the Kagwa's] child," (406), Kinder Garten also has a bigger goal in mind. Kinder Garten's father, a "wild-looking old white man" (TC 328), explains to Apollo:

> There was a time in this country when a man like him [Kinder Garten, C.L.] could be sure his children would do better than he had done. Once that was the birthright of every white man in America. But not anymore. Suddenly men like my son were being passed over in the name of things like "fairness" and "balance." Where's justice in that? [...] We could channel that monster's power into our own deliverance. That was our right, our heritage. That's why we came to America! (TC 369-370)

Being a descendent of Norwegian immigrants and of the original servants of the troll, Kinder Garten feels cheated out of his family's American Dream, by what he thinks is a dwindling of white privilege and the demise of a white birthright, to racial, cultural, and social supremacy. In his quest to restore his "birthright," Kinder Garten renews his family's deal with the troll and starts a new round of sacrificing the "yellow, white, and red" children of immigrants—the perfect victims for a racist like him, who thinks that "[i]mmigrants have many children" (TC 365) and all of these children will potentially grow up und demand "fairness" and "balance," further cheating him and his children out of their presumed natural right to supremacy. This construction of a white Savage Villain, with an explicit connection to the racist violence involved in claiming and defending white privilege and supremacy in today's United States, should not be dismissed as "strained allusions to Donald J. Trump, Fox News and the far right, which seem to have blown in from some neighboring land" (Senior n.p.); rather, LaValle exploits the conventional "one-yet-many" characteristics of the Savage Villain, to the point at which we cannot help but re-read the entire novel, through the lens of the intricate and destructive workings of white racism.

In this respect, the novel's Civil Hero, Apollo, has to fight for the survival of his Black family against innumerable faceless but—as in the case of Kinder Garten—very encroaching, well-connected, and technology-savvy white racist antagonists: Apollo comes of age during "the era of Bernhard Goetz shooting black boys on the subway and many white folks in the city cheering him on," and in a society in which "[e]very kid with excess melanin became a superpredator, even boys with glasses and a backpack full of books" (TC 19). In this world, as Natalie Beach (n.p.) points out in her tongue-in-cheek review of *The Changeling*, "[i]t's not enough [for a Civil Hero, C.L.] to face down monsters while going about [his] daily business, there are also the challenges a man of color deals with every day. It makes you wonder: Would Hercules have been able to complete his 12 labors under the threat of stop-and-frisk?" Walking "through white suburbs at night," *while being Black*—to borrow the ironic phrase so present in today's media—lets Apollo and his friend Patrice muse that Black men "can be heroes. But heroes like us don't get to make mistakes" (TC 299). Not without irony, LaValle promptly delays his Civil Hero's quest, by letting a "police car" come "down Park Lane South as casual as a puma"—of course, this is not a coincidence but qualified by LaValle as just another face of racism and, very likely, of Kinder Garten's ten thousand men: "This part of Forest Hill is still called Little Norway. You were never going to blend in. [...] Especially at night," one of the police officers informs Apollo (TC 333). His fight against the Savage Villain and his urgent quest to find his wife and child are over for the night. Black Civil heroes "like him [don't] get to make mistakes" (TC 333), in a world of "so many white people" (TC 165). What is more, the systemic and everyday racism that the Black Civil Hero—as much as the African American man—encounters, or, according to Saidiya Hartman, "the scenes of subjection" that must be resisted, transgressed, and transformed continuously, has not just begun with Donald Trump's election; racism in *The Changeling* has its origins in the first wave of immigration from Europe and has, since then, been merely camouflaged and hidden from plain sight by "Glamour," "an old kind of magic [and] an illusion to make something appear different than it really is" (TC 247). In this respect, the election of Donald Trump to the presidency of the United States, or shall I say, the white supremacy-inspired deal with a real-life troll, only unmasked the illusions of a post-racial U.S. society—the "golden palace" has been unmasked as "[a] ruined castle" (TC 247).

Despite the intricate and systemic workings of white supremacy and racism in the social fabric of the United States, which *The Changeling* constructs and displays, the novel does not allow for a (Afro-)pessimistic reading. Indeed, it is LaValle's reiteration of the SV/CH Gotheme that allows him to create an (almost) optimistic ending to his fantastic narrative. Facing off with the real-life "goddamn troll" (TC 424), Civil Hero Apollo, equipped with a mattock and reunited with Damsel Emma (who brings a change of clothes for Brian and an iPad), can successfully overcome the Savage Villain and destroy both Kinder Garten (in the singular) and the gigantic troll. In perfect fairy tale manner, Apollo cuts the swallowed-whole baby, unscathed, from the beast's intestines, and the reunited family takes the bus home on a free ticket "from the NYPD" (TC 431). While Kinder Garten's ten thousand men are still out there, the troll and, thus, his most immediate claim to white supremacy have been slain by the Black Civil Hero. The future momentarily looks as bright and victorious as "a chariot pulling the sun across the sky" (TC 431); to thwart today's villains and menaces of white supremacy, "the novel reveals, we need today's heroes—not the son of Zeus but the son of a Ugandan immigrant, a new kind of warrior who can fend off fiends and then go home to cook dinner for his family" (Beach n.p.). In many respects, *The Changeling* can thus be read as a fictionalization of LaValle's self-proclaimed optimism. In a 2009 article for *Bookforum*, he states that he is

> tired of all the dourness and doomsaying; of the grimace that's required whenever we discuss [black nationalism] and blackness in general; of the countless humorless men and women who scold every impulse toward comfort or laughter or, dare I say it, optimism. I'm sick of the same old forecast for blackness: gloom followed by clouds of hail. (LaValle, "Beyond the Skin Trade" n.p.)

The Changeling refrains from envisioning a "happily ever after" for Apollo and his family but opts for a "happily today" (TC 431), that is, for "a life full of adventure" (430) in the present tense, in which obstacles and antagonisms can be overcome, by countering them jointly as a close-knit family unit and from within conservative gender roles. LaValle, in sum, envisions an optimistic and—maybe necessarily so—fantastic narrative of the futurity and survival of Black man- and parenthood in the United States generally and during the Trump administration particularly. Fending off and defeating white racist trolls, trespassing into the Black families online and offline, becomes the key quest for a Black men and father. While LaValle still opts for optimism in 2017, *The Changeling*'s overarching question functions as the sword of Damocles, constantly threatening to crush the Kagwa's renewed sense of belonging and familiar bliss: "No matter what we do, the world finds its way in. So then how do we protect our children?" (TC 246). In a world of white racist trolls, longing for their share of white privilege and supremacy, the consequences of this intrusion are more often fatal than they are reversible with the help of a mattock and an iPad.

The last novel in my inevitably sketchy overview of the contemporary African American Gothic is Andre Duza's small press genre publication, *WZMB* (2014).[5] *WZMB* is a rather curious post-apocalyptic zombie novel that is narrated in the form of transcripted "video-clips of The Martin Stone Show" (*WZBM* 5), a thinly-veiled stand-in for the controversial U.S. talk radio show, *The Howard Stern Show*, to whose hosts, producers, guests, and callers Duza has also dedicated his novel. While I will have a lot more to say about zombies in Gothic fiction, and especially in African American Gothic fiction, in my analysis of Colson Whitehead's *Zone One*, a brief look into Duza's take on the genre and the SV/CH Gotheme is possible, without risking too many repetitions and redundancies later on. Duza's zombies closely resemble the mainstream WASP American zombies that are currently undergoing a massive revival—even a *Zombie Renaissance*, as Laura Hubner (et al.) have recently titled, in all branches of American popular culture, including TV (think *The Walking Dead, Z Nation, iZombie*) and film productions (such as *28 Days Later*, the *Resident Evil* film series), literature (*Pride and Prejudice and Zombies, World War Z*), computer games (*Resident Evil, Left4Dead, State of Decay*), and comic books (*The Walking Dead, Plants vs. Zombies,* etc.), but also in art, music, and fandom. This extremely successful revival of zombie texts has been explained by a majority of scholars (Kyle William Bishop, Warren St. John, and Laura Hubner to name just three) in relation to 9/11 and the paranoid and xenophobic fear that it inspired. According to Warren St. John,

> [i]t does not take much of a stretch to see the parallel between zombies and anonymous terrorists who seek to convert others within society to their deadly cause. The fear that anyone could be a suicide bomber or hijacker parallels a common trope of zombie films, in which healthy people are zombified by contact with other zombies and become killers. (n.p.)

Bishop goes so far as to assert that "a post-9/11 audience can hardly help but perceive the characteristics of [the zombie genre] through the filter of terrorists threats and apocalyptic reality" (*American Zombie Gothic* 30). While zombie texts "are doing

---

5   As of today, *WZMB* has only been reviewed critically twice (by Ben Arzate for *CulturedVultures.com* and by Michael Noe for *Splatterpunkzine*), and no scholarly voices have engaged with the novel yet.

exactly what Romero started in the 1960s" (Bishop, *American Zombie Gothic* 31)—give or take today's zombies' enhanced speed, strength, and ghoulishness—the North American audiences watch, play, and read zombie "themes and motifs through different lenses than they would have before" 9/11 (Dendle qtd. in Bishop, *American Zombie Gothic* 31).

What critics like Bishop and Dendle only hint at will be of the utmost importance for my own engagement with texts of the zombie renaissance: the relation between the zombie trope, a WASP American target audience, and racism. That racism and xenophobia were fueled by the Bush administration and the mass media, in the wake of the attacks on the World Trade Center in 2001, goes almost without saying; however, the anti-Black racism, which is so dominant in the WASP American zombie trope,[6] both predates and outlives the social and cultural rupture of 9/11. It is the invisibilization of rampant anti-Black racism, vis-à-vis the 9/11 paranoia, that inspired Will Smith's controversial commentary on the effects of the September 11 attacks on African Americans. Interviewed by a major German newspaper (*Frankfurter Allgemeine Sonntagszeitung*, August 8, 2004) about whether or not 9/11 had changed anything for him personally, Smith answered:

> No. Absolutely not. When you grow up black in America you have a completely different view of the world than white Americans. We blacks live with a constant feeling of unease. And whether you are wounded in an attack by a racist cop or in a terrorist attack, I'm sorry, it makes no difference. (29; trans. by Ray D. http://medienkritik.typepad.com/blog/2004/08/will_smith_in_f.html)

As if in dialogue with Smith, Duza and Whitehead trigger and play with allusions to 9/11 in their zombie novels, while negotiating anti-Black racism and white abjectorship. In *WZMB*, the majority of humanity has been infected with a mysterious, rapidly spreading virus that has turned the living into the flesh-eating living dead since the day of the outbreak—"9/6" (*WZMB* 65); other than in *Zone One*, for example, "the zombies themselves aren't really the important part of the novel" (Noe n.p.) but feature mainly as part of the setting, the backdrop against which Duza can intertwine his negotiation of The Howard Stern Shown in a post-9/11 America, torn to shreds between religious fanaticism on the one hand and white political hardliner and opportunists on the other. As a matter of fact, the zombies in *WZMB* are not part of Duza's version of the SV/CH Gotheme.

Instead, *WZMB*, evokes (somewhat comparable to LaValle's *The Changeling*) a mock villainy first, which motivates and helps to uncover the novel's savage villainy. The mock villainy in Duza's novel is the "Left Hand of God," a sect of religious fanatics led by Mother Margaret (known in The Martin Stone Show as the frequent—and always deemed annoying—caller "Maggie from Lancaster"), whose

---

6   See Chapter 7.3.

"sole purpose is to ensure that God's plan of the Biblical End of Days is carried out" and not hindered by survivors, a vaccine, or a hope-inspiring radio show (WZMB 209). Mother Margaret is an "older Black woman with a long face that eschews warmth for authority, eyes that radiate lunatic devotion, and hair resembling a ceremonial headdress" (WZMB 273). Her Left Hand of God "parishioners" dress up zombies "in a loincloth and a crown of thorns fashioned from barbed wire" and nail them "to a 10-foot wooden cross at the center of the alter," so that they can "file past and kiss" the zombies feet in religious ecstasy (WZMB 102f.); they also use "decoys to infiltrate settlements and destroy them from the inside out by using suicide bombers, or turning members against each other or tampering with the medicine or food supply" (WZMB 209). Throughout the plot, Duza makes certain that Mother Margaret, with her naturally-grown "ceremonial headdress," must be read as a Black female Christian fanatic, yet, the manifold allusions to religiously motivated suicide bombers and mass-shooting sprees hint both at Islamic terrorism and at the infectious spreading of (religious) fanaticism of all varieties, in the wake of a traumatic event such as "9/6" in the novel, or 9/11 in the United States.

It is this context that Duza gradually uncovers the real Savage Villain in WZBM and, therefore, where we can confront his intertwinement of 9/11 and an ongoing und unchanging anti-Black racism in one character: Morgan Brand, "the billionaire weapons developer" (WZMB 15) and "GOOD man" (WZMB 242). Brand controls the Brand compound and its social policies, the Brand security forces, and The Martin Stone Show, "[b]roadcasting on Brand 96 on the Brand Satellite Channel and Brand 103 for those of you with access to video" (WZMB 34); he "doesn't give a fuck about you unless you can help him push his agenda, which, I'm [Dave, head of security and veritable CH, C.L.] afraid to say has more to do with power than that humanitarian bullshit he's been shoveling down your throats" (WZMB 245). Yet, fully in line with other Savage Villains, Brand stands in for a much larger problem, is but one head of a massive hydra. The Brand policies, regulating all aspects of the society of survivors, are based on racist and unethical medical experimentation, for which the old man "spare[s] no expenses" (WZMB 66). Brand supports and outfits the medical research of "Dr. Franklin Hammond (Caucasian, 56)" (WZMB 63), a doctor of the mad scientist variety, who is working on a mind-controlling device to be implanted in the brains of zombies and who is thus actively "push[ing] the boundaries of what would have been deemed ethical before 9/6" (WZMB 68). When Hammond, "stone-faced [and] unaffected," describes his medical team's torturous testing on "Bob Marley," "a dark-skinned man, dead but living, cut in half at the waist" (WZMB 70), before breaking out in laughter when his team poses as zombies, dancing the "'THRILLER' by Michael Jackson" (WZMB 77), the anti-black racism underlying the Brand policies and notions of progress and hope becomes tangible.

Again, these unethical and racist medical practices cannot be reduced to the mad delusions of a single mad scientist or his old white patron. Rather, a large team of willing collaborators, who have "worked together in the past" (WZMB 65), make use of "the sudden surplus of test subjects [...] since things like ethics have gone out of the window" (WZMB 67). "I don't think anybody's going to complain," comments Martin Stone on the unethical and overtly graphic torture of black bodies (WZMB 68), the reduction of Black bodies to flesh. In *WZMB*, Duza fittingly sets Dr. Hammond's medical facility "in an old meat processing plant" (WZMB 69) that "[l]ooks like a medieval dungeon" (WZMB 70), where "Dr. Hammond-stein" (WZMB 71) and his team routinely test, torture, and dispose of zombies in the name of medical research. Their most impressive result to date is "not a cure" (WZMB 70) but making a zombie drag "a weighted sled with two 45lb plates sitting on top" (WZMB 76) through the meat processing plant, via mind control. In other words, before being rendered "a pile of bodies that have worn out their usefulness" (WZMB 77), the Brand zombies are subjected to a post-apocalyptic version of chattel slavery.

Duza's construction of the Savage Villain, as an all-powerful and all-pervasive WASP American force of ethically unhinged military and medical authorities, ties in seamlessly with the history of racism "in medicine, misconduct in human research, the arrogance of physicians, and government abuse of Black people" in the United States (Gamble 1773). Directly relatable to the medical experimentation on and outright torture of African Americans, in the name of medical and scientific progress—think of the antebellum use of slaves and free Black people as subjects for medical experimentation and dissection, the experimental gynecological operations conducted by Dr. J. Marion Sims, the Tuskegee Syphilis Study, and the coerced sterilization procedures, in the name of racial purity and eugenics, for example[7]—*WZMB* foregrounds anti-Black racism as a continuous evil and mundane occurrence that all but started with the apocalypse and "9/6." In a nutshell, *WZMB* envisions a post-"9/6" world, in which zombies function as both legitimization and fuel for the ongoing unethical and racist medical research of white authorities. In this respect, Duza repositions 9/11 as a WASP American cover-up story for a history of rampant anti-Black racism and the routine practice of Black abuse and torture, in the name of scientific progress. Read from this perspective, the religious fanatics of *The Left Hand of God* and their world-ending cause appear almost justified—if it were not for Zombie Jesus.

In the following two subchapters, I will provide a much more detailed reading of the Savage Villain/Civil Hero Gotheme in two contemporary African American Gothic novels, namely in Toni Morrison's *A Mercy* and Colson Whitehead's *Zone One*.

---

7   For a first overview of anti-Black racism in North American medical institutions, see Vanessa Northington Gamble's 1997 article, "Under the Shadow of Tuskegee: African Americans and Health Care."

While my (however limited) overview in this subchapter already indicates the prevalence of a reiterated and therefore complicated—yet continuously racialized and racializing—SV/CH Gotheme in the contemporary African American Gothic novel, only a second round of close readings of the Gotheme can really argue for or against the assumption of an unchanged, conventionally fixed, and intrinsic raciality at the core of the Gothic writing strategy. Thus far, we must note a uniquely African American Gothic writing strategy that reiterates the SV/CH Gotheme, vis-à-vis its raciality, and functionalizes it in an unflinching and often self-reflective discursive battle against white abjectorship and anti-Black racism in WASP (speculative/Gothic) literature and in the United States' larger social and cultural fabric.

6.2 "Are You Afraid? You Should Be": Tony Morrison's *A Mercy*

> "The history of blackness is a testament to the fact that objects can and do resist."
> (Fred Moten, In the Break 1)

When Maria I. Diedrich contextualizes and discusses Sabine Broeck's epistemical reading of African American women's work,[8] in her contribution to *Sabine Broeck—Plotting against Modernity: Critical Interventions in Race and Gender*, she draws special attention to Broeck's 2006 article, "Trauma, Agency, Kitsch and the Excess of the Real: *Beloved* Within the Field of Critical Response." In this lesser-known article, Broeck not only "sift[s] through a rich history of secondary literature whose authors have almost unanimously agreed on enthusiastically greeting *Beloved* as a breakthrough moment for African American and/or postcolonial post-Middle Passage cultural reconstruction" (Broeck, "Trauma" 240); she also offers what Diedrich calls "a radical re-reading of *Beloved*" (Diedrich, "The Burden" 269). Refusing to follow the prevailing trend of "kitsch" analyses, which strip the Pulitzer Prize-awarded novel of inner ambiguities and narrative excess, until it becomes a quasi-therapeutic text "that ultimately articulates the possibility of working through and healing the trauma of slavery" (Nehl 56), Broeck argues:

> What *Beloved* does is create a post-haunted African American community as a historical self, a subject in possession of memory, a subject able to negotiate

---

8   Diedrich is particularly interested in Broeck's ceaseless deconstruction of the "role of gender as a modern western paradigm" (Broeck, "Enslavement" 37), vis-à-vis its repositioning in the dominant white discourses of enslavement and abjection, that is, as "a category from which black females [qua their discursively constructed ontological status of "things"/"chattel," C.L.] were ex-scribed" (Broeck, "The Challenge" 20). See Diedrich, "'The Burden of Our Theories' Genealogies': Lessons in Decolonization of Gender" 266.

> society on its own terms but beyond that, it is wise enough to leave the excess of the historical real in place, to write, as it were, "against itself." [...] The community which will have forgotten Beloved might include the implied reader who ignores the text's excess, reads for the plot *only*. That the novel is characterized by a deep ambiguity in terms of its structure (plot versus unplotted fragments), its protagonists (realist and surrealist), its language (mimetic syntax versus semiotic ruptures), and its ethical and aesthetic claim to address historical trauma (as curable by narrativization or as excessive to it), is a challenge which has been met with surprising critical neglect in favor of following *Beloved*'s and its author's lure in readerly identificatory desire. (Broeck, "Trauma" 252, original emphasis)

Concluding her commentary on Broeck's reading of *Beloved*, Diedrich is the first to connect the literary and cultural scholarship's reconciliatory and ultimately reductive reception practice with the "powerful black feminist reflection [...] and intertextual intervention" (Nehl 57) that is *A Mercy*. She asks provocatively:

> who can help re-reading *A Mercy*, Toni Morrison's return to enslavement at its colonial beginnings, as an invention of memory in the flesh, as a discourse on enslavement so fiercely embracing its momentum of negativity that any attempt of escaping into redemption kitsch reception goes up in flames with Florens's writing on the walls? (Diedrich, "The Burden" 269)

Following Diedrich's lead, Markus Nehl explicates further this "momentum of negativity," by positioning *A Mercy* in "a constructive discussion with Afro-pessimism about the meaning of (anti-)blackness," vis-à-vis "Morrison's exploration of the meaning of 'thingification' and the novel's rendering of Florens's experiences of antiblack racism" (Nehl 57). Nehl also claims that *A Mercy* can be understood as a self-reflective commentary on and intervention against the repetition of a reception that—at the expenses of complexity, ambiguity, and narrative excess—would aim at "giving a coherent account of Florens's life and of working through and closing the wounds of slavery" (Nehl 57).

Indeed, only a handful of other scholars emphasize *A Mercy*'s negativity—or pessimism—mostly by highlighting the "frustration, if not failure" of Florens's quest (Conner 147), within "the historically derived and institutionalized systems of ideas and practices in which [she is] caught" (Moya 158), as well as the "futile sadness of the novel's conclusion" (Peterson, "Eco-Critical Focal Points" 12) that foreshadows deterministically and dramatically "the racialization of the United States [... and] predicts the future entanglement of American economic interests and slavery" (Cantiello, "From Pre-Racial to Post-Racial" 173). The vast majority of scholarship, however, once again engages in what Broeck would probably criticize as yet another round of reconciliatory kitsch reception.

While risking undue simplification of complex arguments and analyses, I want to differentiate between two basic branches of optimistic and reconciliatory—even "kitschy"—scholarship on *A Mercy*: The first branch engages in what Jessica Wells Cantiello has argued for the mass of reviews on the novel, that is, "the tendency to emphasize certain comparisons, particularly the semantic relationship between Morrison's use of *pre-racial* to describe the novel's late seventeenth-century racial landscape and the media's use of *post-racial* to describe Obama's America" (Cantiello 165). By reading *A Mercy* as inexorably tied to Morrison's endorsement of Barak Obama, his election in 2008 (the novel was published in the U.S. on November 11, 2008, i.e. one week after Obama's election) and, more importantly, to the then hoped-for and often-presumed eve of a post-racial America, a number of reviewers and scholars emphasize "these types of connections at the expense of a more complex and complete analysis of the text" (Cantiello 166). Stephanie Li, for example, reads *A Mercy* as describing "the history of our nation's racist language as well as the foundation for our contemporary 'race-specific, race-free' discourse [Li's terminology for a post-racial but not color-blind discourse, C.L.]" and argues that "even as skin color is used as a convenient sign of degradation for religious zealots and avaricious traders, the interracial cooperation in the Vaark household offers the promise of a 'race-specific, race-free' home" (Li 15). In her article, "Contextualizing Toni Morrison's Ninth Novel: What Mercy? Why Now?," Justine Tally bases her analysis on the assumption "that the era of massive subjugation and racial apartheid in the U.S. has indeed ended, or is at least in its last throes" (63). On this basis, Tally reads Jacob Vaark as alluding "to the foundations of the future U.S. as a secular, tolerant society" (66) and his last home, the "imitation plantation house in the North," as "a veritable 'White House'" (63), onto whose floors and walls Black story telling is now etched. Charles Tedder, to add one last example to this branch of optimistic, or kitschy, scholarship, claims that "the novel suggests that Americans in the post-racial or post-cultural age are the orphaned children who are 'still falling' through the contingencies of cause and effect, still haunted by the colonial proclamation" (158); however, Tedder is certain, while many colonial-time "systems are still in place today," *A Mercy* offers a historical foundation for "an ethos of human kindness" and, therefore, "a context for living in the present" (157). Morrison herself, who is known for "read[ing] her reviews" (Morrison, "The Spirit" 50) and following the scholarship on her work, quipped at a reading in November 2008: "I have to tell you, I really like President-Elect Obama, but I wish he'd stay out of my book reviews and things" (Morrison, "America" 23).

The second branch of optimistic and reconciliatory scholarship on *A Mercy*, in the vast majority of cases, reads *A Mercy* in direct comparison and "as a prequel to Morrison's masterpiece *Beloved*" (Vega-González, "Orphanhood" 120). Instead of finding that Morrison's ninth novel "so fiercely embrac[es] its momentum of negativity," to borrow Diedrich's phrase once more ("The Burden" 269), as to counter all pseudo-therapeutic and trauma-healing approaches to the text, this type of scholarship finds "self-love," "communal love and female bonding" in *A Mercy* and reads Florens as "at last, a free woman" (Gallego-Durán 113). Also focusing on Florens's development, Susana Vega-González concludes that the young Black slave girl "finally learns to own herself and thus to soar in her newly-acquired emotional and spiritual freedom" ("Orphanhood" 131). Jami Carlacio goes even further and muses that "because she [Florens] herself has completed the journey to selfhood, she may be able to hear that which she could not hear before": the voice and narrative of her mother (146). The underlying assumption of this focus on a teleological development of Florens toward selfhood, (at least inner) self-liberation, and, more generally, a happy ending, is made explicit in Maria Rice Bellamy's article, "'These Careful Words...Will Talk to Themselves': Textual Remains and Reader Responsibility in Toni Morrison's *A Mercy*." Bellamy argues that, "in order to heal the deep-seated wounds of slavery in the American consciousness," (18) to bring "healing to unresolved traumas" (29), "Morrison positions her readers to enter the middle space with her characters" (18):

> Thus, we become Florens, the lost child, and hear *my mother* speaking words of love. We become the mother speaking love to other lost children. The contemporary reader then becomes the bridge across the chasm that separates mother and child and holds them in the love they could not share with each other, thus healing their tormented souls. (18)

While not explicitly including the healing of Morrison's readership, Gene Melton, II, argues in a similar direction and stylizes the blacksmith as both "a god-like creator [...], an artist" and "a healer" (38), who provides "the painful, all-too-human salvation Florens needs," directly on par with "a minha mãe's sacrifice years before" (40). Without a doubt, readings like Melton's and Bellamy's indicate how the critical reception of *A Mercy* has taken over the key arguments already presented in the reconciliatory "kitsch" reception of *Beloved*, thus "slid[ing] into an almost mythical, certainly naive faith in the social and individual 'cure' the novel can preside over" (Broeck, "Trauma" 247). Especially problematic and therefore in need of scholarly critique is the explicit (as in the case of Bellamy's analysis) or implicit (such as the readings by Melton, II and Jami Carlacio) assumption that a direct identification "of postmodern, contemporary white European and American novel readers [...] with the violated but mute black body of slavery" (Broeck, "Commentary" 26) is not only readily achievable but also aimed for by the author. This pseudo-emphatic identification of white readers with, for example, Douglass's Aunt Hester, Sethe's ripped open back, or Florens's ripped apart family has been termed "pornotroping" by Hortense Spillers, as early as 1987 ("Mama's Baby" 206).

Engaging critically with reconciliatory and overly simplistic readings of *A Mercy*, my own analysis of the novel will return to the "pessimistic" readings outlined above. Positioning her narrative in the crucial time and place, where the "new nation imagined itself into being" (Bryan, "Written on the Walls," 89), by firmly connecting the "hierarchy of race" legally, socially, and culturally to the institution of slavery and, thus, by becoming "inevitably yoked to Africanism" (Morrison, *Playing* 38), Morrison self-reflectively constructs the discursive birth of the Africanist Savage Villain. By tracing the circulation and adaptation of European proto-Gothic discourses on American soil and to American needs, Morrison drags her readers into the creation of the Black Gothicized abject, of the Africanist Savage Villain, constructed in and through the WASP discursive gaze. Having thus forged the link between Blackness, savage villainy, and chattel slavery, Morrison closely follows Afro-Pessimistic ontological arguments, thereby establishing a racial binary along the lines of Blackness and non-Blackness, the latter including white and non-white races (such as the Native American character Lina and the "mongrelized" Sorrow/Complete, *A Mercy* 195).

This, however, is only one side of Morrison's narrativized grappling with the origins of the Africanist Savage Villain. I will argue that Morrison's construction of the discursive birth of the Africanist Savage Villain in/through the white gaze—from its very beginning(s)—includes Black resistance and Black reiteration practices. In this crucial respect, Morrison re-mythologizes the Black Gothicized abject, up to the point at which the WASP Gothic Africanist Savage Villain is no longer thinkable, without also reading it as a form of Black resistance and agency. Thus, *A Mercy* reiterates the Africanist Savage Villain, in order to effectively and self-reflectively bridge the gap between key Afro-Pessimistic assumptions (especially the ontological link between Blackness and enslaved chattel and, therefore, the racial binary between Blackness and non-Blackness) and the possibility of Black resistance and agency (not least qua reiteration of the Gothic).

To break down this complex argument into manageable parts, I will mainly focus on the three key Gothic scenes of *A Mercy*: Jacob Vaark's visit to the Jublio plantation, Florens's encounter with the Puritans in Widow Ealing's home, and the climactic encounter of Florens and the blacksmith. Through close readings of the Gothicized elements in these scenes, I will show how Morrison creates a discursively and racially fluid "proto-Gothic" that negotiates its not yet conventionalized tropes and binaries (such as the Civil Hero/Savage Villain Gotheme), on the basis of power and subversion. In these scenes, what/who is and what/who is not "Gothicized" becomes a matter of perspective and, more specifically, a matter of racialization. While we witness that the WASP "collective needs to ally internal fears and to rationalize external exploitation [as] American Africanism—a fabricated brew of darkness, otherness, alarm, and desire" (Morrison, *Playing* 38), Morrison concurrently introduces Black reiteration and resistance into the proto-Gothic's fluid discourse. In the end, *A Mercy* constructs a newly mythologized point of origin of American literature's obsession with the Gothicized Africanist presence: Since before the Gothic was conventionally (and racially) fixed in the mid-eighteenth century—with all the denigrating and racist implications I have previously discussed—it has been a discourse of Black resistance and Black (creative) agency.

A Proto-Gothic on American Soil: Fluid Discourses Between Power and Subversion

Following the first-person stream of consciousness and present-tense introductory tour de force of Florens's "confession [...] full of curiosities" (AM 1),[9] talking voices—"I like talk. Lina talk, stone talk, even Sorrow talk. Best of all is your talk" (AM 2)—and the dread of "mothers nursing greedy babies" in "the white air" of "hell" (AM 6), Morrison switches over to a more chronologically structured, third-person narration, which she focalizes through Jacob Vaark. Taken together, Florens's and Jacob's perspectives construct what in filmmaking would be called an "establishing shot": By showing/narrating the relationship between key characters, objects, and the setting, Morrison establishes the context and multi-perspectivity of the novel. This multi-perspectivity, however, should not be mistaken as a display of a multiplicity of equally authoritative voices and perspectives. By framing Jacob's account through Florens's ongoing narration, Morrison clearly positions her protagonist's Black voice as the key authority of the narration. What is more, from the start, she uses this biased multi-perspectivity to set up *A Mercy*'s Gothic—or proto-Gothic—subtext as a negotiation of WASP discursive abjection and Black resistance.

The events of the novel take place over a period of roughly eight years (from 1682 to 1690) and are set in the American colonies of Virginia, Maryland, and in what is present-day upstate New York. Thus, "zeroing in on the precise historical time and place at which the previous social and juridical fluidity that has characterized early American colonial society was beginning to harden" (Moya 138), Morrison depicts a "society with slaves," on the brink of turning not only into a "slave society" (Berlin 9) but also into America's "peculiar institution," that is, into a society and economy based on chattel slavery. Coalescing historical events and contemporaneous juridical novelties, this turning point is narrated extradiegetically through Jacob Vaark's perspective and is connected to the 1676 Bacon's Rebellion in Virginia:

> In this territory he could not be sure of friend or foe. Half a dozen years ago an army of blacks, natives, whites, mulattoes—freedmen, slaves and indentured—had waged war against local gentry led by members of that very class. When that "people's war" lost its hopes to the hangman, the work it had done—which included the slaughter of opposing tribes and running the

---

9   In-text citations marked with "AM" refer to Toni Morrison's *A Mercy*.

Carolinas off their land—spawned a thicket of new laws authorizing chaos in defense of order. By eliminating manumission, gatherings, travel and bearing of arms for black people only; by granting license to any white to kill any black for any reason; by compensation owners for a slave's maiming or death, they separated all whites from all others forever. (AM 8)

The "territory," which the novel navigates, is a chaotic, Gothicized wilderness, a "thicket" "spawned" out of "slaughter" and violent expulsion; a territory of incarceration ("eliminating manumission, gatherings, travel") and racial segregation,[10] of hangmen, killing and maiming "in defense of order." In this "disorganized world" (AM 23), Jacob, while firmly positioned on the side of "all whites" and "with the relative safety of his skin" (AM 9), cannot readily differentiate between "friend and foe"—not so much because of the interracial quality of the insurrection six years prior, but because the unflinching "interests of the gentry's profits" (AM 8) have created a proto-capitalistic "mess," in which, "suddenly, from behind felled trees a starving deserter with a pistol might emerge, or in a hollow a family of runaways might cower, or an armed felon might threaten" (AM 9). Firmly situated in this wilderness of violence, racial segregation, and "profits" is the Gothicized Jublio plantation, to which Jacob has "been invited, rather summoned" (AM 12) by the Portuguese plantation and slave owner, Senhor D'Ortega.

The Jublio plantation can best be described as a proto-Gothic mansion. Erected roughly 100 years prior to Walpole's *Castle of Otranto*, Jublio appears to be a supratemporal transplant from Europe, that is, a trope drawing on the contemporary reader's extensive cultural knowledge of the Gothic conventionality, while remaining firmly situated in the seventeenth-century American setting.[11] Situated in the midst of a wilderness infested with "mud snakes" (AM 12), "the sweetish rot of vice and ruined tobacco" (AM 26) "cloak[s] Jublio like balm" (AM 13). The main house's exterior is "prideful" (AM 13), "ornate" (AM 25), and reeks of "pagan excess" (AM 25); in the interior, "surrounded by graven idols" (AM 14) and "candles [burned]

10 Note that the racial segregation constructed in this passage is peculiar: The concluding statement, "they separated all whites from all others forever," stands in contrast to the previous listing of restrictions for and measures against "black people" only. By drawing the race line between "all whites" and "all others," Morrison separates a (thus far) undefined group of "all whites" from the previously defined group of "black people." Thus, I already read an implicit Afro-Pessimistic stance in this passage.
11 When Morrison declares Jublio's "grand pillars suitable for a House of Parliament" (AM 13), she either self-reflectively or unknowingly makes this supratemporal adaptation explicit: While the capitalization points toward London's Westminster Palace, the Palladian style, which dominated the west façade before the buildings had been rebuilt in the Neogothic design following the fire of 1834, was created by John Vardy between 1755 and 1770; in the seventeenth century, there were no "grand pillars" on the exterior of the Parliamentary estate. See Christine Riding, et al. *The Houses of Parliament: History, Art and Architecture*.

in midday" (AM 17), "[s]tone-quiet" (AM 17) children live as animatedly "as tombs" (AM 15). Surrounded by rows of run-down slave quarters, from the start, Jublio's peculiar rotten smell is implicitly connected to D'Ortega's "passel of slaves"; when Jacob is finally introduced and invited to inspect the plantation's slaves, Morrison picks up the Gothic pace: The slaves' loud silence about "the scars, the wounds like misplaced veins tracing their skin," "the facial brand," and about what created the "shockproof" eyes of female slaves reverberates like an all-encompassing "roar he could not hear," quickly turning into the nauseating panic of being buried under "an avalanche" (AM 20). Jublio, in other words, is constructed as a "sweetish" and seductive but ultimately rotten and doomed blend of pride, excess, and slavery.

It is crucial to note, however, that this Gothicized construction of Jublio is dependent on—and controlled by—the perspective of Jacob Vaark. Morrison self-reflectively comments on Jacob's effort to Gothicize Jublio, in accordance with his increasing dislike of and disgust (AM 21) for D'Ortega. Jacob "entertain[s] himself by conjuring up" Gothicized imagery, and it "amuse[s] him to divine the worst while he endure[s] the foolish, incomprehensible talk and inedible dishes" (AM 17/18). Thus, Jacob can as readily conjure up a Gothic, nightmarish plantation as he can re-envision it as a manifestly destined dream "of a grand house of many rooms rising on a hill above the fog" (AM 33), a "house that size" and shape "but fair" and "pure, noble even, because it would not be compromised as Jublio" is (AM 25). The Gothic, in other words, is laid open to be a discursive practice performed and controlled (in this scene) by a WASP man. This, to a certain extent, also holds true for the Savage Villain/Civil Hero Gotheme; yet, as we will see time and again in *A Mercy*, there is never only one voice to listen to or one perspective to negotiate.

Approached from Jacob's focalized perspective, villainy on the Jublio plantation reads very much like the prototypical early British Gothic: A Mediterranean man with a "narrow grasp of the English language" (AM 16), more precisely a Portuguese Catholic member of the newly "rich gentry" (AM 25), a "loud and aggressive" (AM 14), "vain, [and] voluptuous" (AM 17) "substitute for a man" (AM 24) unable "to accommodate certain kinds of restraint" (23), leads a reign of terror in a remote location. In an "embroidered silk and lace collar" (AM 15), the "curdled, arrogant" Papist (AM 23) beats and tortures his slaves and demands "more than cooking" from his female slaves (AM 24). Confronted with this villain, Jacob is (self-) stylized as the Civil Hero: Riding in with "muddy boots" and hands still bloody from saving an innocent creature in need (AM 18), the uncompromised, "fair," "pure," and "noble" (AM 25) "commoner" and occasional "raw boy" (AM 23) goes "head to head with rich gentry" (AM 25), until "rank tremble[s] before courage" (AM 23). "[C]al_ed on to rescue" (AM 31) Florens from the hands and lust of the villain, "this ill-shod child that the mother was throwing away," he "rescue[s]" her, just as he had "rescue[d]" "the curly-haired goose child, the one they called Sorrow" years before (AM 32).

Despite equipping Jacob with discursive control over the construction and/or deconstruction of the SV/CH Gotheme in this scene, Morrison creates a constant Black Gothic undercurrent to Jacob's "feeling of license" that comes with the "newly recovered recklessness" (AM 24) of racial whiteness, in the otherwise "disorganized world" (AM 23). While this Black Gothic undercurrent will ultimately be explained (to a certain extent) through Florens's authorship of the narrative, including all its voices and perspectives, it must also, and more importantly, be understood as a textual means of the novel to write "against itself" (Broeck, "Trauma" 252). The white gaze and its discursive power to construct or deconstruct Gothicized places and peoples with a "feeling of license"—and *A Mercy* will not stop at having summoned the villainous Mediterranean man of the early British Gothic—are not accepted but met with resistance and subversion.

Most readily accessible is this Black Gothic undercurrent of the Jublio scene in the subversion of the (self-)stylized Civil Hero into yet another corrupted head of the systemically villainous hydra of slavery. Consider in this respect the following longer passage that concludes Jacob's (only) chapter:

> The sky had forgotten completely its morning fire and was tricked out in cool stars on a canvas smooth and dark as Regina's hide. He gazed at the occasional dapple of starlight on the water, then bent down and placed his hands in it. Sand moved under his palms; infant waves died above his wrists, soaking the cuffs of his sleeves. By and by the detritus of the day washed off, including the faint trace of coon's blood. As he walked back to the inn, nothing was in his way. [...] And the plan was a sweet as the sugar on which it was based. And there was a profound difference between the intimacy of slave bodies at Jublio and a remote labor force in Barbados. Right? Right, he thought, looking at a sky vulgar with stars. Clear and right. The silver that glittered there was not at all unreachable. And the wide swath of cream pouring through the stars was his for the tasting. (AM 33)

Up to this point in the novel, Jacob can readily be characterized as "cloaked in self-delusion" (Moya 152), or as one "of Morrison's white knights," who are "ignorant rather than good" (Mayberry 172). Thus far, Jacob has hidden behind naivety, when claiming that his purchase of a mail-order bride "was necessary" (AM 32), that he traded two girls out of mercy, and, "outright and deliberately" only bought one woman (AM 32). In his "Virginia version of Noah's ark" (Mayberry 174), the two indentured homosexual servants (Willard and Scully) are another necessity, this time for keeping his women in check (as a "frequently absent master [is] invitation and temptation," not least "to escape," AM 32), without posing the threats of "rape or rob" (AM 32). This scene, however, essentially rewrites and Gothicizes the self-stylized Civil Hero into a veritable villain, who, with a "cool" mind, decides to invest in the rum trade and, thus, into the large-scale trading, 'breeding,' torture, and exploitation of "mulattoes, creoles, zambos, mestizos, lobos, chinos, coyotes [...] being produced" and "controlled" in Barbados (AM 28). Washing "the faint trace of coon's blood" off of his hands—and here Morrison insinuates the double meaning of "coon," as a diminutive of "raccoon" and a racial slur for Black people[12]—"infant waves die[...] above his wrists." His plan may seem clear, right, and "sweet as the sugar," and the "labor force in Barbados" may feel as "remote" as the black night sky, yet death is already on his hands, and dead infants' blood already soaks "the cuffs of his sleeves." The future is a B/black "vulgar" horn of plenty, a "smooth and dark" "canvas," through which a "wide swath" has been cut—the sweet "cream pouring through" this swath, which now belongs to Jacob, it is "his for the tasting." The violated and exploited Black slave body becomes the canvas onto which this image of white violent vulgarity is drawn (or cut). Jacob, thus, is turned into a Gothic double of D'Ortega's "vain [and] voluptuous" (AM 17) villainy; he becomes another head of the hydra of slavery, a willing beneficiary directly responsible for the systemic exploitation and violation of the enslaved population of Barbados and for the transatlantic slave trade, as well as its "thousandfold men walking the waves, singing wordlessly" (AM 120).

By re-positioning the presumed Civil Hero as yet another white villain, Morrison closely follows a key Black Gothic writing strategy, prevalent in Black and African American (Gothic) texts from Equiano onward. In this scene, Jacob's failing as Civil Hero creates a gap in the Gothic plot that threatens to unbalance the Go-theme. In effect, the systemic and lawful villainy, based on which the slaveholding class oversees as the building of the "grand house of many rooms rising on a hill" (AM 33), appears to overpower the plot, to reign supreme and—seemingly—unchallenged. In the course of the novel, as we will see in the following, Morrison refills this gap of civil heroism and, as a matter of fact, constructs a force of veritable resistance to the systemic villainy of slavery.

"[I]t scares me it scares me": The Birth of the Africanist Savage Villain in the Puritan's Home

As if it were a direct inspiration for *A Mercy* generally, and for the scene focusing on Florens's consequential stay in Widow Ealing's home particularly, Morrison argues in *Playing in the Dark: Whiteness and the Literary Imagination*: "What rose up out of

---

12   Morrison foreshadows this double meaning of "coon" in this passage, when she lets Jacob rescue "a young raccoon stuck in a tree break," which, upon being thus rescued, "limp[s] off, perhaps to the mother forced to abandon it or more likely into other claws" (AM 9). The "coon" (meaning both a little raccoon and a racial slur for Black person), in other words, foreshadows Florens, who is abandoned by her mother, out of utter despair over her daughter's future as D'Ortega's sex slave, ending up in the "claws" of Jacob and in his 'peculiar' version of Noah's Ark.

collective needs to ally internal fears and to rationalize external exploitation was American Africanism—a fabricated brew of darkness, otherness, alarm, and desire that is uniquely American" (38). We have already encountered the villainous, Gothic underside of the collective need to rationalize the exploitation and enslavement of peoples. By drawing on the early British Gothic's construction of the villainously unrestrained, Catholic Mediterranean man and blending it with its WASP American double, the equally unrestrained, economically ambitious, white Protestant man who considers his advancement in the New World a Manifest Destiny, Morrison has staked out the fertile ground on which the "internal fears" will fall and grow into the "brew of darkness, otherness, alarm, and desire" that translates to the Africanist Savage Villain in the American Gothic tradition. In effect, Florens, the presumed "rescued" but invariably enslaved Black girl, is turned into "a canvas smooth and dark" (AM 33), onto which "other claws" (AM 9), this time belonging to a Puritan community on a witch hunt, can inscribe its internal fears in a WASP discourse of abjection and thingified savage villainy.

When Florens enters Willow Ealing's home, in an unnamed village with "a tiny steeple on a hill" and a distinct "burn smell, like pinfeathers singed before boiling a fowl" (AM 104), she enters an already Gothicized space. "Evil" and "danger" lurk "about" (AM 105), Florens is informed, as soon as she crosses the threshold into the "the single lit house" (AM 104) and into the space of a potentially demonic "she-wolf" (AM 105). With her flesh "cut to ribbons," so that the "dark blood beetling down her legs [...and] pouring over her pale skin" may prove the skew-eyed widow's daughter is neither she-wolf nor "demon," and summoned by "the Black Man" that the neighbors "say they have seen" (AM 107), the widow's desperate "bloodwork" (AM 108) becomes comprehensible, vis-à-vis the all-encompassing "burn smell": Looking for shelter and food, Florens has stumbled into the spatial and temporal vicinity of the Salem witch trials.[13] Employing Gothic features in a distinctly, yet comically, exaggerated fashion, Morrison confronts the local Puritan witch hunters, "a man, three women and a little girl" (AM 108/109), with Florens, once Widow Ealing has completed "the bloodwork" and, thus, figuratively and literally, has managed to "push[...] the goat out of the door" for the time being (AM 108,

---

13   Between 1692 and 1693, about 200 men and women were accused of witchcraft in Salem, Massachusetts and its surrounding communities; 20 people were eventually executed as witches, but, contrary to popular belief, none of the "witches" was burned at the stake. In accordance with English law, nineteen of the victims of the Salem witch trials died by hanging, one was pressed to death with stones, and a number of accused witches died in prison while still awaiting their trial. The popular (and broadly marketed) Gothic narrative of burnings at the stake in Salem was most likely inspired by European witch trials, where both execution by fire and cremation were practiced according to medieval codes of law between the fifteenth and eighteenth centuries. For a detailed introduction to the Salem witch trials, see Marilynne K. Roach, *The Salem Witch Trials: A Day-by-Day Chronicle of a Community Under Siege* (2002).

the goat is a symbol for the devil). Having "never seen any human this black," the Puritans "have shock," as Florens understands: The "sweet" little girl screams and hides, the "women gasp," and the "man's walking stick clatters to the floor causing the remaining hen to squawk and flutter" (AM 109). While Florens can be seen and readily rationalized as being an "Afric" and "as black as others," the Puritans accept the "little girl['s] shaking and moaning" as a testimony against Florens: She is "Afric and much more," a "minion" of "[t]he "Black Man" (AM 109).

At this point, Florens is accused of witchcraft (qua her skin color's relation to "the Black Man"), and Widow Ealing's already suspicious family is potentially doomed by affiliation. Only when Florens pulls out her mistress's letter to prove that she is in fact "nobody's minion but [her] Mistress" (AM 109, sic!) does this Gothicized ascription—and with it the tone of the narrative—change fundamentally:

> The man looks at me, looks again at the letter, back at me back at the letter. Again at me, once more at the letter. [...] They point me to a door that opens onto a storeroom and there, standing among carriage boxes and a spinning wheel, they tell me to take off my clothes. Without touching they tell me what to do. To show them my teeth, my tongue. They frown at the candle burn on my palm [...]. They look under my arms, between my legs. They circle me, lean down to inspect my feet. [...] The little girl is back, not sobbing now but saying it scares me it scares me. (AM 111)

The mistress's letter triggers a scene that blends (sentimental) narrative elements of slave markets and auction block inspections with the "internal fears" of colonial orthodox Puritanism of the late seventeenth century. Placed among other movable property in the storeroom, Florens's personhood and humanity are discursively deconstructed in and through the penetrating WASP gaze, until the former Black girl (and potential minion of the devil) is fully "thingified" and reduced to the ontological status of chattel. This "scene of subjection," as Saidiya Hartman would conceptualize it (*Scenes* 38), closely reflects Florens's mother's experience of being inspected and sold as "not a person" but as "negrita" (AM 163) in Barbados. To a certain extent, Morrison thus "anticipates a society in which the concepts of slavery and race are closely intertwined and blackness is equated with inferiority," as Nehl argues (65); more significantly, however, is Morrison's blending of WASP discursive abjection with the Gothic that anticipates more than 300 years of WASP cultural productions, in which B/blackness will be equated with the uncontrollable threat of the Africanist Savage Villain. Since the letter positions Florens as an enslaved and nameless "female person" (AM 110), the Puritans feel (and legally are) entitled to use her as an uncanny black canvas, onto which their fearful WASP discourses of otherness and abjection can be inscribed. Taken together, Florens is not only robbed of her former appellation of a "female person" but also becomes a scary Black "thing apart" (AM 113): "*It* scares me *it* scares me" (AM 111, my emphasis, C.L.).

As in the previously discussed scene (Jacob's visit to the Jublio plantation), the Widow Ealing scene also has a Black Gothic undercurrent that effectively both reiterates and "writes against" the domineering and Gothicizing WASP gaze. All but being transformed "into a weaker and more vulnerable person" (Nehl 65), Florens may be standing "[n]aked under their examination" (AM 111), vulnerable to the white arbitrary and violating gaze "across distances without recognition," but she gazes back. Watching "for what is in their eyes," Florens recognizes something with less cognitive abilities than "[s]wine [...] when they raise their heads from the trough" (AM 111) and neither averts her eyes when she is "inspect[ed]" nor does she ridicule the women who "look away," out of fear she might "come close to love and play" like "the bears" in the wilderness (AM 111). Following Florens's escape from Widow Ealing's home (and the loss of her mistress's letter to the Puritans), Morrison reiterates the discursive birth of the Africanist Savage Villain in a climactic passage:

> I am a thing apart. With the letter I belong and am lawful. Without it I am a weak calf abandon by the herd, a turtle without shell, a minion with no telltale signs but a darkness I am born with, outside, yes, but inside as well and the inside dark is small, feathered and toothy. [...] Sudden it is not like before when I am always in fright. I am not afraid of anything now. The sun's going leaves darkness behind and the dark is me. (AM 113)

It is important to note the parallelisms between this reiterative construction and the previously discussed scene (AM 111). Again, the letter enables the discursive inscription of the Black canvas; this time, however, the black on B/black lettering creates an all-dark picture, and "the dark is [Florens]." Rather than re-inscribing herself as a "thing," Florens chooses to envision her "drain[ing]" humanity as vulnerable animals: she becomes "a weak calf abandon[ed] by the herd," and—annulling all simplistic conflations with domesticated farm animals—"a turtle without shell." Picking up on the Puritan's fear of "the Black Man," it is Florens who connects her previously inspected and discursively distorted "outside" darkness with an "inside dark that is small, feathered and toothy" and "not afraid of anything." No longer "in fright," Florens blends in with the "darkness" that the "sun's going leaves [...] behind," knowing that she "can spring out of the darkness and bite" (AM 113). Thus, Morrison's construction of the discursive birth of the Africanist Savage Villain in/through the white gaze—from its very beginning(s)—includes Black resistance and Black reiteration practices. In this key scene, Morrison lets the Black Gothicized abject reiterate its own abjection, until the WASP Gothic Africanist Savage Villain is deconstructed and replaced by "the clawing feathery thing" (AM 113) of Black resistance and agency. At this point of the novel, the reiteration concludes in an optimistic, hopeful stance. Hoping for an intraracial connection with her lover, the free blacksmith, who has "the outside dark as well" (AM 113), Florens concludes her blending into wilderness and darkness by blending in with the blacksmith and his home: "[...] the dark is me. Is we. Is my home" (AM 113). As we will see below, it is this latter conflation that will cause the violent eruption of the (reiterated) Africanist Savage Villain in the blacksmith's home.

Before heading over to the blacksmith's "little cabin" (AM 133) with a newly fearless Florens, we must return to the gaping hole that the unmasked villain Jacob Vaark left in the SV/CH Gotheme, that is, to Morrison's reiteration of the Civil Hero. In the Widow Ealing episode, this position is filled temporarily by the intraracial cooperation of two Gothicized and discursively othered (Jane) or abjected (Florens) young women. Understanding that there is no hope for a savior, riding in to save them from being harmed by the people "who will decide" and who are solely entitled to own the "knowing," even if that means accusing a girl of witchcraft to get her mother's "pasture they crave" (AM 107), the women are left to their own agency and courage. Jane, who understands that she is as much or as little a "demon" as Florens is a "minion" of the devil (AM 112), "[r]isks it all to save" (AM 158) Florens, by aiding her escape. Florens's B/blackness, on the other hand, distracts the witch hunters lastingly from Jane's possibly demonic eye. Having exchanged kisses, Jane comments bemusedly and full of relish on their joint subversion of the Puritans' power and discourse, by claiming the ascription of "demon" (as Florens will claim her "thingified" savagery): "Are you a demon I ask her. Her wayward eye is steady. She smiles. Yes, she says. Oh, yes" (AM 112). Though differently attacked and preyed upon, vis-à-vis their different races, Jane and Florens succeed temporarily, by cooperating across the color line against the same oppressor. While *A Mercy* will significantly trouble any utopia of a powerful, interracial female community, within otherwise nightmarish territories through the progressive destruction of the Vaark homestead, it is a powerful (ful)filling of the Civil Hero's plot function for the time being.

The Africanist Savage Villain in the Blacksmith's Home

When Florens finally reaches the blacksmith's house, she shimmers significantly and constantly between two Gothicized ascriptions: She is the vilified and thingified Gothic abject that the Puritans have rendered her discursively; and she is the "the clawing feathery thing" (AM 113), born out of both her resistance against the white gaze and her own discursive agency. In Morrison's proto-Gothic constructiveness, Florens's function is also fundamentally in flux, meandering seemingly chaotically between Savage Villain, Civil Hero, and Damsel in Distress.

Her longed-for lover, a skilled, free Black male artisan, known only by his profession as "the blacksmith," is a character even more in flux than Florens, and the only major recurring character who does not focalize a chapter of *A Mercy*. Following Moya's insightful argument, I read the blacksmith's function "as a cipher—an empty placeholder onto which the other characters project their desires, anxieties, and judgments" (146). Moya summarizes:

> For Florens, Blacksmith is God made flesh—her savior, her safety, and her lover. For Willard Bond, Blacksmith is evidence of the existence of injustice: Blacksmith's freedom and ability to demand wage for his labor excites in Willard a resentful desire for increased status. For Linda, Blacksmith is loss personified; as the living embodiment of carnal temptation, Blacksmith reminds Lina of her own loss of freedom, as well as of the possibility of losing Florens. For Rebekka, Blacksmith is the anchor that holds her and her husband together. (146)

We can easily add to this list even more perspectives: For the young foundling Malaik, the blacksmith is a foster father who provides a home; for Sorrow, he is a healer, a savior, and a symbol for the kind of affectionate intimacy she has experienced herself (AM 126); for Jacob, he is a skilled artisan and befriended settler. Morrison's positioning of the blacksmith undoubtedly "invites us to interrogate the historically- and culturally-situated schemas that guide each character's perception of" the blacksmith and of each other (Moya 146). What is more, the functionalization of a free, "too shiny, way too tall" (AM 58), fully-Black male character as a textual cipher must be understood as an important aspect of Morrison's radical reiteration of the Africanist Savage Villain. Put bluntly, the blacksmith (violently and discursively) refuses to be the Africanist Savage Villain. Only by setting her novel in the late seventeenth century and rendering the blacksmith an intangible cipher in the multiperspectivity of the narrative can Morrison construct a blank canvas and cipher out a strong, male Black body, from which discourses and imaginations can be drawn that are not directly associated with the threat of the Africanist Savage Villain. Yet, Morrison does not negate these associations of the Black male body with the Gothicized abject; rather, through the ongoing discursive processes of the legal, social, and cultural conflation of race with slavery and Blackness with chattel, the blacksmith is positioned on the verge of becoming forcefully redefined as an Africanist Savage Villain.[14] That is why he "must maintain a clear demarcation between his free blackness and Florens's enslaved blackness" (Babb, "E Pluribus" 154), even if this means rejecting Florens, in a scene of intra-Black violence and

---

14   It is this positioning of the blacksmith, "on the verge" of the nascent WASP discourses of the Africanist Savage Villain, that has caused scholarship to analyze the character in polarly opposing directions: Either he is read as the healer who heals and saves Florens from her internalized slave status, qua his rejection of her (see e.g. Melton 37), or, as in the case of Ruth Bienstock Anolik's 2011 article, "Haunted Voices, Haunted Text: Toni Morrison's *A Mercy*," he is read as a "murderous villain" (422), an instantiation of "Satan" (424), and, ultimately, an "inhuman monster" (435).

racism. After having struck Florens in the face, the blacksmith resorts to discursive violence, and "[e]ach word" he uses "cuts" right into Florens, forcing her to her knees, and "killing" her: "[Y]ou are a slave. [...] Your head is empty and your body is wild. [...] You are nothing but wilderness. No constraint. No mind. [...] [A] slave by choice" (AM 139).

What is important to note here is that the blacksmith's discursive violence both targets Florens's "wilderness" and repositions her as a "slave by choice," although the latter is not constructed as the force, or, point of origin, of her "wilderness." This point of origin remains clearly und indisputably located in WASP discursive realms of the Jublio Plantation and the Puritan village. As a matter of fact, in Florens's encounter with the blacksmith, she is far from being reduced to a passive and permanent damsel in distress: It is Florens's own violence that triggers this fierce encounter—she hides young Malaik's precious doll, dislocates his shoulder, and causes him, upon fainting, to hit his head on "the table corner" (AM 138). Now confronted with the blacksmith's rage, Florens "curl[s] up on the floor" but is in control of herself and her unafraid and potent "clawing feathery thing" (AM 113): "I hold down the feathers lifting" (AM 138). Only when she understands that the blacksmith will not and cannot provide her with an identity and a space of racial and familial belonging—a "face [...] in blue water" (AM 140)—does Florens let go and "[f]eathers lifting, [she] unfold[s]" (AM 140). Through the blacksmith's intraracial discursive denigration of her, Florens finally becomes the "thing apart" of WASP discursive abjection. Apart and abject from racial whiteness, from Blackness, from family, and from community, the Black slave girl becomes a veritable Africanist Savage Villain: "I am wilderness. I am. Is that a tremble on your mouth, in your eye? Are you afraid? You should be" (AM 155).

The ensuing violence in which Florens likely kills the blacksmith with his own tools is, therefore, first and foremost based on and contextualized with the systemic degradation and violence of slavery and the nascent WASP discursive practices surrounding and legitimizing it. Yet, the novel does not allow us to read Florens's violence as an act of resistance against the oppressing system. By attacking a free Black man and a Black child (rather than D'Ortega, the Puritans, or her cured but "not well" mistress, Rebekka, AM 157), Florens violently and with potential fatal consequences does "a wrong thing:" she "wrest[s] dominion over another," to both avenge and undo the "wicked thing" of having willingly "give[n] dominion of [her]self to another" (AM 165). In a 2008 interview, Morrison weighs in on this point in Florens's development, by quipping: "She turns into something fairly feral, a tough-minded person who's willing to stand up for herself [...]. Too bad about the guy, but at least she's meaner. And she might survive this" (Morrison, "The Spirit" 54).

"I am wilderness. I am." Scratching Black Resistance and Agency into the Africanist Savage Villain

Florens leaves the battlefield at the blacksmith's cabin "barefoot, bloody but proud" (AM 146) and returns to the Vaark farm as a creature somewhere between "ghost and soldier" (AM 150). To the amazement of Scully, Florens's pervious "defenselessness, eagerness to please and, most all, a willingness to blame herself for the meanness of others" have given way to a daunting display of power and "un-rapeability"—Florens has "become untouchable" (AM 150). Yet, as Yvette Christiansë observes, "Morrison is never simply recuperative and never triumphalist, thus avoiding the conservatism of such gestures" (60). In fact, Florens may have become "untouchable," but she is neither unexploitable nor unsalable. Back at the farm and under the control of a newly "infidel" mistress (AM 157) and the close-by Anabaptists, "the clawing feathery thing" (AM 113) must "promise to lie quietly in the dark" and to "never again unfold [its] limbs to rise up and bare teeth" (AM 1). Reinstated as a slave, rising up and baring teeth against her white oppressors would mean certain death. In order to survive, Florens quiets down her discursively claimed wilderness and does chores, cleans, builds, and cleans some more (AM 156), before being ordered to sleep among the other "tools" in "the storeroom" (AM 157). Subversion and resistance with 'folded limbs' would mean creeping out of the storeroom furtively at night, in order to scratch her story into the walls and floors of Jacob's semi-completed and decaying grand manor.

Florens's act of writing directly reflects—and self-reflectively comments on—her reiteration and claiming of the Africanist Savage Villain. Read in this way, Florens's forceful scratching of her narrative into Jacob's version of the Jublio plantation with a nail (AM 156) is her first physical and discursive grappling with the hierarchizing and dehumanizing WASP discourses of power and race, to which the system of slavery gets more and more readily tied. In other words, Florens finally uses her "claws [to] scratch and scratch" (AM 140) the real cause for her oppression: "Realizing that she has no legitimate claim to place, she not only inserts herself into the home by occupying it, but she marks it as her own. She writes herself and her belonging into being," as Anissa Wardi concludes (34).

Yet again, Morrison denies Florens's authorship both triumph and lasting impact. Whenever she is outside of the house, she "spend[s] haunting time" in (AM 141), Florens is constructed as the epitome of "a thing apart." As a thingified chattel, Florens sleeps in the storeroom, while Lina, Sorrow/Complete and her baby sleep in the cowshed; and as a chattel, she is the only one put "up for sale" ("[b]ut not Lina," and Rebekka tries to "give away [Sorrow] but no one offers to take her," AM 157). Thus reduced to a "shadow" (AM 141) on the rapidly dissolving Vaark homestead, Florens's ontological status as a chattel sets her apart from all others, including both non-Black races and free Black people. With no one to share her story, and utterly aware of her status as the abject, Florens "might even burn down the house and, with it, the story that she has been writing" (Christiansë 60). Paradoxically, what does remain, when Florens burns down Vaark's manor and her own narrative, is Florens. She has found a way to survive in a system that thrives on the social (and willingly accepts the physical) death of the Black body. Florens states: "I am become wilderness but I am also Florens. In full. [...] Slave. Free. I last" (AM 159). Florens 'is,' she exists, and she will survive. She has reiterated and claimed WASP discursive appellations of racial denigration and violence as a means of self-empowerment and resistance; she is wilderness but also Florens, slave, free. In her final and ultimate self-positioning, Florens thus remains in flux; the paradoxical tension of her identity (which is also the tension between the Savage Villain, the Civil Hero, and the Damsel in Distress) is not resolved but claimed and literally inscribed.

It is important to not read Florens's self-positioning ("Slave. Free. I last") as a nod toward reconciliation—the presumable construction of a physically and legally enslaved Black woman whose inner resistance against WASP racial discourses liberates her spiritually (slave but free)—which in turn may trigger a renewed wave of reconciliatory kitsch analyses in the scholarly field. Morrison outright refuses to facilitate any sort of identification of, or with, the Black protagonist, along the lines of victimhood, trauma, and healing. I thus concur fully with Nehl's conclusion that, ultimately, "*A Mercy* is not about healing but about the impossibility of successfully working through, and thus leaving behind, the trauma of slavery" (78). In sum, *A Mercy* positions itself as an African American "testament to the fact that objects can and do resist" (Moten 1). The contemporary African American Gothic is the ideal writing strategy to narrate this testament—not in spite of the Gothic's conventional centering of the highly problematic racialized and racializing SV/CH Gotheme but because of it.

6.3 "Pheenie Optimism"—with Zombies!: Colson Whitehead's *Zone One*

"Unfortunately, 'post racism' is also a myth, like unicorns and black people who survive to the end of a horror movie." (Simien 10)

"In the midst of so much death and the fact of Black life as proximate to death, how do we attend to physical, social, and figurative death and also to the largeness that is Black life, Black life insisted from death?" (Sharpe 17)

When it comes to positionality within the twenty-first century's "Zombie Renaissance,"[15] Colson Whitehead's *Zone One* is a somewhat troublesome text. At first glance, the novel follows the conventional premise of a contemporary zombie narrative. Set mainly in a near-future dystopic rendering of New York City's Lower Manhattan district, *Zone One* explores the fate of protagonist and expert marksman Mark Spitz, over the course of the walled-off zone's final days, before a zombie horde tears down one of humanity's remaining barricades, mauls the living, and creates more living dead. This apparent conventionality has left many critics wondering about, and even apologizing for, Whitehead's flirtation with the zombie genre. Whitehead, the recipient of numerous grants and awards dedicated to literary merit and excellency,[16] has shocked his critics to the extent that "review after review counterposes serious literature to genre fare" (Swanson 379), often without an awareness of the backwardness and outright absurdity of such a distinction.[17] Glen Duncan's review for the *New York Times*, to give just one example, equates the seriousness and cultural value of zombie fiction with that of pornography, claiming: "A literary novelist writing a genre novel is like an intellectual dating a porn star" (Duncan n.p.). What Duncan fails to see, however, is that Whitehead is not merely enjoying the presumed gory extravagance of the zombie genre, nor is he simply giving in to "his own horror fandom" (Swanson 380). Rather, he uses the zombie trope's multilayered history of social criticism and racial connotations to deconstruct one of the Gothic's most persistent binaries: the Savage Villain/Civil Hero Gotheme. This deconstruction makes *Zone One* a challenging and boundary-pushing text for zombie (and/or Gothic) genre fans and critics alike. Whitehead's further deconstruction of the zombie trope's natural habitat—the near-future dystopia—does not result in a revival of utopianism and/or (Afro)futurism, but, ins-

---

15 Chapter 7.1 outlines the mainstream WASP American zombie trope's renaissance in all branches of American popular culture, including TV and film productions, computer games, comic books, literature, art, music, and fandom. It does so within the context of discussing Andre Duza's post-apocalyptic zombie novel *WZMB*. See Hubner, Leaning, and Manning (eds.), *The Zombie Renaissance in Popular Culture* (2015); also Bishop (5).

16 Critics most often refer to Whitehead's receipt of the MacArthur Fellowship "Genius" Grant in 2002, which is one of the most prestigious grants in the United States, awarded to individuals in any field who have shown "extraordinary originality and dedication in their creative pursuits." The MacArthur Foundation especially emphasized Whitehead's "willingness to take the intellectual risks necessary to expand the boundaries of contemporary writing" and expressed their belief that he would make "further contributions to American literature" (cf. The MacArthur Foundation https://www.macfound.org/fellows/702/). Since 2002, and over the course of accumulating numerous prestigious awards and grants—among them his recent Pulitzer Prize win for *The Underground Railroad*—Whitehead has undoubtedly confirmed that this early belief in his boundary-pushing contributions to American literature was well-founded.

17 See for example Barton (2011), Charles (2011), Chiarella (2011), Kois (2011), and Ness (2011).

tead, results in a quintessentially Afro-Pessimistic novel that portrays the inevitable dead-end of the WASP America's post-racial fantasies that peaked during the presidency of Barack Obama.[18]

Zone One embarks "from the tensions between an ontological and structural 'fact' of blackness, on the one hand, and a discursive, constructed, performative, and identificatory blackness on the other" (Linscott 105). Whitehead establishes this tension against the backdrop of a seemingly post-apocalyptic and post-racial U.S. society, which, in its government-issued belief that survivors of the human-zombie conflict have completely surpassed race, gender, and class prejudices, in fact only re-stages, re-performs, and re-constructs anti-Black racism and the socially-dead Black abject. In the process of reiterating and, more specifically, reiteratively deconstructing the Savage Villain/Civil Hero Gotheme, Zone One ceases to work like a generic white American-mainstream zombie novel; rather, while Whitehead's novel features zombies, it resists the Gothic's racialized binaries. Since the Gothic cannot sidestep its intrinsic raciality, Whitehead paradoxically sidesteps the Gothic, through his creation of a zombie novel that features carefully un-Gothicized versions of Gothic characters, props, and settings.

Contrary to Glen Duncan's criticism, Whitehead's reiterative deconstruction works not despite but because of his use of the zombie trope. The zombie is the only conventional Gothic trope that does not originate in white discourse and literature but in Haitian lore. Scholar Toni Pressley-Sanon summarizes the original Haitian zombie figure and its initial entry to the white American imagination:

> Unlike the flesh-eating zombie of the contemporary popular imagination, the original zombie, a figure that emerges out of Haitian lore, was a sightless, mindless slave who had been raised from the grave and forced to reside in a liminal

---

18   In its most simple postulation, Sherrow O. Pinder argues, "post-raciality promotes the idea that the election of the first black man, Barack Obama, as the president of the United States proves that the United States has moved beyond race" (63). This view, however, is consistent with a larger set of beliefs that "the majority of White Americans have held for well over a decade: that African Americans have achieved, or will soon achieve, racial equality in the United States despite substantial evidence to the contrary" (Dawson and Bobo 247). The fact that anti-Black racism and racist violence (the full extent of which can only be hinted at by high-profile individual cases like the murders of Trayvon Martin and Tamir Rice) continued to routinely occur in the United States during the Obama presidency unmasks post-raciality as a WASP fantasy. Furthermore, that this white "dream of post-raciality was only a prelude to the recurring nightmare of institutional and existential anti-black violence, etched not only in our memory but unfolding before us" (Frankowski xi), became first apparent in the onslaught of anti-Black propaganda and violence during the Obama presidency, doubtlessly culminating in the 2016 presidential election of a man unapologetically racist (see also Chapter 5.1).

state in order to work for his master until physical death[19] released him from his torment. With no will of his own and no memory of his past life, he was a figure to be pitied, rather than feared. It is this zombie that entered the American imagination in the 1930s during the US marine invasion and subsequent occupation of Haiti, at a time when the United States was trying to figure out what to do with its own "Negro problem." The zombie was the perfect embodiment of the monstrous black who had been successfully contained and controlled. As a figure who was fully under the command of his or her master, the zombie was the prefect representation of white men's desire for the subservient black laborer that they needed in order to feel secure, not only in the United States but on an international front. As such, the zombie recalls the condition of the chattel slave [...]. (30)

The import of the Haitian zombie figure into U.S. cinema[20] must be understood in the context of contemporaneous white American race and eugenics discourse. Amid the African American population's push for political and social equality, images of indefinitely enslaved Black bodies, devoid of free will, served as useful fodder for white supremacy's agenda. The common denominator in all white American renderings of the zombie trope is the Gothicized Black abject. The Haitian zombie figure was

> [...] first refashioned as occult exotica by W.B. Seabrook and others in the early twentieth century in the form of "white zombies"; then shifting shape into Romero's silent, implacable ghouls and the more vocal variety with a comical fetish for brains; finally, metamorphosing into a malleable monster that can assume different forms (running or slowly lurching in pursuit, ghoulishly feeding or rabidly murderous, purposefully seeking or mindlessly wandering). Far from being an enslaved soulless corpse strictly under the control of a *bokor*, the zombie, once unleashed, freely ranges over cities and countries, in massive hordes that overwhelm organized resistance, no matter how expert or militarized. (Ahmad 131).

---

19 Pressley-Sanon refers here to the zombie's second physical death. Depending on the folkloric tradition, this second death can either be brought about by God's merciful collection of the soul or by human hands, for example, by feeding the zombie salt. For an excellent introduction to the Haitian zombie and its migration to U.S. popular culture, see Ann Kordas's 2011 article, "New South, New Immigrants, New Zombies: The Historical Development of the Zombie in Popular Culture."

20 Until the 1980s, the fictional zombie (not to be confused with ethnographic accounts of the Haitian folkloric zombie, the most noteworthy being Zora Neal Hurston's 1938 study *Tell My Horse*) was featured almost exclusively in white American films, specifically in low-budget B movies.

As Toni Pressley-Sanon, Gerry Canavan, Jessica Hurley, and others have argued, the distinction between human and zombie, between life and the liminal state of the living dead, "is always a racial one" (Hurley 312). In the Haitian zombie-slave narrative, the white American discursive racialization of Haitian bodies hearkened back to chattel slavery and its commodification of Black human beings, meaning the erasure of personhood and agency and, thus, being 'zombified.' In U.S. popular culture's white gaze, this Blackness took on contagious qualities, embodying the threat of miscegenation and racial decline. In the construction of the zombie, Blackness becomes an unflinching visual presence. Despite the title of the 1932 film *White Zombie*, the white damsel in distress never becomes enslaved by the white zombie master, while all the fully-fledged zombies are Black men. From the 1940s onward, the zombification of a white damsel became not only racially imaginable but a popular horror trope; the zombie, in American cinema, turned into an almost exclusively white figure. Yet, as Anne Anlin Cheng has shown, the seemingly pure, clean surface of the white zombified body is continuously revealed to be ruptured and rotting, infected with B/blackness underneath (101). Becoming a zombie means becoming a vessel for contagious Blackness. The imagery of a horde of contagious, uncontrollably violent B/black bodies, threatening to overrun and (racially) infect white civilization, plays into the Savage Villain/Civil Hero Gotheme. In other words, the adaptation of the Haitian zombie figure for American audiences meant fitting the formerly tragic figure into the white American binary, equating Blackness with savagery and civilizational decline and whiteness with civic order and virtue.

By both exposing and drawing upon the dichotomized tradition on which today's zombie trope is based, Whitehead circumnavigates the intrinsic raciality of the white SV/CH Gotheme. In summary, *Zone One* is an Afro-Pessimist allegory of WASP post-racial fantasies that explores and self-reflexively performs, through the reiterative deconstruction of the SV/CH Gotheme, the possibility of Black survival and resistance to unceasing (even after the apocalypse) white abjectorship and white supremacy. Whitehead's literary strategy—writing from within, against, and even outside the Gothic conventions of racial denigration and white abjectorship—allows for a restrained optimism in an otherwise Afro-Pessimistic novel. *Zone One* pushes the zombie trope outside the boundaries of conventional Gothicized raciality (the SV/CH Gotheme), to achieve an intra-discursive emergence "unthought." Whitehead's boundary-pushing novel therefore provides a solution to a key problem of this project. The Gothic is intrinsically racialized and racializing, as it is conventionally bound to the SV/CH Gotheme. However, *Zone One* indicates that the zombie can be excavated from the Gothic's vast corpus of conventional characters, props, and settings and reiterated deconstructively, to create a strategically un-Gothicized narrative.

To make this complex argument about *Zone One*, I rely not only on research on the zombie trope and its origins in Haitian lore but also on secondary literature regarding the novel itself. Most likely due to early consensus that Whitehead's novel is "a zombie novel," which, however, is not "*about* zombies" (Swanson 379, his emphasis; again, this can be tied back to the many reviews dismissing the generic zombie narrative), these two perspectives have so far only been connected superficially and in passing, if at all.

First and foremost, *Zone One* is currently read as a post-9/11 novel. While Whitehead himself has stated that he "wasn't directly writing about 9/11 in *Zone One*" (Naimon, "A Conversation with Colson Whitehead" n.p.), critics such as Tim S. Gauthier, Kyle William Bishop, Erica Sollazzo, Walton Muyumba, and others argue that "Whitehead intends to link the zombie-apocalypse to the terrorist attacks of September 2001" (Gauthier 111). Since "the title linguistically echoes 'Ground Zero,' the area directly impacted by the attacks" (ibid.), many readings understand the novel as "transcend[ing] pulp fiction by piercingly exploring the national trauma of September 11" (Bishop 90). New York City is depicted "as an infected biological body" that can never be cured, or un-wounded, "through propagandistic nostalgia and heavy-handed commercialization" as the United States witnessed in the wake of 9/11 (Bishop 91). Gauthier conflates Whitehead's zombie horde (he does not consider Whitehead's differentiation between "skels" and "stragglers") with Islamic terrorists and *Zone One*'s Buffalo-based government with the administration of George W. Bush:

> There is no questioning of how and why the zombie outbreak occurred. Scientists are hard at work only on figuring out how to destroy the zombies and end the pandemic. Most of all, there is no hint of self-interrogation. The echoes of 9/11 ring most strongly here. The Bush administration was far more concerned and determined to destroy al-Qaeda than to understand the conditions that brought the extremist organization into existence [...]. (118)

While it is—at least to a certain extent—"tempting to read all recent zombie narratives through the critical lens of 9/11" (Bishop 90), this type of allegorical comparison, largely detached from both the novel and the real-life political complexities in the aftermath of the terrorist attacks on the World Trade Center, is inevitably oversimplified. Erica Sollazzo avoids the oversimplification of a one-sided allegorical reading, arguing that Whitehead has constructed a tripartite allegory that "draws from three real-world 'apocalypses'—the 9/11 terrorist attacks, the financial crisis, and accelerating gentrification—to demonstrate the insidious effects of excessive corporate influence" (457). Sollazzo interprets the zombie trope in *Zone One* as an economic allegory:

> The zombie figure performs several symbolic tasks in this context. The ravenous "skel" comes to stand for both the consumer and the corporation; the nostalgic "straggler" comes to stand for both the customer and the mindless corporate employee. In the end, Whitehead's dystopia is dominated by market forces—in other words, by distinctly *nonhuman* values. (480, original emphasis)

How these "nonhuman values" of the market, as well as the paradoxical crossings of consumer/corporation and customer/employee, can be connected back to the "real-world 'apocalypse'" of 9/11 remains largely unexplored in Sollazzo's article.

In my own reading of *Zone One*, I understand 9/11 as a fruitful context, however not quite in the sense of the scholars briefly introduced above. I argue that Whitehead, like Andre Duza in *WZMB*, uses 9/11 to portray a presumably post-racial society as a white American discourse, from which African Americans are excluded, vis-à-vis anti-Black racism and white abjectorship. My analysis connects strongly to a handful of articles that firmly position the novel in the post-racial discourse and debate so prevalent during the Obama era. Arguing that *Zone One* "embraces radical narrative closure as an alternative to futurist narratives of crisis" (Sorenson 560), Leif Sorensen discusses the novel's suggestion of "the shocking possibility of an absolute ending" (561), concluding that "[t]he austere bleakness of Whitehead's imagined apocalypse is a powerful expression of dissent from the commitment of futurism that permeates contemporary culture" (ibid). The "import of Whitehead's critical reworking of the contemporary zombie narrative," according to Sorensen, arises from the "moment in which the apocalyptic and pre-apocalyptic worlds collapse into one another, suggesting that the death-world has already arrived" (587). *Zone One* thus forces its readers out of their comfort zone of presumed post-raciality and to confront, in Mark Spitz's words, "the monstrous we overlook every day" (Z 297).[21] Derek C. Maus also picks up on Whitehead's conflation of the living and the living dead as a means to powerfully express his dissent against white America's commitment to post-racial historical revisionism. While positioning the novel as the "most pessimistic of his [Whitehead's] novels" (121), Maus concludes his reading of *Zone One* in a hopeful tone:

> If the world's problem has been a traumatic connection to a past that no longer works, the novel's last line may either chronicle Mark Spitz's last living steps or his first steps into a radically different future: 'Fuck it, he thought. You have to learn to swim sometime. He opened the door and walked into the sea of the dead' ([Z] 259). If he learns to swim, the irony of his nickname disappears, leaving open-ended space for a whole new range of identities (120).

---

21 In-text citations marked with "Z" refer to Whitehead's *Zone One*.

Maus, in other words, thinks that the protagonist can escape the appellative racism inscribed throughout the novel, even in his very name (the nickname "Mark Spitz" refers to the white Olympic swimmer and is given to the protagonist in the course of a racist "black-people-can't-swim" pun (Z 287). This optimism stems from Maus's reading of the novel's ending as being ambiguous, refraining from indicating whether the protagonist will die and be merged with the zombie horde or if he will survive in an identity (re-)forming "open-ended space." In her 2015 article, "History Is What Bites: Zombies, Race, and the Limits of Biopower in Colson Whitehead's *Zone One*," Jessica Hurley does not share Maus's optimism. Noting the manifold "visual tensions between whiteness and blackness in Hollywood representations of the zombie" as markers of racism and the discursive operations of biopower (in Foucault's sense), Hurley argues that the zombie trope in *Zone One* functions as "the return of a repressed history of racial trauma in a contemporary moment in which biopower operates increasingly under the sign of the 'post-racial'" (311). She states:

> The contemporary fantasy of the post-racial produces this specific nightmare as its material unconscious: the walking dead, embodying in their disintegrating bodies the ongoing violence of modern racialization and its disavowal, impossible to contain within the past, the post-. (Hurley 330)

While I regard Hurley's article as groundbreaking, especially in its negotiation of the racialized tradition of the zombie trope and its direct relevance to Whitehead's *Zone One*, her argument that repressed "traumatic racial histories" (312) return, in presumably post-racial times, rests on two premises that I cannot share. Firstly, Hurley reads Whitehead's zombies—she hardly distinguishes between "skels" and "stragglers" here— "not only as a kind of monster, but also as a kind of ghost" (314). This argumentative maneuver allows her to further stress the zombie's haunting presence as a reminder of traumatic history; however, it also all but dismisses her previous analysis of the racially Black zombie trope in white Hollywood film productions and, subsequently, in white American literature. Secondly, to (re-)establish race as a core quality of this simple ghost-like presence, Hurley juxtaposes racialized zombies and Mark Spitz, whom she analyzes as a "literally post-racial (in the sense of deracinated) protagonist" (313). Qua Mark Spitz being "named after a white swimmer" and the revelation that, all along, he has "been black only in the final pages of the novel" (ibid.), Hurley positions him in a *bildungsroman*-type quest: Confronted with "the reality of the undead," that is, with the unburied racial bodies that post-racial discourses "pretend [...] never existed" (330), Mark Spitz learns to decode the language and relentless presence of the living dead as "the disposed-of Other" (ibid.), without being or becoming one of them. My own analysis foregrounds Whitehead's deconstructive reiteration of the zombie trope and its racialization, while it strongly encourages a reading of Mark Spitz as a Black protagonist who, from the start, is subjected to the discursive workings of anti-Black racism. The racial abjection of Mark Spitz, inscribed in his very name, blurs the boundaries between him and the zombies, to the point that his union with "the sea of the dead" (Z 259) becomes a logical consequence of the plot, as well as of the "straggler" ontology projected onto him.

My argument for reading *Zone One* as an Afro-Pessimistic novel that addresses white American post-racial fantasies, which developed out of fear of Black resistance, rests on two premises. First, I trace how Whitehead creates and then reiteratively deconstructs the SV/CH Gotheme to depict the unending presence of the socially-dead Black abject in a supposedly post-racial society. Second, I address *Zone One*'s exploration of the (im)possibility of Black survival and resistance in the death-worlds of white discourse and abjectorship, which leads to the key question of the possibility (and desirability) of an intra-discursive emergence of "unthought" in contemporary African American Gothic fiction.

As mentioned at the beginning of this subchapter, at first glance, *Zone One* follows the conventional premise of a contemporary zombie narrative. *Zone One* employs the white American SV/CH Gotheme on one level, only to deconstruct it on another. On the first level, Whitehead constructs a conventional zombie narrative of walled-off survivors, fighting the unceasing onslaught of the infectious walking dead. Employing the white American SV/CH Gotheme, Whitehead's "plague-era" (Z 15) zombies are cannibalistic "legions of the damned," (Z 29) consisting of horrific "monsters" (Z 16) with "dark, gory muzzle[s], the telltale smear produced when a face burrowed deep into live flesh" (Z 15). Whitehead divides his zombies into "average skels" (Z 33)—the cannibalistic group of zombies that "twist their bodies in unison," as if following a "dumb choreography" (Z 20) to feed jointly on their human prey—and "harmless stragglers" (Z 33)—"the things" (Z 77) that form "a succession of imponderable tableaux" (Z 48) that stay immobile and completely oblivious to both the world and their possible prey forever. Counterbalancing the savage horde of the cannibalistic undead is the civil heroism of the "American Phoenix" (Z 79). Erecting barricades between their "civilization" inside safe havens, such as "Happy Acres" and "Zone One" and "this savage new reality" (Z 18) "out in the wild" (Z 40), the American Phoenix establishes a "steadfast binary" (Z 27) that creates "a single Us now, reviling a single Them" (Z 231). Confronted with the apocalyptic zombie horde, the "good little pheenies" (Z 43) stick together, in the firm belief that, faced with the nonhuman Other, they have finally surpassed "racial, gender, and religious stereotypes" (Z 231).

The binary of a single Us/humans versus a single Them/zombies is established as much through gun power and physical barricades as it is through 'the new language" of "reconstruction" (Z 79). Through slogans such as "We Make Tomorrow!" (Z 48) and patriotic songs like "Stop! Can You Hear the Eagle Roar? (Theme from *Reconstruction*)" (Z 110), the Buffalo-based interim government engages in spreading "the new optimism" (Z 35), by discursively "rebranding survival" (Z 79). Most importantly, the new language insists that survivors "[m]ustn't humanize them" (Z 158), encouraging both violent language (as in the fun pastime activity "Name That Bloodstain!") and excessive "sadism" (of "[s]kel mutilation," for example) as acceptable forms of "popular amusement" (Z 81) and as "a healthy outlet" (Z 82) for pent-up emotions. Again, true to the SV/CH Gotheme, the American Phoenix's actions are motivated by fighting for a "return to Eden" (Z 53) and for the propagandistic purity of the damsels in distress. The three mysterious babies, the "Tromanhauser Triplets" (e.g. Z 45), function in particular as the epitome of innocence and "localized hope" (Z 42) and, consequently, as "the reserve tank" (Z 41), on which the American Phoenix's operations run. The slogans "Do it for Cheyenne" Tromanhauser and "[y]ou're never on your own" (Z 193) reflect how rhetoric can serve as fuel.

On this level of Whitehead's (de)construction of the SV/CH Gotheme, Mark Spitz is an almost archetypal civil hero. At the bottom of the American Phoenix's hierarchy—"[f]irst Buffalo [...], then the military, then civilian populations, and finally the sweepers" (Z 18)—he stands out as the hard-boiled, hands-on action hero, who refuses to succumb to the "hope-delivery system sent down from Buffalo" and "that pheenie bullshit" (Z 26). Meanwhile, he seemingly survives effortlessly on his own, even when confronted with an "impossible" horde of "the massing dead" (Z147): "He had the ammo. He took them all down" (Z 148). In this respect, Mark Spitz "[i]sn't like the rest of them" (Z 26) because he is a better marksman, a tougher yet morally superior fighter and independent thinker among simple-minded and oftentimes outright sadistic "pheenies."

It is, however, upon Mark Spitz's climactic display of civil heroism and action-hero-type masculinity that Whitehead creates a rupture and turning point in the conventional zombie plot, which culminates in a reevaluation of the entire narrative, effectively forcing the reader to enter the second, deconstructive level of *Zone One*'s SV/CH Gotheme. When Mark Spitz single-handedly takes down a horde of skels on a bridge on I-95, instead of jumping off the bridge with his comrades, he does not become a hero and subject of propagandistic pheenie anecdotes of heroism and courage; rather, he is ridiculed, denigrated, and nicknamed simply for being Black. In his moment of greatest strength and masculinity, the protagonist is nicknamed "Mark Spitz" because his refusal to jump off the bridge is reduced to "the black-people-can't-swim thing" (Z 231). Being a Black man excludes him from civil heroism, thus subjecting him to racist ridicule and denigration instead; the potentially dangerous and ultra-masculine action hero with a gun and plenty of ammunition is reduced to a harmless, even childlike, non-swimmer and a racist insider joke. What is more, Whitehead uses this rupture of the uncovered racist nickname to lay bare the ongoing and persistent reduction of Mark Spitz to the ontological level of a straggler:

If he'd been able to explain the extent of what was happening in his brain that day they nicknamed him Mark Spitz, the host of maniac, overlapping processes, perhaps he'd have earned a different moniker, one suitable for the completely bloodless processes inside him. (Z 144)

When Whitehead explicitly reveals that Mark Spitz is Black, in the last third of the novel, his continuous self-recognition in the stragglers starts to fall into place, making the character "finally complete, in a way" (Z 144). Mark Spitz is the only character in the novel whose individual Post-Apocalyptic Stress Disorder—or, "PASD in its sundry tics, fugues, and existential fevers"—allows him "to see in different spectra" (Z 30) the humanity and individuality of the dehumanized hordes of zombies. Every time Mark Spitz happens to cross paths with a straggler or a skel, he cannot help but ponder their former human existences and names. Mark Spitz, Gauthier argues, "sees the human in the zombie [...] and the zombie in the human (at one point he thinks of Gary as more zombie than anything else)" (121). Without an air of superiority in his observations and, more importantly, with a clearly rehumanizing stance, Mark Spitz recognizes himself in the zombies, muses on his own possible haunting grounds as a future straggler, and, thus, develops a sense of "mutuality, some fellow-feeling" (Gauthier 121): "He was a ghost. A straggler" (Z 155).

When the protagonist refuses to buy into the American Phoenix's propaganda and their distinction between "Us" and "Them," understanding "that they are not you," "the whole thing breaks down" (Z 158). The American Phoenix's discourse and its "props of civilization" (Z 137) can no longer hide what their "Reconstruction" really means. Just like the first period of Reconstruction after the Civil War, which attempted to redress the inequities of slavery and its political, social, and economic legacies but which really re-established and re-legitimized antebellum anti-Black racism, in a society of Jim Crow laws and racist violence, this second "return to the things before" (Z 135) allows "the new skinheads" (Z 141) and "[t]he secret murderers, dormant rapists, and latent fascists [... to freely] express their ruthless natures" (Z 197). America's reconstruction of itself, as "a well-organized muck with a hierarchy" (Z 162), is legitimized as being "pure-blooded American bad-assery" (Z 139). This hierarchy, again, is a racial hierarchy. Mark Spitz, qua his Blackness, is excluded from "pure-blooded American bad-assery"—no matter how bad-ass his actions are; he inevitably becomes reinstated in the ontological position of a straggler.

Whitehead's *Zone One* visualizes the white abjectorship leading to Mark Spitz's straggler ontology—the most fitting fictionalization of a socially-dead Black abject that I have encountered to date—by constantly exposing Mark Spitz to the "evanescent currents of white flakes" (Z 186). The machinery of the American Phoenix incinerates the innumerous zombie bodies, and "white smoke and ash" with "constancy and pervasiveness" covers Mark Spitz's "skin and the pavement" (Z 187) "like snow" (Z 186), until it even becomes "assimilated into his body" (Z 187). Mark Spitz is aware of the intricate workings of white abjectorship on and under his skin, "he despise[s] it," as a "particular face of his PASD" (Z 187). Here and throughout the novel, we can read "PASD" and "past" as being synonyms. Mark Spitz has learned to "[r]esist" (Z 24), as "a survivalist even at a tender age" (Z 9), when growing up Black on Long Island meant exposing his "shabby suburban self" to the "constant jostling of strangers, who cut him off, scowled at his tentative steps, [...] and render him defenseless so they could devour him" (Z 206). Whenever young Mark Spitz could not hide in the "black stations" (Z 210), "down in the dark [where] no citizen was more significant or more decrepit than another" (Z 214), to "catch his breath" and "prepare himself for the next engagement" (Z 210), he had to rely on his "cockroach impersonation, the infinite resilience of said critters he had down cold" (Z165).

Past and present, the pre- and post-apocalyptic United States merges into one "persistent vegetative state" of "a flatlined culture" (Z 217), based on white supremacy and white abjectorship. In this culture of the American Phoenix, self-fashioned as post-racial and post-stereotypical, the Black male protagonist is under constant threat, however, not because of the zombies. Rather, it is the "prevailing delusions" of post-raciality, the "pandemic of pheenie optimism," both "inescapable" and suffocating—"a contagion in its own right" (Z 13)—that discursively erases the Black person behind the racist nickname "Mark Spitz," rendering him a socially-dead abject, a straggler, even before the plague. The contagious disease rampant in the United States is dehumanizing, anti-Black racism; the post-racial discourse of the American Phoenix in the novel (as much as of the white American public, especially during the Obama administration) is unmasked as only another face of white abjectorship and white supremacy.

In effect, the re-individualized, re-humanized, and pitiable zombies cease to function as the Savage Villain, appearing in the role of victims subjected to the cruel sadism of sweepers like Gary and the American Phoenix propaganda machine, whose genocidal campaign is equipped with an arsenal of weapons of mass destruction and efficient incinerators ("the Coakley has proven itself a most worthy recruit," Z 187). In this respect, Whitehead re-inscribes the Haitian-type tragic slave-zombie into the plot. If we consider that Whitehead's zombie terminology, his differentiation between "skel" and "straggler," is also white police jargon for "criminal/thug" and "beggar," the allegorical potential of his zombies falls into place: Skels and stragglers stand in for the racially and socially marginalized, just as Mark Spitz stands in for the straggler.

By dissolving the binary between zombies (in the end, *Zone One* collapses the difference between skels and stragglers, by constructing a very animated and deadly straggler, fittingly described as "the fortune-teller," Z 223) and the protagonist, between zombie plague and "pheenie optimism," between past and present, pre- and post-apocalypse, Whitehead reiteratively deconstructs the SV/CH Gotheme, to the point that the conventional Gothic/zombie plot breaks down. Rather than letting the protagonist either survive or die involuntarily, Mark Spitz, discursively reduced to the ontology of a straggler, willingly gives up his last shred of individuality—his "unrivaled mediocrity" that has enabled his survival as a "cockroach" thus far—and unites physically and discursively with "the sea of the dead": "fuck it, he thought. You have to learn to swim sometime. He opened the door and walked into the sea of the dead" (Z 259).

This conclusion of the novel can paradoxically be read as both the epitome of *Zone One*'s Afro-Pessimistic stance and a veritable form of Black resistance against the discursive, anti-Black violence that the protagonist has been subjected to throughout. Either Mark Spitz commits suicide, by joining the zombie horde as a logical conclusion to his discursive and ontological descent into 'stragglerness,' or *Zone One* positions Mark Spitz's suicide against the propagandistic needs and discursive power of the American Phoenix. The first reading casts the ending as both nihilistic and bitingly ironic: A post-racial American utopia is only imaginable when every single American has been turned into a zombie; hoping for a better future, the Black protagonist might as well join the zombie horde. The second reading affords Mark Spitz more agency: Rather than letting white abjectorship decide his status as (socially as well as physically) alive or dead, he claims this right for himself: "killing yourself in the age of the American Phoenix was a rebuke to its principles," because how can "We Make Tomorrow!" if someone destroyed "the delusion that we'll make it through" (Z 202)? In this respect, Mark Spitz's walking into "the sea of the dead" forces the surviving pheenies to confront the American Phoenix's delusional propaganda and to understand that there is no making "it through," because there is no difference between before and after. Given that Mark Spitz was a straggler all along, he might as well join the other "ambassadors of nil" (Z 245), to continue lurching and straggling through Zone One.

In many ways, Whitehead's *Zone One* reflects and fictionalizes Achille Mbembe's concept of the "Necropolis" (his eponymous essay is commonly cited as the progenitor of Afro-Pessimism). Co-joining the notions of "biopower" of Michel Foucault and Giorgio Agamben, "Necropolis" claims that "the ultimate expression of sovereignty resides, to a large degree, in the power and the capacity to dictate who may live and who must die" (11). In America, black social death is depicted as being necessary for white sovereignty (i.e. the American Phoenix) to flourish—now, just as it was during times of slavery. For Afro-Pessimism and for *Zone One*, the Black Necropolis, or "death-world," is an undeniable structural fact that precedes any performative, constructed, or anti-essentialist blackness. When we consider how Whitehead collapses the pre- and post-apocalypse, indicating that the plague of anti-Blackness both precedes and outlives the interregnum of the American Phoenix and the zombies, his version of the Black Necropolis seems even more pessimistic than Agamben's (and even Mbembe's) original notion. Leif Sorensen argues:

> The novel undoes Agamben's distinction between an earlier version of politics, for which the city served as *nomos*, and the biopolitical order of modernity, in which the camp replaces the city. If the city has always been a predatory death-world that feeds on his citizens, even Agamben's despairing account of modernity is overly optimistic (587).

That the narrator neither comments on Mark Spitz's motivation nor his fate in "the sea of the dead," leaving us with an ambiguous vision of Mark Spitz's death/walking with the zombies, fictionalizes the only tentative optimism that remains possible in Zone One's bleak Afro-Pessimistic framework: "a living death is as much a death as it is a living" (Sexton, "The Social Life" 69).

It is in this regard that Whitehead's construction of a Black "death-world," plagued by the "pandemic of pheenie optimism" (Z 16), must still be understood as an exploration of the (im)possibility of Black survival and resistance. By deconstructing the SV/CH Gotheme, this otherwise Afro-Pessimistic (even nihilistic) novel indeed envisions escape, at least on a meta-fictional level: Whitehead reiteratively deconstructs the racialization of the SV/CH Gotheme, without deconstructing the zombie trope per se. *Zone One* no longer works as a generic zombie novel, but it still is—and undeniably so—a novel featuring zombies, just one existing outside of Gothic conventionality and binaries. Whitehead uses the zombie against itself. Based on the trope's origins in Haitian negotiations of chattel slavery, Whitehead reiteratively deconstructs the white American zombie and, with it, the SV/CH Gotheme that lies at its core. He not only shows how white abjectorship discursively (re-)creates Blackness as the zombified Black abject, but he forces the reader to participate in this zombification of the Black man, in the abjection of "Mark Spitz" so prevalent in—and inescapable through—the protagonist's very name. By writing the Haitian tragic slave-zombie back into the zombie narrative, he renders the death-world itself, and the white abjectorship behind the process of zombification, as the truly monstrous and horrific aspect of his novel. This forces us to confront not just the dehumanizing race discourse, controlling the white American pop-cultural zombie narrative, but also the everyday banality and mediocrity with which white abjectorship operates on all levels of society and at all times. For the zombie narrative specifically, and for the American Gothic more generally, this translates to the possibility of discursive unthought. By reiteratively and self-reflectively deconstructing the white American zombie trope, vis-à-vis its intrinsic raciality, Whitehead does not allow the reader to buy the pop-cultural zombie narrative at face value. Without seeing in the zombie both the Black abject and white abjectorship at its core becomes impossible. This must be seen as an extension of the possibilities of both the zombie genre and the American Gothic. In an interview with Alexis Madrigal, Whitehead argues for his extension of the genre, explaining his reiteration strategy as follows:

> You take what you want from a genre, deform it, steal from it, pay homage, and at the same time, if you're doing it right, you are extending the possibilities of that genre, reinvigorating it. I wanted to be true to a Romero-style version of existential zombie dread, but of course the fun part of being a writer is making up shit. (Madrigal n.p.)

Unfortunately, the creative potential of a Gothic trope to be discursively unthought against and from within itself is not only connected to an individual author's virtuosity but also, and most importantly, to the zombie trope's unique history. Rather than engaging with the SV/CH Gotheme's long racial and literary history, the zombie trope offers a unique shortcut that Whitehead exploits reiteratively. By tapping directly into the zombie's origin in Black folklore, Whitehead can extricate the trope from the white American SV/CH Gotheme. This allows him to both depict and think outside the boundaries and binaries of white abjectorship and its conventional reliance on the Gothicized Black abject. That the zombie trope has only very recently (since the 1980s, roughly) made its appearance on the American literary stage must be seen as another important factor in this process of discursive unthinking. This apparent limitation also bears enormous potential for the future engagement of African American authors with the zombie and with Black quasi-Gothic tropes we have not encountered in white American Gothic texts thus far.

Epilogue: The American Gothic, Raciality, and the Possibility of Reiterative "Unthought"

> "As a metaphor for transacting the whole process of Americanization, while burying its particular racial ingredients, this Africanist presence may be something the United States cannot do without. Deep within the word 'American' is its association with race." (Morrison, Playing 47)

On November 20, 2013, an episode of the popular United States television game show, *Family Feud*, aired, featuring an exchange between African American host Steve Harvey and a white female contestant, "Christie." The exchange instantaneously went viral on the Internet as being one of the most awkward, even racist, moments in the history of the show. Asked by Harvey to "name something you know about zombies," Christie hits the buzzer and enthusiastically says: "Black!" Visibly shocked by the answer, Harvey turns to the wall stiffly muttering, "... They're Black. Okay," while Christie meanders between self-conscious backtracking ("I don't know if they're white ... or ... I just ... probably ...") and insisting, "It's up there, it's up there!" Still, with his back to Christie, Harvey says to her: "You shut up, lady!" When "Black" is not one of the top six answers "up there" on the screen, the two competing teams, the audience, and Harvey are visibly relieved; Christie is disappointed. Responses to Christie's zombie answer ranged from ridicule and disbelief, for the hilarious "kneejerk response" (Moore n.p.), to an outright controversy over racism on TV, as noted in the *Observer*'s article, "Is this *Family Feud* Contestant Being a Zombie Racist?" (Grant n.p.) Was Christie being racist? If so, why did her racism only spill out uncontrollably when she was asked about her knowledge of zombies?

The first thing that came to my mind when I watched the exchange between Christie and Harvey online (years after its first airing on TV) was: "Christie is right!" My second thought was: "But, she doesn't know it." Zombies are Black; their Blackness "is indeed the defining feature of the zombie no matter what the skin color of its body's original owner" (Hurley 315). Born out of the abhorrent violence and dehumanizing race discourses on Haitian sugar plantations, the ur-zombie of Black Haitian lore is a stand-in for the nightmare of the indefinite enslavement of Black bodies rendered completely powerless. In the context of Jim Crow, lynchings, the Ku Klux Klan, and eugenics in the United States, this understanding of the term zombie fell on fertile ground and spawned into a multiplicity of pop-cultural adaptations. The key to unlocking the WASP American zombie's Gothic potential, that quality of balancing entertainment with gooseflesh for a predominately white audience, was its integration into the WASP American Savage Villain/Civil Hero Gotheme. While the WASP American zombie trope—on its surface—has become almost exclusively white-skinned, becoming a zombie now translates into being infected with and turned into a vessel for contagious Blackness. Following the racial logic of the Savage Villain/Civil Hero Gotheme, the tragic slave-zombie is replaced by the B/black contagious horde of uncontrollable violent bodies threatening to overrun and (racially) infect white civilization. Christie's cultural consciousness correctly makes this connection between B/blackness and the zombie trope. For me, the awkwardness is triggered by two things. First, Christie makes this connection unreflectively, from within the WASP American discourse that renders her haplessly complicit rather than intentionally revelatory. Second, neither Harvey nor the *Family Feud* audience seems aware of the anti-Black racism that is an intrinsic quality of the currently predominant WASP American version of the zombie trope. With my study on the intrinsic raciality of the American Gothic, past and present, WASP American and African American, I hoped to elucidate how and why popular Gothic tropes are both racialized and racializing, and why it is both difficult and crucial for a white consumer of Gothic texts (in its broadest sense)—like Christie and myself—to become aware of the anti-Black racism at the very heart of one of the most popular and bestselling writing strategies to date.

Let me review the logic and key findings of my study in broad strokes. Taken together, the three parts of *Savage Horrors: The Intrinsic Raciality of the American Gothic* set out to address four decisive and far-reaching questions:

1. What holds the diversity of texts summarized as "the American Gothic" together?
2. Is the common denominator the racialized and racializing SV/CH Gotheme?
3. If so, how is the SV/CH Gotheme employed in Gothic novels by African American authors, who, according to the WASP American Gothic's conventionality, belong in the racial category of the abject, that is, of the Africanist Savage Villain?
4. Is creative and discursive "unthought" possible? In other words, is it thinkable that a future Christie answers a *Family Feud* task, such as "name something you know about zombies," without instantaneously equating the monstrous with Blackness?

Epilogue: The American Gothic, Raciality, and the Possibility of Reiterative "Unthought"

In "Part I: The Gothic and the Savage Villain/Civil Hero Gotheme," I developed a working definition of the Gothic as an ideologically and generically ultra-adaptable writing strategy that is based on a stable canon of Gothemes, that is, of conventionalized structural binaries. Based on my analysis of the Gothic's origins in eighteenth-century British literature and culture, I positioned the Savage Villain/Civil Hero Gotheme, a racial dichotomy based on the structural opposition between a racialized other/Gothicized abject and the contrastingly racialized norm of civilization, at the heart of the Gothic. The Gothic conveys and quotes racial stereotypes, but it has the potential to quote with a twist. This twist can either describe a new context, genre, etc., in which the conventions are employed, or it can describe the discourse-altering reiteration an author undertakes. In other words, some Gothic texts repeat old and painfully racialized stereotypes in new contexts, thereby strengthening the underlying discriminating discourse. Other Gothic texts function as consciously critical narratives, making visible—and working toward changing—the hateful discourse.

I then outlined the history of the SV/CH Gotheme in WASP American Gothic texts. I did so by first looking at its early nineteenth-century transfer from British to American contexts. I then analyzed the SV/CH Gotheme in the imprinting phase of the WASP American Gothic, and I traced its development from an initial type of Savage Villainy as the Native American "other" to the momentous shift to the Africanist Savage Villain as the Gothicized Black abject. I then found that the Africanist Savage Villain swallowed and replaced the Native American SV, due to greater political, social, and cultural urgency and actuality, up to the point at which WASP American Gothic literature focused solely on the Africanist Savage Villain (while the Nobel Savage became the stock stand-in character used to depict the Native American "other" in WASP American literature). Making the transition to the contemporary WASP American Gothic, I analyzed the continuous presence of the racialized and racializing SV/CH Gotheme in a number of recent novels, before focusing in-depth on Stephen King's *The Girl Who Loved Tom Gordon* and Karen Russell's *Swamplandia!*. At the end of "Part II: The 'Savage Villain/Civil Hero' Gotheme: WASP Origins and Iterations," it became clear that the SV/CH Gotheme is a constant trope in WASP American Gothic fiction, past and present. The uncomfortable realization that the continuity of race in WASP American Gothic texts—more specifically, of the dehumanized and Gothicized Black abject/the Africanist Savage Villain—directly fuels the arguments of Afro-Pessimism concluded the second part of my study, leading directly to the third part.

"Part III: 'You say I am wilderness. I am'—Black Origins and African American Reiterations" keeps in mind the Afro-Pessimistic implications of the previous part and pursues the SV/CH Gotheme in the Black Atlantic and African American texts. Delivering a blow against scholarship that theorizes the African American Gothic as a merely reactive, "anti-gothic" (Smethurst 29) type of writing, I traced the uniquely Black reiteration tradition of the SV/CH Gotheme in Olaudah Equiano's *The Interesting Narrative*. I established a second, alternative point of origin for the American Gothic, outside the cultural and geographic boundaries of WASP-dominated North America and inside the Black Atlantic. In my subsequent analyses of numerous nineteenth-century and contemporary African American Gothic texts, I traced the continuous presence of the SV/CH Gotheme in complex reiteration contexts and in terms of discourse-strategic efforts. The SV/CH Gotheme remains a continuous presence in African American Gothic literature; however, the way it is simultaneously strategically utilized, reiterated, and critically (re-)integrated into two writing traditions (Black and WASP American) significantly complicates the Gotheme and the Gothic writing strategy. Finally, I focused on Toni Morrison's *A Mercy* and Colson Whitehead's *Zone One* to trace the authors' creative and reiterative exploitation of the SV/CH Gotheme's intrinsic raciality and the possibility of discursive "unthought" in two recent novels that are—maybe necessarily so—both Afro-Pessimistic and Gothic.

Taken as a whole, my study established that the SV/CH Gotheme and, thus, raciality (generally) and the Black abject (more specifically) are at the core of the American Gothic. This has direct implications for the paradigmatic concept of "the American Gothic." If the continuous presence of the SV/CH Gotheme alone is at stake, then we can and must speak of "the American Gothic"; here, "American," in Morrison's sense, already implies the American Gothic's intrinsic "association with race" (Morrison, *Playing* 47). Furthermore, considering that the "American" in "American Gothic" has been most consistently considered to be the terminological equivalent to "white" or "WASP American Gothic," the umbrella term fittingly expresses the countless echoings and iterations of the Savage Villain in WASP American Gothic fiction. Thus, it helps expose WASP American Gothic fiction as being one form of the structural violence inscribed in what Wilderson calls "the rubric of antagonism (an irreconcilable struggle between entities, or positions, the resolution of which is not dialectical but entails the obliteration of one of the positions)" (*Red* 5). Recent WASP American bestsellers, such as Anne Rice's *Prince Lestat and the Realms of Atlantis*, Stephen King's *The Girl Who Loved Tom Gordon*, or Karen Russell's *Swamplandia!*, unequivocally demonstrate how persistent and appealing racialized Gothic dichotomies, generally, and the Gothicized Black abject, more specifically, still are. They also show that the apparent lack of a "physical" Poesque B/black Savage Villain in a WASP American text does not entail a de-racialization of the SV/CH Gotheme or the refutation of the Africanist presence. Indeed, all of the discussed contemporary WASP American Gothic novels functionalize the Africanist presence, that "fabricated brew of darkness, otherness, alarm, and desire" (Morrison, *Playing* 38), by continuing to conflate blackness and Blackness, savage villainy, and the B/black body from the discursive position of white abjection.

However, if we want to stress the innovative, discourse-altering potential that the creative use of the ultra-adaptable writing strategy has in the hands of writers such as Harriet Jacobs or Colson Whitehead, then the term "American Gothic" is crassly over-simplified. A more careful differentiation between various types of "Gothics"—here, for example, antebellum female African American Gothic and early twenty-first century male African American Gothic—is mandatory. This terminological sub-differentiation also helps draw more attention to the most problematic, or disheartening, finding of my study: While Black and African American writers, past and present, make use of the Gothic writing strategy as a means to reiterate critically, and in a potentially discourse-altering way, the underlying racial stereotypes, this ongoing, transcultural exchange with both Black Gothic origins and the WASP American Gothic's (problematic racial) conventionality appears to be a one-way street. In WASP American Gothic texts, harmful and hateful racialized tropes and stereotypes—especially tangible in the Africanist SV, that is, in the Gothicized Black abject—have continued to reign supreme since the early nineteenth century. At best, reiterative change, in which WASP American Gothic is constructed outside the racialized and racializing constraints of the SV/CH Gotheme, appears to be a creative project for the future generation of WASP Gothic writers. At worst, achieving that change seems to be impossible.

In this polarizing contrast between the ongoing African American reiterative and (potentially) discourse-altering practice and the WASP American Gothic's intrinsic raciality, we must question whether or not the SV/CH Gotheme can be reiterated outside the boundaries of race. We must also determine whether or not an intra-discursive emergence of "unthought" is possible and/or desirable. In my study, only Colson Whitehead's reiteration of the WASP Gothic's zombie trope, vis-à-vis the Haitian ur-zombie—itself a unique constellation within the Gothic tradition, as I outlined in the previous chapter—opens up space for some optimism. While Whitehead does not reiterate the zombie outside the boundaries of race *per se*, he successfully dismantles the Gothicized Black abject (that is, the Africanist SV), by exposing, even annulling, the process of white discursive abjection that lies at the core of the Gotheme. Within this vein of reiterative critical Gothic writing—by African American, Native American, Asian American, or Hispanic American authors, to name just four types, currently thriving on "American Gothics"—I see the greatest potential for discursive unthought and, thus, for a future Gothic liberated from the intrinsically racialized and racializing SV/CH Gotheme.

In the field of Gothic scholarship, for those of us who make a living by tending to the monsters in our closets, while knowing well that they really reflect the broader fears and anxieties lurking outside our front doors, this hope is hardly relevant. As Terrence Rafferty reminds us, "[w]ith every fashion in horror, it's worth asking, Why do we choose to fear this, and why now? The answers can be more unsettling than the stories themselves" ("The State" n.p.). In the era of the blatantly racist

Trump presidency, faced not so much with a rise in but with a brutal continuity of xenophobia and anti-Black racism and violence in the streets, as well as in medial discourse (notwithstanding the #BlackLivesMatter movement), why would African American authors not choose racialized otherness to portray an angst-inducing real-life battle against white supremacy and anti-Black racism?

Works Cited

Adorno, Theodor W. *Negative Dialektik*. Suhrkamp, 1966.
Aguirre, Manuel. "The Roots of the Symbolic Role of Woman in Gothic Literature." *Exhibited by Candlelight: Sources and Developments in the Gothic Tradition*. Eds. Valeria Tinkler-Villani, Peter Davidson, and Jane Stevenson. Rodopi, 1995. 57–64.
Ahmad, Aalya. "Gray is the New Black: Race, Class, and Zombies." *Generation Zombie: Essays on the Living Dead in Modern Culture*. Eds. Stephanie Boluk and Wylie Lenz. McFarland, 2011. 130–146.
Albright, Richard S. *Writing the Past, Writing the Future. Time and Narrative in Gothic and Sensation Fiction*. Lehigh University Press, 2009.
Alcott, Louisa May. *The Inheritance*. Penguin, 1998.
Althans, Katrin. *Darkness Subverted. Aboriginal Gothic in Black Australian Literature and Film*. University Press, 2010.
Althusser, Louis. *Lenin and Philosophy, and Other Essays*. Trans. Ben Brewster. New Left Books, 1971.
Ammons, Elizabeth. *Edith Wharton's Argument with America*. Georgia University Press, 1980.
Anderson, Benedict. *Imagined Communities. Reflections on the Origin and Spread of Nationalism*. Rev. ed. Verso, 2006.
Andrews, William L. *To Tell a Free Story: The First Century of Afro-American Autobiography, 1760–1865*. University of Illinois Press, 1986.
Andrews, William L. "Introduction." *From Fugitive Slave to Free Man: The Autobiographies of William Wells Brown*. Ed. William L. Andrews. University of Missouri Press, 2003.
Anolik, Ruth Bienstock and Douglas L. Howard, eds. *The Gothic Other. Racial and Social Constructions in the Literary Imagination*. McFarland, 2004.
—, ed. *Demons of the Body and Mind. Essays on Disability in Gothic Literature*. McFarland, 2010.
—. "Haunting Voices, Haunted Text: Toni Morrison's A Mercy." *21st-Century Gothic: Great Gothic Novels Since 2000*. Ed. Daniel Olson. Scarecrow, 2011. 418–31.

Anthony, Ted. "King's 'Unplanned' Offspring Is the Reader's Joy." *Jefferson City News Tribune Online*. 25 April 1999. <www.newstribune.com/stories/042599/ent0425990026.html> (last accessed 20 January 2014).

Appiah, Kwame Anthony. "No Bad Nigger: Blacks as the Ethical Principle in the Movies." *Media Spectacles*. Eds. Marjorie Garber, Jann Matlock, and Rebecca L. Walkowitz. Routledge, 1993. 77–90.

—. "Race." *Critical Terms for Literary Study*. Eds. Frank Lentricchia and Thomas McLaughlin. 2nd ed. The University of Chicago Press, 1995. 274–305.

Armitt, Lucie. *History of the Gothic: Twentieth-Century Gothic*. University of Wales Press, 2011.

Arnzen, Michael A. "Childhood and Media Literacy in *The Girl Who Loved Tom Gordon*." *The New York Review of Science Fiction* 14.8 (2002): 1, 8–11.

Arrivé, Mathilde. "Interview with Navajo-Laguna Novelist and Filmmaker Aaron Albert Carr." *Revue de recherché en civilisation américaine* 2 (2010): 1–18.

Ashcroft, Bill, Gareth Griffiths and Helen Tiffin. *The Empire Writes Back: Theory and Practice in Post-Colonial Literatures*. 2nd ed. Taylor and Francis, 2002.

—. *Post-Colonial Studies: The Key Concepts*. 2nd ed. Routledge, 2007.

Atwood, Margaret. *Strange Things: The Malevolent North in Canadian Literature*. Clarendon, 1995.

Auerbach, Nina. *Woman and the Demon: The Life of a Victorian Myth*. Harvard University Press, 1984.

—. *Our Vampires, Ourselves*. University of Chicago Press, 1995.

Austen, Jane. *Northanger Abbey*. Ed. Marilyn Butler. Penguin, 1995.

Babb, Valerie. "*E Pluribus Unum?* The American Origins Narrative in Toni Morrison's *A Mercy*." *MELUS* 36.2 (2011): 147–164.

Bailey, Dale. *American Nightmares: The Haunted House Formula in American Popular Fiction*. University Press, 1999.

Baker, Houston A. Jr. *Blues, Ideology, and Afro-American Literature: A Vernacular Theory*. University of Chicago Press, 1984.

Baker, Lee D. *From Savage to Negro: Anthropology and the Construction of Race, 1896–1954*. University of California Press, 1998.

Bakhtin, Mikhail M. *The Dialogic Imagination. Four Essays*. Ed. Michael Holquist. Trans. Caryl Emerson and Michael Holquist. 15th ed. University of Texas Press, 2004.

Balchin, Nigel. *The Anatomy of Villainy*. Collins, 1950.

Baldick, Chris and Robert Mighall. "Gothic Criticism." *A Companion to the Gothic*. Ed. David Punter. Blackwell, 2000. 209–228.

Banks, L.A. *Minion. A Vampire Huntress Legend (1)*. St. Martin's Griffin, 2003.

—. *Bad Blood. A Crimson Moon Novel (1)*. St. Martin's Paperbacks, 2008.

Banta, Martha. "The Ghostly Gothic of Wharton's Everyday World." *American Literary Realism* 27 (1994): 1–10.

Bardi, Abigail R. *The Gypsy as Trope in Victorian and Modern British Literature*. Digital Repository at the University of Maryland, 2007.

Barnett, Louise K. *The Ignoble Savage: American Literary Racism, 1790–1890*. Greenwood Press, 1975.

Barthes, Roland. *Mythologies*. Transl. by Annette Lavers. New York: Hill and Wang, 1972.

Beach, Natalie. "The Thriller You Won't Be Able to Put Down." *Oprah.com*. Web. http://www.oprah.com/oprahsbookclub/the-changeling-by-victor-lavalle (last accessed 10 June 2018).

Beckford, William. *Vathek*. Oxford University Press, 1998.

Beecher-Stowe, Harriet. *Uncle Tom's Cabin*. Bantam Dell, 2003.

—. *A Key to Uncle Tom's Cabin: Presenting the Original Facts and Documents Upon Which the Story Is Founded*. Dover Publications, 2015.

Behdad, Ali. *A Forgetful Nation: On Immigration and Cultural Identity in the United States*. Duke University Press, 2005.

Bellamy, Maria Rice. "'These Careful Words...Will Talk to Themselves': Textual Remains and Reader Responsibility in Toni Morrison's *A Mercy*." *Contested Boundaries: New Critical Essays on the Fiction of Toni Morrison*. Ed. Maxine L. Montgomery. Cambridge Scholars, 2013. 14–32.

Berenstein, Rhona J. *Attack of the Leading Ladies: Gender, Sexuality, and Spectatorship in Classic Horror Cinema*. Columbia University Press, 1996.

Bergland, Renée L. *The National Uncanny: Indian Ghosts and American Subjects*. University Press of New England, 2000.

Berlin, Ira. *Generations of Captivity: A History of African American Slaves*. Harvard University Press, 2004.

Bickham, Troy. *Savages Within the Empire: Representations of American Indians in Eighteenth-Century Britain*. Clarendon Press, 2006.

Birke, Dorothee. "Challenging the Divide? Stephen King and the Problem of 'Popular Culture.'" *The Journal of Popular Culture* 47.3 (2014): 520–536.

Birkerts, Sven. "Gothic Feminism." *Mirabella* 3:2 (1991), 40–44.

Birkhead, Edith. *The Tale of Terror. A Study of the Gothic Romance*. Constable and Company, 1921.

Birney, James and Lewis Tappan. "Alabama Beacon versus James Williams." *The Friend of Man* 3.14 (19 September 1838). *Cornell University Archive*. Web (last accessed 10 August 2017).

Bishop, Kyle William. *American Zombie Gothic: The Rise and Fall (and Rise) of the Walking Dead in Popular Culture*. McFarland, 2010.

Blackall, Jean F. "Imaginative Encounter: Edith Wharton and Emily Brontë." *Edith Wharton Review* 9 (1992): 9–11.

Blockett, Kimberly. "Writing Freedom: Race, Religion, and Revolution, 1820-1840." *The Cambridge History of African American Literature*. Eds. Maryemma Graham and Jerry W. Ward, Jr. Cambridge University Press, 2011. 116–133.

Bloom, Harold. "For the World of Letters, It's a Horror." *Los Angeles Times*. 19 September 2003. Web. <http://articles.latimes.com/2003/sep/19/opinion/oe-bloom19> (last accessed 12 August 2015).

Blum, Virginia. "Edith Wharton's Erotic Other-World." *Literature and Psychology* 33.1 (1987): 12–29.

Bodziock, Joseph. "The Cage of Obscene Birds: The Myth of the Southern Garden in Frederick Douglass's *My Bondage and My Freedom*." *The Gothic Other: Racial and Social Constructions in the Literary Imagination*. Eds. Ruth Bienstock Anolik and Douglas L. Howard. McFarland, 2004. 251–263.

Booth, Wayne C. *The Rhetoric of Fiction*. Second ed. University of Chicago Press, 1983.

Botting, Fred. "In Gothic Darkly: Heterotopia, History, Culture." *A Companion to the Gothic*. Ed. David Punter. Blackwell, 2000, 5–14.

Botting, Fred. *Gothic*. 11th ed. Routledge, 2006.

Boyarin, Jonathan. *Storm from Paradise: The Politics of Jewish Memory*. University of Minnesota Press, 1994.

Brabon, Benjamin A. and Stéphanie Genz, eds. *Postfeminist Gothic: Critical Interventions in Contemporary Culture*. Palgrave Macmillan, 2007.

Brabon, Benjamin A. "The Spectral Phallus: Re-Membering the Postfeminist Man." *Postfeminist Gothic. Critical Interventions in Contemporary Culture*. Eds. Benjamin A. Brabon, and Stéphanie Genz. Palgrave Macmillan, 2007. 56–67.

Bradford Warner, Anne. "African American Literature, Beginnings to 1919." *The Companion to Southern Literature: Themes, Genres, Places, People, Movements, and Motifs*. Eds. Joseph M. Flora and Lucinda H. MacKethan. Louisiana State University Press, 2002. 10–15.

Brantlinger, Patrick. "Imperial Gothic: Atavism and the Occult in the British Adventure Novel, 1880–1914." *English Literature in Transition* 28.3 (1985): 243–252.

—. *Rule of Darkness. British Literature and Imperialism, 1830–1914*. Cornell University Press, 1988.

Breton, André. *Le Manifeste du Surréalisme*. 1924. *Manifestoes of Surrealism*. Trans. Richard Seaver and Helen R. Lane. University of Michigan Press, 1969.

Brodkin, Karen. *How Jews Became White Folks: And What That Says about Race in America*. Rutgers University Press, 1999.

Broeck, Sabine. "The Challenge of Black Feminist Desire: Abolish Property." *Black Intersectionalities: A Critique for the 21st Century*. Eds. Monica Michelin and Jean Paul Rocchi. Liverpool University Press, 2013. 211–224.

—. "Trauma, Agency, Kitsch and the Excesses of the Real: *Beloved* within the Field of Critical Response." *Sabine Broeck—Plotting against Modernity: Critical Interventions* in *Race and Gender*. Eds. Karin Esders, Insa Härtel, and Carsten Junker. Ulrike Helmer Verlag, 2014. 239–257.

—. "Commentary (In Response to Michel Feith)." *Black Studies Papers* 1.1 (2014): 25–28.

—. "Enslavement as Regime of Western Modernity: Re-Reading Gender Studies Epistemology through Black Feminst Critique." *Sabine Broeck—Plotting against Modernity: Critical Interventions in Race and Gender*. Eds. Karin Esders, Insa Härtel, and Carsten Junker. Ulrike Helmer Verlag, 2014. 34–51.

Brogan, Kathleen. *Cultural Haunting: Ghosts and Ethnicity in Recent American Literature*. University Press of Virginia, 1998.

Brookhiser, Richard. "The Numinous Negro: His Importance in Our Lives; Why He Is Fading." *National Review*. 20 Aug. 2001. Web. http://www.nationalreview.com/article/220766/numinous-negro-williumrex (last accessed 1 April 2017).

Brown, Charles Brockden. "Novel-Reading." *Literary Magazine* 1 (1804): 401–405.

—. *Three Gothic Novels: Wieland, Arthur Mervyn, Edgar Huntly*. Penguin Putnam, 1998.

Brown, William Wells. *From Fugitive Slave to Free Man: The Autobiographies of William Wells Brown*. Ed. William L. Andrews. University of Missouri Press, 2003.

Brown, William Wells. *Clotel; or, The President's Daughter*. Ed. M. Giulia Fabi. Penguin Books, 2004.

Brown, William Wells. "A Lecture Delivered before the Female Anti-Slavery Society of Salem: At Lyceum Hall, Nov. 14, 1847." *William Wells Brown: A Reader*. Ed. Ezra Greenspan. University of Georgia Press, 2008. 107–129.

Brox, Ali. "'Every Age Has the Vampire It Needs': Octavia Butler's Vampiric Vision in *Fledgling*." *Utopian Studies* 19.3 (2008): 391–409.

Bruhm, Steven. "The Contemporary Gothic: Why We Need It." *The Cambridge Companion to Gothic Fiction*. Ed. Jerrold E. Hogle. Cambridge University Press, 2002. 259–276.

Bryan, Eugenia P. "Written on the Walls: Reflections of Shifting Definitions of Slavery and Self in Toni Morrison's *A Mercy*." *Afterimages of Slavery: Essays on Appearances in Recent American Films, Literature, Television and Other Media*. Eds. Marlene D. Allen and Seretha D. Williams. McFarland, 2012. 89–109.

Bryant, Howard. "Don't Expect Protests in Baseball—It's a White Man's Game by Design." ESPN.com. Web. http://espn.com/mlb/story/_/id/17537499 (last accessed 21 September 2016).

—. *Shut Out: A Story of Race and Baseball in Boston*. Routledge, 2002.

Buntline, Ned. *The Mysteries and Miseries of New York: A Story of Real Life*. Dublin: James M'Glashan, 1849. Archive.org. Web (last accessed 11 August 2016).

Burke, Edmund. *Reflections on the Revolution in France, and on the Proceedings in Certain Societies in London Relative to That Event: in a Letter Intended to Have Been Sent to a Gentleman in Paris*. 1790. The Project Gutenberg eBook of Burke's Writings and Speeches. Volume the Third. Web (last accessed 4 December 2013).

Burnham, Michelle. "Is There an Indigenous Gothic?" *A Companion to American Gothic*. Ed. Charles L. Crow. Blackwell, 2014. 225–237.

Busey, Christopher L. "Examining Race from Within: Black Intraracial Discrimination in Social Studies Curriculum." *Social Studies Research and Practice* 9.2 (2014): 120–131.

Butler, Judith. *Excitable Speech. A Politics of the Performative*. Routledge, 1997.

—. *Bodies That Matter: On the Discursive Limits of Sex*. Taylor and Francis, 2010.

Butler, Octavia E. *Fledgling*. Grand Central, 2005.

Bryant, Cedric G. "'The Soul Has Bandaged Moments': Reading the African American Gothic in Wright's *Big Boy Leaves Home*, Morrison's *Beloved*, and Gomez's *Gilda*." *African American Review* 39.1 (2005): 541–553.

Cantiello, Jessica Wells. "From Pre-Racial to Post-Racial? Reading and Reviewing *A Mercy* in the Age of Obama." *MELUS* 36.2 (2011): 165–183.

Canup, John. *Out of the Wilderness: The Emergence of an American Identity in Colonial New England*. University Press of New England, 1990.

Carby, Hazel V. *Reconstructing Womanhood: The Emergence of the Afro-American Woman Novelist*. Oxford University Press, 1987.

Carens, Timothy L. "The Civilizing Mission at Home: Empire, Gender, and National Reform in *Bleak House*." *Dickens Studies Annual* 26 (1998): 121–145.

Carlacio, Jamie. "Narrative Epistemology: Storytelling as Agency in *A Mercy*." *Toni Morrison: Paradise, Love, A Mercy*. Ed. Lucille P. Fultz. Bloomsbury, 2013. 129–146.

Carretta, Vincent and Philip Gould. "Introduction." *Genius in Bondage: Literature of the Early Black Atlantic*. Eds. Vincent Carretta and Philip Gould. The University Press of Kentucky, 2001. 1–13.

—. *Equiano, the African: Biography of a Self-Made Man*. University of Georgia Press, 2005.

—. "The Emergence of an African American Literary Canon, 1760–1820." *The Cambridge History of African American Literature*. Ed. Maryemma Graham and Jerry W. Ward, Jr. Cambridge University Press, 2011. 52–65.

Carroll, Noel. *The Philosophy of Horror, Or, Paradoxes of the Heart*. Taylor and Francis, 1990.

Cassuto, Leonard. *The Inhuman Race. The Racial Grotesque in American Literature and Culture*. Columbia University Press, 1997.

Castronovo, Russ. "The Art of Ghost-Writing: Memory, Materiality, and Slave Aesthetics." *In Search of Hannah Crafts: Critical Essays on The Bondwoman's Narrative*. Eds. Henry Louis Gates, Jr. and Hollis Robbins. Basic Books, 2004. 195–212.

Cavallaro, Dani. *The Gothic Vision. Three Centuries of Horror, Terror and Fear*. Continuum, 2002.

Chaplin, Sue. *Gothic Literature. Texts, Contexts, Connections*. York Press, 2011.

Charles, Ron. "Love at First Bite." *The Washington Post*. 30 October 2005. Web (last accessed 3 June 2018).

Chartier, Roger, eds. *A History of Private Life. Passions of the Renaissance*. 7th ed. Belknap Press 2003.

Cheng, Anne Anlin. "Skins, Tattoos, and Susceptibility." *Representations* 108.1 (2009): 98–119.

Child, Lydia Maria. "The Quadroons." *The Online Archive of Nineteenth-Century U.S. Women's Writings*. Ed. Glynis Carr. Web. www.facstaff.bucknell.edu/gcarr/19cusww/ lb/q.html (last accessed 7 October 2017).

Christiansë, Yvette. *Toni Morrison: An Ethical Poetics*. Fordham University Press, 2013.

Clark, Emily. "The Tragic Mulatto and Passing." *The Palgrave Handbook of the Southern Gothic*. Eds. Susan Castillo Street and Charles L. Crow. Palgrave Macmillan, 2016. 259–270.

Clery, Emma J. *The Rise of Supernatural Fiction, 1762-1800*. Cambridge University Press, 1995.

—. and Robert Miles, eds. *Gothic Documents. A Sourcebook. 1700-1820*. Manchester University Press, 2000.

Cohen, Jeffrey Jerome. "Monster Culture (Seven Theses)." *Monster Theory: Reading Culture*. Ed. Jeffrey Jerome Cohen. University of Minnesota Press. 3–25.

Coleridge, Samuel T. "Review of *The Monk*." *Critical Review* 19 (February 1797): 194–200.

Collings, Michael R. "Qua Vadis, Bestsellasaurus Rex?" *The Stephen King Story: A Literary Profile*. Ed. George Beahm. Andrews and McMeel, 1991. 210–223.

Conner, Marc C. "'What Lay Beneath the Names': The Language and Landscapes of *A Mercy*." *Toni Morrison: Paradise, Love, A Mercy*. Ed. Lucille P. Fultz. Bloomsbury, 2013. 147–165.

Cooper, James Fenimore. *The Last of the Mohicans*. Penguin, 1994.

Cornelius, Laurie. "Into the Swamp: An Examination of Folk Narrative Structures and Storylines in Karen Russell's *Swamplandia!*." *Women of Florida Fiction: Essays on 12 Sunshine State Writers*. Eds. Tammy Powley and April Van Camp. McFarland Books, 2015. 26–37.

Costanzo, Angelo. *Surprising Narrative: Olaudah Equiano and the Beginnings of Black Autobiography*. Greenwood, 1987.

Cox, Amy Ann. "Aiming for Manhood: The Transformation of Guns into Objects of American Masculinity." *Open Fire: Understanding Global Gun Cultures*. Ed. Charles Fruehling Springwood. Berg, 2007. 141–152.

Cox, Jeffrey N. "Gothic Drama". *The Handbook to the Gothic*. Ed. Marie Mulvey-Roberts. 2nd ed. Palgrave Macmillan, 2009. 73–75.

Crafts, Hannah. *The Bondwoman's Narrative*. Ed. Henry Louis Gates, Jr. Warner Books, 2003.

Cruea, Susan M. "Changing Ideals of Womanhood During the Nineteenth-Century Woman Movement." *General Studies Writing Faculty Publications* (2005). Paper 1. Web. http://scholarworks.bgsu.edu/gsw_pub/1 (last accessed 10 August 2017).

Curry, Tommy J. *The Man-Not: Race, Class, Genre, and the Dilemmas of Black Manhood.* Temple University Press, 2017.

Davenport-Hines, Richard. *Gothic. Four Hundred Years of Excess, Horror, Evil and Ruin.* North Point Press, 1998.

Davidson, Cathy N. *Revolution and the Word: The Rise of the Novel in America.* Oxford University Press, 2004.

—. "Olaudah Equiano, Written by Himself." *Novel* 40.1 (2006): 18–51.

Davis, Arthur. "Introduction." *Clotel; or, the President's Daughter: A Narrative of Slave Life in the United States, by William Wells Brown.* Collier Books, 1970. vii–xvi.

Davison, Carol Margaret. "African American Gothic." *The Encyclopedia of the Gothic: Volume II, L–Z.* Eds. William Hughes et al. Blackwell, 2013.

Davison, Carol Margaret. *History of the Gothic: Gothic Literature 1764–1824.* University of Chicago Press, 2009.

Dawson, Michael C., and Lawrence D. Bobo. "One Year Later and the Myth of a Post-racial Society." *Du Bois Review: Social Science Research on Race* 6.2 (2009): 247–249.

Day, William P. *In the Circles of Fear and Desire: A Study of Gothic.* University of Chicago Press, 1985.

Demoor, Marysa. "Male Monsters or Monstrous Males in Victorian Women's Fiction." *Exhibited by Candlelight: Sources and Developments in the Gothic Tradition.* Eds. Valeria Tinkler Villani, Peter Davidson, and Jane Stevenson. Rodopi, 1995. 173–182.

Derrickson, Teresa. "Race and the Gothic Monster: The Xenophobic Impulse of Louisa May Alcott's 'Taming a Tartar.'" *ATQ* 15.1 (2001): 43–58.

Derrida, Jacques. *Limited INC.* Northwestern University Press, 1988.

De Voogd, Peter. "Sentimental Horrors: Feeling in the Gothic Novel." *Exhibited by Candlelight: Sources and Developments in the Gothic Tradition.* Eds. Valeria Tinkler Villani, Peter Davidson, and Jane Stevenson. Rodopi, 1995. 75–88.

Dew, Thomas Roderick. *Review of the Debate in the Virginia Legislature of 1831 and 1832.* The Library of Congress. Web. Archive.org (last accessed 1 August 2016).

D'Haen, Theo. "Postmodern Gothic." *Exhibited by Candlelight: Sources and Developments in the Gothic Tradition.* Eds. Valeria Tinkler Viviani, Peter Davidson, and Jane Stevenson. Rodopi, 1995.

Dickens, Charles. *Bleak House.* Penguin Classics, 2003.

Diedrich, Maria I. *Ausbruch aus der Knechtschaft: Das Amerikanische Slave Narrative Zwischen Unabhängigkeitserklärung und Bürgerkrieg.* Steiner, 1986.

—, Henry Louis Gates, Jr., and Carl Pedersen, eds.: *Black Imagination and the Middle Passage.* Oxford University Press, 1999.

—. *Cornelia James Cannon and the Future of the American Race.* University of Massachusetts Press, 2010.

—. "'The Burden of Our Theories' Genealogies': Lessons in Decolonization of Gender." *Sabine Broeck—Plotting against Modernity: Critical Interventions in Race and*

Gender. Eds. Karin Esders, Insa Härtel, and Carsten Junker. Ulrike Helmer Verlag, 2014. 266–270.

Dobson, Joanne. "Reclaiming Sentimental Literature." *American Literature* 69.2 (1997): 263–288.

Douglass, Frederick. *Narrative of the Life of Frederick Douglass, an American Slave, Written by Himself.* Norton, 1996.

Doyle, Laura. *Freedom's Empire: Race and the Rise of the Novel in Atlantic Modernity, 1640-1940.* Duke University Press, 2008.

Dryden, John. *The Works of John Dryden: Prose 1691-1698: De Arte Graphica and Shorter Works, Volume XX.* University of California Press, 1989.

DuCille, Ann. "The Shirley Temple of My Familiar." *Transition* 73 (1997): 10–32.

Duncan, Glen. "A Plague of Urban Undead in Lower Manhattan." *The New York Times* (28 October 2011). Web. https://www.nytimes.com/2011/10/30/books/review/zone-one-by-colson-whitehead-book-review.html (last accessed 5 July 2018).

Duza, Andre. *WZMB.* Deadite Press, 2014.

Edmundson, Mark. *Nightmare on Main Street. Angels, Sadomasochism, and the Culture of Gothic.* Harvard University Press 1999.

Edwards, Justin D. *Gothic Passages. Racial Ambiguity and the American Gothic.* University of Iowa Press, 2002.

—. and Agnieszka Soltysik Monnet. "Introduction. From Goth/ic to Pop Goth." *The Gothic in Contemporary Literature and Culture: Pop Goth.* Eds. Justin D. Edwards and Agnieszka Soltysik Monnet. Routledge, 2012. 1–18.

Eggers, Dave. *The Circle.* Penguin, 2013.

Elbert, Monika and Bridget M. Marshall, eds. *Transnational Gothic.* Ashgate, 2013.

Ellingson, Ter. *The Myth of the Noble Savage.* University of California Press, 2001.

Ellis, Kate. *The Contested Castle: Gothic Novels and the Subversion of Domestic Ideology.* University of Illinois Press, 1989.

Ellis, Markman. *The History of Gothic Fiction.* Reprint. Edinburgh University Press, 2003.

Equiano, Olaudah. *The Interesting Narrative and Other Writings.* Ed. Vincent Carretta. Penguin Books, 2003.

Ernest, John. *Resistance and Reformation in Nineteenth-Century African-American Literature: Brown, Wilson, Jacobs, Delany, Douglass, and Harper.* University of Mississippi Press, 1995. 20–54.

—. "African American Literature and the Abolitionist Movement, 1845 to the Civil War." *The Cambridge History of African American Literature.* Eds. Maryemma Graham and Jerry W. Ward, Jr. Cambridge University Press, 2011. 91–115.

Esplugas, Celia. "Gypsy Women in English Life and Literature." *The Foreign Woman in British Literature: Exotics, Aliens, and Outsiders.* Eds. Marilyn Demarest Button and Toni Reed. Greenwood Press, 1999. 145–158.

Fabi, M. Giulia. "Explanatory Notes." *Clotel; or, The President's Daughter*. Ed. M. Giulia Fabi. Penguin Books, 2004. 249–285.

—. "Introduction." *Clotel; or, The President's Daughter*. Ed. M. Giulia Fabi. Penguin Books, 2004. vii–xxviii.

Fassin, Didier. "Racialization: How to Do Races with Bodies." *A Companion to the Anthropology of the Body and Embodiment*. Ed. Frances E. Mascia-Lees. Blackwell, 2011. 421–434.

Fedorko, Kathy A. *Gender and the Gothic in the Fiction of Edith Wharton*. Alabama University Press, 1995.

Felman, Shoshana. "Turning the Screw of Interpretation." *Yale French Studies* 55/56 (1977): 94–207.

Fiedler, Leslie. *Love and Death in the American Novel*. Stein and Day, 1960.

Figliola, Samantha. "Reading King Darkly: Issues of Race in Stephen King's Novels." *Into Darkness Peering: Race and Color in the Fantastic*. Ed. Elisabeth A. Leonard. Greenwood, 1997. 143–158.

Foreman, P. Gabrielle. "The Spoken and the Silenced in *Incidents in the Life of a Slave Girl* and *Our Nig*." *Callaloo* 13 (1990): 313–324.

Foster, Thomas A. "The Sexual Abuse of Black Men under American Slavery." *Journal of the History of Sexuality* 20.3 (2011): 445–464.

Foucault, Paul-Michel. "Orders of Discourse." Translated by Robert Sawyer. *Social Science Information* 10/2 (April 1977). Reprinted with the title "The Discourse on Language." *Archaeology of Knowledge*. Routledge Classics, 2002.

—. *Archaeology of Knowledge*. Routledge Classics, 2002.

Frankowski, Alfred. *The Post-Racial Limits of Memorialization: Toward a Political Sense of Mourning*. Lexington Books, 2015.

Frederick, Bonnie. "Harriet Beecher Stowe and the Virtuous Mother: Argentina, 1852–1910." *Journal of Women's History* 18.1 (2006): 101–120.

Frederickson, George M. *The Black Image in the White Mind: The Debate on Afro-American Character and Destiny, 1817-1914*. Harper and Row, 1971.

Freud, Sigmund. "Das Unheimliche." *Imago. Zeitschrift für Anwendung der Psychoanalyse auf die Geisteswissenschaften* V (1919): 297–324.

—. "The Uncanny." *The Standard Edition of the Complete Psychological Works of Sigmund Freud*. Vol. XVII (1917-1919). *An Infantile Neurosis and Other Works*. Ed. James Strachey. Vintage, 2001. 219–256.

Frye, Katie. "The Case against Whiteness in William Wells Brown's Clotel." *Mississippi Quarterly: The Journal of Southern Cultures* 62.4 (2009): 527–540.

Frye, Northrop. *The Secular Scripture. A Study of the Structure of Romance*. Harvard University Press, 1976.

Gallego-Durán, Mar. "'Nobody Teaches You to Be a Woman': Female Identity, Community and Motherhood in Toni Morrison's *A Mercy*." *Toni Morrison's A Mercy:*

Critical Approaches. Eds. Shirley A. Stave and Justine Tally. Cambridge Scholars, 2011. 103–118.

Gamble, Vanessa Northington. "Under the Shadow of Tuskegee: African Americans and Health Care." *American Journal of Public Health* 87.11 (1997): 1773–1778.

Gamer, Michael. *Romanticism and the Gothic. Genre, Reception, and Canon Formation*. Cambridge University Press, 2000.

Gates, Henry Louis Jr. *The Signifying Monkey: A Theory of African American Literary Criticism*. Oxford University Press, 1988.

—, ed. *The Classic Slave Narratives*. Signet, 2012.

Gauthier, Tim S. "Zombies, the Uncanny, and the City: Colson Whitehead's *Zone One*." *The City Since 9/11: Literature, Film, Television*. Ed. Keith Wilhite. Fairleigh Dickinson University Press, 2016. 109–125.

Gelder, Ken. "Postcolonial Gothic." *The Handbook of the Gothic*. Ed. Marie Mulvey-Roberts. Second edition. Palgrave Macmillan, 2009. 219–220.

Gilbert, Sandra M. and Susan Gubar. *The Madwoman in the Attic. The Woman Writer and Nineteenth-Century Literature*. Yale University Press, 1979.

Giles, Paul. "Narrative Reversals and Power Exchanges: Frederick Douglass and British Culture." *American Literature* 73.4 (2001): 779–810.

Goddu, Teresa A. *Gothic America. Narrative, History, and Nation*. Columbia University Press, 1997.

—. "The African American Slave Narrative and the Gothic." *A Companion to American Gothic*. Ed. Charles L. Crow. Wiley-Blackwell, 2014. 71–83.

Golden, Thelma. "Introduction." *Freestyle: The Studio Museum in Harlem*. Eds. Christine Y. Kim et al. The Studio Museum of Harlem, 2001.

Gonzales, Susan. "Director Spike Lee Slams 'Same Old' Black Stereotypes in Today's Films." *Yale Bulletin and Calendar* 29.21 (2001). Web. http://yale.edu/opa/arc-ybc/v29.n21/story3.html (last accessed 10 May 2016).

Gordon, Jean and Veronica Hollinger. "Introduction: The Shape of Vampires." *Blood Read. The Vampire as Metaphor in Contemporary Culture*. Eds. Jean Gordon and Veronica Hollinger. University of Pennsylvania Press, 1997. 1–7.

Gould, Philip. "Early Print Literature of Africans in America." *The Cambridge History of African American Literature*. Eds. Maryemma Graham and Jerry W. Ward, Jr. Cambridge University Press, 2011. 39–51.

Graham, Sarah. "Unfair Ground: Girlhood and Theme Parks in Contemporary Fiction." *Journal of American Studies* 47.3 (2013): 589–604.

Grant, Drew. "Is This Family Feud Contestant Being a Zombie Racist?" *Observer*. 20 November 2013. Web. http://observer.com/2013/11/is-this-family-feud-contestant-being-a-zombie-racist/ (last accessed 10 July 2018).

Gray, Frances. "Fireside Issues: Audience, Listener, Soundscape." *More Than a Music Box: Radio Cultures and Communities in a Multi-Media World*. Ed. Andrew Crisell. Berghahn Books, 2006. 247–262.

Gray, Thomas R. *The Confessions of Nat Turner (1831)*. Electronic Texts in American Studies. Paper 15. Web. http://digitalcommons.unl.edu/etas/15 (last accessed 10 October 2019).

Greaves, Sharron. "Shirley Temple: Dimples, Dichotomies and the Great Depression." *The 1930s: The Reality and the Promise*. Eds. J. Bret Bennington, Zenia Sacks DaSilva, Michael D'Innocenzo, and Stanislao Pugliese. Cambridge Scholars, 2016. 171–180.

Greeson, Jennifer R. "The 'Mysteries and Miseries' of North Carolina: New York City, Urban Gothic Fiction, and *Incidents in the Life of a Slave Girl*." *American Literature* 73.2 (2001): 271–309.

Grigsby, Daryl Russell. *Celebrating Ourselves: African Americans and the Promise of Baseball*. Dog Ear Publishing, 2010.

Gronniosaw, James Albert Ukawsaw. *A Narrative of the Most Remarkable Particulars in the Life of James Albert Ukawsaw Gronniosaw, an African Prince, as Related by Himself* (W. Gye, 1770). Documenting the American South. Web. http://docsouth.unc.edu/neh/gronniosaw/menu.html (last accessed 10 August 2017).

Gross, Louis S. *Redefining the American Gothic: From Wieland to Day of the Dead*. Uni Research Press, 1989.

Grossman, Jay. "'A' Is for Abolition?: Race, Authorship, *The Scarlet Letter*." *Textual Practice* 7.1 (1993): 13–30.

Gruesser, John Cullen. *Confluences: Postcolonialism, African American Literary Studies, and the Black Atlantic*. The University of Georgia Press, 2005.

Guerrera, Tania. *Thoughts and Transformations*. Writers Club Press, 2003.

Haggerty, George E. *Gothic Fiction/Gothic Form*. Pennsylvania State University Press, 1989.

—. *Queer Gothic*. Chicago: University of Illinois Press, 2006.

Hall, Stuart: "The Rediscovery of 'Ideology': Return of the Repressed in Media Studies." *Culture, Society and the Media. Part 1: Class, Ideology and the Media*. Eds. Michael Gurevitch, Tony Bennett, James Curran and Janet Woollacott. Methuen, 1982. 50–90.

—. *Representation. Cultural Representations and Signifying Practices*. 8th ed. Sage Publications, 2003.

Halttunen, Karen. "Gothic Imagination and Social Reform: The Haunted Houses of Lyman Beecher, Henry Ward Beecher, and Harriet Beecher Stowe." *New Essays on "Uncle Tom's Cabin."* Ed. Eric Sundquist. Cambridge University Press, 1986. 107–134.

Hand, Elizabeth. "Anne Rice's Vampire Chronicles Is Looking a Little Long in the Tooth." *The Washington Post*. 9 December, 2016. Web (last accessed May 5, 2018).

Hartman, Saidiya. *Scenes of Subjection: Terror, Slavery, and Self-Making in Nineteenth-Century America*. Oxford University Press, 1997.

—. *Lose Your Mother: A Journey along the Atlantic Slave Route*. Farrar, Straus, Giroux, 2007.

Harris, Jason Marc. "Absurdist Narratives in the Sunshine State: Comic, Criminal, Folkloric, and Fantastic Escapades in the Swamps and Suburbs of Florida." *NDiF* 10.1 (2012): 32–84.

Hatch, Kristen. *Shirley Temple and the Performance of Girlhood*. Rutgers University Press, 2015.

Havard, John C. "Slavery and the Emergence of the African American Novel." *The Cambridge Companion to Slavery in American Literature*. Ed. Ezra Tawil. Cambridge University Press, 2016. 86–99.

Hawthorne, Nathaniel. *The Scarlet Letter*. New American Library, 1999.

—; Susan Manning, ed. *The Marble Faun*. Oxford: Oxford University Press, 2002.

Heather, Peter. *The Goths. The Peoples of Europe*. Blackwell, 1996.

Hébert, Kimberly G. "Acting the Nigger: Topsy, Shirley Temple, and Toni Morrison's Pecola." *Approaches to Teaching Stowe's Uncle Tom's Cabin*. Eds. Elizabeth Ammons and Susan Belasco. The Modern Language Association of America, 2000. 184–198.

Hendershot, Cyndy. *The Animal Within: Masculinity and the Gothic*. University of Michigan Press, 1998.

Henry, Frances and Carol Tator. "Critical Discourse Analysis: A Powerful but Flawed Tool?" *Race, Racialization and Antiracism in Canada and Beyond*. Ed. Genevieve Fuji Johnson and Randy Enomoto. University of Toronto Press, 2007. 117–130.

Herstig, Brian and Alice Wybrew. "*The Killing Moon* by N. K. Jemisin (Review)." *Fantasy Book Review*. Web. http://www.fantasybookreview.co.uk/NK-Jemisin/The-Killing-Moon.html (last accessed 10 June 2018).

Hicks, Heather J. "Hoodoo Economics: White Men's Work and Black Men's Magic in Contemporary American Film." *Camera Obscura* 18.2 (2003): 27–55.

Hidalgo, Alexandra. "Bridges, Nodes, and Bare Life: Race in *The Twilight Saga*." *Genre, Reception, and Adaptation in the Twilight* Series. Ed. Anne Morey. Ashgate, 2012. 79–94.

Hochschild Jennifer L. and Vesla Weaver. "Policies of Racial Classification and the Politics of Racial Inequality." *Remaking America: Democracy and Public Policy in an Age of Inequality*. Eds. Joe Soss, Jacob Hacker, and Suzanne Mettler. Russell Sage Foundation, 2007. 159–182.

Hoeveler, Diane Long. "The Female Gothic, Beating Fantasies and the Civilizing Process." *Comparative Romanticism: Power, Gender, Subjectivity*. Eds. Larry H. Peer and Diane Long Hoeveler. Camden House, 1998. 103–132.

Hogle, Jerrold E. "Introduction." *The Cambridge Companion to Gothic Fiction*. Ed. Jerrold E. Hogle. Cambridge University Press, 2002, 1–21.

—. "Teaching the African American Gothic: From its Multiple Sources to *Linden Hills* and *Beloved*." *Approaches to Teaching Gothic Fiction: The British and American Traditions*. Eds. Diane Long Hoeveler and Tamar Heller. MLA, 2003. 215–222.

Holman, Matthew M. "Trisha McFarland and the Tough Tootsie: Coping with Fear in *The Girl Who Loved Tom Gordon*." *Stephen King's Contemporary Classics: Reflections on the Modern Master of Horror*. Eds. Philip L. Simpson and Patrick McAleer. Rowman and Littlefield, 2015. 75–84.

Holmes, Trevor. "Becoming-Other: (Dis)Embodiments of Race in Anne Rice's *Tale of the Body Thief*." *Romanticism on the Net* 44 (2006).

Hood, Robert E. *Begrimed and Black: Christian Traditions on Blacks and Blackness*. Augsburg Fortress, 1994.

Horace. *Of the Art of Poetry. A Poem*. Transl. the Earl of Roscommon. H. Hills, 1709.

Horáková, Erin. "*The Killing Moon* by N. K. Jemisin (Review)." *StrangeHorizons.com*. 16 July 2016. http://strangehorizons.com/non-fiction/reviews/the-killing-moon-by-n-k-jemisin/ (last accessed 10 June 2018).

Horner, Avril. "Heroine." *The Handbook to the Gothic*. Ed. Marie Mulvey-Roberts. Palgrave Macmillan, 2009. 115–119.

Howells, Coral A. *Love, Mystery, and Misery. Feeling in Gothic Fiction*. Athlone Press, 1978.

Hubner, Laura, Marcus Leaning, and Paul Manning. *The Zombie Renaissance in Popular Culture*. Palgrave Macmillan, 2015.

Hughey, Matthew W. "Cinethetic Racism: White Redemption and Black Stereotypes in 'Magical Negro' Films." *Social Problems* 56.3 (2009): 543–577.

Hume, Robert D. "Gothic Versus Romantic: A Revaluation of the Gothic Novel." *PMLA* 84 (1969): 282–290.

Hurley, Jessica. "History Is What Bites: Zombies, Race, and the Limits of Biopower in Colson Whitehead's *Zone One*." *Extrapolation* 56.3 (2015): 311–333.

Ignatiev, Noel. *How the Irish Became White*. Routledge, 2009.

Irr, Caren. "The Space of Genre in the New Green Novel." *Studia Neophilologica* 87.1 (2014): 82–96.

Jacobs, Edward H. *Accidental Migrations. An Archaeology of Gothic Discourse*. Bucknell University Press, 2000.

Jahoda, Gustav. *Images of Savages. Ancient Roots of Modern Prejudice in Western Culture*. Routledge, 1999.

Jacobs, Harriet. *Incidents in the Life of a Slave Girl, Written by Herself*. Penguin Books, 2000.

Jemisin, N. K. "Dreaming Awake." Web. http://nkjemisin.com/2012/02/dreaming-awake/ (last accessed 10 June 2018).

—. *The Killing Moon*. Orbit, 2012.

John, Warren St. "Market for Zombies? It's Undead (Aaahhh!)." *The New York Times*. 26 March 2006. Web. https://www.nytimes.com/2006/03/26/fashion/

sundaystyles/market-for-zombies-its-undead-aaahhh.html (last accessed 30 June 2018).

Johnson, Samuel. *The Rambler* 4 (31 March 1750). Reprinted in *The Yale Edition of the Works of Samuel Johnson*. Eds. Walter J. Bate and Albrecht B. Strauss. Vol. 3. Yale University Press, 1969. 54–59.

Jones, Miriam. "*The Gilda Stories*: Revealing the Monsters at the Margins." *Blood Read: The Vampire as Metaphor in Contemporary Culture*. Eds. Joan Gordon and Veronica Hollinger. University of Pennsylvania Press, 1997. 151–167.

Jordan, Winthrop D. "American Chiaroscuro: The Status and Definition of Mulattoes in the British Colonies." *The William and Mary Quarterly* 19.2 (1962): 183–200.

Kádár, Judit Ágnes. *Going Indian: Cultural Appropriation in Recent North American Literature*. PUV, 2012.

Kant, Immanuel. *Observations on the Feeling of the Beautiful and Sublime and Other Writings*. Eds. Patrick Frierson and Paul Guyer. Cambridge University Press, 2011.

Kaye, Heidi. "Gothic Film." *A Companion to the Gothic*. Ed. David Punter. Blackwell, 2000. 180–192.

Kazanjian, David. *The Colonizing Trick: National Culture and Imperial Citizenship in Early America*. University of Minnesota Press, 2003.

Kent, Brian. "Christian Martyr or Grateful Slave? The Magical Negro as Uncle Tom in Frank Darabont's *The Green Mile*." *The Films of Stephen King: From "Carrie" to "Secret Window."* Ed. Tony Magistrale. Palgrave Macmillan, 2008. 115–128.

Ketton-Cremer, Robert Wyndham. *Horace Walpole: A Biography*. 3rd ed. Methuen, 1964.

Khair, Tabish. *The Gothic, Postcolonialism and Otherness. Ghosts from Elsewhere*. Palgrave Macmillan, 2009.

Kimmel, Michael. *Manhood in America: A Cultural History*. The Free Press, 1996.

King, Stephen. *The Girl Who Loved Tom Gordon*. Pocket Books, 2000.

—. *Different Seasons*. Hodder and Stoughton, 2007.

Kilgour, Maggie. *The Rise of the Gothic Novel*. Routledge, 1995.

Kliger, Samuel. *The Goths in England: A Study in the Seventeenth and Eighteenth Century Thought*. Harvard University Press, 1952.

Knutson, Lin. "Monster Studies: Liminality, Home Spaces, and Ina Vampires in Octavia E. Butler's *Fledgling*." *University of Toronto Quarterly* 87.1 (2018): 214–233.

Kohn, Abigail A. *Shooters: Myths and Realities of America's Gun Cultures*. Oxford University Press, 2004.

Kordas, Ann. "New South, New Immigrants, New Zombies: The Historical Development of the Zombie in Popular Culture." *Race, Oppression and the Zombie: Essays on Cross Cultural Appropriations of the Caribbean Tradition*. Eds. Christopher M. Moreman and Cory James Rushton. McFarland, 2011. 41–53.

Krauthammer, Anna. *The Representation of the Savage in James Fenimore Cooper and Herman Melville*. Peter Lang, 2008.

Kreiger, Georgia. "Playing Dead: Harriet Jacobs's Survival Strategy in *Incidents in the Life of a Slave Girl*." *African American Review* 42.4 (2008): 607–621.

Kristeva, Julia. *Desire in Language: A Semiotic Approach to Literature and Art.* Columbia University Press, 1980.

Kucich, John J. *Ghostly Communion: Cross-Cultural Spiritualism in Nineteenth-Century American Literature.* University of New England Press, 2004.

Langan, John. *The Fisherman.* Word Horde, 2016.

Lannon, Linnea. "Stephen King: Too Many Books, Not Enough Awards?" *Oregonian.* 19 June 1991. Web. <http://www.lexis-nexis.com/> (last accessed 8 July 2015).

Lant, Kathleen M. and Theresa Thompson, eds. *Imagining the Worst: Stephen King and the Representation of Women.* Greenwood, 1998.

LaValle, Victor. "Beyond the Skin Trade: How Does Black Nationalism Stay Relevant in the Age of Barack Obama?" *Bookforum* April/Amy 2009. Web (last accessed 10 June 2018).

—. *The Changeling.* Spiegel and Grau, 2017.

Lawrence, David H. *Studies in Classic American Literature.* Reprint. The Viking Press, 1964.

Leab, Daniel. *From Sambo to Superspade: The Black Experience in Motion Pictures.* Seeker and Warburg, 1975.

Leavis, Frank R. *The Great Tradition: George Eliot, Henry James, Joseph Conrad.* 1960. Reprint. Chatto J. Windus, 1973.

Lee, Robert A. *Gothic to Multicultural. Idioms of Imagining in American Literary Fiction.* Rodopi, 2009.

Lenhardt, Corinna. "'Washington's troops skinned dead Indians from the waist down and made leggings from the skins'—Reiterating Villainy in Native American Gothic Fiction." *Villains and Heroes or Villains as Heroes?: Essays on the Relationship Between Villainy and Evil.* Ed. Luke Seaber. Inter-Disciplinary Press, 2012. 111–128.

—. "'As Bones Dig Mass Racial Graves'—The Gothic Excess of Multiraciality in Larissa Lai's Long Poem 'Nascent Fashion'." *Anglistentag 2015 Paderborn: Proceedings.* Eds. Christoph Ehland, Ilka Mindt, and Merle Tönnies. WVT, 2016. 157–167.

—. "Wendigos, Eye Killers, Skinwalkers: The Myth of the American Indian Vampire and American Indian 'Vampire' Myths." *Gothic Matters: A Special Edition (No. 6) of Text Matters: A Journal of Literature, Theory and Culture* 23 (2016): 195–212.

Lévi-Strauss, Claude. *Structural Anthropology.* Trans. Claire Jacobson and Brooke Grundfest Schoepf. Basic Books, 1963.

—. *The Raw and the Cooked: Introduction to a Science of Mythology.* Harper and Row, 1969.

Levine, Robert S. "Trappe(d): Race and Genealogical Haunting in *The Bondwoman's Narrative*." *In Search of Hannah Crafts: Critical Essays in the Bondwoman's Narrative*. Eds. Henry Louis Gates, Jr. and Hollis Robbins. Basic Books, 2004. 276–294.

—. "Reading Slavery and 'Classic' American Literature." *The Cambridge Companion to Slavery in American Literature*. Ed. Ezra Tawil. Cambridge University Press, 2016. 137–152.

Levy, Maurice. *Le Roman "Gothique" Anglais, 1764-1824*. Assn. des Pubs. de la Faculte des Lettres et Sciences Humaines de Toulouse, 1968.

—. "Gothic and the Critical Idiom". *Gothic Origins and Innovations*. Eds. Allan L. Smith and Victor Sage. Rodopi, 2007. 1–15.

Lewis, Matthew. *The Monk*. Oxford University Press, 1998.

Li, Stephanie. *Signifying without Specifying: Racial Discourse in the Age of Obama*. Rutgers University Press, 2012.

Ligon, Glenn. *Study for Frankenstein #1*. 1992. Oil stick and gesso on canvas, 30 1/8 x 22 in. Saint Louis Art Museum, St. Louis, Missouri, U.S.A.

Limerick, Patricia Nelson. *The Legacy of Conquest*. Norton, 1987.

Linscott, Charles P. "Introduction: #BlackLivesMatter and the Mediatic Lives of a Movement." *Black Camera* 8.2 (2017): 75–80.

Löffler, Marie-Luise. "'She Would Be No Man's Property Ever Again': Vampirism, Slavery, and Black Female Heroism in Contemporary African American Women's Fiction." *Images of the Modern Vampire: The Hip and the Atavistic*. Eds. Barbara Brodman and James E. Doan. Fairleigh Dickinson University Press, 2013. 113–128.

Loggins, Vernon. *The Negro Author: His Developments in America*. Columbia University Press, 1931.

Long, Diane Hoeveler. *Gothic Feminism: The Professionalization of Gender from Charlotte Smith to the Brontës*. Pennsylvania State University Press, 1998.

Lornezo, María M. García. "The Unwhitening of Discourse: The Gothic in African American Literature." *Western Fictions, Black Realities: Meanings of Blackness and Modernities*. Eds. Isabel Soto and Violet Showers Johnson. LIT, 2011. 47–60.

Louisiana Division/New Orleans Public Library. "Yellow Fever Deaths in New Orleans, 1817-1905." Web. http://nutrias.org/facts/feverdeaths.htm (last accessed 26 September 2017).

Lundegaard, Erik. "The Girl Who Loved Tom Gordon." *Erik Lundegaard's Book and Movie Reviews*. April 1999. Web. <home.earthlink.net/ elundegaard/girlwholoved.html> (last accessed 20 January 2014).

Madrigal, Alexis. "Bookforum Talks with Colson Whitehead." *Bookforum* (17 October 2011). Web. https://www.bookforum.com/interview/8491 (last accessed 5 July 2018).

Magistrale, Tony. *Stephen King: America's Storyteller*. ABC-Clio, 2010.

Malchow, Howard L. *Gothic Images of Race in Nineteenth-Century Britain*. Stanford University Press, 1996.

Malin, Irving. *New American Gothic*. Illinois: Southern Illinois University Press, 1962.

Manzanas, Ana María and Jesús Benito. *Intercultural Mediations: Hybridity and Mimesis in American Literatures*. Lit Verlag 2013.

Marino-Faza, Maria. "More than Human: Reading the Doppelgänger and Female Monstrosity in Television Vampires." *Posthuman Gothic*. Ed. Anya Heise-von der Lippe. University of Wales Press, 2017. 125–142.

Marrant, John. *A Narrative of the Lord's Wonderful Dealing with John Marrant, a Black, (now going to preach the Gospel in Nova-Scotia), born in New-York, in North America*. Archive.org (last accessed 10 August 2017).

Martin, Robert K. and Eric Savoy. *American Gothic: New Interventions in a National Narrative*. University of Iowa Press, 2009.

Masterson, John. "Floods, Fortresses, and Cabin Fever: Worlding 'Domeland' Security in Dave Eggers's *Zeitoun* and *The Circle*." *American Literary History* 28.4 (2016): 721–739.

Mason, Clifford. "Why Does White America Love Sidney Poitier So?" *The New York Times*. 10 September 1967. Web. http://nytimes.com (last accessed: 10 May 2016).

Massé, Michelle. *In the Name of Love: Women, Masochism, and the Gothic*. 2nd ed. Cornell University Press, 1992.

Maturin, Charles Robert. *Melmoth the Wanderer*. Penguin, 2000.

Maus, Derek C. *Understanding Colson Whitehead*. The University of South Carolina Press, 2014.

Mayberry, Susan Neal. "Visions and Revisions of American Masculinity in *A Mercy*." *Toni Morrison: Paradise, Love, A Mercy*. Ed. Lucille P. Fultz. Bloomsbury, 2013. 166–184.

Mbembé, Achille. "Necropolis." Translated by Libby Meintjes. *Public Culture* 15.1 (2003): 11–40.

McAleer, Patrick. *The Writing Family of Stephen King: A Critical Study of the Fiction of Tabitha King, Joe Hill, and Owen King*. McFarland, 2011.

McBride, Dwight. *Impossible Witnesses: Truth, Abolitionism, and Slave Testimony*. New York University Press, 2001.

McDowell, Deborah. "In the First Place: Making Frederick Douglass and the Afro-American Narrative Tradition." *Critical Essays on Frederick Douglass*. Ed. William L. Andrews. G. K. Hall, 1991. 192–215.

McDowell, Margaret B. "Edith Wharton's Ghost Stories." *Criticism* 12 (1970): 133–152.

Mechling, Jay. "An American Culture Grid, with Texts." *American Studies International* 27.4 (1989): 2–12.

Melton, Gene II. "The (Neo) Slave Narrative in Black and White: Toni Morrison's Re-Envisioning of Masculinity in *A Mercy*." *Contested Boundaries: New Critical Essays on the Fiction of Toni Morrison*. Ed. Maxine L. Montgomery. Cambridge Scholars, 2013. 34–52.

Mengham, Rod. "British Fiction of the War." *The Cambridge Companion to the Literature of World War II*. Ed. Marina MacKay. Cambridge University Press, 2009. 26–42.

Meyer, Stephenie. *Twilight*. Little, Brown and Company, 2005.

—. *New Moon*. Atom, 2006.

Michaud, Marilyn. *Republicanism and the American Gothic*. University of Wales Press, 2009.

Milbank, Alison. "Female Gothic". *The Handbook to Gothic Literature*. Ed. Marie Mulvey Roberts. New York University Press, 1998. 53–57.

Miles, Robert. *Racism*. Routledge, 1989.

Miles, Robert. "Review of *Gothic*, by Fred Botting." *Gothic Studies* 1 (1999): 119–120.

—. "'Tranced Griefs': Melville's *Pierre* and the Origins of the Gothic." *ELH* 66.1 (1999): 157–77.

—. *Gothic Writing 1750–1820: A Genealogy*. 2nd ed. Manchester University Press, 2000.

—. "Europhobia: The Catholic Other in Horace Walpole and Charles Maturin." *European Gothic: A Spirited Exchange, 1760–1960*. Ed. Avril Horner. Manchester University Press, 2002. 84–103.

—. "Eighteenth-Century Gothic." *The Routledge Companion to Gothic*. Eds. Catherine Spooner and Emma McEvoy. Routledge, 2007. 10–18.

Modleski, Tania. "In Hollywood, Racist Stereotypes Can Still Earn Oscar Nominations." *The Chronicle of Higher Education*. 17 March 2000. Web. https://www.chronicle.com/article/In-Hollywood-Racist/3429 (last accessed 10 June 2019).

Moers, Ellen. *Literary Women*. Doubleday, 1977.

Mogan, David, Scott P. Sanders and Joanne B. Karpinski. *Frontier Gothic. Terror and Wonder at the Frontier in American Literature*. Associated University Press, 1993.

Montesquieu, Charles-Louis de Secondat. *The Spirit of the Laws*. Trans. Thomas Nugent (1750). Vol. I. Bell and Sons, 1878. Reprinted in: Clery, Emma J. and Robert Miles, eds. *Gothic Documents: A Sourcebook. 1700-1820*. Manchester University Press, 2000. 61–62.

Moore, A. "Awkward Racist Response to 'Family Feud' Zombie Question Causes Outrage." *Atlanta Black Star*. 21 November 2013. Web. http://atlantablackstar.com/2013/11/21/awkwardly-racist-response-family-feud-zombie-question-causes-outrage/ (last accessed 10 July 2018).

Morais, Betsy. "Sharing Is Caring Is Sharing." *The New Yorker*. 30 October 2013. Web. https://www.newyorker.com/tech/elements/sharing-is-caring-is-sharing (last accessed 10 February 2018).

Morris, Susana M. "Black Girls Are from the Future: Afrofuturist Feminism in Octavia E. Butler's *Fledgling*." *Women's Studies Quarterly* 40.3/4 (2012): 146–166.

Morrison, Toni. *Playing in the Dark. Whiteness and the Literary Imagination*. Vintage, 1993.

—. *Beloved*. Vintage, 2005.

—. *A Mercy*. Chatto and Windus, 2008.

—. "The Spirit and the Strength." Interview by Kevin Nance. *Poets and Writers* (Nov.-Dec. 2008): 47–54.

—. "America Before Slavery Meant Race." Interview by David L. Ulin. 19 November 2008. *Town Hall Journal* 72.1 (2009): 22–23.

—. "No Place for Self-Pity, No Room for Fear." *The Nation*. 23 March 2015. Web. https://www.thenation.com/article/no-place-self-pity-no-room-fear/ (last accessed 10 August 2017).

Morrow, Bradford and Patrick McGarth. "Introduction." *New Gothic. A Collection of Contemporary Gothic Fiction*. Ed. Bradford Morrow and Patrick McGarth. Vintage, 1992. xi–xiv.

Moten, Fred. *In the Break: The Aesthetics of the Black Radical Tradition*. University of Minnesota Press, 2003.

Moya, Paula M. L. *The Social Imperative: Race, Close Reading, and Contemporary Literary Criticism*. Stanford University Press, 2016.

Mudge, Bradford K. "The Man with Two Brains: Gothic Novels, Popular Culture, Literary History." *PMLA* 107.1 (1992): 92–104.

Mulvey, Christopher. "Freeing the Voice, Creating the Self: The Novel and Slavery." *The Cambridge Companion to the African American Novel*. Ed. Maryemma Graham. Cambridge University Press, 2004. 17–33.

Mulvey-Roberts, Marie, ed. *The Handbook to the Gothic*. 2nd ed. Palgrave Macmillan, 2009.

Munro, Joyce Underwood. "The Invisible Made Visible: The Fairy Changeling as a Folk Articulation of Failure to Thrive in Infants and Children." *The Good People: New Fairylore Essays*. Ed. Peter Narváez. University Press of Lexington, 1997. 251–283.

Naimon, David. "A Conversation with Colson Whitehead." *Tin House*. 21 September 2012. Web. https://tinhouse.com/q-and-a-colson-whitehead/ (last accessed 5 July 2018).

Napier, Elizabeth R. *The Failure of Gothic: Problems of Disjunction in an Eighteenth-Century Literary Form*. Clarendon Press, 1987.

Nehl, Markus. *Transnational Black Dialogues: Re-Imagining Slavery in the Twenty-First Century*. Transcript, 2016.

Neocleous, Mark. "The Political Economy of the Dead Marx's Vampires." *History of Political Thought* 24.4 (2003): 668–684.

Nilsen, Sarah. "White Soul: The 'Magical Negro' in the Films of Stephen King." *The Films of Stephen King: From "Carrie" to "Secret Window."* Ed. Tony Magistrale. Palgrave Macmillan, 2008. 129–140.

Noe, Michael. "*WZMB* by Andre Duza (Book Review)." *Splatterpunkzine*. 7 June 2016. Web. https://splatterpunkzine.wordpress.com/2016/06/07/wzmb-by-andre-duza-book-review/ (last accessed 10 June 2018).
Norden, Eric. "Playboy Interview: Stephen King." *Playboy* 6/June (1983): 65–82, 230–239.
Nordius, Janina. "Slavery and the Gothic." *The Encyclopedia of the Gothic*. Eds. William Hughes, David Punter, and Andrew Smith. Blackwell, 2013. 629–632.
Norwood, Kimberly Jade, ed. *Color Matters: Skin Tone Bias and the Myth of a Postracial America*. Routledge, 2014.
Nudelman, Franny. "Harriet Jacobs and the Sentimental Politics of Female Suffering." *English Literary History* 59 (1992): 939–964.
O'Keefe, Deborah. *Good Girl Messages: How Young Women Were Misled by Their Favorite Books*. Continuum, 2001.
Okorafor-Mbachu, Nnedi. "Stephen King's Super-Duper Magical Negroes." *Strange Horizons*. 25 October 2004. Web. http://www.strangehorizons.com/2004/20041025/kinga.shtml (last accessed 5 July 2015).
Olney, James. "'I Was Born': Slave Narratives, Their Status as Autobiography and as Literature." *Callaloo* 20 (1984): 46–73.
Otter, Samuel. "'Race' in *Typee* and *White-Jacket*." *The Cambridge Companion to Herman Melville*. Ed. Robert S. Levine. Cambridge University Press, 1998. 12–36.
—. "Stowe and Race." *The Cambridge Companion to Harriet Beecher Stowe*. Ed. Cindy Weinstein. Cambridge University Press, 2004. 15–38.
Parkinson, Marc H. "Fantastic." *The Routledge Dictionary of Literary Terms*. Eds. Peter Childs and Roger Fowler. 3rd ed. Routledge, 2006. 82–84.
Person, Leland S. "The Dark Labyrinth of Mind: Hawthorne, Hester, and the Ironies of Racial Mothering." *Studies in American Fiction* 29.1 (2001): 33–48.
Peterson, James Braxton. "Eco-Critical Focal Points: Narrative Structure and Environmentalist Perspectives in Morrison's *A Mercy*." *Toni Morrison's A Mercy: Critical Approaches*. Eds. Shirley A. Stave and Justine Tally. Cambridge Scholars, 2011. 9–21.
Pinder, Sherrow O. *Colorblindness, Post-raciality, and Whiteness in the United States*. Palgrave MacMillan, 2015.
Pitt, William. *Correspondence of William Pitt, Earl of Chatham*. Eds. William Stanhope Tylor and John Henry Pringle. Vol. II. John Murray, 1838.
Poe, Edgar A. *Tales of the Grotesque and Arabesque*. Vol. I. Lea and Blanchard, 1840.
—. *The Narrative of Arthur Gordon Pym and Related Texts*. Oxford University Press, 2008.
Policante, Amedeo. "Vampires of Capital. Gothic Reflections between Horror and Hope". *Cultural Logic*: Spec. issue of *Works and Days* 30.1 (2012): 213–224.
Poole, W. Scott. *Monsters in America. Our Historical Obsession with the Hideous and the Haunting*. Baylor University Press, 2011.

Powley, Tammy. "Gators, Goggles and Giant Shells: Fantasy and Florida in the Short Stories." *Women of Florida Fiction: Essays on 12 Sunshine State Writers*. Eds. Tammy Powley and April Van Camp. McFarland Books, 2015. 13–25.

Praz, Mario. *The Romantic Agony*. 1930. Transl. Angus Davidson. Oxford University Press, 1970.

Pressley-Sanon, Toni. "Addressing the 'Negro Problem': Rethinking the Coon and the Mammy in *King of the Zombies* and *Revenge of the Zombies*." *Black Camera* 8.1 (2016): 27–54.

Pugliatti, Paola. "A Lost Lore: The Activity of Gypsies as Performers on the Stage of Elizabethan-Jacobean Street Theatre." *English Renaissance Scenes: From Canon to Margins*. Eds. Paolo Pugliatti and Alessandro Serpieri. Peter Lang, 2008. 259–310.

Punter, David. *The Literature of Terror. A History of Gothic Fictions from 1765 to the Present Day. Volume I. The Gothic Tradition.* Longman, 1996.

— and Glennis Byron. *The Gothic*. Blackwell, 2004.

Pye, Henry J. *A Commentary Illustrating the Poetics of Aristotle*. 1786. Rpt. in *Novel and Romance 1700-1800: A Documentary Record*. Ed. Ioan Williams. Routledge, 2012. 252–256.

Radcliffe, Ann. *The Italian, or, the Confessional of the Black Penitents*. Oxford University Press, 1968.

Rafferty, Terrence. "The State of Zombie Literature: An Autopsy." *The New York Times*. 5 August 2011. Web. https://www.nytimes.com/2011/08/07/books/review/the-state-of-zombie-literature-an-autopsy.html (last accessed 10 July 2018).

—. "The Latest and Best in Horror." *The New York Times*. 26 October 2016. Web. https://www.nytimes.com/2016/10/30/books/review/graveyard-apartment-and-more-horror.html (last accessed 5 May 2018).

Railo, Eino. *The Haunted Castle: A Study of the Elements of English Romanticism*. Routledge and Kegan Paul, 1927.

Reed, Ishmael. *Flight to Canada*. Simon and Schuster, 1998.

Reid-Pharr, Robert F. "The Slave Narrative and Early Black American Literature." *The Cambridge Companion to the African American Slave Narrative*. Ed. Audrey Fisch. Cambridge University Press, 2007. 137–149.

Rice, Anne. *Memnoch the Devil*. Random House, 1995.

—. *Prince Lestat and the Realms of Atlantis*. Arrow Books, 2016.

Richardson, Elaine B. *African American Literacies*. London, New York: Routledge, 2003.

Riding, Christine, et al. (eds). *The Houses of Parliament: History, Art and Architecture*. Merrell, 2000.

Ringe, Donald. *American Gothic: Imagination and Reason in Nineteenth-Century Fiction*. University Press of Kentucky, 1982.

Rintoul, Suzanne. "Review Essay: 'Gothic Anxieties: Struggling with a Definition.'" *Eighteenth-Century Fiction* 17.4 (2005): 701–709.

Roach, Marilynne K. *The Salem Witch Trials: A Day-by-Day Chronicle of a Community Under Siege.* Cooper Square Press, 2002.

Roberts, Bette B. "The Horrid Novels: *The Mysteries of Udolpho* and *Northanger Abbey.*" *Gothic Fictions: Prohibition/Transgression.* Ed. Kenneth W. Graham. AMS Press, 1989. 89–111.

Roberts, Siân Silyn. *Gothic Subjects: The Transformation of Individualism in American Fiction, 1790-1861.* University of Pennsylvania Press, 2014.

Robinson, Timothy M. "Octavia Butler's Vampiric Vision: *Fledgling* as Transnational Neo Slave Narrative." *Vampires and Zombies: Transcultural Migrations and Transnational Interpretations.* Eds. Dorothea Fischer-Hornung and Monika Mueller. University Press of Mississippi, 2016. 61–82.

Romkey, Michael. *American Gothic.* Del Rey, 2004.

Royle, Nicholas. *The Uncanny.* Manchester University Press, 2003.

Russell, Karen. *Swamplandia!* Vintage Books, 2011.

Rutman, Darrett B. and Anita H. Rutman. "'Of Agues and Fevers': Malaria in the Early Chesapeake." *William and Mary Quarterly* 33.3 (1976): 31–60.

Sadleir, Michael. "The Northanger Novels: A Footnote to Jane Austen." *The English Association Pamphlet* 68 (1927).

Sage, Victor. "Introduction." *The Gothick Novel. A Casebook.* Ed. Victor Sage. Palgrave Macmillan, 1990, 8–28.

Sanborn, Geoffrey. *Plagiarama!: William Wells Brown and the Aesthetics of Attractions.* Columbia University Press, 2016.

Sánchez-Eppler, Karen. "Gothic Liberties and Fugitive Novels: *The Bondwoman's Narrative* and the Fiction of Race." *In Search of Hannah Crafts: Critical Essays in the Bondwoman's Narrative.* Eds. Henry Louis Gates, Jr., and Hollis Robbins. Basic Books, 2004. 254–275.

Savoy, Eric. "The Rise of American Gothic." *The Cambridge Companion to Gothic Fiction.* Ed. Jerrold E. Hogle. 6th ed. Cambridge University Press, 2008. 167–188.

Schopp, Andrew. "From Misogyny to Homophobia and Back Again: The Play of Erotic Triangles in Stephen King's *Christine.*" *Extrapolation* 38.1 (1997): 66–79.

Schulze-Engler, Frank. "Introduction." *Transcultural English Studies. Theories, Realities, Fictions.* Eds. Frank Schulze-Engler and Sissy Helff. Rodopi, 2009. ix–xvi.

Scott, Anthony O. "A Golden Dollop of Motherly Comfort." *The New York Times,* 16 Oct. 2008. Web. http://movies.nytimes.com/2008/10/17/movies/17bees.html?_r=0 (last accessed 24 October 2012).

Sedgwick, Eve Kosofsky. *The Coherence of Gothic Conventions.* Arno Press, 1976.

Sekora, John. "Black Message/White Envelope: Genre, Authenticity, and Authority in the Antebellum Slave Narrative." *Callaloo* 32 (1987): 482–515.

Senior, Jennifer. "In *The Changeling*, the Dark Fears of Parents, Memorably Etched." *The New York Times*. 20 June 2017. Web. https://www.nytimes.com/2017/06/20/books/reviewchangeling-victor-lavalle.html (last accessed 10 June 2018).

Septo, Robert B. "Sharing the Thunder: The Literary Exchanges of Harriet Beecher Stowe, Henry Bibb, and Frederick Douglass." *Harriet Beecher Stowe's Uncle Tom's Cabin: A Casebook*. Ed. Elizabeth Ammons. Oxford University Press, 2007. 113–130.

Sexton, Jared. "The Social Life of Social Death: On Afro-Pessimism and Black Optimism." *Time, Temporality and Violence in International Relations: (De)Fatalizing the Present, Forging Radical Alternatives*. Eds. Anna M. Agathangelou and Kyle D. Killian. Routledge, 2016. 69–74.

Shapiro, Stephen. *How to Read Marx's Capital*. Pluto Press, 2008.

Sharpe, Christina. *In the Wake: On Blackness and Being*. Duke University Press, 2016.

Shelly, Mary Wollstonecraft. *The Annotated Frankenstein*. Eds. Susan J. Wolfson and Ronald L. Levao. Belknap Press of Harvard University Press, 2012.

Shindler, Dorman T. "Baseball Tied to Wilderness Survival." *DenverPost.com*. 25 April 1999. <63.147.65.175/books/skgirl0425.html> (last accessed 20 January 2014).

Simien, Justin. *Dear White People: A Guide to Interracial Harmony*. Atria, 2014.

Singley, Carol. *Edith Wharton: Matters of Mind and Spirit*. Cambridge University Press, 1995.

Sivilis, Matthew Wynn. "American Gothic and the Environment, 1800–Present." *The Gothic World*. Eds. Glennis Byron and Dale Townshend. Routledge, 2013. 121–131.

Smethurst, James. "Invented by Horror: The Gothic and African American Literary Ideology in Native Son." *African American Review* 35.1 (2001): 29–40.

Smith, Alan Gardner. "Edith Wharton and the Ghost Story." *Modern Critical Reviews: Edith Wharton*. Ed. Harold Bloom. Chelsea House, 1986. 89–97.

Smith, Allen L. "American Gothic." *The Handbook to Gothic Literature*. Ed. Marie Mulvey Roberts. New York University Press, 1998. 2–10.

Smith, Andrew, William Hughes and Jonathan Taylor. *Empire and the Gothic. The Politics of Genre*. Palgrave Macmillan, 2003.

—. *Victorian Demons: Medicine, Masculinity, and the Gothic at the Fin-de-Siècle*. Manchester University Press, 2004.

Smith Foster, Frances. *Witnessing Slavery: The Development of Ante-bellum Slave Narratives*. 2nd ed. The University of Wisconsin Press, 1994.

Sollazzo, Erica. "'The Dead City': Corporate Anxiety and the Post-Apocalyptic Vision in Colson Whitehead's *Zone One*." *Law & Literature* 29.3 (2017): 457–483.

Sorensen, Leif. "Against the Post-Apocalyptic: Narrative Closure in Colson Whitehead's *Zone One*." *Contemporary Literature* 55.3 (2014): 559–592.

Sowerby, Robin. "The Goths in History and Pre-Gothic Gothic." *A Companion to the Gothic*. Ed. David Punter. Blackwell, 2000. 15–26.

Spillers, Hortense J. "Mama's Baby, Papa's Maybe: An American Grammar Book." *Black White and in Color: Essays on American Literature and Culture.* (Spillers). The University of Chicago Press, 2003. 203–229.

Spooner, Catherine, and Emma McEvoy, eds. *The Routledge Companion to Gothic.* Routledge, 2007.

Springer, Marlene. *Ethan Frome: A Nightmare of Need.* Hall, 1993.

Stampone, Christopher. "'[H]eroic bravery in more than one battle': The Creation of Heroes in William Wells Brown's Multi-Edition *Clotel.*" *African American Review* 49.2 (2016): 75–91.

Stauffer, John. "Frederick Douglass's Self-Fashioning and the Making of a Representative American Man." *The Cambridge Companion to the African American Slave Narrative.* Ed. Audrey Fisch. Cambridge University Press, 2007. 201–217.

Stevens, David. *The Gothic Tradition.* 5th ed. Cambridge University Press, 2004.

Stoker, Bram; Jae Lee. *The Illustrated Dracula.* Viking Studio, 2006.

Strasen, Sven-Knut. "Marxistische Literaturtheorie." *Metzler Lexikon Literatur- und Kulturtheorie. Ansätze, Personen, Grundbegriffe.* Ed. Ansgar Nünning. 5th ed. Metzler, 2013. 482–485.

Sucur, Slobodan. "Gothic Literature." *The Literary Encyclopedia.* Web. (last accessed 17 May 2013).

Summers, Montague. *The Gothic Quest: A History of the Gothic Novel.* Fortune Press, 1938.

Sundquist, Eric. "Faulkner, Race, and Forms of American Fiction." *Faulkner and Race.* Eds. Doreen Fowler and Ann J. Abadie. University Press of Mississippi, 1987. 1–35.

Sullivan, Kate. "Stephen King's Bookish Boys: (Re) Imagining the Masculine." *Michigan Feminist Studies* 14 (2000): 29–57.

Swanson, Carl Joseph. "'The Only Metaphor Left': Colson Whitehead's *Zone One* and Zombie Narrative Form." *Genre* 47.3 (2014): 379–405.

Sweeney, Toni V. "Prince Lestat and the Realms of Atlantis: The Vampire Chronicles." *New York Journal of Books.* 12 December, 2016. Web. https://www.nyjournalofbooks.com/book-review/prince-lestat (last accessed 5 May 2018)

Tacitus, Publius Cornelius. *Germania.* 3rd ed. Patmos, 2003.

The Sickly Taper. Web. <http://www.thesicklytaper.com> (last accessed 20 June 2018).

Tally, Justine. "Contextualizing Toni Morrison's Ninth Novel: What Mercy? Why Now?" *Toni Morrison's A Mercy: Critical Approaches.* Eds. Shirley A Stave and Justine Tally. Cambridge Scholars, 2011. 63–83.

Tedder, Charles. "Post Racialism and Its Discontents: The Pre-National Scene in Toni Morrison's *A Mercy.*" *Contested Boundaries: New Critical Essays on the Fiction of Toni Morrison.* Ed. Maxine L. Montgomery. Cambridge Scholars 2013. 144–159.

Tomc, Sandra. "Dieting and Damnation: Anne Rice's *Interview with the Vampire*." *Blood Read. The Vampire as Metaphor in Contemporary Culture*. Ed. Joan Gordon and Veronica Hollinger. University of Pennsylvania Press, 1997. 95–113.

Tracy, Ann B. "Contemporary Gothic." *The Handbook of the Gothic*. Ed. Marie Mulvey-Roberts. 2nd ed. Palgrave Macmillan, 2009. 109–111.

Tracy, Susan J. *In the Master's Eye: Representations of Women, Blacks, and Poor Whites in Antebellum Southern Literature*. University of Massachusetts Press, 2009.

Truitt, Brian. "LaValle's *The Changeling*: A Creepily Good Modern Fairy Tale." *USA Today*. 13 June 2017. https://eu.usatoday.com/story/life/books/2017/06/13/the-changeling-a-novel-victor-lavalle-book-review/102515950/ (last accessed 10 June 2018).

Turcotte, Gerry. "Australian Gothic." *The Handbook of the Gothic*. Ed. Marie Mulvey-Roberts. 2nd ed. Palgrave Macmillan, 2009. 277–287.

Van Leer, David. "Reading Slavery: The Anxiety of Ethnicity in Douglass's *Narrative*." *Frederick Douglass: New Literary and Historical Essays*. Ed. Eric Sundquist. Cambridge University Press, 1990. 118–140.

Varma, Devendra P. *The Gothic Flame. Being a History of the Gothic Novel in England*. Arthur Baker, 1957.

Vega-González, Susana. "Orphanhood in Toni Morrison's *A Mercy*." *Toni Morrison's A Mercy: Critical Approaches*. Eds. Shirley A Stave and Justine Tally. Cambridge Scholars, 2011. 119–135.

Velie, Alan R. "Gerald Vizenor's Indian Gothic." *MELUS* 17.1 (1991-1992): 75-85.

Verney, Kevern. *Black Civil Rights in America*. Routledge, 2004.

Vogrinčič, Ana. "The Novel-Reading Panic in 18th- Century in England: An Outline of an Early Moral Media Panic." *Medij. Istraž.* 14.2 (2008): 103–124.

Wald, Priscilla. "Hannah crafts." *In Search of Hannah Crafts: Critical Essays in the Bondwoman's Narrative*. Eds. Henry Louis Gates, Jr. and Hollis Robbins. Basic Books, 2004. 213–230.

Wallace, Diane and Andrew Simth, eds. *The Female Gothic: New Directions*. Palgrave Macmillan, 2009.

Walonen, Michael K. "The Socio-Spatial Dynamics of Theme Parks in Contemporary Transatlantic Fiction." *Literature Interpretation Theory* 25.3 (2014): 259-270.

Walpole, Horace. "Letter to Sir Horace Mann. April 27. 1753." *The Letters of Horace Walpole*. Vol. II. Ed. J. Wright. Richard Bentley, 1840. 469–472.

—. *The Castle of Otranto. A Gothic Story*. Oxford: Oxford University Press, 1998.

Walter, Natasha. *Living Dolls: The Return of Sexism*. Virago, 2010.

Wardi, Anissa. "The Politics of 'Home' in *A Mercy*." *Toni Morrison's A Mercy: Critical Approaches*. Eds. Shirley A. Stave and Justine Tally. Cambridge Scholars, 2011. 23–41.

Warner, Samuel. "Authentic and impartial narrative of the tragical scene which was witnessed in Southampton County (Virginia) on Monday the 22d of August last, when fifty-five of its inhabitants (mostly women and children) were inhumanly massacred by the blacks!" *The Gilder Lehrman Institute of American History.* Web. <http://www.gilderlehrman.org/collections> (last accessed 1 August 2016).

Watt, Ian. *The Rise of the Novel*. 2nd ed. University of California Press, 2001.

Watt, James. *Contesting the Gothic: Fiction, Genre and Cultural Conflict, 1764–1832.* Cambridge University Press, 1999.

Weier, Sebastian. "Consider Afro-Pessimism." *Amerikastudien/American Studies Quarterly* 59.3 (2014): 419–433.

Wein, Toni. *British Identities, Heroic Nationalism, and the Gothic Novel, 1764–1824.* Palgrave Macmillan, 2002.

Weinstock, Jeffrey Andrew. "American Monsters." *A Companion to American Gothic.* Ed. Charles L. Crow. Wiley Blackwell: 2014. 41–55.

—. "American Vampires." *American Gothic Culture: An Edinburgh Companion.* Eds. Joel Faflak and Jason Haslam. Edinburgh University Press, 2016. 203–221.

Weld, Theodore Dwight, ed. *American Slavery as It Is: Testimony of a Thousand Witnesses.* Cambridge University Press, 2015.

Welsch, Wolfgang. "Transculturality – The Puzzling Form of Cultures Today." *Spaces of Culture: City, Notion, World.* Eds. Scott Lash and Mike Featherstone. Sage, 1999. 94–213.

—. "Was ist eigentlich Transkulturalität?" *Hochschule als transkultureller Raum? Beiträge zu Kultur, Bildung und Differenz.* Eds. Lucyna Darowska, Thomas Lüttenberg and Claudia Machold. Transcript, 2010. 39–66.

West, Elizabeth. "American Studies and the 'Racial Fault Line': Response to Sebastian Weier's 'Consider Afro-Pessimism.'" *Amerikastudien/American Studies Quarterly* 59.3 (2014): 439–442.

Wester, Maisha L. *African American Gothic: Screams from Shadowed Places.* Palgrave Macmillan, 2012.

Welter, Barbara. "The Cult of True Womanhood: 1820–1860." *American Quarterly* 18.2 (1966): 151–174.

White, Armond. "Twilight: Bronte Never Dies." *New York Press,* 21 Nov. 2008. Web. <http://nypress.com/twilight-bronte-never-dies/> (last accessed 10 September 2016).

Whitehead, Colson. *Zone One.* Doubleday, 2011.

Whittier, John Greenleaf. "The Opium Eater" (1833). *Perseus Digital Library.* Web (last accessed 10 August 2017).

Wilderson III, Frank B. *Red, White & Black: Cinema and the Structure of U.S. Antagonisms.* Duke University Press, 2010.

—. "The Black Liberation Army and the Paradox of Political Engagement." *Postcoloniality Decoloniality-Black Critique: Joints and Fissures.* Eds. Sabine Broeck and Carsten Junker. Retrieved online: http://www.illwilleditions.noblogs.org (last accessed: 14 August 2015).

Williams, Anne. *Art of Darkness: A Poetics of Gothic*. University of Chicago Press, 1995.

Williams, James. *Narrative of James Williams, an American Slave, Who Was for Several Years a Driver on a Cotton Plantation in Alabama*. Documenting the American South. http://docsouth.unc.edu/fpn/williams/menu.html (last accessed 10 August 2017).

Williamson, Joel. *New People: Miscegenation and Mulattoes in the United States*. Free Press, 1980.

Williamson, Peter. *French and Indian Cruelty: Exemplified in the Life and Various Vicissitudes of Fortune, of Peter Williamson*. N. Nickson: 1757. Retrieved online: https://archive.org/details/frenchindiancrue00will (last accessed 19 June 2015).

Wilson, Natalie. "Civilized Vampires Versus Savage Werewolves: Race and Ethnicity in the *Twilight* Series." *Bitten by Twilight: Youth Culture, Media, and the Vampire Franchise*. Eds. Melissa A. Click, Jennifer Stevens Aubrey, and Elizabeth Behm Morawitz. Peter Lang, 2010. 55–70.

Wilt, Judith. *Ghosts of the Gothic: Austen, Eliot, Lawrence*. Princeton University Press, 1980.

Winter, Kari J. *Subjects of Slavery, Agents of Change. Women and Power in Gothic Novels and Slave Narratives, 1790–1865*. University of Georgia Press, 1992.

Williams, Linda. *Playing the Race Card: Melodramas of Black and White from Uncle Tom to O.J. Simpson*. Princeton University Press, 2001.

—. "Why, Eight Years After It Ended, *The Wire* Remains America's Best Example of Racial Melodrama." http://www.huffingtonpost.com/lind-williams/why-eight-years-after-it_b_6063376.html. 01 Feb 2015 (last accessed: 10 May 2016).

Wisker, Gina. *Horror Fiction. An Introduction*. Continuum, 2005.

Wolff, Cynthia Griffin. *A Feast of Words: The Triumph of Edith Wharton*. Oxford University Press, 1977.

Wolfram, Herwig. *Die Goten. Von den Anfängen bis zur Mitte des sechsten Jahrhunderts. Entwurf einer historischen Ethnographie*. 5th ed. Beck, 2009.

Wollstonecraft, Mary. *A Vindication of the Rights of Woman: With Strictures on Political and Moral Subjects*. J. Johnson, 1792. Retrieved online: http://www.gutenberg.org/ebooks/3420 (last accessed 10 May 2015).

Wolstenholme, Susan. *Gothic (Re)Visions: Writing Women as Readers*. Suny Press, 1993.

Yellin, Jean Fagan. "Hawthorne and the American National Sin." *The Green American Tradition: Essays and Poems for Sherman Paul*. Ed. H. Daniel Peck. Louisiana State University Press, 1989. 75–97.

Young, Elizabeth. *Black Frankenstein: The Making of an American Monster*. New York University Press, 2008.

Young, Hershini Bhana. "Performing the Abyss: Octavia Butler's *Fledgling* and the Law." *Studies in the Novel* 47.2 (2015): 210–230.

Ziegler, Robert. "Lost and Found in Karen Russell's *Swamplandia!*." *Notes on Contemporary Literature* 42.1 (2012): 8–12.

Social and Cultural Studies

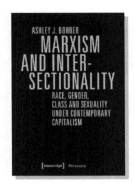

Ashley J. Bohrer
Marxism and Intersectionality
Race, Gender, Class and Sexuality
under Contemporary Capitalism

2019, 280 p., pb.
29,99 € (DE), 978-3-8376-4160-8
E-Book: 26,99 € (DE), ISBN 978-3-8394-4160-2

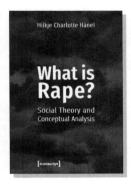

Hilkje Charlotte Hänel
What is Rape?
Social Theory and Conceptual Analysis

2018, 282 p., hardcover
99,99 € (DE), 978-3-8376-4434-0
E-Book: 99,99 € (DE), ISBN 978-3-8394-4434-4

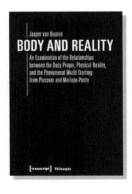

Jasper van Buuren
Body and Reality
An Examination of the Relationships
between the Body Proper, Physical Reality,
and the Phenomenal World Starting from Plessner
and Merleau-Ponty

2018, 312 p., pb., ill.
39,99 € (DE), 978-3-8376-4163-9
E-Book: 39,99 € (DE), ISBN 978-3-8394-4163-3

**All print, e-book and open access versions of the titles in our list
are available in our online shop www.transcript-verlag.de/en!**

Social and Cultural Studies

Sabine Klotz, Heiner Bielefeldt,
Martina Schmidhuber, Andreas Frewer (eds.)
Healthcare as a Human Rights Issue
Normative Profile, Conflicts and Implementation

2017, 426 p., pb., ill.
39,99 € (DE), 978-3-8376-4054-0
E-Book: available as free open access publication
E-Book: ISBN 978-3-8394-4054-4

Michael Bray
Powers of the Mind
Mental and Manual Labor
in the Contemporary Political Crisis

2019, 208 p., hardcover
99,99 € (DE), 978-3-8376-4147-9
E-Book: 99,99 € (DE), ISBN 978-3-8394-4147-3

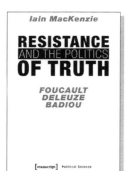

Iain MacKenzie
Resistance and the Politics of Truth
Foucault, Deleuze, Badiou

2018, 148 p., pb.
29,99 € (DE), 978-3-8376-3907-0
E-Book: 26,99 € (DE), ISBN 978-3-8394-3907-4
EPUB: 26,99 € (DE), ISBN 978-3-7328-3907-0

**All print, e-book and open access versions of the titles in our list
are available in our online shop www.transcript-verlag.de/en!**